PITT A  [

ESSAYS AND LETTERS

BY

J. HOLLAND ROSE, Litt.D.

READER IN MODERN HISTORY, THE UNIVERSITY OF CAMBRIDGE

LONDON
G. BELL AND SONS, LTD.
1912

CHISWICK PRESS : CHARLES WHITTINGHAM AND CO.
TOOKS COURT, CHANCERY LANE, LONDON.

PREFATORY NOTE

THE following Essays, dealing with the characters and careers of Pitt and Napoleon, are new, with the exception of those entitled "The True Significance of Trafalgar," and "General Marbot and his Memoirs." I acknowledge with gratitude the valuable advice given by Professor Oman, LL.D., on the "Waterloo" Essay; by Mr. Julian Corbett, LL.M., on the "Invasion" Essay; and by Mr. C. R. Fay, M.A., Fellow of Christ's College, Cambridge, on Pitt's "Bill for the Relief of the Poor"; also Mr. A. M. Broadley's help in communicating the new letter of Pitt on the Walmer Volunteers.

In the second part of this volume I have grouped together important new letters illustrative of the career of Pitt. My thanks are especially due to His Grace the Duke of Portland for communicating the correspondence of Pitt with the third Duke of Portland; to the Earl of Harrowby for a similar service respecting Pitt's correspondence with the first Earl of Harrowby; also to Earl Stanhope and E. G. Pretyman, Esq., M.P., for permission to search for and utilize letters of Pitt and others contained in the archives at Chevening and Orwell Park respectively.

J. H. R.

January 1912.

CONTENTS

PART I. ESSAYS

PART II. LETTERS

PITT AND NAPOLEON

PART I

ESSAYS

THE ORATORY OF PITT

IN his dialogue on the perfect orator Cicero sets forth two ideals. Crassus, the representative of the more cultured and florid style, maintains that the perfect speaker must not only possess the physical and mental qualifications necessary for success in the art, but that he needs also to be versed in poetry, science, politics, attainments of all kinds, so that from his well-filled armoury he may overwhelm his opponent and fascinate his auditors by charms of bewildering variety. The other chief disputant, the successful pleader, Antonius, demurs to these claims as excessive, and, while admitting that the orator must be not quite a tyro or novice in any business of life, declares that his aim must be to convince and persuade: "He is one who, both in forensic and in general cases, can employ language pleasing to the ear and maxims suitable to carry conviction."[1] As the discussion proceeds, it is clear that Cicero inclines to the wider theory, even while his commonsense defers to the practical advice of the pleader. In truth both methods are needed. The cultured and magnificent style sways the minds of men at great crises; but economy of effort is the prime condition of success on more ordinary occasions. Doubtless Cicero intended to advise young aspirants to master the essentials of the art for use in forensic cases, in the hope that the inspiring, if unattainable ideals set forth by Crassus would lead the best of them to

---

[1] Cicero, "De Oratore," i, ch. xlix.

acquire the learning and imbibe the graces which wing the loftiest shafts.

Alone, perhaps, among English orators Pitt satisfied the two ideals set forth by Cicero. Reared by the side of Chatham, hearing day by day the recital of a chapter of the Bible or some other classic, and trained to an almost pedantically careful use of his mother-tongue, he grew up in a rhetorical forcing-house such as Crassus would have wonderingly approved. Before proceeding to Cambridge he ranged over classical and English literature, became an adept in mathematics, and showed skill in versification. At the university his intercourse was in the main restricted to the austere circles presided over by his private tutor, Wilson, and by the tutor of his college, the Rev. Dr. Pretyman, with occasional relaxations in the society of young men destined for a parliamentary career. Among his favourite studies was Civil Law, lectures on which he called "instructive and amusing." But his chief joy was attendance at the debates in Parliament which hammered out the last scintillations of the genius of Chatham.

Yet this training in the magnificent style was happily balanced by training as a barrister. After the death of his father, he had perforce to bestow much time on the study of law, which Burke declared to be more invigorating to the mind than all the other kinds of learning put together.[1] He even undertook a few briefs and won commendation for his closely-argued statements. All this was but preliminary to the parliamentary career which alike realized his hopes and ripened his powers. His maiden speech of 26th February 1781 astonished all who heard it; and thenceforth he swayed the House of Commons during a quarter of a century which vibrated also to the tones of Fox and Sheridan.

It is far from easy to illustrate in an essay the qualities of the oratory of Pitt, which depended for its effect, not so much on isolated outbursts as on a cumulative and finally overwhelming pressure. His nature being less fiery and magnetic than that of Chatham, he relied on continuous argument and cogent appeals rather than on lightning flashes; and the reader is at times apt to ask—where is the touch of genius in all this? The answer must be that it pervades the whole speech; it is in the under-

---

[1] Burke, "Speech on American Taxation," 19th April 1774.

lying reasoning, in the stately march of the reasoning, in the unfailing vigour of its serried periods, and in the union of grace and strength, of elevated thought and noble diction. These powers, present from the first, steadily matured. His rhetoric is not remarkable for the sudden unfolding of almost unsuspected powers whereby Mirabeau astonished the States-General of France in 1789. What it was in 1781 it remained in essence, though endowed with greater vitality and grace, down to the month after Trafalgar, when his two sentences uttered at the Lord Mayor's banquet summed up for ever the achievements of the past and winged all thoughts towards the duties and glories of the future.

Those who heard his maiden speech in Parliament were most impressed by its perfection of form. Burke and Fox were loud in their praise; Lord North pronounced it the best first speech he had ever heard; and Storer, an equally good judge, declared that the delivery was marked by a becoming confidence far removed from pert self-assurance, so that there was not a word or a look one would wish to correct.[1] This is the more remarkable as Pitt had sharply inveighed against the sinecures attached to the King's Civil List. Not content with insisting on the need of economy, he boldly declared the object of the present proposal to be the reduction of the influence of the Crown—

An influence which is more to be dreaded because more secret in its attacks and more concealed in its operations than the power of prerogative. . . . It ought to be remembered that the Civil List revenue was granted by Parliament to His Majesty for other purposes than personal gratification. It was granted to support the power and the interests of the Empire, to maintain its grandeur, to pay the judges and the foreign Ministers, to maintain justice and support respect; to pay the great officers that were necessary to the lustre of the Crown; and it was proportioned to the dignity and opulence of the people. It would be an ungracious task to investigate the great difference that there is between the wealth of the Empire when that revenue was granted and the wealth at the present time. It would serve, however, to show that the sum of revenue which was necessary to the support of the common dignity of Crown and people at that time, ought now to be abated as the neces-

---

[1] So, too, in 1796, Horner (a harsh critic) admitted his " wonderful fluency and correctness, approaching to mechanical movement." He blamed his action as one who sawed the air with his whole body (F. Horner, " Mems.," i, 11).

sities had increased. The people, who granted that revenue under the circumstances of the occasion, are justified in resuming a part of it under the pressing demand of an altered situation. They clearly feel their right, but they exercise it with pain and regret. They approach the throne with bleeding hearts, afflicted at the necessity of applying for retrenchment of the royal gratifications; but the request is at once loyal and submissive. It is justified by policy, and His Majesty's compliance with the request is inculcated by prudence as well as by affection.

That one who had barely attained to manhood should venture to assail the Monarch and the still unbroken phalanx of the King's Friends caused surprise; that he displayed no agitation in the midst of so desperate a tilt aroused enthusiasm; and experienced members saw in that calmly confident demeanour, that equable flow of words, that faultless grace of delivery, sure signs of the advent of an athlete of debate.

A not unkindly destiny willed that Pitt's championship of Reform and steadfast opposition to the Fox-North Coalition of the year 1783 should entail uphill fights against large majorities. The courage which appeared in his first daring utterance was tempered by a long succession of struggles, seemingly hopeless, were it not that the nation inclined to his side. What could be more vigorous than the speech of 21st February 1783 in defence of the preliminary terms of peace with France, Spain, and America? It was delivered under unfavourable conditions. The terms, however necessary, were deemed humiliating; and the threatened union of Fox with North promised to overthrow the Ministry of Earl Shelburne, in which Pitt was Chancellor of the Exchequer. Yet in masterly style he showed that a peace was rendered inevitable by the recklessness and incompetence of Lord North, whose successors now secured terms far from unfavourable. Then, adverting to the rumoured Coalition of Fox and North, he said: "I repeat, then, Sir, that it is not this treaty, it is the Earl of Shelburne alone whom the movers of this question are desirous to wound. This is the object which has raised this storm of faction; this is the aim of the unnatural Coalition to which I have alluded. If, however, the baneful alliance is not already formed, if this ill-omened marriage is not already solemnized, I know a just and lawful impediment, and, in the name of the public safety, I here forbid the banns."

No more thrilling metaphor has been used in Parliament. Occasionally Pitt's metaphors and allusions were somewhat too

literary and recondite to strike home.[1] Classical quotations even
in that age cannot have been familiar to the mass of the members, and therefore did not call forth that immediate and overwhelming response at which the orator should aim. To hit the
golden mean, a metaphor should be neither too lofty for speedy
comprehension, nor too common for the dignity of the occasion.
That of Pitt recalled the challenge which always arouses a flutter
of anxious interest; and lest it should seem too trite a phrase
for the present emergency, he winged and barbed it with the
nobly patriotic addition "in the name of the public safety."
Such a metaphor is worth a battery of arguments. They soon
become blurred, while words that trace out the situation in
strokes of fire burn into the memory. The glow of that phrase
shed lustre upon Pitt throughout his contest with the large but
discordant *cohue* of the Coalition. The speeches which he levelled
against that unnatural union and in defence of his Administration which succeeded it have lost much of their interest; but
they abound in vigorous arguments based upon the needs of the
nation, and helped to secure from that final court of appeal the
triumphant verdict of May-June 1784. So far from the truth is
it that his speeches were merely parliamentary. Like Chatham,
he often appealed away from Parliament to the people.

The success of an orator depends largely on his ability to win
the good opinion of his audience; and Pitt, who had studied
Cicero to good effect, often sought to gain this advantage. On
one occasion at least, he departed from the precepts of the
ancients by placing this personal appeal not first, but last. It was
in the great speech of 21st February 1783, when the fate of the
Shelburne Ministry trembled in the balance and an adverse vote
implied for him a return to the Bar.

It has been the great object of my short official existence to do the
duties of my station with all the ability and address in my power, and

---

[1] A case in point is his retort on 23rd January 1784 to General Conway,
who had charged him with bribing the country. After indignantly denying
the calumny, "he concluded—so runs the report—in a tone of high and
elevated sentiment, and with a classical text expressive of its being inconsistent with dignity to attend to either their rash slanders or their modest
questions." Evidently the classical text went high over the heads of the
reporters and of their helpers. Wraxall (iii, 12) says that Pitt, out of regard
for the country members, cited the Classics not more than nine or ten times
in his career, a very doubtful estimate.

with a fidelity and honour which should bear me up, and give me confidence, under every possible contingency or disappointment. I can say with sincerity, I never had a wish which did not terminate in the dearest interests of the nation. I will at the same time imitate the honourable gentleman's candour, and confess, that I too have my ambition. High situation, and great influence, are desirable objects to most men, and objects which I am not ashamed to pursue, which I am even solicitous to possess, whenever they can be acquired with honour, and retained with dignity.[1] On these respectable conditions, I am not less ambitious to be great and powerful than it is natural for a young man with such brilliant examples before him to be. But even these objects I am not beneath relinquishing, the moment my duty to my country, my character, and my friends, renders such a sacrifice indispensable. Then I hope to retire, not disappointed, but triumphant; triumphant in the conviction that my talents, humble as they are, have been earnestly, zealously and strenuously employed to the best of my apprehension in promoting the truest welfare of my country.

. . . You may take from me, Sir, the privileges and emoluments of place, but you cannot and you shall not take from me those habitual and warm regards for the prosperity of Great Britain which constitute the honour, the happiness, the pride of my life, and which, I trust, death alone can extinguish. And, with this consolation, the loss of power, Sir, and the loss of fortune, though I affect not to despise them, I hope I soon shall be able to forget.

> Laudo manentem. Si celeres quatit
> Pennas, resigno quae dedit, . . .
> . . . . . . probamque
> Pauperiem sine dote quaero.[2]

The memoir-writer, Sir Nathaniel Wraxall, who heard this peroration, describes the artifice adopted by Pitt as he approached the middle words of the passage—

> Et mea virtute me involvo.

Feeling them to be in excess of his merit, the orator paused for a moment, fixed his eyes on the ground, and passed his handker-

---

[1] A hit at the unnatural Coalition, which was neither honourable nor dignified.

[2] Horace, "Odes," iii, 29. "If she (Fortune) abides, I commend her. If she shakes her fleet pennons for flight, I resign her gifts . . . and hail hones dowerless Poverty as mine."

chief once or twice over his lips. Then, as if recovering from temporary embarrassment, he declaimed the final words, emphasizing them by blows upon the table in front. In the judgement of Wraxall no more masterly or beautiful piece of oratorical acting was to be found in antiquity.[1] The verdict shows how far the standard of taste has changed since that time. A member who in this matter-of-fact age should have recourse to such a device would be voted a pedant and a prig.

In the main, however, the oratory of Pitt inclined to the austere rather than to the florid style. Differing from Burke, who poured forth profusely the treasures of his fancy, and from Sheridan, equally lavish of wit, Pitt sought to persuade the reason rather than to captivate the imagination or raise a laugh. Not that he was destitute of these powers; for his friends agree that in private he excelled in sprightly repartee. On one occasion, at least, he gave fancy the rein. Fox, censuring the King's Speech of 5th December 1782, had ironically quoted against the Prime Minister the lines—

> You've done a noble turn in nature's spite;
> For tho' you think you're wrong, I'm sure you're right.

In reply Pitt levelled at Fox the following parody—

> The praise he gives us in his nature's spite;
> He wishes we were wrong, but clearly sees we're right.

In general, however, his speeches want the touches of humour or irony which light up the subject and entrance an audience. Where in his speeches should we find so mordant a simile as that which Disraeli, on 3rd April 1872, flung at the Gladstone Cabinet in the days of its waning popularity? " As I sat opposite the Treasury Bench, the Ministers reminded me of one of those marine landscapes not very unusual on the coast of South America. You behold a range of exhausted volcanoes. Not a flame flickers on a single pallid crest." Possibly Pitt curbed his satirical powers in the belief that only by the adoption of a mature seriousness could he make up for the disadvantage of his youth. To this motive we may refer the rebuke which, in his twenty-third year, he administered to Burke, then in his

---

[1] Wraxall, iii, 11, 12.

fifty-second year, for flippant comments on the King's Speech above referred to:

> The gay flowers of a brilliant and exuberant fancy are proper for their season, for hours of jollity and recreation. I shall be happy to share in the delights of that fertile imagination which has so long been the wonder and pleasure of this House; but I cannot consent to indulge myself in admiring "the beautiful motes which people the sunbeam," when my mind is occupied with objects so serious and important as those now before the House. . . . I rise therefore to bring back the House to sobriety and seriousness, and to tell them that this is neither a fit time nor a proper subject for the exhibition of a gaudy fancy or the wanton blandishments of theatrical enchantment. It is your duty and business to break the magician's wand, to dispel the cloud, beautiful as it is, which has been thrown over our heads, and to consider solemnly and gravely the very perilous situation of the country.

Rarely has youth bestowed on maturity a graver censure, and yet in words which hinted that the speaker could at will almost vie with his opponent in wealth of imagination and grace of diction. Pitt had his reward. True, we miss in his orations that free outpouring of philosophic thought and lively fancy which by turns instructs, surprises, and delights readers of Burke. But, though Pitt was sometimes sententious and rarely dull, he gained his end, which was to prove his case to the satisfaction of Parliament and of the nation at large. Nevertheless, his speeches, while adapted to present needs, arouse the interest which ever belongs to the stately treatment of great themes. Among the best specimens of this kind of oratory in the early part of his career are, his description of his India Bill on 6th July 1784 (one of the most luminous surveys of the affairs and needs of that Empire), his three speeches of the session of 1785 on the proposed commercial regulations with Ireland, that of 18th April 1785 on Reform, that of 13th June 1786 on the Warren Hastings case, and the series of financial statements, among which the most memorable is that of the 29th March 1786, on the introduction of the Sinking Fund. In these orations there is no straining after effect; the language is clear and forcible; the development of the theme, orderly ; the refutation of opponents, vigorous; the conclusion, cogent. In his financial statements Pitt towers above all Chancellors of the Exchequer, except perhaps Peel and Gladstone, who followed where he led the way. Never before had a statesman succeeded in handling complicated statistics in an interesting manner. Wilberforce remarked on the ill fortune of Pitt in having frequently to speak "upon subjects of a low and vulgarising quality, such as the excise on tobacco, wine, etc., topics almost incapable, with propriety, of an association with wit or grace, especially in one who was so utterly devoid of all disposition to seek occasions for shining."[1] Apparently, Wilberforce did not discern the merits of Pitt's speeches on finance, which, despite their lack of ornament, rank among the triumphs of the oratorical art. The inquiry into the nation's resources and the conditions of prosperity is so luminous, the recommendations are so sound, the refutation of opponents is so fair and convincing, as to open up fresh vistas of thought, amidst which the eye discerns the dissolution of the old and the advent of the new as at the bidding of a Prospero. What, for instance, could be better than this reply to the prophets of woe who foretold ruin to overtaxed, high-priced Britons from the approximation to Free Trade with Ireland ι which Pitt proposed in 1785:

It is said that our manufactures are all loaded with heavy taxes. It is certainly true. But with all that disadvantage they have always been able to triumph over the Irish in their own markets, paying the additional ten per cent. on the importation to Ireland, and all the charges.

But the low price of labour [in Ireland] is mentioned Will that consideration enable them to undersell us? Manufacturers think otherwise. There are great obstacles to the planting of any manufacture. It will require time for arts and capital; and the capital cannot increase without the demand also; and in an established manufacture improvement is so rapid as to bid defiance to rivalship. In some of our manufactures, too, there are natural and insurmountable objections to their competition. In the woollens, for instance, by confining the raw material to this country, the manufacture is confined also. There may be some branches in which Ireland may rival and perhaps beat England; but this ought not to give us pain. We must calculate from general, not from partial views, and above all things not look on Ireland with a jealous eye. It requires not philosophy to reconcile us to a competition which will give us a rich customer instead of a poor one. Her prosperity will be a fresh spring to our trade.[2]

[1] "Private Papers of Wilberforce," 79.
[2] The final sentences doubtless refer to the *dictum* of Adam Smith ("Wealth of Nations," bk. iv, ch. iii, pt. ii): "A nation that would enrich

By passages like these Pitt shed on statistics the ennobling light of his serene faith in the progress of humanity. Far from being "of a low and vulgarising quality," finance became in his hands a means of stimulating thought and effort. Perhaps the most original of his speeches are those on this subject, which Burke had touched only at the fiery point of American taxation, and where Sheridan would have seemed but an interloper clad in motley.

The effect of a speech depends not only on the lucid, vigorous and suggestive treatment of a great theme, but fully as much on beauty of language, variety of illustration, and power of appealing to the sense of humour, or sympathy, or of indignation. In beauty of diction Pitt takes high rank. His choice of consecutive vowel sounds shows a delicate and exacting ear. Examples of this felicity may be found in the extract quoted at the end of page 13. The sounds are pleasingly varied, and the avoidance of monotony is seen in the use of the word "savageness" instead of "savagery," which would offend the ear just before the word "ferocity." Pitt was careful to avoid the sonorous jingles which pompous speakers affect by the reiterated use of words ending in —"tion." Nowhere in his speeches is there a phrase like that used by the Earl of Beaconsfield in his first speech in the House of Lords: "It is in this way only we can secure an amelioration in the condition of the population of the Ottoman Empire." Examples of the nicety of Pitt in the choice of sounds will be noticed by the reader in the course of this essay.

Perhaps the periods of Pitt are somewhat too regular, his tones too uniform, to satisfy the admirers of Chatham, Burke, and Fox. In the greatest efforts of Chatham the flash of the levin now and again delights or appals the eye. Those of his son shine with a fainter though more lasting radiance. His diction also lacks the magical power of enriching, amplifying, or illustrating thought in which Burke stands supreme. Rarely does there shine forth in the speeches of Pitt a simile as glowing as that in which Burke describes the decline of Chatham and the rise of Townshend. "Even then, Sir, before this orb was entirely set, and while the western horizon was in a blaze with his descending glory, on the opposite quarter of the heavens arose another

itself by foreign trade is certainly most likely to do so when its neighbours are all rich, industrious, and commercial nations."

luminary, and, for his hour, became lord of the ascendant." [1] Still less had Pitt the power of etching a scene such as vivifies Burke's attack on the noisy rhetoricians of Paris. "Because half-a-dozen grasshoppers under a fern make the field ring with their importunate chink, while thousands of great cattle reposed beneath the shadow of the British oak, chew the cud and are silent, pray do not imagine that those who make the noise are the only inhabitants of the field." [2] Probably, too, Pitt deemed it beneath his dignity to imitate the homely words with which Burke sometimes surprised the House, as when he described the clatter of white-sticks and yellow-sticks about the head of an economical reformer who should try to abolish them; or, again, when he inveighed against "the miserable inventions of the wretched runners for a wretched cause, which they have fly-blown into every weak and rotten part of the country, in vain hopes that, when their maggots had taken wing, their importunate buzzing might sound something like the public voice." [3] Such an image Pitt would have scorned as vulgar. Nevertheless, his speeches would have gained by occasionally dipping from the heights of St. Stephen's to the level of the street and the home. That a personal touch relieved the strain of an almost Miltonic elevation of sentiment and style is often apparent in the speeches of the most human and most forcible of English orators, John Bright. In one of his Philippics against the Crimean War occurred the following interlude: "We all know what we have lost in this House. Here, sitting near me, very often sat the member for Frome. I met him a short time before he went out, at Mr. Westerton's, the bookseller's, near Hyde Park Corner. I asked him whether he was going out. He answered, he was afraid he was—not afraid in the sense of personal fear; he knew not that—but he said, with a look and a tone I shall never forget, ' It is no light matter for a man who has a wife and five little children.' The stormy Euxine is his grave; his wife is a widow, his children fatherless." As has been well pointed out,[4] the effect of the climax is enhanced by the preceding personal and local touches, which, trivial though they

[1] Burke, "Speech on American Taxation."
[2] Burke, "Reflections on French Rev.," a passage which is essentially rhetorical.
[3] Burke, "Speech on American Taxation."
[4] C. A. Vince, "John Bright," p. 212.

are, make the mind vividly receptive to the pathos of the last overwhelming utterance.

On a lower plane than this noble passage are the personal invectives of Fox. The speeches of the Whig orator are far looser in texture than those of Pitt. Wraxall avers that Fox paid little attention to the sequence of his arguments, from a conviction that one third of the members were either asleep or were absent at dinner; and he states that, at any considerable influx (or signs of awakening?), he would go over the same ground, often to the manifest annoyance of those who had heard their fill. Nevertheless, so manly was his bearing, so powerfully did he first state, and then tear in pieces, the assertions of opponents, and so skilfully did he "hit the House between wind and water"—to use a phrase of Burke—that all defects were forgotten. In truth, Fox had a signal advantage over Pitt. After the year 1783 the leaden weight of official responsibility weighed on the younger orator, while Fox, condemned to an almost hopeless opposition, could let his lively fancy roam at will. Attack is always more inspiriting than defence; and for this reason the speeches of leaders of the Opposition generally afford better reading than those of Prime Ministers. True, these positions on the whole suited the peculiar talents of Pitt and Fox; and if Fox may almost be termed the Napoleon of debate, assuredly Pitt was its Wellington. · Fox, however, could generally choose time and place for an attack; and this is an immense tactical advantage. Never, surely, has an assault been delivered with more energy than that of Fox upon the Westminster Scrutiny. In fullness of technical knowledge, masterly development of the attack, and skilful play upon every feeling which could tell against the Government, his speech of 8th June 1784 stands unrivalled. Above all it pulsates with manly indignation against ministerial pressure exerted upon a single member unprovided with funds for the contest. Few passages have moved Parliament more deeply than these:

Not to him [Pitt], but to its true cause do I attribute this shameful attack; to that black, that obstinate, that stupid spirit, which by strange infatuation pervades and has pervaded the counsels of this country throughout the whole course of this unfortunate and calamitous reign; to that weak, that fatal, that damnable system, which has been the cause of all our disgraces and all our miseries; to those secret advisers who hate with rancour and revenge with cruelty. To those malignant men whose character it is to harass the object of their enmity with a relentless and insatiable spirit of revenge; to those, Sir, and not to the right honourable gentleman do I impute this unexampled persecution. . . .

But if the right honourable gentleman neglects his duty, I shall not forget mine. Though he may exert all the influence of his situation to harass and persecute, he shall find that we are incapable of unbecoming submissions. There is a principle of resistance in mankind, which will not brook such injuries; and a good cause and a good heart will animate men to struggle in proportion to the size of their wrongs and the grossness of their oppressors.

The inconsistency of the two passages does not much impair their effectiveness. In fact, this masterly diatribe owes much of its force to the glowing appeal for personal sympathy; and here Fox succeeded to an extent scarcely attainable by Pitt. The Prime Minister seldom trenched on the domain of personalities. Even in his speeches on the French Revolution, which often vibrated with passion, the personal note is usually absent. There is no reference to Robespierre or Marat instinct with the concentrated loathing which inflates the well-known diatribe of Macaulay against Barère. The following outburst, of 1st February 1793, uttered eleven days after the execution of Louis XVI, is characteristic of the style of Pitt:

France has trampled under foot all laws human and divine. She has at last avowed the most insatiable ambition and greatest contempt for the law of nations, which all independent States have hitherto professed most religiously to observe; and unless she is stopped in her career, all Europe must soon learn their ideas of justice, law of nations, models of government, and principles of liberty from the mouth of the French cannon.

On 21st January 1794, the anniversary of that execution, he uttered these words:

We are called in the present age to witness the political and moral phenomenon of a mighty and civilized people formed into an artificial horde of banditti, throwing off all the restraints which have influenced men in social life, displaying a savage valour directed by a sanguinary spirit, forming rapine and destruction into a system, and perverting to their detestable purposes all the talents and ingenuity which they derived from their advanced stage of civilization, all the refinements of art and the discoveries of science. We behold them uniting the utmost savageness and ferocity of design with consummate contrivance and skill in execution, and seemingly engaged in no less than a conspiracy to exterminate from the face of the earth all honour, humanity, justice, and religion.

Again, on 7th June 1799, in language more pictorial than usual, he calls the French Government "an insupportable and odious tyranny, holding within its grasp the lives, the characters and the fortunes of all who are forced to own its sway. . . . The French Republic is dyked and fenced round with crime, and owes much of its present security to its being regarded with a horror which appals men in their approaches to its infamous battlements."

Strange to say, it was Bonaparte who called forth his keenest antipathy. Replying to Erskine on 3rd February 1800, shortly after the rejection by the Government of the tentative and probably illusory offers of peace by the First Consul of France, the Prime Minister passed in rapid review the phases of French policy, painting in vivid colours the acts of aggression, often stained with perfidy, at the expense of neighbouring lands. He then proceeded as follows: "This is the first and moving spirit of the French Revolution: . . . it has equally belonged to Brissot, to Robespierre, to Tallien, to Reubell, to Barras, and to every one of the leaders of the Directory, but to none more than to Bonaparte, in whom all their powers are united." After demonstrating his share in the plunder of Italy and Switzerland, in the unscrupulous *coup d'état* of Fructidor (1797), and the high-handed seizure of Malta and Egypt, Pitt added these words:

His hold upon France is the sword, and he has no other. Is he connected with the soil, or with the habits, the affections, or the prejudices of the country? He is a stranger, a foreigner, and an usurper; he unites in his own person everything that a pure Republican must detest, everything that an enraged Jacobin has abjured, everything that a sincere and faithful Royalist must feel as an insult. If he is opposed at any time in his career, what is his appeal? *He appeals to his fortune;* in other words to his army and his sword. Placing, then, his whole reliance upon military support, can he afford to let his military renown pass away, to let his laurels wither, to let the memory of his achievements sink in obscurity? . . . Is it nothing, with a view to influence or example, whether the fortune of this last adventurer in the lottery of Revolutions shall appear to be permanent?

A lighter effort is his raillery at Sheridan. On 6th March
1805 the Whig orator brought forward a motion for repealing
Pitt's "Additional Force Act" of the previous year, pointing it
with reckless comments on the incompetence of the Ministry.
After treating the question at issue, Pitt thus turned the tables
on Sheridan:

The honourable gentleman seldom condescends to favour us with a
display of his extraordinary powers of imagination and of fancy; but
when he does come forward, we are prepared for a grand performance.
No subject comes amiss to him, however remote from the question
before the House. All that his fancy suggests at the moment, or that he
has collected from others, all that he can utter in the ebullition of the
moment, all that he has slept on and matured, are combined and produced for our entertainment. All his hoarded repartees, all his matured
jests, the full contents of his common-place book, all his severe invectives,
all his bold hardy assertions, all that he has been treasuring up for days,
for weeks and months, he collects into one mass which he kindles into a
blaze of eloquence, and out it comes altogether, whether it has any
relation to the subject or not. Thus it is, with his usual felicity, that the
honourable gentleman finds a new argument for the repeal of the
present Bill, because the House and the country have less confidence
in the present than even in the late Ministers. . . .

But the most telling of Pitt's retorts was that flung back at
Tierney on 17th February 1800. That opinionated and for the
time self-constituted leader of the Whigs had annoyed the Prime
Minister by challenging him to state in one sentence, " without his *ifs* and *buts*, and special pleading ambiguity," what was
the object of the war, which he (Tierney) asserted to be for the
restoration of the House of Bourbon. At once Pitt took up the
gauntlet, and in one word declared the object of the war to be
" security." Then, turning to the charge respecting the Bourbons,
he said:

He [Tierney] has assumed the foundation of the argument, and has
left no ground for controverting it, or for explanation, because he says
that any attempt of explanation upon this subject is the mere ambiguous
unintelligible language of *ifs* and *buts*, and of special pleading. Now,
Sir, I never had much liking to special pleading; and if ever I had any,
it is by this time almost entirely gone. He has besides so abridged
me of the use of particles that, though I am not particularly attached
to the sound of an *if* or a *but*, I would be much obliged to the honour-

able gentleman if he would give me some to supply their places. Is this, however, a light matter that it should be treated in so light a manner? The restoration of the French monarchy I will still tell the honourable gentleman I consider as a most desirable object because I think that it would afford the strongest and best security to this country and to Europe. *But* this object may not be attainable; and *if* it be not attainable, we must be satisfied with the best security which we can find independent of it. Peace is most desirable to this country, *but* negotiation may be attended with greater evils than could be counterbalanced by any benefits which would result from it. And *if* this be found to be the case; *if* it afford no prospect of security; *if* it threaten all the evils which we have been struggling to avert; *if* the prosecution of the war afford the prospect of attaining complete security; and *if* it may be prosecuted with increasing commerce, with increasing means, and with increasing prosperity, except what may result from the visitations of the seasons; then I say that it is prudent in us not to negotiate at the present moment. These are my *buts* and my *ifs*. This is my plea, and on no other do I wish to be tried by God and my country.

No more crushing reply has been heard in the House of Commons. One knows not whether to admire most the mental alertness which could on the instant frame an answer full of wit and wisdom, or the beauty of the language, or the cumulative force of the period, which marches from the trivial to the last indignant outburst. Especially admirable from our present standpoint is the arrangement of sentences which develop the *but* and *if motif*. At first they are short and almost snappish, leading up, however, to others more sonorous, stately, and proportioned to the rising grandeur of the theme. The words swell and the phrases lift their crests until the final wave sweeps all before it, Tierney and his crew being scarcely visible—

Rari nantes in gurgite vasto.

The effect of these outbursts of eloquence was singularly enhanced by the personality of the speaker. If Pitt had not his father's power of browbeating by a frown, or of cowing by a flash of anger in those hawk-like eyes, he yet swayed the House by a dignity of bearing and an indefinable authority possessed by none of his contemporaries. Lord Monboddo summed up the impression produced by this perfection of form in the statement that " Pitt spoke, Fox barked, and Lord North screamed." The periods of Pitt were like those which Cicero wrote, and such as no contemporary could either speak or write.[1] Erskine, the most forcible of pleaders at the Bar, shrank from a parliamentary duel with Pitt.[2] It is said that on one occasion when the great jurist was inveighing against the Ministry, Pitt abashed him by ostentatiously tearing in pieces notes of a reply which he had begun to prepare. The incident may seem trivial, but it points to the existence of that last reserve of power which places the great orator above the able speaker, the power of personality.

In beauty of language and elevation of thought, Pitt's well-known speech of 2nd April 1792 on the abolition of the Slave Trade transcended all efforts even in that golden age of eloquence; but, as I have elsewhere quoted largely from it,[3] I pass on to a passage which well illustrates his power of investing a subject with dignity. It occurs in the exordium of his speech of 21st April 1800 on the proposed union of the British and Irish Parliaments:

If we wish to accomplish the great work that we have undertaken, we must look to the whole of this important and complicated question, we must look at it in a large and comprehensive point of view; we must consider it as a measure of great national policy, the object of which is effectually to counteract the restless machinations of an inveterate enemy [France], who has uniformly and anxiously endeavoured to effect a separation between two countries whose connection is as necessary for the safety of the one as it is for the prosperity of the other. We must look to this as the only measure we can adopt which can calm the dissensions, allay the animosities, and dissipate the jealousies which have unfortunately existed; as a measure whose object is to communicate to the sister kingdom the skill, the capital, and the industry which have raised this country to such a pitch of opulence; to give her a full participation of the commerce and of the constitution of England; to unite the affections and resources of two powerful nations; and to place under one public will the direction of the whole force of the Empire. . . .

In deciding on this question, we ought to be actuated by another feeling, a feeling which it is not necessary for me to state, because the magnanimity of every gentleman must have suggested it to his own mind. In the union of a great nation with a less, we must feel that we ought not to be influenced by any narrow views of partial advantage.

[1] "Corresp. of Wilberforce," i, 33. [2] Wraxall, iii, 409.
[3] Rose, "William Pitt and National Revival," p. 470.

We must refute by our conduct . . . the idea that we have any other object in view than that of promoting the mutual advantage of both kingdoms. We must show that we are not grasping at financial advantages, that we are not looking for commercial monopoly; we must show that we wish to make the Empire more powerful and more secure by making Ireland more free and more happy. These, Sir, are the views; these are the only views, with which I could ever have proposed this measure; and it is with these views alone that it can be rendered effectual to its object, and establish mutual harmony and confidence between the two nations.

In Cicero's treatise, " De Oratore," Crassus declares that the great orator is he who can speak judiciously, in set form, elegantly, from memory, with dignity of action, on any subject that requires elucidation. The claim may seem excessive; and he who would satisfy it would be, not a parliamentary orator, but a professional rhetorician. In the opinion of some, Pitt is open to this charge. Macaulay in his generally unfair estimate of Pitt, represents him as a driveller in military affairs, content to send forth England's forces to defeat so long as his splendid declamation won triumphs at Westminster. A perusal of the speeches of Pitt on the true policy of the first and second coalitions, or of his able statements on national defence in the summer of 1804, will reveal the falsity of this slander. Coleridge, followed by Lecky, commented on the poverty of thought in the speeches of Pitt. The criticism smacks of the study and leaves out of count the imperative needs of Westminster. It was the fate of the noble orations of Burke to fall flat owing to the superabundance of the imaginative gifts which now constitute their charm. He thought in aphorisms and his speech scintillated similes; but that intellectual galaxy dazzled or bewildered the House. Compared with Burke, Pitt was sparing of generalizations and similes, though they occurred often enough to dignify his orations and charm his audience. In fact the great merit of his speeches is the balance of their qualities. They took a middle course between the Pegasus flight of Burke and the pedestrian efforts of Grenville. While his sonorous cadences satisfy the ear of an artist, his periods, like his thoughts, were rarely, if ever, too complex for the halting wits of the country squires who formed the bulk of the members.

Here he compares favourably with Gladstone, whose subtle intellect, extreme conscientiousness, love of distinctions and reservations, often involved his statements in conditional clauses which not unnaturally incensed the Tierneys of his day. In other respects, if we allow for differences of temperament and creed, the oratory of the founder of the Union and of the proposer of the Home Rule Bill of 1886 has much in common. Theirs were the essential gifts of charming ear and eye by silvery speech and vigorous action, of marshalling vast masses of facts with ease and clearness, of surrounding even unattractive themes with the halo of intellectual superiority, of convincing the reason and enthralling the fancy, and of merging these powers in a unity where beauties of detail disappear in the symmetrical dignity of the whole. In truth, the architectonics of the speeches of Pitt resemble the design of an Ionic or Corinthian temple, not devoid of ornament, but impressive in its simplicity and in a completeness which defies alteration. Other styles have other merits. In majesty of diction and thrilling power the orations of Chatham stand unequalled; in debating dexterity and passionate declamation those of Fox have not been surpassed; those of Burke will always attract men of letters, those of Sheridan journalists; but the most perfect example of the union of grace and force, of stately rhetoric and convincing argument fused in the white heat of patriotism, is to be found in the speeches of Pitt the Younger.

PITT AND EARL FITZWILLIAM

THE dispute between Pitt and the second Earl Fitzwilliam, which complicated affairs in Ireland early in 1795, arose out of the union of the Portland Whigs with Pitt's followers in the previous summer. The accession of a number of influential and expectant statesmen produced more than the usual amount of haggling about the distribution of the spoils of office; but so great was the desire of Pitt to form a truly national party, capable of facing the increasing difficulties of the time, that he sought to humour his exigent allies. Their leader, the Duke of Portland, demanded the Home Office for himself, and the Irish Viceroyalty for the Whig magnate, the Earl Fitzwilliam, to whom that appointment was prematurely offered by the Prince of Wales and Fox during the Regency Crisis of 1789. Cheated of their hopes at that time by the recovery of the King from the attack of insanity which had produced that orgy of Cabinet-making, Portland and Fitzwilliam now revived their claims with better chances of success. Fitzwilliam had recently joined the Cabinet as Lord President, but he longed for the Irish Viceroyalty, and it is clear from Pitt's letter to the Duke of 2nd July 1794, quoted in the sequel, that His Grace laid stress upon that appointment. In view of the democratic ferment in England and the collapse of the campaign in Flanders consequent on the Austrian defeat at Fleurus, Pitt could not refuse the request, even though it involved the recall from Dublin Castle of his old friend of Cambridge days, the Earl of Westmorland. He, however, stipulated that some honourable position must be found for Westmorland, and on the same understanding the King sanctioned the change. Pitt's letters of 2nd and 3rd July to Portland showed an earnest desire to meet his wishes; but unexpected difficulties arose, the result being that the appointment of Fitzwilliam remained in abeyance for several weeks.

In such circumstances the conduct of a Viceroy-elect should

be marked by tactful reserve. That of Fitzwilliam showed incredible levity. On 4th August he wrote to Grattan, the fervent champion of Irish nationality, asking him and his friends, the Ponsonbys, for their support during his approaching Viceroyalty. In a postscript he admitted that his appointment was not settled and that the present offer was therefore premature.[1] Nevertheless, without marking his letter "private," he began to arrange for what was a complete change of system in Ireland. Grattan seems to have behaved with equal imprudence in revealing this State secret. At any rate it is certain that busybodies at Dublin soon buzzed about the news of the approaching departure of Westmorland in a way which vastly increased the difficulties of an already trying situation. On 23rd October he complained bitterly to Pitt of the slight inflicted on him and the harm done to the King's cause by putting Ireland in the hands of those who had recently sought to hold His Majesty in thraldom. By that time it was believed that there would soon be drastic changes at Dublin; and Westmorland, while appreciating Pitt's efforts to secure for him either the Presidency of the Council or the Privy Seal at Westminster, expressed deep pain at his opening the door to almost revolutionary changes in Ireland. The following words about Portland are significant: " Is it indiscretion only, without consultation with you, to appoint a Lord Lieutenant? Is it indiscretion only to insult the existing Lord Lieutenant without pretence? Is it indiscretion only to form a plan of removing the King's servants and changing the system of measures? "[2] Dundas, also, who had been removed from the Home Office to the War Office in order to make way for Portland, expressed to Pitt keen resentment at the conduct of their new allies. Writing at Walmer on 13th October, he charged them with "abominable swindling, of which the Old Baillie provides no example."[3] Pitt's reply on the morrow shows dignified reserve, but evinces deep pain at the narrow personal spirit displayed by the Portland Whigs at so grave a crisis. He also resolved on no account to allow Fitzwilliam to dismiss that Protestant stalwart, Lord Fitzgibbon, from the office of Vice-Chancellor of Ireland.[4] This change, and the removal of another staunch supporter of the Government, John Beresford from the

[1] " Grattan Memoirs," iv, 173.   [2] Chevening MSS.
[3] Pretyman MSS. quoted by Lord Ashbourne, " Pitt," p. 184.
[4] Stanhope, " Pitt," ii, 283. Fitzgibbon soon became Earl of Clare.

Revenue Board and other emoluments, were those on which the opponents of Westmorland set most store.

But the questions at stake in Ireland were far more than political or personal; they were also religious. The French Revolution, with its almost magical power of energizing diverse impulses, now prompted the Roman Catholic Irishry to struggle for a recognition of their creed in the Parliament at Dublin. Hitherto none but Protestants could enter the portals at St. Stephen's Green. The Romanists chafed at their exclusion; and agrarian grievances, especially that of tithe to the Established Church, further tended to band together the Presbyterians of Ulster with the Celtic substratum of the other three provinces. Hence the Society of United Ireland, formed in 1791 by the able young Ulsterman, Wolfe Tone, succeeded in marshalling three-fourths of the population against the privileged oligarchy entrenched at Dublin Castle. As has been shown elsewhere,[1] Pitt did much in the years 1792-3 to lessen the grievances of Roman Catholics, but latterly Westmorland had embarked on a policy of coercion which seemed to end their hopes during his regime. Pitt had forbidden his making an official pronouncement which closed the door to hope; but the position was becoming intolerable; and on general grounds much could be said in favour of the adoption of the principles of religious equality.

Nevertheless, there was every need of caution before setting about so important a change in the midst of the excitement then prevailing; and it was here that Fitzwilliam went astray. His unofficial action in approaching Grattan was such as to excite hopes for the satisfaction of which he had no official warrant. In his excuse it must be said that, though fifty-six years of age, he had little experience of public life, and he seems to have lacked the power of self-suppression so eminently needful during the time of waiting. Family influence and wealth were his chief recommendations. As nephew and heir of the Marquis of Rockingham, and husband of Lady Dorothy Cavendish, he possessed a unique claim to supremacy in the Whig phalanx which sought to guard and control the throne. Among them personal ability was less desirable than a strong sense of family and party solidarity. In these virtues Fitzwilliam was rich. He also inherited the bureaucratic notions ingrained in the old Whig families, and therefore regarded himself, with his

[1] Rose, "William Pitt and the Great War," ch. xvi.

great territorial and family influence in Ireland, as the necessary
executant of the policy of concession initiated by Portland in
his brief Viceroyalty twelve years previously. The powers of a
Lord Lieutenant were extensive; and a member of the Whig
oligarchy may almost be pardoned for looking on Ireland as a
political preserve during his tenure of that exalted office. Westmorland had good reason to warn Pitt that a Lord Lieutenant
could always find means to dismiss whom he would; and he
added the striking words: "Either make up your mind to give
it [Ireland] to that party or keep it for yourself. There is no
medium—believe me." [1]

The Duke of Portland also maintained that he had joined the
Cabinet only on the understanding that the new Lord Lieutenant
should be a man in whom he had confidence; and as Portland
favoured concession to the Roman Catholics, this understanding, if it were so distinct as to be binding, implied a change of
system at Dublin. Evidently the Duke and Fitzwilliam believed
that they were to have a free hand; and, as we have seen, their
confidence was soon shared by the Ponsonbys and Grattan, who,
in their resolve to compass the overthrow of the ultra-Protestant
clique, proceeded to London in September 1794, and succeeded
in gaining the ear of Lord Loughborough, Lord Chancellor of
Great Britain. Lady Arden, wife of the Attorney-General, at a
dinner given by Loughborough to Grattan and others, heard a
conversation which betokened a complete change of system at
Dublin. Sir Richard Pepper Arden therefore wrote to Pitt urgently begging him to beware of committing that Government to
men who had behaved badly to the King at the Regency Crisis.
Pitt does not seem to have attached much importance to the
matter, so we may judge from a sentence of his letter of 24th
September 1794 to his brother, Lord Chatham: "I have heard a
variety of reports relative to Lord Fitzwilliam going to Ireland
immediately, but not a step has been taken towards creating
the vacancy." [3] This, of course, merely implies that no suitable
post had yet been found for Westmorland. But while arrangements at Court were thus delayed, Loughborough made overtures to the Portland Whigs and their Irish supporters. How
far Pitt authorized them I have not discovered. It was an

[1] Pitt MSS. 331. Westmorland to Pitt, 18th and 23rd October 1795.
[2] See Rose, "William Pitt and the Great War," p. 341, for Arden's letter.
[3] Pitt MSS., 103. Stanhope (ii, 260) omits this sentence.

indiscretion to allow him to intervene at all; for the Lord Chancellor, once an impecunious barrister of East Lothian, Alexander Wedderburn by name, had run a signally devious course before settling down with dignity on the woolsack. In his earlier days his shifts and turns aroused no less contempt for his faithlessness than admiration at their easy grace; but by the year 1794 those devices were almost forgotten, and he was looked upon as a Ulysses who, on reaching home, had put far from him the wiles of war and navigation. Whether George III, no inexpert judge, held this opinion may be doubted; for, on hearing of his death in 1805, he compiled the regal epitaph: "Then he has not left behind him a greater knave in all my dominions."

Such was the man who now acted as go-between for Pitt and Fitzwilliam. The following new letters of Loughborough to Pitt show that it was he who suggested the conference between the leaders, and besought him to go as far as possible in the way of concession. By the middle of October Portland, Fitzwilliam and the other Whig recruits had threatened to leave the Cabinet if their demands were not complied with, and in view of the urgency of the political crisis Pitt could not defy them to do their worst. To this time we may refer the following undated letters:[1]

Bedford Square, Friday, 11 a.m.

MY DEAR SIR,

Late as it was when I left you last night I could not help writing the enclosed paper, tho' there can be nothing in it which has not occurred to you. I cannot renounce the hope that a free conference would settle all this business, the real importance of which bears no sort of proportion to the mischief it may produce. One immediate consequence is quite evident; if it is not settled, the impossibility of keeping Ireland composed. That will be the first, but not the greatest, of the train of evils that must follow; and that consideration very much diminishes the value of any point that can be made with respect to that Government, and raises the value of every mode of conciliation that can be devised. There is hardly any arrangement that could be more disadvantageous to the Irish Administration than a direct rupture, or endanger their situations more. From the turn of the note you received yesterday, I suspect that a party pride has a much greater effect than either sense or duty should allow in a business on which the public safety is so deeply staked. That, I am sure, will not obstruct in your

[1] Pitt MSS., 328.

mind any accommodation that would secure the publick object, however irksome it must be to be harassed with difficulties arising from such a cause. I am obliged to stay at home the early part of this morning, but about two o'clock I hope to be able to call upon you.

Yours ever most entirely,

LOUGHBOROUGH.

MEMORANDUM OF LORD LOUGHBOROUGH

[After asserting that the danger of a disruption of the Administration of this country must and could be averted by a candid explanation between the two parties, Loughborough states that the undefined term, "new system," as applied to Ireland, has complicated the negotiation. But it only implies a desire to unite in the Government of Ireland "all the respectable interests of that country;" it implies "a spirit of conciliation, a disposition to acquire friends, to extinguish, not to create opposition." A new system must refer both to men and measures in Ireland. He believes that the men chosen by the one side will be received with perfect cordiality by the other. He continues]: "The persons in Ireland of the most consideration amongst those who have stood apart from Government are Mr. Grattan, the Mr. Ponsonbys, Mr. Conolly, the Duke of Leinster. To attach the first, it is only necessary to govern well. The Mr. P[onsonbys] might both be placed in the highest degree of consideration, which would necessarily follow from their connection with the Lord Lieutenant; and there could be no difficulty in finding situations, without the necessity of any harsh unqualified and precipitate removals, for all those whom the judgment of the chief Governor on the spot would lead him to adopt. That confidence is implied in his appointment, could not be withheld from him without endangering the Government, and most assuredly is not meant to be in any degree narrowed in the present instance. The power of removal must also be inherent in the office; for no government could be carried on with credit and efficacy if any person forming a part of it held [it] by such a tenure as to enable him to counteract it with safety. But the exercise of his power requires great moderation and caution especially in the case of a new-formed Administration, when a consider-able portion of power and influence must of necessity pass from those who have been in the possession of both. Every removal would require either to be qualified by some accommodation, or distinctly to mark (*sic*) the specific cause and prevent the alarm that might be excited by it in others.

"With respect to measures, those that may be proposed must probably have the same tendency with the measures that have for some time been adopted by the English Government, the circumstances not being materially changed. It is therefore unlikely that any difference in principle should exist. Difference of opinion as to the extent or form is to be settled by discussion, and it requires only to be stated what the measures are in order to judge whether that difference can extend very far. The most necessary step is that the persons chiefly concerned should invite each other to an open and full explanation of their intentions regarding both men and measures. That once done, all conditions would be totally unnecessary and in some degree unfit. The public ought only to know that no difference subsisted; what had been agreed should only be known by its effects. No man would then be disquieted either by unreasonable apprehensions or extravagant hopes, and all would be the better disposed to be reconciled to each other and to their respective situations, as from the certain knowledge that an entire confidence had been re-established amongst the principals, no hope would be left for the gratification of the humour or interest of particular persons."

Very noteworthy is the skill with which Loughborough insinuates that the new system, advocated by Fitzwilliam and demanded by Grattan, was not a new system at all, but merely the adoption of a friendly spirit, together with a few changes of persons at Dublin which doubtless could be arranged to the advantage of everyone concerned. Equally deft is the suggestion that the new Lord Lieutenant must have a free hand, though, of course, he would act with moderation. In fact, his measures would not differ materially from those adopted by the British Government, and there would therefore be no difference of principle, while details might be settled by friendly discussion. Such a discussion should not be accompanied by conditions. These plausible suggestions might have deceived a novice; but it is strange that Pitt did not at once put a stop to Loughborough's parade of the olive branch. Apparently he did not. Unfortunately no account survives of Loughborough's conference with Fitzwilliam and Grattan. The only other letter of Loughborough surviving in the Pitt MSS. refers to it only in general terms. He seems to have shown to them the paper which he drew up for Pitt. Probably, after inducing Pitt to give some kind of assent to his statement, he thereafter persuaded them to do the same. The blessings invoked on the peacemaker shed a halo on the following letter to Pitt:

Sat' mng.
MY DEAR SIR,

I saw Ld Fitzwilliam and Mr. Grattan last night; the conversation spread into a pretty considerable detail, the grounds of which were perfectly conformable to the principles expressed in the paper. I read it over, and it was agreed to be a very just state (*sic*) of his intentions— adopted indeed entirely, with the very slight alteration of the word *desirous* to *willing*—to state his sentiments. I did not fix any further meeting because it appeared to me that there was a wish first to talk with the Duke of P[ortland], and on Monday we shall all meet. I will call upon you as soon as I can.

Yours most entirely,
LOUGHBOROUGH.

I have found no account of Loughborough's interviews. Indeed Pitt soon excluded him from these negotiations, probably because he detected his aim of enticing Ministers into vague and therefore dangerous concessions. From the first Pitt displayed a discreet reserve towards Fitzwilliam and his future supporters at Dublin. At a dinner given by the Duke of Portland, at which Grattan, the Ponsonbys, and Sir John Parnell were present, the Prime Minister behaved most affably to Parnell; but to his remark commending the union of Irish Catholics with Protestants, he replied, " Very true, Sir, but the question is, whose will they be? " [1] To Grattan also his demeanour was equally cordial and cautious. The son and biographer of the great Irishman ventures to assert that Pitt throughout this affair resolved to cheat Ireland; but the facts disprove this reckless and unproven slander.[2] Pitt's letters to Windham, one of the new Whig Ministers, evince a desire to go far in the way of concession to his allies and therefore to Grattan; but he was resolved not to allow Fitzwilliam a free hand at Dublin, still less to dismiss Fitzgibbon and Beresford. On 16th October, after conferring with Grattan, Windham assured Pitt that, if he would sacrifice the C[hancellor], —— might be saved. The dash probably hints at Beresford, who, however influential at Dublin, was a less redoubtable fighter than the Chancellor, Fitzgibbon. As for his own feelings, Windham stated his desire to remain in the Cabinet. Nevertheless, if Pitt's support of the ultra-Protestants at Dublin led Portland to resign, he (Windham) must also go out. It is clear, then, that Loughborough's efforts to whittle down differences of principle had no effect with Pitt, though they probably gave rise to the stories of his duplicity

---

[1] " Mems. of Grattan," iv, 175.
[2] Stanhope, " Pitt," ii, 285-7, with letters.

which gained ready belief at Dublin. Grenville also stood firm, and on 24th October wrote that the reports about a change of system at Dublin had blown over, though in the meantime they had wrought infinite harm.[1] Not until 14th November did the King receive Lord Mansfield's acceptance of the Presidency of the Council, an arrangement which enabled Westmorland to become Master of the Horse, and Fitzwilliam Lord Lieutenant of Ireland.[2] At once Pitt wrote to Portland requesting a second meeting of those concerned in the last appointment, or, failing that, a private interview beforehand:

Downing Street, Friday night, Nov. 14, 1794.[3]

MY DEAR LORD,

I have had some conversation this evening with Lord Fitzwilliam, Lord Spencer and Lord Grenville, on the subject of Ireland. They have agreed to resume it here at twelve to-morrow; and, being very desirous to lose no time in endeavouring to adjust satisfactorily the points which remain for discussion, I trouble Your Grace with this information in the hope that it may not be inconvenient to you to be present at this meeting, or that you will have the goodness to name the time which suits you best, when I may have the pleasure of seeing you on the subject of it. I am, etc.,

W. PITT.

There is no sign of anxiety in this letter. Still less does it breathe the spirit of intrigue. Evidently Pitt deemed the question capable of adjustment by ordinary means; but, unfortunately, owing to difficulties at Court, it was not until 10th December 1794 that Fitzwilliam attended the King's levee to kiss hands on his appointment to the Viceroyalty.

Some time in December there was held an important meeting at which Pitt and Grenville discussed with the new Whig Ministers the future policy of Fitzwilliam at Dublin. Grenville committed to writing a full description, which saw the light first in the year 1898 in Lord Ashbourne's work on Pitt, and, *in*

---

[1] "Buckingham Papers," ii, 317. A passage which corrects the misstatement of Mr. Bryce ("Two Centuries of Irish History," ch. v) that Portland accepted office on condition of a complete change of system at Dublin. Burke's long letters of 16th to 28th October to Windham ("Windham's Diary," 321-333) display ignorance of certain facts of the case. They have been largely followed by Lecky.

[2] The King to Pitt, 14th November 1794. See p. 230 of this volume.

[3] From Mr. Doulton's MSS.

extenso, in the "Dropmore Papers" published in the following year. The account is far too long for quotation in full; but the following sentences are essential. The first refers to the preliminary discussions; the others, to the conference held at Downing Street:

After much discussion on the subject of Lord Fitzgibbon's removal, that idea was renounced, and the most explicit assurances were given by Lord Fitzwilliam that he had not in view the establishment of any new system in Ireland, but that he was desirous of strengthening his Government by the accession of Mr. Ponsonby and his friends, and the support of Mr. Grantham. . . .

At the conference, "Mr. W. Ponsonby was proposed by Lord Fitzwilliam for Secretary of State. It was objected that this office ought to be annexed to that of Chief Secretary [for Ireland]. . . . In answer to these objections Lord Fitzwilliam strongly urged the necessity of his bringing forward Mr. W. Ponsonby, for which he said there was no other opening. It was then proposed to him that Mr. Ponsonby might be made Keeper of the Signet, and the office of Secretary of State be annexed to that of Chief Secretary. And this arrangement was, after much difficulty and discussion, agreed to by Lord Fitzwilliam. . . . No mention was made at this conversation of Mr. Curran; nor was it known to some of the persons there present that Lord Fitzwilliam had ever thought of proposing that gentleman for Solicitor-General till after Lord Fitzwilliam's arrival in Ireland, when that arrangement became the subject of public discussion there.

". . . Nothing was intimated in this conversation of any idea of removing Mr. Beresford, nor was even his name mentioned by Lord Fitzwilliam.

". . . At the close of it [the conversation] Lord Fitzwilliam, who had brought to the meeting a memorandum of matters to be talked of, was repeatedly asked whether there were any other points to be discussed, or any new measures to be proposed. The answer was that he knew of none."[1]

The other important topic discussed at the conference was the

---

[1] "Dropmore Papers," iii, 36-8. Lord Ashbourne, "Pitt," 187-9. Mr. Fortescue ("British Statesmen of the Great War," pp. 107-9) makes no reference to this all-important document.

Fitzwilliam afterwards stated that in one of his conversations with Pitt he had announced his intention of dismissing Beresford; but Pitt denied that this was so. The King at the end of his letter of 29th January 1795 to Pitt states (in a sentence omitted by Earl Stanhope) that Fitzwilliam had paid no attention to what was understood at the time of his departure.

proposal of Fitzwilliam to nominate George Ponsonby as Attorney-General in place of Wolfe. This was vetoed; and the new Viceroy was instructed to defer to the opinion of the King's Government in London on so weighty a matter as the granting of further concessions to Roman Catholics.

What, then, must have been the surprise of Ministers when they heard of the proceedings of Fitzwilliam on his arrival at Dublin? Landing on Sunday evening 4th January, he was confined to his room by indisposition the whole of the next day. On Tuesday he transacted business. On Wednesday he sent Daly to warn John Beresford, head of the Revenue Department, of his coming dismissal; for he (Beresford), having made the fortunes of Fitzgibbon and other high officials, had virtually the Law, the Church, and the Army almost under his hands. Daly advised Beresford quietly to retire. It afterwards transpired that Fitzwilliam on the Tuesday raked up charges of financial irregularities, and was also prepared to accuse him of duplicity towards Pitt, in what matter is not known. On 15th January the Lord Lieutenant wrote to Grenville that Beresford was satisfied with this arrangement and promised his support.[1]

Beresford had said nothing of the kind. He wrote at once to his old friend, Lord Auckland, urging him to appeal to Pitt for fair play; and on 23rd January he set out for London.[2] The Prime Minister saw the gravity of the crisis; for, as he told George Rose, the dismissal of Beresford "would be an open breach of a most solemn promise." It was more than that; it portended the change of system which Fitzwilliam had agreed to waive. Beresford's later letters to Auckland show that Fitzwilliam and the Ponsonbys were bent on making a clean sweep at Dublin Castle. By dint of several unfair dismissals they succeeded; and Ponsonby, when under the influence of Lord Shannon's vinous hospitality, declared that he had long worked to this end and now had the reins in his hands.[3] This was so. When viewed at large, these changes seem a preparation for a

[1] "Dropmore Papers," iii, 9.

[2] Pitt MSS., 325. Auckland adds in a note, "Received January 15, 3 p.m.; wrote to Mr. Pitt, 5 p.m."

[3] "Beresford Corresp.," ii, 60. The only letter of any importance from Fitzwilliam to Pitt is a request for a pecuniary grant to the Chief Baron, Yelverton, whom Fitzwilliam had raised to a peerage. He makes it almost a question of confidence (Pitt MSS., 328).

measure of religious equality too long delayed. On examination, there emerge unmistakable signs that that curse of Irish politics, family jobbery, was only to reappear in a Whig guise.

On the larger question at issue, Fitzwilliam's conduct is more defensible. He found the country in a ferment on the Catholic question. True, this was largely the result of his own blazing indiscretions and those of Grattan. There had been few signs of an agitation on that question until the autumn.[1] But then the shadows of coming change at Dublin caused general excitement; and in the winter of 1794-5, when the disgraceful collapse of the Allies in Holland chilled the hearts of all loyalists, there was little show of resistance. Presbyterian Ulster had made common cause with the Catholics in demanding the abolition of all religious disabilities. In February, when the Dutch fleet was in the hands of the French, rumours of an invasion became rife; and in these circumstances it was not unnatural for Fitzwilliam to feel that the time had come for granting the last of the Catholic claims.

Yet his conduct was such as to illustrate the difference between obstinacy and firmness. While clinging to his preconceived notions, he displayed no resourcefulness or courage in meeting a threatening situation. He did little or nothing to dissuade Grattan from proposing a Bill for Catholic Emancipation, though his recent promise to Ministers should have bound him to that course of action. Further, a man of magnanimous nature would have appealed to Irishmen to sink their differences for the present in face of a common danger. But Fitzwilliam, after depressing the spirits of the loyal, now had not the nerve or the tact to enliven them. On the contrary, his acts and his passivity alike gave new life to malcontents. His letters to Portland and Pitt exhaled discouragement and dismay. He warned them that Government could not cope with the discontent, which amounted to veiled rebellion. Clearly, Fitzwilliam was out of his place at Dublin. Unfortunately owing to stress of weather a long delay occurred in the despatch of the mails for England, namely from 10th to 23rd January,[2] a fact which fully explains "the astounding neglect of duty," of the Pitt Ministry against

---

[1] "Beresford Corresp.," ii, 44.
[2] Beresford to Auckland, 19th January (Pitt MSS., 325). At the close he says he will sail by the first packet which sails. He did not sail until 23rd January.

which Lecky declaimed.[1] On 28th January Grenville wrote to Fitzwilliam in friendly terms, hinting, however, that the dismissals at Dublin were not quite consonant with the former assurances of the Earl.[2] A few days later the Duke of Portland sent off official rebukes drawn up in a far harsher tone.

To what are we to ascribe this change? Mainly, I think, to the intervention of the King. On 5th February, after the Drawing Room at St. James's, Portland handed to him letters from Fitzwilliam announcing the proposal to admit Roman Catholics to the Irish Parliament and his concurrence with it. George did not say much at the time; he smothered his feelings, slept on them, and on the morrow fired off a double-shotted volley at Pitt. The Duke, he said, had undoubtedly sought to sound his sentiments in view of the Cabinet meeting on the 7th. He (the King) felt the utmost surprise at the conduct of the Viceroy, who, after three weeks' stay in Ireland ventured "to condemn the labours of ages," and to set at defiance the judgement of all men of property in that land. Every land must have a Church Establishment. In Ireland there were few Romanists of standing who could sit in Parliament. Grattan's measure would therefore "disoblige the greater number to benefit a few." Besides being a peevish attempt to humiliate the friends of Ireland, it trenched on the domain of conscience. "I cannot conclude (wrote the King) without expressing that the subject is beyond the decision of any Cabinet of Ministers." In fact it would be better to change the Administration at Dublin rather than admit so dangerous an innovation.[3]

These closing words were of terrible import. They closed the door against Catholic Emancipation for that reign and forbade the Cabinet even to discuss a matter which soared above their jurisdiction into the realm of conscience. Ministers had not placed a veto on the discussion of this question at some future time; but now the King did; and his intervention must have stiffened the attitude of the Cabinet. The proceedings of the Cabinet meeting of 7th February are not known. But on the following day Portland charged Fitzwilliam to do all in his power to postpone the Catholic Question; and on 9th February the Prime Minister wrote to the Viceroy blaming the dismissal

[1] Lecky, vii, 70.   [2] "Dropmore Papers," iii, 13.

[3] Stanhope, ii, App., pp. xxiii-xxv.

of officials both as a breach of promise and as burdening the Irish revenue with a needless number of pensions.[1] The letter contained no reference to Grattan's proposals, but dwelt merely on the personal questions at stake. The omission probably resulted from his writing in a way which supplemented the more formal missive of Portland. In any case, the Lord Lieutenant haughtily informed Pitt that he must choose between him and Beresford; and to Portland he declared that he would not be the man to put off the Catholics, and "by doing so raise a flame in the country that nothing short of arms would be able to keep down."

It is clear, then, that his resignation resulted, not merely from the dismissals (as Grattan recklessly stated[2]) but also from his tacit encouragement of a measure which he had promised to hold back. That both causes were operative appears in the letter of George Rose to the Bishop of Lincoln (28th February): "... Mr. Pitt has said nothing to me lately about Ireland, but I conceive it utterly impossible for Lord Fitzwilliam there, because he said he positively went not (*sic*) if Beresford should be restored, on which Mr. Pitt peremptorily insists; there can be no doubt of his coming away on other grounds, such as Catholic measures, etc."[3]

On 25th February, after receiving a further letter from Pitt in the same sense as the former,[4] the Lord Lieutenant informed Fitzgibbon that the opposition shown to him on the Catholic Question and Beresford's removal had decided him to retire within a week.[5] Circumstances prevented his departure until near the end of March, when, instead of leaving as quietly as possible, he took the advice of Grattan and departed in a manner which evoked a great popular ovation. With the utmost effusiveness the men of Dublin dragged his carriage to the quay, and openly threatened to subvert the authority of his successor, Earl Camden.

---

[1] "Stanhope Misc.," i, 19-23.

It has been suggested that Fitzgibbon secretly influenced the King's decision. But his letter of 14th February to Beresford shows that he intended to send over Grattan's Bill with legal comments respecting the King's Coronation oath. The King evidently formed his judgement on the letters of Fitzwilliam shown to him by Portland on 5th February. See, however, Lecky, vii, 103. The oft-quoted assertion that no petition was sent in against Grattan's proposals is incorrect. The Corporation of Dublin and a few other bodies sent in protests.

[2] "Grattan Memoirs," iv, 195.   [3] Pretyman MSS.
[4] "Stanhope Misc.," i, 23.   [5] "Beresford Corresp.," ii, 74.

For these commotions Fitzwilliam must be held responsible. Before his departure he wrote to his old friend of Eton days, the Earl of Carlisle, two long letters sharply impugning the good faith of the Pitt Ministry, justifying his own acts, and accusing Beresford of malversation of the public funds.[1] It is said that he intended these letters to be printed at Dublin only for private circulation. Of course they at once became public, thereby pouring oil on the flames of strife in Ireland. The populace at once accused Pitt and Portland of perfidy and lauded Fitzwilliam to the skies as a true friend of Ireland, who was recalled for dismissing a dishonest official and favouring a measure of religious equality. With all the evidence now before us, we must pronounce him guilty of a breach of promise to the Pitt Cabinet and of acts so indiscreet and perverse as to shake the very foundations of Government. Perhaps the worst act of the Earl's public life was the citation, in the letter to the Earl of Carlisle, of a passage from a confidential despatch of the Duke of Portland. In it the Home Secretary declared that the postponement of Catholic Emancipation would prove to be "the means of doing a greater service to the British Empire than it has been capable of receiving since the Revolution [of 1688] or at least since the Union [with Scotland]." Probably Portland here referred to the hoped-for Union of the British and Irish Parliaments, which Pitt desired to effect by means of the great, though as yet unorganized, influence of the Roman Catholics in Ireland. It is, however, unfair to accuse Pitt of keeping back that reform merely as a bribe; for there were larger issues than appeared on the surface. To admit Catholic members to St. Stephen's Green was a real danger to Protestant institutions in Ireland. To include them in the future national Parliament at Westminster, where they must form a minority, could involve no such danger. But, as it is the habit of mankind to lose sight of wider considerations in the mean motives which everyone can understand, the postponement of that measure was deemed a cunning deferment of a dainty morsel in order to garnish the unpalatable dish which he had in store.

To sum up, Pitt did not handle the Fitzwilliam affair either firmly or judiciously. Even in those leisurely days the delay of more than five months from its inception to the actual appoint-

[1] For this insult Beresford challenged Fitzwilliam. They met "near Kensington," but a peace officer prevented the duel.

ment of Fitzwilliam must be pronounced slovenly in the extreme. So soon as the Earl began heedlessly to foreshadow coming events at Dublin, there was obvious need of promptly coming to a clear understanding with him. Far from doing so, Pitt allowed Loughborough to have a hand in the negotiations with Fitzwilliam and Grattan, the result being that the question was involved in a cloud of specious verbiage which raised the hopes of Irish malcontents and the demands of their Whig allies, so as to threaten the overthrow of the Government. Ultimately, and largely owing to the good sense and forbearance of Grenville, the issue stood forth clearly; and the December conference of Ministers with Fitzwilliam left not a shadow of doubt in any mind but his that he was precluded from making any important change at Dublin without the consent of the British Government. If this agreement had been framed in August, instead of December, a vast amount of mischief would have been avoided. Accounts of this dispute published before the year 1898 assume that Fitzwilliam had a free hand at Dublin.[1] We now know that the reverse was the case.

Therefore, while Pitt is open to the charge of weak and dilatory procedure, the verdict on Fitzwilliam must be far more severe. His conduct at Dublin contravened his recent agreement with Ministers, and he must be held responsible for the turmoil which ensued. Finally his conduct at the time of leaving Ireland and his reckless charges against the Cabinet and Beresford bear the stamp of a small and peevish nature which scrupled not to increase the difficulties of his successor. The marvel is that he was ever again asked to join an Administration; and it is a sign both of the generosity of Pitt and of the gravity of the national crisis in the month of May 1804 that he advised his appointment as one of the Secretaries of State in the national Administration which was vetoed by the King. Fitzwilliam did not reciprocate this magnanimity. Wilberforce, in the year 1827, found him still obsessed by " deadly hostility " to the memory of Pitt, whom he accused of a rooted dislike to him.[2] The statement implies a lasting vindictiveness in him who made it.

---

[1] *E.g.*, Lecky, vii, 41 *et seq.*
[2] " Life of Wilberforce," v, 280. See, too, " Rutland Papers " (Hist. MSS. Commiss.), iii, 229, for Lord Sydney's comments on the peevish tone of Fitzwilliam's speeches.

Finally, we may judge of the rights and wrongs in this painful dispute by the subsequent conduct of the other Whig Ministers. Portland, Spencer and Windham knew all the details of the case. Yet, after the recall of Fitzwilliam, they continued to support Pitt, and manifested their sense of the Earl's misconduct by a chilling demeanour towards him. The editor of the " Grattan Memoirs " explains this away by the voluminous statement that the artful and insincere policy of Pitt had completely succeeded.[1] On the contrary, the clamour raised by Fitzwilliam's hasty conduct told fatally against the policy of firmness tempered by moderation, which Pitt looked on as preparatory to further measures of conciliation and of a closer political union of the two islands.

[1] " Grattan Mems.," iv, 211.

WAS PITT RESPONSIBLE FOR THE QUIBERON DISASTER?

THE answer to this question cannot be given offhand. It demands careful examination of the motives which led to the Quiberon enterprise, of the events attending it, and of the causes, both obvious and secret, which ruined it. I shall therefore endeavour in this essay to set forth the state of French politics which induced Pitt to help the French Royalists, also the plans for rousing Brittany from Quiberon as a base, and the events which determined the issue. In a question which has aroused furious feeling, the more objective the treatment, the better.

Many influences conspired to strengthen the royalist reaction which swept over France after the end of the Reign of Terror. Tallien and the other Jacobins, who overthrew Robespierre by the *coup d'état* of 10 Thermidor (28th July 1794), had no thought of ruling with clemency. It was the force of public opinion, now at last set free, which swept them back towards moderation, which the ardour of the French nature promised to transform into royalism. By that time the golden visions of 1789 had faded away into drab reality; and amidst the misery of the winter of 1794-5 many would have echoed the pithy comment of an old woman—" Ah, sir, under Robespierre we poor people suffered, but in silence; now we suffer just as much, but we can speak about it." The populace never uttered the once sacred watchwords of the Revolution without a sneer or a grimace. At the theatres they hissed down the Marseillaise and called for anti-revolutionary songs. Two-thirds of the National Convention posed as Moderates, a term which thinly veiled a preference for monarchy. Everywhere the churches were reopened, and the Sunday services were crowded, the Jacobinical day of rest, *le Décadi*, being ignored. In fact the general craving for political security awakened an almost universal regret for the once detested *ancien régime*. It was therefore natural that Pitt, in his resolve to abate the claim of France to her " natural frontiers "— the Rhine, the Alps, the Pyrenees, and the ocean—should make use of the French Royalists or Moderates who decried the Jacobinical policy of aggrandizement.[1]

The course of British politics also inclined Pitt to pay more heed to the requests of the French *émigrés*. In July 1794 their friend and champion, Windham, entered the Cabinet as Secretary at War conjointly with Henry Dundas; so that the policy of a royalist crusade, trenchantly advocated by Burke and Windham, now had an official exponent. Further, there soon arrived in London Comte Joseph de Puisaye, a man of commanding stature and persuasive power, who had long and stoutly warred against the Republic in Brittany. These services, it is true, counted for little among the " pure " Royalists who surrounded the exiled French princes, the Comte de Provence and the Comte d'Artois. To those reactionary cliques he, a champion of constitutional royalty, was merely a tool to be used for a time, and then flung aside.[2] But his reason and moderation commended him to Pitt and Windham, and his letters to Pitt, which began at the close of September 1794, show how extensive was the support in arms and money thenceforth given to the Bretons. At that time 122 officers and 150 privates, all Royalists, sailed from Southampton with munitions of war. Puisaye remained behind to organize further expeditions on funds supplied by Pitt and Windham. These piecemeal tactics move military historians to contempt; but it is clear that the northwest of France was roused in that way. Canton after canton was won for the royalist cause in the winter of 1794-5, when the allies were retreating from Holland into Germany. Puisaye's lieutenants then wrote to him that the whole province was with them; that the republican troops were few and ill-paid, and could easily be seduced. On 22nd December the Council of the Royal Army of Brittany urged Puisaye to return at once, and, if possible, bring powerful succour from England. They are especially needed. " A prince of the blood of France, the

---

[1] In the autumn of 1793 Pitt sought to come into touch with the Bretons, who had thrown off the Republican yoke. For his letter of 25th November 1793, to the Earl of Moira, then in command of an expedition in the Solent, destined to help the Bretons, see the " Quarterly Review " for 1912.

[2] E. Daudet, " L'Emigration," i, 281.

émigrés en masse, all those in England to be obliged to come; the *émigré* corps raised by England; 12,000 British troops."[1]

To send so large a force as this to one of the most dangerous coasts of Europe during the storms of winter was scarcely feasible, even if the men and the ships had not been needed for the Dutch and colonial campaigns. Carnot and his colleagues doubtless counted on this, and decided to push hard the Duke of York's force then retreating through Holland. They also held out the olive branch to the Bretons; and it is probable that the very easy terms which they offered to the brave Breton leader, Charette, in the so-called Peace of la Jaunaie, were a device for warding off a military collapse in the West, while they threw all their energies into the Dutch campaign. The conditions which Charette and some of his lieutenants imposed at Nantes, and those embodied in the subsequent treaty of 20th April, always had an air of unreality.[2] Could the Republic carry out conditions utterly at variance with its previous claims? Was not the whole proceeding a device for gaining time until the troops set free by the hoped-for peace with Prussia and with Spain were available for service in the West? Such were the questions whispered secretly by Jacobins and Chouans. As for the sturdy gamekeeper Stofflet, the rival of Charette, he acceded to the peace most grudgingly; and incidents, such as the murder of two Royalists by the garrison of Laval, threatened a speedy end to this pretended reconciliation. On their side Charette and Stofflet probably counted on help from England, and, still more, on the Royalist reaction now rapidly gaining strength at Paris.

Accordingly Puisaye assured Pitt that, if British help were given effectively, the Bretons would rise as one man and throw off the republican yoke for ever. Ministers took him at his word, and procured powers from Parliament for raising regiments from among the French *émigrés*, who came over in swarms after the Jacobin conquest of Holland. If only the declared Royalists had been enrolled, all might have gone well. But, on the advice of Puisaye, Ministers decided to admit deserters from the republican armies in Holland and Germany, and thus to form eight regiments of 1,550 men each. The uniform was to be scarlet with white facings; the flag the *fleur-de-lys*.[3] As

---

[1] "Dropmore Papers," iii, 537, 538.   [2] "Ann. Reg." (1795), p. 177.
[3] *Ibid.*, pp. 163-7.

deserters came in very slowly, Puisaye hit upon another still more questionable device, namely, of enrolling those prisoners of war in England who volunteered for the royal army; and again the Cabinet acted on his advice. In his "Memoirs" he justifies his conduct on the ground that, up to the time of the Quiberon expedition, men enrolled in this way had done their duty.[1]

Another device which Pitt adopted, probably at the instance of Puisaye, was the printing of royal *assignats*. So far back as 20th September 1794 Puisaye and his staff of the royalist army in Brittany had decreed, by virtue of powers conferred on them by the French princes, that paper money should be issued for the support of their troops, the republican *assignats* being denounced as illegal and worthless. Asserting that the issue of money belonged solely to the King or Regent, Puisaye called on the loyalists to honour the paper notes soon to be circulated, as these only would be recognized at the restoration of monarchy.[2] Puisaye's journey to England was probably in part connected with the manufacture of these notes; and certainly the Royalists regarded the issue by the Republic of *assignats* on the security of the lands seized by the Revolutionists as a confirmation of an act of robbery which must be thwarted by all possible means. Among them forged *assignats* had a prominent place. Pitt and his colleagues allowed their fabrication for use with the Duke of York's army in French Flanders; for that date appears at the bottom of the pattern copy which has survived. The notes were manufactured at Haughton Paper Mills near Hexham, Langley Paper Mill near Durham, and at a mill near Dartford. A distinction must, however, be drawn between the forged *assignats* and those which bore a mark ensuring their identification when the king "came to his own again." Probably both kinds were manufactured in England, and with the knowledge of Pitt.[3]

---

[1] "Puisaye Mems.," ii, 594-603; v, 39-49. Other royalist leaders had adopted the same plan. See Forneron, "Hist. des Emigrés," ii, 13, 14. In view of the well-known fact that these prisoners of war enlisted in order to get back to France, why do Sorel (iv, 365), and Fortescue (iv, pt. i, 415) say that they were *forced* into the service?

[2] See the decree in the "Puisaye Papers," B.M. Add. MSS. 8072.

[3] Note by Mr. Maberly Phillips in the "Journal of the Institute of Bankers," May, 1894; also "Notes and Queries" (Second Series, vi, 255); Doubleday's "Financial History of England," and "Newcastle Weekly

During the spring of 1795 the British Ministry spent money freely in order to further the royalist movement in Brittany. On 8th April Puisaye, in a letter to Pitt, refers to an agreement for advancing the sum of £3,000 a month for the Breton cause, the half of which he desires may be paid to him or his commissary, Prigent, every fortnight in the way that Windham and Huskisson prescribe.[1] Even up to the month of June the situation in la Vendée and Anjou was far from clear. Charette was quietly mustering his bands, as if for a struggle, while Stofflet, always at feud with him, observed the peace with the Republic. In Brittany, a royalist leader, Cormatin, reluctantly observed the peace;[2] and it was questionable whether the peasants would rise *en masse* until the crops were garnered. The omens being so doubtful, was it desirable to send an expedition to the Breton coast? Was it not better to struggle on in North Germany in hopes of help from Austria and Russia? Or were not the colonial enterprises, dear to Dundas, preferable to the risks of trusting to leaders so little trustworthy as Charette now seemed to be? Here was the problem confronting Pitt and his colleagues. It became more acute as Spain showed signs of defection from the monarchist league. Worse still, on 16th May, the Dutch Republic came to terms with France. Thenceforth an attack from the Dutch navy was only a matter of time.

In this perplexing state of things, when every week brought new calls upon our little army, very few British troops were sent to Brittany. Ministers had been collecting a force of French *émigrés* at Portsmouth and Southampton, under the Earl of Moira and General Doyle. But I have found no decisive proof that up to the date 12th June Pitt intended to despatch the force to Brittany. On that day the Foreign Minister, Grenville, wrote to the Earl of Bute, British Ambassador at Madrid, urging him to encourage the Spanish court to persevere in the

Chronicle" (Supplement), 14th April 1894. I have not been able to find one of these royalist *assignats*. If their distinguishing mark was not wholly concealed (and how could it be if they were redeemable at the Restoration?) I think that they can no more be censured than Jefferson Davis' "Confederate notes."

[1] Pitt MSS., 169. See, later on, Windham's letter of 3rd July 1795 to Pitt as to the help in money destined for Charette.

[2] Cormatin, Sorilhac, Boishardy, and six other leaders signed a protest against the peace, as undoing in one day the toil of years. It is in B.M. Add. MSS., 37,859.

royalist cause, seeing that an expedition would very soon proceed to Brittany, thus leading to risings elsewhere in France,
and causing a powerful diversion in favour of Spain.[1]

There were therefore solid reasons why Pitt should persevere
with the royalist expedition: but unfortunately it was weakened
by the causes noted above, and also by the resolve of George III
to detain in Hanover a large part of the British and subsidized
forces. There was the less excuse for this as Prussia, in the
Treaty of Basle (5th April 1795), agreed to include the whole of
North Germany in a system of neutrality which would have
guarded Hanover from attack if the pride of George could have
stooped to acknowledge this trying form of protection. Unfortunately he delayed to do so, though Ministers brought pressure
to bear upon him. On 23rd May Cornwallis wrote to Ross that
the idea of neutrality for Hanover, however unpleasant, must be
acquiesced in as a military necessity. " It may not be easy," he
adds, " to make [the King] hear cool and dispassionate reason,
but still Ministers must do their duty."[2] George, however, would
not give way. So late as 28th August Dundas complained to
Grenville that as many as 30,000 British and subsidized troops
were kept idle in Hanover; but a few days later the Cabinet
drew up a minute requiring that the British cavalry should be
withdrawn. To this the King yielded an angry assent, but too
late to save the situation in the west of France.[3] In truth,
George disliked the *émigrés* and persistently used his influence
against efforts on their behalf. In view of the sharp criticisms
recently levelled at Pitt for neglecting the Quiberon expedition,[4]
it is well to remember the opposition which he encountered in
the highest quarters. If any Englishman be responsible for the
disaster, it is the King himself.

The reasons for not entrusting this first expedition to the
Comte d'Artois have been ascribed by French royalist writers
to Pitt's design of ruining the enterprise. Viewing the matter
calmly, we can see that he acted from motives of prudence. It
is incorrect to assert, as Earl Stanhope did,[5] that he urged the
prince to lead the expedition, but that, while not refusing out-

---

[1] " F. O.," Spain, 37.   [2] " Cornwallis Corresp.," ii, 289.
[3] See the King's letter of 9th September 1795 later in this volume: also
" Dropmore Papers," iii, 128, 134.
    Fortescue, " British Statesmen of the Great War," 111, 114, 115.
[5] Stanhope, " Pitt," ii, 336.

right, the prince threw difficulties in the way. The letters of the Comte d'Artois show that he was anxious to take the lead. On 3rd May he wrote to the Duc d'Harcourt, his factotum in London: " I would sacrifice everything rather than miss the opportunity of realizing the expedition, which forms the object of all my wishes, and which I consider more than ever as a measure most desirable for the interest and glory of England, as for the salvation of my country."[1] Harcourt informed the Government of the wishes of the Prince. But how could the British Government risk the life of one who was so near the succession to the French throne on a small and tentative expedition, the reception of which in Brittany was wholly uncertain? On 19th June Grenville informed Artois that the object of the first expedition was merely to convey arms and stores to the Bretons. No large force would be sent. But when the Bretons and Vendéans had taken up arms, then would be the time for him to put himself at their head without too much compromising his personal safety.[2] Puisaye, then, was to act the part of forerunner, merely holding the Quiberon Peninsula as a base for future operations on a larger scale. If all went well the Prince was to appear. The subsequent conduct of Artois leads us to suppose that he fully appreciated this care for his safety.

Pitt, however, may have been actuated by another motive. Possibly he desired to give to Puisaye the opportunity of asserting the constitutional principles of 1791 as against the reactionary creed of the Comte d'Artois and Charette. The British Ministers favoured the cause of the Moderates at Toulon; and, whatever the Bretons might think, the greater part of France disliked the antediluvian views of Artois. Certainly the choice of Puisaye, though it confirmed the previous choice of the French princes for their army in Brittany, provoked angry protests from the *émigrés*.[3] But who would have been acceptable to those homeless, waspish swarms?

---

[1] " F. O.," France, 44.

[2] Note the following words: " L'intention de cet envoi est plutôt de protéger le débarquement des provisions et des munitions militaires que Sa Majesté envoie aux royalistes de la Bretagne que de tenter une entreprise militaire avec une force si peu considérable " ("F. O.," France, 44). The construction put on this letter by E. Daudet (" L'Emigration," i, 296) is quite unwarrantable.

[3] " Mémoires du Marquis Louis de Bouillé," ii, ch. xxxv; " Dropmore Papers," iii, 89, 94-101.

In his memoirs Puisaye noted several proofs of the earnest-
ness of Pitt and his colleagues in the royalist cause. Their
preparations, though tardy, were thorough. They placed at
the head of the British regiments designed to reinforce
Puisaye, a man who was the soul of honour, the Earl of Moira;
and the admirals who were told off to protect the convoy
were men of high reputation, Bridport and Sir John Borlase
Warren. Sir Sidney Smith, cruising off the north coast of
Brittany, also actively exerted himself to mislead the enemy
as to the point of attack. On 17th June 1795 Warren weighed
anchor in the Solent with his convoy, having on board some
3,800 French Royalists. They consisted of Hervilly's regiment
(1,200), Dresnay's (700), Hector's regiment of naval officers and
seamen (700), La Chatre's (600), and 600 artillerymen, mostly
refugees from Toulon.

At first all went well. Bridport dealt a sharp blow at a
squadron of the enemy off l'Orient and captured three sail-of-
the-line, one being " Le Tigre," destined to win fame off Acre.
The rest of the fleet he drove into l'Orient and blockaded it
there. The coast having been thus cleared, Warren felt his way
in hazy weather towards Quiberon:

> The sickle sweep of Quiberon Bay
> Whose beach once ran with loyal blood.

He cast anchor there on 27th June. Four ships which had
parted company soon arrived.

The Quiberon Peninsula stretches southwards into the Bay
of Biscay. In shape it is not unlike Portland; but, though larger
and more fertile, it is lower in contour and more hooked in
shape, enclosing a deep bay which forms one of the best road-
steads in France. The peninsula contained several hamlets of
fisher-folk, who named the outer sea *la mer sauvage*. The bay
was then in part commanded by two weak batteries not far from
the tip of the tongue, while a stronger fort, then called " Fort
Sansculottes," dominated the long and narrow isthmus. Such
was the place whence the royalist movement was to gather
itself up and sweep eastwards to the demolition of Jacobinism.

Disputes had begun while the force was at sea. By some
unaccountable blunder Dundas and Windham (always more or
less at variance) in their instructions of 6th June to Puisaye
appointed him commander of the French regiments in British

pay, from the time of disembarkation; whereas the Admiralty despatch of the same date appointed the Comte d'Hervilly to that command, Puisaye accompanying the expedition as adviser. It is possible that Ministers meant to designate Puisaye to the supreme command of the whole force, which, it was hoped, would speedily gather around the nucleus now sent. If so, the instructions were drafted with gross carelessness. The results were deplorable. Hervilly, a hot-tempered, brave and ambitious man, at once asserted his claim to command, and at first refused to allow the disembarkation.[1] The arrival of favourable news from Tinténiac and Boisberthollet, the scouts of the expedition, overbore his objections, and the disembarkation took place on the mainland not far from the mysterious cromlechs of Carnac (27th June). Then came a scene which revealed the real feelings of the Bretons. Scarcely were the first troops ashore before men, women, and children streamed to the beach uttering cries of welcome, and bringing food and wine to their deliverers. The next day witnessed a ceremony which testified to the piety prompting the crusade. The venerable Bishop of Dol and a band of priests, who had come in order to rouse that great province for the orthodox creed, celebrated mass in the open air before thousands of adoring worshippers. Yet even here signs of feud were not wanting. Hervilly, scornful of the rustics, and mistrusting their eager rush for arms, held his paid regiments aloof from the volunteers even in the act of worship.

Nevertheless, Puisaye was full of hope. On that day he wrote to Windham, begging for the sum of £40,000 to enable him to support the army of 80,000 men which would soon be under his command. He also sent to Calonne, the once famous Minister of Finance, now rusticating in his villa at Wimbledon, the following urgent missive:

Depart, Sir, and announce to our Princes the first successes of our expedition. Tell them that they will soon have an army of 80,000 men ready to die for them. I can enter into no details, not having a moment to spare. But I will limit myself henceforth for some days to writing with the sword.

---

[1] See B.M. Add. MSS., 7975, for the instructions; also Puisaye, "Mems.," vi, 60; L'Abbé Robert, "Expéd. de Quiberon," ch. ii. In B.M. Add. MSS., 8079, are some notes of Puisaye, *inter alia*, on "Projets des intrigans pour porter l'Expédition à la Vendée." Probably Hervilly was among them.

Calonne received this enthusiastic message very coolly and sent it on to Pitt, adding the curious comment, that he hoped the Comte d'Artois would share Puisaye's views, but he (Calonne) refused to take any action in a matter in which he desired not to be involved.[1] Nevertheless, the news of the successful landing and the prospect of a general rising in Brittany, decided Pitt, Windham, and Spencer to lose no time in sending for Artois. A frigate was at once dispatched to bring him from his residence near Bremen.[2]

The confidence of Puisaye seemed well founded. Armed bands from the interior of Brittany soon appeared, and by 29th June Warren reported that some thousands of peasants had joined the array. Arming and enrolling occupied the first days. Then, on 3rd July Puisaye and Hervilly led some 8,000 men, including British marines, along the isthmus towards the fort, while Warren ranged his frigates alongside. The commander at once surrendered with his 600 men. The greater number went as prisoners to the ships; but several of them, deserters from the old *Régiment de la Reine* to the republican levies, manifested a desire to return to their allegiance; and Hervilly was credulous enough to enrol them.[3] The *fleur-de-lys* and the Union Jack were hoisted side by side over the fort, now re-named Fort Penthièvre. Warren landed guns from the " Thunderer " in order to strengthen its batteries. He also helped the operations of the Royalists along the coast by means of gun-vessels and armed *chassemarées*. On 10th July he described the royal army as 14,000 strong; he took on board more bands of prisoners, and sent the whole number to England under convoy of warships.[4]

The next six days witnessed an utter change. Already there were acute divisions at headquarters; Hervilly persistently thwarted Puisaye's plan for a rapid march into the interior,

---

[1] Pitt MSS., 119.   [2] " Dropmore Papers," iii, 89.

[3] The Report sent by the Marquis de la Jaille to "Monsieur" thus describes this incident: " M. d'Hervilly avoit grossi son régiment de près de 200 hommes pris parmi les prisonniers faits à Quiberon. Cette mesure était dangereuse; elle fut blâmée et généralement rejettée par tous les autres chefs de corps. Ces nouveaux prédicants ne tardèrent pas à travailler avec succès l'opinion des soldats engagés dans les prisons d'Angleterre" (B.M. Add. MSS., 8079).

[4] Adm. (Chan. Fleet, 103). M. l'Abbé Robert (" L'Expédition de Quiberon," 1894), amidst his diatribes against the perfidy of Pitt, does not mention the important services of the British Navy at Quiberon up to 21st July 1795.

which would sweep the scattered bands of Republicans into the royalist net. Thus, time was given for them to rally under one of the ablest of French leaders. General Hoche, "the saviour of the Republic," was at this time twenty-seven years of age. Rouget de Lisle, the composer of the "Marseillaise," has described the impression produced on him in those critical days at Quiberon by the towering frame, soldierly bearing, and calm steadfast gaze of the young hero, whose features were set off by "a superb scar" that spread across his forehead. To see Hoche in repose was to esteem, almost to love, him. To see him amidst the rage of battle was to fear the pent-up powers controlled by that terrible will. Speedily he rallied the "blues" near the town of Auray, some ten miles inland, and recovered that important post for the Republic.

Meanwhile the "whites" persisted in futile inaction and demoralizing quarrels. The *émigrés* and the peasants often fell out. On one occasion a noble, on entering a tent at dusk, called out to another, "Who is that fellow there?"—"Only a *Chouan,*" came the scornful reply, "one sees none but peasants here." Finally the *émigrés* and the peasants had to be enrolled in separate bodies, which eyed each other askance. Is it surprising that these discordant leaders and suspicious bands lost ground to Hoche? Hervilly, who now virtually commanded the expedition, committed the strange blunder of exposing the untrained Chouans to the first onsets of the Republicans, while he kept the best troops in the peninsula. Mainly owing to this foolish disposition of his troops, he was driven out of the fortified lines at the village of Ste. Barbe near the neck of the peninsula. He then rallied his men in and beyond the isthmus, where they had the support of British gunboats.

Everything now depended on a speedy diversion from the interior of Brittany. For this purpose Puisaye had sent by sea, with a convoy of British ships, some three or four thousand Chouans under his faithful friend, Tinténiac, to rouse the country and take Hoche's troops in the rear. The expedition arrived safely at the mouth of the River Vilaine, and seemed likely to succeed, when, on 11th July peremptory orders of a contrary tenour arrived from the secret royalist agency at Paris. Purporting to emanate from Artois himself, they bade Tinténiac make for St. Brieuc or St. Malo in the north of Brittany. It is now generally admitted that these orders were given (probably by Duverne de Praile) in order to discredit Puisaye, to whom the royalist agency at Paris was bitterly hostile.[1] In any case, whether the outcome of stupidity or of bigotry, they helped to wreck the campaign. Tinténiac turned away from his appointed task, and fell in one of the many skirmishes that attended his march northwards. His place was then taken by Georges Cadoudal, who did nothing for the relief of Puisaye.

Unconscious of this mishap, Puisaye placed some hope in the Vendéans, some sixty miles to the south. Their brave leader, Charette, though barely thirty-five years of age, had acquired a complete hold over those fanatical peasants. At his command they took up arms or skulked in their woods. Faithful unto death for Church and King, they asked nothing better than to slay or be slain under his leadership. Money he needed not. If his men did not do their utmost, he himself beat them; and they then did better. His opinion about Puisaye stands fully revealed in the account of the long interview which he had with Grenville's envoy, the Baron de Nantiat, during the critical days that decided the fate of the Royalists at Quiberon.

Pitt and Grenville have been reproached with doing little or nothing to ensure united action in Brittany. But they sent Nantiat for this very purpose. Difficulties detained him at Nantes, then firmly held by the Republicans; and not until 23rd July could he make his way, in the disguise of a mason, to the Breton camp, a few leagues to the southward. The suspicions long nursed by Charette soon came to light. Could it be that the British Ministers, who had so long abandoned him, were now about to send help? Nantiat strove to allay these feelings, and proved to him that some of the stores sent to la Vendée must have miscarried; certainly Windham and Grenville desired to do their utmost for him. We may remark here that Charette's suspicions were directed against Puisaye, not against the Pitt Ministry; for only three days before he had written to Whitehall asking for help in arms and stores. In that letter he sought to explain away his recent parleys with the Republicans on the ground that they had promised to concur with him in the restoration of royalty, and that he found himself grossly deceived.[2] There must have been a large fund of simplicity in Charette.

[1] E. Daudet, "L'Emigration," i, 317; Forneron, "Les Emigrés," ii, 111; Puisaye, "Mems.," vi, 429.

[2] "Nous n'avons posé nos armes un instant que parcequ'on nous avoit

On 23rd July he sought to play a game of bluff with Nantiat. He declared that he wanted no money from England. His chief needs were a few cannon, horses, and stores; above all, powder, powder, powder. " Ah," he cried, " if the English had only given me half of what they gave Puisaye, who will do nothing at Quiberon." Questioned as to this, he said that six of his officers were there in disguise at the disembarkation and stayed there eight days. They saw the lack of discipline, the heedless offer of arms to all who applied for them, the quarrels, the delays, and the final retirement towards the peninsula. Above all, Puisaye had not informed Charette of his plans, his force, or his arrival.[1] Report described that leader as eating oysters on the coast when he should have been routing Hoche's detachments. And why did not the Comte d'Artois come to inflame the hopes of the Royalists?[2] Nantiat replied that Monsieur burned to do so; but that the British Cabinet wished him not to land until he could do so with safety. Would not 80,000 faithful troops form an impenetrable rampart? asked the fierce Breton. As for Puisaye, he would have nothing to do with him. In fact, the Vendéans could not stir until they had reaped the harvest.

This important interview reveals the causes that led to the failure at Quiberon. Charette's suspicion of Puisaye hindered the unity essential to success. Had Artois been at hand and enjoined united action, this might have been attained. As it was, the Quiberon effort remained without the support on which the British Ministers had reasonably counted.

Meanwhile, Pitt, on hearing news of the unsteadiness of the Chouans in the fights at Auray and Carnac, prepared to despatch 3,000 British troops in support of Puisaye. Moira, too, by 13th July had overcome his hesitations as to accepting a command of some 7,000 British infantry, supported finally by a band of *émigrés* and the 3,000 horsemen still in Hanover.[3] His instructions bade him declare after landing that the aim of the expedition

promis de concourir au rétablissement de la royauté. Non seulement trompés dans notre attente, mais menacés dans la personne de nos chefs, dont quelques uns ont été indignement égorgés," etc. (" F. O.," France, 44). Despatched on 19th July, it was received on 25th August

[1] " Dropmore Papers," iii, 112. This contradicts Puisaye's assertions (" Mems.," vi, pt. i, 99, 120 *et seq.*).

[2] On 30th June Charette wrote to the Comte d'Artois that la Vendée had taken up arms and would fight to the death (B.M. Add. MSS. 37859).

[3] " Dropmore Papers," iii, 90, 100.

was the restoration of Louis XVIII, and that England in return for this help, expected to gain some French possession, but not in Europe. Artois was to proceed to Brittany at once, Moira's force being auxiliary to that which the prince would command. A secret letter of 15th July expressed the hope that His Royal Highness would display towards his misguided subjects "those sentiments of generosity, lenity and moderation which His Britannic Majesty's servants have so strongly recommended."[1]

Within a week Hoche ruthlessly shore asunder the whole scheme. While Moira was embarking the British infantry at Southampton, the Republicans entrenched themselves before the village of Ste. Barbe, thus threatening the neck of the Quiberon Peninsula. An eye-witness describes the eager energy of "the blues" in labouring at the trenches at that point, while "the whites" wasted their energies in quarrels. The feud between Puisaye and Hervilly was now at its height. The latter had at first counselled dilatory tactics and was mainly responsible for the retirement to the Quiberon Peninsula. But now he swung round to the other extreme and advised an attack on Hoche's lines at Ste. Barbe, at the very time when a squadron hove in sight, bringing a body of 1,500 *émigrés* from North Germany.[2]

There was some method in this madness. Puisaye and Hervilly had not heard of the diversion of Tinténiac's corps, and believed it to be on the point of assailing Hoche in the rear. They also did not know of the ill success of an attack on Hoche's left, near the village of Carnac, made by Vauban.[3] Thus, heedless of the succour near at hand, and trusting in the support of Tinténiac and Vauban, the Royalists filed along the narrow ridge of shingle, deployed on the mainland, and very early on the 16th July rushed on the lines of the Republicans. At first their ardour carried all before it. They swept through two lines. But Hoche, skilfully unmasking batteries on the two wings, raked their ranks with a terrific fire that laid low hundreds of the noblest sons of France. Their onset withered away. No signs of help appeared beyond those impenetrable ranks. After daring their utmost against enemies triple their number they fell back in utter exhaustion to the isthmus, losing men at

---

[1] "W. O.," 176.

[2] Louis de Bouillé ("Mems.," ii, 277), ascribes this change to Hervilly's resolve to have the credit of victory for himself alone.

[3] Vauban, "Mems. sur la Vendée," 120-130.

every step under the sabres of the republican horse. At the narrow neck, where bands of panic-stricken peasants nearly blocked the way with their carts and live stock, the crush became frightful, and the little force must have perished outright, had not Warren, after withdrawing the remnant of Vauban's force, sent in his gun-vessels to beat off the pursuit. As to the effectiveness of his action at this crisis a Frenchman, the Marquis de la Jaille, thus testifies: "The indefatigable Sir John Warren, after having re-embarked the troops of M. de Vauban, had sent his gun-vessels towards the shingle ridge (*falaise*): he arranged them with such skill that they crushed and completely stopped the enemy's columns: he landed the English soldiers who took part in M. de Vauban's expedition; and for the second time the army owed its safety to the valour of the English and the foresight of the commodore."[1]

Not long after this pitiable rout the 1,500 veteran *émigrés* from North Germany landed. They found the peninsula crowded with desperate men and wailing women. None but a hero could save the situation; and their commander, the young Comte de Sombreuil, was merely a chivalrous young officer, endowed with no special gifts. His position had in it every element of pathos. He had torn himself from the arms of his bride at London to lead loyal Brittany in triumph to Paris. He found demoralized bands cowering on a peninsula, guarded only by gun-vessels and a single fort. Everything depended on the possession of this fort, and Sombreuil demanded that his men should hold it. With unpardonable perversity Hervilly refused, from fear of offending his own corps of *émigrés*. He ought to have known that the newly enrolled prisoners of war were wholly untrustworthy. One or two men slipped away nightly to the enemy. So weak a watch was kept on the isthmus that, on the night of the 19th July, only one deserter was caught, while thirty slipped past. One of the traitors, David Goujon by name, offered to lead Hoche's men along the rocks at low tide to a place where they could scale the walls of the fort.

Accordingly, on the night of 20th July, Hoche led his men in three columns towards the isthmus. Furious storms of rain

---

[1] B.M. Add. MSS., 8079. Vauban, "Mems.," 139-140, thus praises Warren: "aussi vrai que valeureux, prêt à tout pour opérer le bien, d'une activité inimaginable."

and hail beat in their faces and brought them to a stand; some
companies lost their way, and after a night of misery they drew
near to the ramparts as the first rays of dawn glinted in the east.
The surprise in front and on the south, at the sheltered side of
the isthmus, failed; for there the faithful Toulonese gunners
opened a deadly fire. Hoche therefore ordered a retreat. But
on the outer side, where the waves lashed the rocks in fury, the
Republicans, guided by a few traitors, crept without hindrance
up to the wall. Hoisted shoulder high, they thrust their
bayonets into the crevices of the masonry, and by sheer skill
and daring clambered to the top. There, where a dozen faithful
men could have hurled them headlong, the friendly arms of
traitors pulled them in. In one band they rushed at the loyal
gunners and cut them down. They hoisted the tricolour, and
Hoche, turning about, ordered an attack which overbore the
faithful remnant.

There was now no time to throw up entrenchments on the
peninsula. To add to the misfortunes of the Royalists, the
storm had obliged Warren to keep his ships and gunboats far
out; and no news of the disaster reached him until it reached
its climax. Remorselessly, then, Hoche pressed his quarry
towards the tip of the peninsula. Sombreuil's men, still full of
fight, contested the advance at every available spot, but they
were hampered by the panic-stricken crowd which swept southwards towards the little Port Allighen. There men and women
rushed into the water, shrieking for the help that did not come
from the ships. At last, Puisaye, after failing to send off his
aide-de-camp, la Jaille, resolved to go himself; and, at a later
time, he declared that he did so on the request of Sombreuil.
However that may be, he put off quickly in a boat so as to save
his confidential papers, and was followed by the curses of his
men. On his departure, and that of Hervilly, who was carried
off to the ships mortally wounded, the defence collapsed. Parts
of the Hervilly and Dresnay regiments went over to the enemy.
Sombreuil, with the faithful troops, had retired to Fort Neuf, on
rising ground near Port Allighen. Unhappily its guns could be
trained only on the friendly British, not on the pursuers. Nevertheless, some of the survivors declared, that if he had held firm
until the tide rose, help would have come from the British warships, and his men could have embarked with little loss under
cover of their fire. He himself, in the last letter that he wrote to

Hoche, stated that, owing to Puisaye's carelessness and cowardice, he had no cartridges; and, on the arrival of guns for the victors, he was fain to trust the generosity of his foes.

The exact truth on this matter will never be known; for the rush of events dazed every brain, and shame at the stampede warped the account of every survivor. La Jaille and Vauban defend Puisaye on the ground that he was not really in command, and acted for the best in saving his papers and soliciting help from the ships. But why then did he not return to rally the panic-stricken masses at Port Orange or Port Allighen, and help on the embarkation? His statement that he would have done so but for the news of the capitulation is far from satisfactory.[1] It seems clear that both he and Sombreuil lost nerve as the horror of the day deepened with broadening light. Sombreuil's band, still some 1,300 or 1,400 strong, was not in a hopeless position. They held a battery which partly screened them from Hoche's attack; and though its cannon were useless, those of H.M. corvette, "Lark," which in the teeth of the gale had worked in near to Port Allighen, searched the approaches to the battery with terrible effect. The twenty-four naval guns (says Vauban) swept an open space across which the assailants passed to attack the little fort. Thus, Sombreuil, however hard pressed from the western shore, could not be surrounded so long as the "Lark" poured in her volleys. Why then, if he had no cartridges, did he not charge with the bayonet towards the open sea?

Certainly all the resourcefulness was among the Republicans. According to Vauban they raised shouts for a capitulation in order to stop the firing of the corvette. Then, under a flag of truce, General Humbert approached and parleyed with Sombreuil.[2] After him came Hoche himself. Those youthful and stalwart champions of warring creeds eyed each other with mutual esteem and admiration. The clemency of Hoche was already well known; and to him, it appears, Sombreuil repeated his proposal to give his own life if his men might be spared. To this Hoche is said to have given a verbal assent, adding that he could do no more, seeing that the final decision must rest with Tallien and Blad, the two *représentants en mission*. Somewhat later they too came on the scene, and promised to do

[1] Puisaye, "Mems.," vi, 524.

[2] Puisaye ("Mems.," vi, 546) gives reasons for thinking that Humbert's sole reason for parleying was to silence the fire of the "Lark."

all in their power to secure pardon from the Convention at Paris. But no incident of this bewildering tragedy is more shrouded in mystery than this question of the capitulation. The *émigrés* certainly believed that their lives would be spared, though some of them (among them Vauban) plunged into the sea, preferring to brave waves and bullets rather than trust their pitiless foes. Several of them reached the corvette, "Lark." Others were picked up by the boats of "La Pomone" and "Galatea."

The following despatch from Warren sets forth the services of his vessels at this time:

H.M.S. "Pomone," Quiberon Bay, July 22, 1799.

I am extremely sorry to inform you that the fort and peninsula of Quiberon was taken the morning of the 21st by assault, at 3 o'clock, owing to treacherous measures. In addition to the misfortune of the place having been surprized by treason, the night being remarkably dark, with a hard gale of wind at N.W., rendered it impossible for the gun-vessels to work up close to shore: as soon as day broke, seeing the fort was taken and the enemy's troops on the march, I dropt down to the south point of the island towards Fort Quiberon, where I made a signal for the frigates to slip, and stationed them alongshore; the "Lark," sloop, and "Pelter," gun-vessel having run close into a sandy bay.

I sent my own boats, as well as those of the men-of-war and *chassemarées*, inshore, and commenced a heavy fire upon the different columns of the enemy who were pressing down on the remainder of the Army, among whom were the regiments of Béon, Damas, and Salm, with part of d'Hector's, under the Comte de Sombreuil, made (*sic*) a most excellent defence until the enemy brought cannon upon their flank when they were obliged to capitulate. I have been able to save about 1,000 troops, with all the generals and staff, [the] greater part of the Corp[s] of Artillery and nine of the Engineers, with 1,400 Chouans, and several regimental colours;[1] and I should have been able to have embarked a greater number, if the masters of the transports had paid the least attention to my signals for their flat-boats, which I repeated with guns four times, without seeing any one having arrived (*sic*).

[He then names with approval Captains Keats and Ogilvey for their work in the embarkation, and Lieut. Tomlinson of the "Pelter" for annoying the enemy during their march along the shore. He continues:]

---

[1] Chassin, ("Hoche à Quiberon"), gives the figures as 900 *émigrés*, 1,400 Chouans, 800 unarmed peasants and women.

I have every satisfaction that no blame whatsoever can attach to the officers and men of the navy in this disastrous affair, as every effort and support was made use of by them in putting the place in a proper state of defence, which nothing but the utmost defection of part of a regiment on guard, whose advanced post deserted and gave the parole and countersign to the enemy, and afterwards fired on their officers, could have effected. I am sorry the loss of the fort puts the enemy in possession of the greater part of our provisions, some valuable articles of clothing, and a few arms, with the cannon taken on the island: the residue I have secured in the transports which are with me; as soon as I have things in order I intend to take possession of the Islands of Hédic and Houat until joined by the army under Earl Moira, who are, I am informed, on their passage; or receive orders to the contrary.[1]

La Jaille, who found refuge on Warren's frigate, adds some significant details about the admiral's conduct respecting the capitulation. Warren, doubting whether it were not a *ruse* to induce him to cease firing, promptly sent to inquire the exact terms. He received an evasive reply, but felt bound to maintain the truce. As the chief effect of the capitulation was to silence the warships and leave the Royalists helpless, Warren became more and more uneasy. On the following day his suspicions deepened; for when he again sent an officer to inquire the conditions, he was insolently informed that there were none.[2] By that time very many of the Royalists had been marched away inland to Auray. Doubtless, Warren would have opened fire on the forts but for the conviction that in that case vengeance must have fallen on the captives.[3]

The last act of the tragedy now opens. It shows us Hoche leaving Quiberon in haste for the revolted districts of North Brittany; while Tallien hurries off to Paris to solicit from the Convention pardon for the prisoners. That gifted and sensitive soldier, Rouget de Lisle, travelled with him, and found his speech full of dignity and clemency. Fortune also willed that they should reach the capital on the first anniversary of the fall of Robespierre. Thoughts of mercy were in all hearts. Disgust

[1] Adm. Chan. Fleet, 103. The details here given correct the exaggerated statement of the losses given by James, "Naval History," i, 279.

[2] B.M. Add. MSS., 8079. The biographers of Hoche deny that there was a capitulation. Daudet, Forneron, l'Abbé Robert (as well as Sombreuil and Vauban), assert there was.

[3] Puisaye, "Mems.," vi, 524, 537.

at the brutal orgies of the Terror formed the theme of every speech. When all the omens pointed to clemency, would not Tallien save the lives of the prisoners huddled together on that wind-swept peninsula or in the Chartreuse of Auray? He is said still to have desired it. But the interview with his wife filled him with dread. That ambitious creature warned him that damning proofs of his intrigues with the Royalists were to hand.[1] One loophole of escape remained, to vindicate the purity of his patriotism by declaiming against the vile offscourings whom the perfidious Pitt had thrown on their coast.

The result was seen a few days later at Auray. Men who had marched quietly to that town, neglecting the chances of escape afforded by their good-natured guards, now heard with indignation their incredible fate. Nevertheless, bravely, as became gentlemen of France, they filed from the Chartreuse, the church, and the prison under the awe-struck gaze of the townsfolk. Two by two, to the tap of drum, with hands bound, but heads erect and eyes flashing defiance, they marched to a long and spongy meadow that fringes the bank of the river. There the butchers were ready. Volleys at short range laid their kneeling forms low, swathe by swathe. Day by day the ghastly work went on, as the military commission at Auray, Vannes, or on the peninsula proceeded with the summary trials. At Vannes fell the men whose fate aroused the most poignant grief. The vengeance of the Republic required the lives of the aged Bishop of Dol, and other chaplains of the royalist army. By the bent form of the bishop there stood the towering figure of young Sombreuil. With unshaken serenity each performed for the other the last sad offices. The noble refused to kneel at the bidding of his enemies. He did so at the advice of the bishop, and then spake these words: " I bend one knee to my God: the other to my King."

These were among the last victims of the holocaust. Many perished on the peninsula, where incredible blundering and treason led to their undoing; but most of them raised their last cry of *Vive le Roi* in the meadow near Auray. Twenty years later, when Louis XVIII came to his own again, the bones were reverently interred; and a *chapelle expiatoire* now rises near *le champ des martyrs* in memory of men who in their death alone

---

[1] Tallien's royalist leanings had long been known. Puisaye, in his first letter to Pitt (30th September 1794) states it as nearly certain that Tallien would soon declare for royalty (Pitt MSS., 169).

were not divided. Perchance those 712 victims achieved more by their death than in their life. The long-drawn-out brutality of the executions, sickening even to the butchers, aroused a furious hatred against the Government which crowned with perfidy a triumph due to treachery. The act cowed only the timid, and therefore it cowed few Bretons and Vendéans. Charette, on hearing the news, decided to end his long balancings. He began a war to the knife by slaughtering 300 Republican prisoners. Thus, the furies of civil strife, fettered in the spring, were let loose once more. The formidable royalist movement of September at Paris, which, but for Bonaparte's cannon, would have overthrown the Convention, had its roots in the loathing inspired by a regime of crass brutality.

A storm of obloquy also broke upon Pitt. Puisaye, whose conduct at the crisis aroused general detestation, was loudly accused of being sold to that Minister, the arch-contriver of ruin. Such a charge is intelligible amidst the ravings of bereaved Royalists, who insinuated that the expedition was deliberately wrecked in order to ensure the massacre of some fifty French naval officers. But it is astounding to find some members of the English Opposition echoing these wild charges. In a violent outburst, which will ever be a stain on his memory, Fox accused Ministers of deliberately sending noble gentlemen to a massacre. The speech of Sheridan was an almost equally disgraceful display of reckless ignorance and eager spite. He declared that, though British blood had not flowed at Quiberon (which was false), yet "British honour had bled at every pore."[1] That Englishmen who knew next to nothing of the facts should utter slanders so diabolical is a striking tribute to the debasing power of partisan malice.

Let us review the facts in the light of the documentary evidence now set forth. It was notorious that for several months the *émigrés* in London had urged the Ministry to send an expedition to the Breton coast. Windham supported their importunities; but Pitt, ever distrustful of the *émigrés*, gave no definite assent until the month of June, when that enterprise promised to create a diversion highly favourable to Spain, and therefore to the royalist cause in general. In face of the schism among the Bretons and Vendéans, and their truce with the Republic,

[1] "Parl. Hist.," xxxii, 159, 170.

an expedition could not have been sent at an earlier date. True, a force had been mustering in the Solent, but Corsica or the West Indies, equally with Brittany, had been thought of as its destination. Finally, Ministers decided to send Puisaye to Quiberon and make it a base of operations for a larger force of *émigrés* and British troops under the lead of Artois, if all went well. Thus, in Pitt's view, the present enterprise was essentially tentative and preparatory.[1] That peninsula was to form a place of arms, unassailable from the mainland so long as the fort was firmly held, and yet, while covered by the fleet, affording the easiest possible access to the mainland. From that starting-point Brittany was to be roused and waverers everywhere encouraged by the moderate royalism of Puisaye. The one inexcusable blunder of the British Government was the assigning of equal powers to Puisaye and Hervilly. On this, and this alone, can the charge of treachery be based; and those who know the incoherence of work in British Departments will readily find a more prosaic explanation. Further, if Pitt had desired to betray their force, he could easily have arranged it by sending a few lines to the Committee of Public Safety at Paris. But, as we have seen, that body and Hoche were quite in the dark as to the point of landing; and at first all went well. Puisaye's ardour therefore flamed forth, and he planned a speedy march into the interior. Hervilly with the paid troops remained in the peninsula, leaving Puisaye's and Vauban's Chouans, with a small force of British marines, to bear the attack of the regular troops of Hoche. Meanwhile Tinténiac's movement against Hoche's rear miscarried owing to contrary orders spitefully sent by the secret royalist committee at Paris; and a similar intrigue kept Charette from sending the help on which the British Ministry and Puisaye reasonably relied. Even so, the disaster would have been averted if Hervilly had waited a few hours for the disembarkation of Sombreuil's troops before making his attack on Hoche's lines at Ste. Barbe; and if, after the repulse, he had replaced the untrustworthy men in the fort by the tried troops of Sombreuil. This it was which led him on his death-bed to accept full responsibility for the disaster.[2]

---

[1] Failure to realize this has betrayed M. Ernest Daudet into the statement (" L'Emigration," i, 297) that Pitt expected to *conquer France* with 5,000 men.

[2] Puisaye, "Mems.," vi, 605-8. The original of Hervilly's confession, with Windham's endorsement, is in B.M. Add. MSS., 8079.

What does Fox's charge of premeditated perfidy imply? It implies in Pitt and his colleagues a singular power of fore-ordaining events; of impelling Puisaye to push boldly on, and of detaining Hervilly in the peninsula. It implies that Ministers foreknew the ill-will of Charette, the resolve of Artois to over-throw Puisaye at the first opportunity, and the action of the secret royalist agency at Paris which diverted Tinténiac from his appointed task. Nor is this all. In the distorting lens of partisanship, Pitt figures as responsible for Hervilly's resolve to enrol part of the republican garrison of Fort Sansculotte; for his attack on Hoche's lines just before the landing of Sombreuil's succouring force; for the actions of deserters from the fort and of traitors within; for the unaccountable collapse at Fort Neuf and the surrender of Sombreuil on verbal assurances; for the craven *volte face* of Tallien at Paris and the wholesale condem-nations of the military commissions at Auray and Vannes. In fine, did Pitt spend £1,120,000 on this expedition in order to rob the future French royalist navy of some fifty officers? [1]

---

[1] The Russian ambassador in London, Vorontzoff (Archives, xvi, 236-248) states that these slanders were soon spread about by the *émigrés*, who (be it remembered) subsisted on money supplied by the British Government. He ably refutes them. D'Andigné afterwards allowed them to be unjust. E. Daudet (" L'Emigration," i, 297) affects to doubt whether the disaster was due to the perfidy or ignorance of the British Government. Chassin (in his scholarly work " La Vendée," ix, 72) absolves Pitt of the charge of perfidy.

BRITISH RULE IN CORSICA

THE need of a good naval base in the Mediterranean led the British Government to put forth several efforts in the course of the eighteenth century. At first they centred in Minorca, with results that are well known.[1] Other islands scarcely came into serious consideration. Our usually friendly relations with the Italian States forbade all thought of the seizure of Corsica, Sardinia, or Elba. As for the conquest of Malta from the Knights of St. John, it would have been alike sacrilegious and cowardly. The aggressive policy of France was, however, to simplify the problem. In the year 1769 she acquired Corsica from the Genoese Republic by far from reputable means; and in 1798 Bonaparte continued at Valetta the policy, inaugurated in the previous year by the partition of Venetia, of seizing small and unoffending neutral States, which previously had been under the protection of Christian law and sentiment.

The outbreak of war with France in February 1793 led Pitt to consider the means of attacking her from the south; and our alliances with Spain, Austria, Naples, and the Kingdom of Sardinia augured well for the proposed attempt to rouse the Royalists of Provence against the Jacobinical Government then struggling to hold its own at Paris. The hold of that faction on Corsica was doubtful despite the desperate efforts of Bonaparte to win over the loyal and religious islanders to the republican cause. Their affections centred in Paoli, who, after a long time of exile spent in England, was devoted to our institutions, and early in that year sent an offer of the crown of Corsica to George III. Signs are not wanting that it was welcomed both at Windsor and Whitehall.

The chief cause for hesitation was the touchiness of the court of Madrid, where some of the Ministers harboured designs on

---

[1] See Mr. Julian Corbett, "England in the Seven Years' War," i, 374-6; i, 174-5, *et seq.*

Corsica. Godoy, Duke of Alcudia, the all-powerful favourite of the Queen, was no less covetous of wealth than suspicious of England. Accordingly, on 25th April 1793 our Foreign Minister, Lord Grenville, wrote to Lord St. Helens, British ambassador at Madrid: "I have said nothing about Corsica in my despatch, but the language of the Duke of Alcudia disconcerts our projects. I tremble for the moment when we come to discuss that tender point of indemnities." Again, on 7th August, after concluding a treaty of alliance with the Court of Naples, Grenville reminded General David Dundas that the objects of the Allies in the Mediterranean ought to be the recovery either of Nice or of Corsica. Sixteen days later, Lord Chatham warned Admiral Hood that if he made an attempt on Corsica, he should secure the help of Captain Masséna, an old Paolist. Further, on 30th November, Grenville expressed regret that the Court of Madrid seemed to retract its former wish, that Corsica should go to England. It is certain, then, that Pitt and his colleagues looked to Corsica as one of the indemnities to be claimed from France at the end of the war. Lord Macartney later on reported that the Comte de Provence (Louis XVIII) made no objection to this plan. But Spain early showed signs of resentment.[1]

The aims of Pitt and his colleagues were doubtless known to Sir Gilbert Elliot, who was to act as the King's Commissioner in the Mediterranean. Elliot, though long an opponent of Pitt, had been so disgusted at the factious conduct of Fox as to espouse the side of the Government, which nominated him as Civil Commissioner, first at Dunkirk, and, on the collapse of that enterprise, at the equally unfortunate post, Toulon. It is singular that so distinguished a statesman as Elliot (the first Earl of Minto) should have begun his official career with two fiascos and next with a lengthier experiment, the failure of which was by superficial observers attributed mainly to him.

In the closing days of 1793, after the evacuation of Toulon, Hood and he resolved to support the Corsican Royalists, and to continue their operations on the coast of Provence from that island as a base. Accordingly, on 12th January 1794 Hood sent Elliot, along with Colonels Moore and Koehler, to confer with Paoli. It was on this mission that the future Sir John Moore

---

[1] "Dropmore Papers," ii, 412; "F. O." Spain, 28. Grenville to St. Helens, 30th November 1793. In "F. O." France, 42, is a long *Mémoire* on the advantages of possessing Corsica, and a plan for securing it.

undertook the first political work in a career which had already been meritorious and was to end in a blaze of glory. The envoys sought to discover the real aims of Paoli, whom Hood suspected of shiftiness, the strength of the French garrisons remaining in the island, and the disposition of the islanders. Elliot and the two colonels found Paoli in a deserted monastery near Pietra Alba, where he lived in simple patriarchal style, surrounded by bands of armed peasants who relieved each other in turn. It afterwards transpired that the French had put a price on his head and that he was very near the end of his resources, a fact which goes far to explain his eagerness for British help.

At the first interview the old general showed his dislike of civilians by opening the conversation with Koehler and Moore; and, on their referring him to Elliot as the King's Commissioner in the Mediterranean, he curtly remarked that he was tired of Ministers and negotiations. Why had not Hood sent him the succour he had promised? However, he calmed down and finally assured them that he would die only happy if he could but see his countrymen under the government or protection of Great Britain. He vouched for their readiness to accept either arrangement, and scouted the notion of consulting them until the French were ousted from their three posts, St. Fiorenzo, Bastia, and Calvi. He spoke as dictator of the island, and his countrymen to a man seemed to acclaim his will as law. Their cheers now, as always, were: "Long live Paoli, the Fatherland, and the English Nation." As for the French garrisons, they were said to number only 1,950 men, along with about 700 Corsican Republicans. Leonati, Paoli's lieutenant, said that the British would need only a few cannon to reduce those garrisons.[1]

Moore soon found cause for distrusting Paoli. Nevertheless, the enterprise seemed so promising that Hood took steps to help him. Though driven aside to Elba by a gale, the fleet on 7th February made St. Fiorenzo Bay on the north-west of Corsica; and General David Dundas, with the able assistance of Moore and Koehler, before long reduced a powerfully constructed tower at Martello Point. That work gave so much trouble that it became the pattern for the many scores of smaller towers, which, under the name of Martello Towers, still diversify parts

---

[1] "Diary of Sir J. Moore," i, ch. ii ; "Mems. of Sir G. Elliot," vol. ii.

of our coastline.[1] The correspondence of Hood with Paoli, preserved in the British Museum, proves that Hood on 17th February sent on shore 10,000 dollars, 50 barrels of gunpowder, and 13,000 musket balls.[2] On that same day the British and Corsicans captured the last of the French batteries defending St. Fiorenzo Bay; but the native levies failed to cut off the retreat of most of the garrison across the hills to Bastia on the east coast. The Corsicans had also grossly understated the strength of the French garrison at that town which numbered 3,500 trained troops. Disputes between Hood and General Dundas led to a spirited protest by the latter against the Admiral's claim to supreme command in the Mediterranean; whereupon he retired home in high dudgeon. Hood's resolve to undertake the siege of Bastia was sharply questioned by eight military officers (including Moore) in a council of war on 20th March. But Hood and the naval officers had their way; and the siege was begun;[3] It was some time before General Sir Charles Stuart arrived to take the command of the troops. The feud between army and navy, which had grown apace at Toulon, entered on a new phase with the appearance of that able but choleric officer.

Meanwhile, despite Paoli's offer of the crown of Corsica to George III, Pitt and his colleagues were acting with much circumspection. Thus, on 7th March, Henry Dundas, one of the Secretaries of State, wrote from Whitehall asking the advice of Paoli as to the terms of the union, on which Ministers could not decide until they heard from him. He, however, assured the Corsicans that "whatever mode of connection may ultimately be established with that island, if the arrangement of its internal government depends upon the country, every reasonable degree of liberty and personal security will be insured to the inhabitants."[4] On 31st March Dundas approved the conduct of Elliot in furthering the plan of a union, but bade him stipulate that the British Governor should have "the supreme executive power, with the command of the military, and with a right of negative of all legislative acts." The constitution and the

---

[1] Fortescue, iv, 182. Sir George Cornwall Lewis derives them (more convincingly, I think) from the Torre di Martello (Hammer Towers) in which the striking of a hammer on a bell gave the warning in case of raids by pirates ("Stanhope Miscellanies," ii, 59).

[2] Brit. Mus. Add. MSS., 22688.

[3] "H. O.," Adm. Medit. (1794).   [4] B. M. Add. MSS., 22688.

fundamental laws of Corsica were to remain unchanged, unless by the act of its Legislature, assented to by George III, and signified by the British Governor.[1]

After gaining the consent of Paoli to these conditions, Hood and Elliot declared themselves empowered to agree to the perpetual union of Corsica with Great Britain, the islanders receiving due guarantees for the maintenance of their constitution, fundamental laws, and religion. Paoli thereupon issued a summons for a Consulta or Parliament to meet at Corte, the old capital in the interior. Three weeks before it met, Bastia succumbed to the joint pressure of the British fleet and the relatively scanty land forces of the Royalists (21st May). As is well known, Commodore Nelson distinguished himself during these operations, and during the siege of Calvi which followed.[2] At the latter place he lost the sight of his right eye. The surrender of Calvi ended the French sway in the island.

The assembly of the Corsican deputies at Corte presented a quaint yet moving spectacle. The members were nearly all chieftains, and they came up to that rock-crowned city, musket at the side, and clad with the trophies of the chase. For once these fierce and factious clans were moved by one impulse. They shouted for Paoli, and almost thrust him into the president's seat. In due course the old man made a telling appeal against France and for union with England. On 19th June this motion passed with enthusiasm, George III being acclaimed unanimously as King, with Sir Gilbert Elliot as Viceroy. In an eloquent speech uttered in French, Elliot expressed his fervent hopes for the future of the two peoples thus happily united. A constitution was soon decreed, which, while democratic in form,[3] gave to the Executive the needful amount of authority. Elliot's powers as Viceroy were nearly on a par with those of the Lord Lieutenant of Ireland, and included the control of the armed forces. This brought him into collision with General Sir Charles Stuart, Commander-in-Chief of the British troops in the Medi-

---

[1] W. O., 70, I. B.

[2] For details see Fortescue, iv, 182-191. As a sign of Hood's brusqueness, note that he thus answered the claim of Pozzo di Borgo, Paoli's agent, to share in the capitulation of Bastia: "I always understood the island of Corsica was to become English and governed in the same manner Ireland is. Consequently, of necessity, the capitulation must be with me alone" (B. M. Add. MSS., 22688).

[3] "Mems. of Sir G. Elliot," ii, 270; Jollivet, 28-32.

terranean, a man whose hotness of temper and impatience of control marred an otherwise promising career. The quarrel arose in part out of an expression by Elliot of a desire to visit the military hospitals. Stuart curtly declared that he would be welcomed as Sir Gilbert Elliot, but not as Governor or Viceroy, for he had no authority over the army. Elliot contested this dictum, and referred the matter to Whitehall. Unfortunately, the Ministerial changes which brought the Duke of Portland to the Secretaryship of State in place of Dundas protracted the usual official delays, and not until 2nd December did the Duke declare decisively in favour of Elliot. Thereupon Stuart threw up his command in high dudgeon (6th January 1795). Major-General Trigge took his place, but proved to be incompetent for his duties.

The need of troops in other quarters, notably in the West Indies, Brittany, and at the Cape of Good Hope, prevented the despatch of the 4,000 or 5,000 men from England whom Ministers had promised for the spring of 1795; and the defence of Corsica depended largely on four battalions of the islanders raised by Elliot. Fortunately a French expedition which set sail for the recapture of Corsica was driven back at a time when the scanty British garrisons were attenuated by fever;[1] but the French sent reinforcements from Brest to Toulon, while few arrived from Plymouth;[2] and the situation encouraged Frenchmen to plan the recapture of an island valued for its supplies of timber and naval stores.

The neglect of Corsica by Pitt and his colleagues (Elliot's despatches usually brought no reply within four or five months), the activity of France, and the sloth of our ally, Spain, weighed on the spirits of the loyal Corsicans and enabled the factious to cavil at British rule. Among a backward, clannish people, the heat engendered by disputes usually rises in proportion to their pettiness. It was so in Corsica. The islanders fretted because the British, as the French before them, made Bastia the capital,

---

[1] "Mems. of Elliot," ii, 297.

[2] Mahan, i, 192; Nelson Despatches, ii, 11-24. Hood (then in England) wrote to Pitt in April 1795 most despondingly about the small reinforcements accorded to the Mediterranean fleet. His tone was so pressing that the Ministry decided not to send him out. In July 1795 he again wrote to Pitt, bemoaning the loss of St. Lucia, also of a large convoy near the Windward Isles. On 2nd December 1795 he requested the Governorship of Greenwich Hospital, which was granted to him (Pitt MSS., 146).

in place of inaccessible Corte. Again, there were ominous mutterings because the old national flag (a Moor's head on a silver ground) was replaced by the British ensign, though the security afforded by the latter at sea might have stilled those insular qualms. The difficulty of administering Corsica received curious illustration from an attempt to institute trial by jury. Pitt hoped that this palladium of liberty would prove a boon in a country where the custom of the vendetta was believed to spring from the corruptibility of judges; but trial by jury proved to be the mother of crime. Rarely could twelve jurymen be brought to agree on a verdict against a prisoner; and, when they did agree, the result was the starting of twelve vendettas against the champions of law and order. In the interests of humanity, therefore, Elliot abrogated trial by jury; and Ministers at home sorrowfully acquiesced.

In the main, however, the storm-centres of the island were Moore and Paoli. It is far from easy to fathom the matters in dispute between them and the Viceroy. Troubles began at Toulon, where Elliot sided with Hood against the soldiery. Stuart took up the feud bequeathed to him by General David Dundas, and passed it on to Moore. Brave and chivalrous almost to a fault, and extremely sensitive to the claims of honour, Moore reminds us of that noble but pathetic figure, Tellheim, in the " Minna von Barnhelm " of Lessing. Like him, Moore was apt to balance the rights and wrongs of a question with an introspection almost Hamlet-like in its nicety; and this peculiarity sharpened his critical faculties until his judgements became censures, and his censures reprimands. " He maintained the right with a vehemence bordering on fierceness." So says his admirer, Colonel Napier. Others sometimes found him more · able to criticise than to act with decision.[1] Certainly in Corsica Moore let his critical faculties run riot. Readers of his " Diary " will infer that Elliot was a vain, meddlesome proconsul, whose absurd mistakes ruined the British Administration. But Moore's statements are grossly one-sided, and he certainly did much to aggravate the difficulties of the Viceroy. When northerners undertake to administer the affairs of the most excitable and factious race in the Mediterranean, its officials ought loyally to support one another. Yet Moore, then Adjutant-General, did

---

[1] See examples in Prof. Oman's " Peninsular War," i, sect. vi.

not scruple to write in his " Diary " about the " little low art " of the Viceroy, of his equating his position with that of the Lord Lieutenant of Ireland merely from a sense of vanity, of his governing now too strictly, now too leniently, but always by means of bribery. Further, how could things work smoothly when Moore sought to persuade Trigge not to let himself be shackled by Elliot? In point of fact it was Moore who managed Trigge. And what can we think of an officer who, though not on the spot, ascribed the failure at Toulon to Admiral Hood's " stupid obstinacy "? [1] This criticism by one who knew next to nothing of the wider causes of that disaster, stamps him as by nature a *frondeur*. Such a man, though admittedly an able officer, was peculiarly dangerous in Corsica, when he began to associate with the opponents of the Government, and openly criticised its proceedings. Accordingly the Viceroy asked that Moore should be recalled. The Duke of Portland complied with the request, and added, with needless severity, that Moore must leave Corsica within forty-eight hours. After passionately protesting against Elliot's conduct, that officer left the island on 4th October 1795. After arriving in London, he saw Pitt, who heard what he had to say against the Viceroy, and then advised him to speak to the Duke of Portland, not in " the language of passion," but to say calmly all that would tend to his justification.[2]

Pitt's cold manner affected Moore somewhat painfully; for he afterwards complained of it to Dundas, only to be informed that the Prime Minister had thought that he (Moore) had been hardly used and should be employed again. It is clear, then, that Pitt valued his services highly (he afterwards used his military advice), but wished to read the hothead a lesson in prudence and official reserve. The resulting statement by Moore did not convince the Duke of Portland. Moore describes the Duke as silent and embarrassed, as if he were struck with the force of arguments which he could not answer. But the Duke was a nervous and silent man. On 30th April, when affairs settled down in Corsica, he thus cumbrously congratulated the Viceroy on the change. " Nothing can more clearly manifest the causes which obstructed the return of the disposition of mind which was necessary for this purpose, or more fully justify the wishes you at last allowed yourself, and I trust not too late, to express for the removal of Colonel Moore and General Paoli, than the

---

[1] Moore, " Diary," chs. v, vi.   [2] *Ibid.*, i, 171-4, 179, 180.

demonstrations of that temper which has universally shown itself since their departure from the island." [1]

The so-called retirement of Paoli to England is a question the merits of which depend on the truthfulness of many individuals of an essentially southern race. Paoli himself is far from trustworthy. Civil war, exile and privations had told on him; and at fifty-five years of age he was no longer the stately and imposing leader who overawed Boswell by his penetrating glances.[2] Age, vanity, a fancy far too lively for his otherwise mediocre abilities, and a truly Corsican proneness to schism and intrigue, made of him a bundle of nerves and prejudices irritating to a northerner, but fascinating to his own kindred. He was the people's idol; and the fact that his influence had brought about the union with England seriously complicated matters. The situation somewhat resembled that which arose in September 1860, when Garibaldi, after freeing Southern Italy, met Victor Emmanuel near the River Volturno; and, unlike the red-shirt chieftain, Paoli did not speedily retire. What position, then, could he possibly hold under Elliot? Fortunately his growing infirmities prevented his acceptance of the Presidency of the Consulta; and a nonentity named Giufferi was chosen. More important was the choice of the head Minister; and here Elliot made the mistake of exalting a skilful, designing advocate, named Pozzo di Borgo. Undoubtedly he was a very able man. The scion of a noble family, endowed with a commanding presence, handsome features, an eloquent tongue, and considerable facility both as a journalist and man of affairs, Pozzo had been the adviser of Paoli during the strife against the Jacobins. But, that being settled, self-interest and difference of character sundered them. Indeed, his gifts were so varied, and his ambition so insatiable, that in that island he could not long be a follower of any chief. And his part once taken, he clave to it with Corsican obstinacy. Such was the *début* of a career which brought him finally into favour with the Czar Alexander I.[3]

In truth, Corsica was too small a sphere for impetuous natures like Paoli, Bonaparte, and Pozzo di Borgo. In that cockpit of the Mediterranean, where the deadly customs of the vendetta were alike the supreme law and the chief check on over-popula-

---

[1] W. O., 70, I. B.   [2] J. Boswell, "An Account of Corsica," p. 315.

[3] Moore calls Pozzo ("Diary," i, 138) "a low, mean-minded man, with some cunning and intrigue, but totally devoid, in my opinion, of talents."

tion, it was difficult for England to succeed where Genoa and France had failed. The people combined the fickleness of the mediaeval Florentines with the independence of islanders and the fighting qualities of mountaineers. Bonaparte summed up the character of his compatriots in the statement that their imagination and their passions were most lively, and that they themselves were extremely difficult to understand.[1] This explains much. At first, of course, the islanders welcomed the British because they ousted the French. But in reality they merely wanted to govern themselves in the rough-and-tumble ways which had so much fascination for Rousseau. Having fulfilled in the person of Bonaparte the Genevese thinker's lucky forecast that they would one day astonish Europe, they were now to reveal the hollowness of his statement that theirs was "the one country in Europe capable of legislation."[2] In point of fact, their ideal was a clannish anarchy which defied all legislation.

The one thing essential for the preservation of anything like order in Corsica was to keep Paoli in a good humour; and, now that his head was in no danger from the French, this was no easy task. The appointment of Pozzo di Borgo to the Presidency of the Council of State was in his eyes an unpardonable sin. For had not he (Paoli) raised Pozzo from obscurity? In vain did the latter consult the old man and flatter him by all possible means.[3] Paoli was inconsolable. From his retreat at Orezza the acrid ferment spread through the mountainous interior. The hillmen were already aggrieved at the choice of Bastia as the seat of Government; and the Corsican deputies, who went to England to lay the crown at the feet of George III, dwelt on this and other matters, until the Duke of Portland lost patience with them and read them a well-deserved rebuke.

Meanwhile, however, the bungling of the Duke's subordinates at Whitehall had given Paoli a handle against Elliot and the British Government. The King had ordered that a miniature of himself set in brilliants and hung from a gold chain should be sent to Paoli. In due course Mr. Pollock of the Treasury delivered to Mr. Richard Stewart, who was setting out to Corsica with despatches, six packages, in one of which the picture was

[1] Napoleon, " Corresp.," ii, 163.
[2] " Contrat Social," bk. ii, ch. x.
[3] Jollivet, *op. cit.*, 157, proves this incontestably.

supposed to be. On his arrival it was missing. Elliot carefully investigated the matter and found that Stewart could not have received the miniature. He forwarded to Paoli Stewart's letter of explanation[1] and ordered close inquiries to be made at Whitehall. But the matter remained in mystery; and this gave to Paoli the opportunity of insinuating that the Viceroy was the thief.

"It is often seen" (says Bacon in his "Essay on Faction") "that a few that are stiff do tire out a greater number that are more moderate." This happened again and again in the French Revolution; and Corsica was now to witness to the truth of the saw. There is every reason to believe that British rule had the tacit approval of the majority. But the restless minority fastened on every incident, until a scratch on a bust came near to rousing a Revolution. The incident came about thus. During a visit of the Viceroy to Ajaccio in June 1795 the officers of one of the Corsican battalions arranged a public ball in his honour at the Town Hall. The function went off brilliantly, and Elliot departed for Bonifacio, charmed by his reception. Meanwhile envious rumour had been at work on a very ordinary accident. A large bust of Paoli had to be removed during the preparations for the ball and sustained a slight injury, a piece of plaster about the size of a sixpence being flaked off from the top of the nose. Soon the story ran that Captain Colonna, an aide-de-camp of the Viceroy, had overthrown the bust, his comrades thereupon stabbing it with their daggers and pitching it away into a cupboard. In vain were the dimensions of the wound measured. In vain did Colonna solemnly declare that he did not enter the Town Hall until the ball began. In vain did Elliot return, hold an inquest on the bust, and set forth the truth. Indignant patriots declared that the honour of Corsica, incarnate in Paoli

---

[1] R. Stewart wrote thus to Elliot from Bastia, on 24th November 1794: "Six days previous to my quitting London, I was informed by the Duke of Portland and by Mr. Pollock of the Treasury that I should be entrusted with despatches to Your Excellency, amongst which would be included H. M.'s picture for Gen[l]. Paoli. On the 21st, the day I left London, Mr. Pollock put into my hands a parcel containing six packages directed for Y. E.; and tho' Mr. Pollock did not mention it at the time, I conceived from what he said that one of them contained the picture alluded to. The six packages I delivered to Y. E.; but from the description you give of the picture and of the chain annexed to it, they could only have been packed in a box; and I am therefore very certain I never received them" (B.M. Add. MSS. 22688).

and therefore in his bust, had been deliberately outraged by the Viceroy and his myrmidons. Pozzo di Borgo was made to figure as an accessory to the "assassination." A *procès verbal* at Ajaccio, drawn up by ardent Paolists, was widely circulated; and the letters of Paoli prove that he sought to make capital out of the affair, with the result that Corsica heaved with passion at the loss of a flake of plaster.[1]

So threatening became the unrest in September 1795 that the Viceroy resolved to remove Paoli. Already, in September 1794, he referred the matter to the British Government, which was aware that the dictator, during the first discussions of a union, had offered, on its accomplishment, to retire to England. After a very trying delay Portland assented to the proposal, and gilded the pill by awarding Paoli £2,000 a year apart from the pension of £1,000 previously accorded. Elliot also accompanied the patriot to the warship that conveyed him to the mainland. But the old man never forgave him or the British Cabinet. In his correspondence there is a long and acrid letter (probably to Sir Charles Stuart) in which he complains that, on his arrival in London, Ministers resented the criticisms that he once more levelled against Elliot.[2] There was reason for their resentment. By that time they had heard from Francis Drake, our envoy at Genoa, of the secret dealings of Paoli with an unfrocked monk, named Pancrazzio d'Istria, who was sent over by Chiappe, a Corsican exile. The report ran that Pancrazzio was to set on foot a scheme for arousing discontent against the taxes and other details of Elliot's administration, the aim being to restore Paoli to power. Such was the report sent to Drake early in September by a secret agent named Timorani. Pitt and his colleagues attached some importance to it; for on 5th October Portland wrote to Elliot that the whole affair "confirmed the suspicion, which you were evidently unwilling to give way to, of Paoli's baseness and treachery. Whether this clue will lead to further discoveries, or whether you will think it right to pursue it, rests solely with you." Portland then promised "a comfortable retreat" for Paoli "on

---

[1] Jollivet, 157-9; Elliot ("Mems.," ii, 319-21). Moore accepted the statements against Colonna; so does his editor on very weak evidence ("Diary," i, 159, 165-9).

[2] B. M. Add. MSS., 22688. Sir C. Stuart wrote to him in equally bitter terms on 2nd November 1796.

the express condition of his withdrawing himself immediately and for ever from Corsica and engaging to pass the remainder of his days in this kingdom."[1] Such, then, was the inglorious ending of Paoli's career. The mural tablet to his memory in Westminster Abbey tells one tale. The British Records tell another and a very different one.

After the removal of Moore and Paoli Corsican affairs proceeded quietly. At the close of 1795 Frederick North, one of Elliot's Secretaries of State, succeeded in framing a treaty with the Dey of Algiers, which not only freed Corsican vessels from the Barbary rovers, but secured the liberation of 195 Corsicans held in bondage. Already Elliot had sent a Frenchman, de Sade, to open up close relations with the Knights of St. John at Malta.[2] Pitt and his colleagues fully approved these overtures; and we learn from Portland's letter of 2nd December 1794 to Elliot, that the Grand Master offered to sell stores and galleys for the defence of Corsica; while the Bailli de la Tour de St. Quentin promised Portland to endeavour to secure the loan of 4,000 Maltese for that purpose.[3] In this he did not succeed; but the promise explains why the Home Government did not for some time send off troops to reinforce the garrison. The incident is also of interest as illustrating the truly prophetic dread of France prevalent among the Knights, and the need of furthering the Mediterranean policy on which Elliot laid so much stress. Thanks to the efforts of a British agent, Sir John Hippisley, at Rome, Elliot succeeded in settling various questions in dispute with the Papacy.[4] Further, an act was passed founding a university at Corte and advanced schools at Ajaccio and Bastia. On 30th April 1796 Portland congratulated Elliot on these efforts, and expressed the hope that Oxford and Cambridge would help Corsica in matters educational.

Up to the month of August 1796 a continuance of British rule in Corsica seemed probable. Work was begun at a naval dock at Ajaccio; but, though the military men had strongly advised the strengthening the defences at Bastia and St. Fiorenzo, Portland forbade those undertakings until sanctioned by the

---

[1] " W. O.," 70, I. B.; " F. O." Genoa, 12. I have published the reports of Timorani " in the " Revue Napoléonienne " for 1910.

[2] " A History of Malta " (1798-1815), by W. Hardman, ed. by J. H. Rose, p. 180.

[3] " W. O.," 70, I. B.   [4] " Castlereagh Corresp.," iii, 476.

Board of Ordnance;[1] and nothing was done. Indeed, on several occasions Elliot wrote bitterly of the apathy of the Home Government. Portland, who corresponded with him, was by nature a balancer. " Portland will look at his nails" (so wrote Elliot), " and raise his spectacles from his nose to his forehead for a fortnight or so before he answers me."[2]   For these delays Pitt must ultimately be held responsible. Owing to party reasons he had raised the Duke to the Home Office, which mismanaged not only internal affairs but also those of Ireland and the colonies; and it was the duty of the Prime Minister to see that Corsica was not neglected. But Pitt lost interest in the war after the autumn of 1795. His one aim now was to secure indemnities for its expense and to gain the best terms possible from France. Probably the peace between France and Spain, and the jealousy of the latter respecting Corsica, convinced him that the island would be a source of more danger than of advantage.

Here we have one of the reasons for the failure of that interesting experiment. The Corsicans soon came to question the continuance of the British occupation. Paoli, on meeting Moore at Cuxhaven in November 1795 expressed a fear that Pitt, under the demoralizing influence of Dundas, would give up Corsica.[3] I have found no proofs of Pitt's opinion on this question. He and his colleagues maintained a prudent reserve; and one cannot argue with certainty from such phrases as—" The possession of Corsica, if it remains with us,"—in one of Grenville's letters.[4] Further, the fact that no public works were pushed on except at Ajaccio, does not imply a resolve to leave Corsica, but rather a prudent economy in money and men at a time when they were more urgently needed elsewhere. It is, however, noteworthy that Pitt in his great speech of 9th December 1795 named Martinique, Cape Nicolas Mole, and the Cape of Good Hope as the three great acquisitions of the war, and made no mention of Corsica.[5]

In the spring of 1796 Government sent thither two fine regiments, one of French *émigrés*, under Edward Dillon (" le beau Dillon"), the other of Swiss under de Rolle. Their arrival strengthened the monarchists at a time when, owing to the brilliant victories of Bonaparte in North Italy, discontent once more be-

---

[1] "W. O.," 70, I. B.   [2] Elliot, "Mems.," ii, 326.
[3] Moore, "Diary," i, 178.
[4] " Dropmore Papers," iii, 12, Grenville to Portland, 26th January 1795.
[5] " Parl. Hist.," xxxii, 585.

came rife. Finally it broke out in a rising near Corte. Elliot tactfully met the demands of the leaders by dissolving Parliament, accepting the resignation of five unpopular officials, and promising to consider the remission of the salt and land taxes. This lenity, which appeased the people for a time, probably resulted from Elliot's doubts as to the intentions of Ministers. Portland, when at last he did write, penned these paralysing words:—" You must remember that the possession of Corsica is not more gratifying to the public than that of Gibraltar, and that the expenses belonging to it are not likely to make it popular. Remember that our worthy countrymen are not foreign politicians."[1]

This is true enough. But what are we to think of a statesman who, on a matter on which the public can form no judgement, hedges and trims according to their varying moods? Resolution and firmness in the early spring of 1796 would have saved England and Europe from an Iliad of war. At that time Bonaparte's communications with France lay along the Italian riviera; and a blow struck at Vado Bay, or Oneglia, would have clogged his operations at the outset. Here again, then, the Ministry failed to act betimes and must share with Austria the responsibility of allowing its ally, Sardinia, to be crushed by the young conqueror. Even up to the middle of May the landing of a small force on that coast would have checked his progress through Lombardy. He had always taken a keen interest in the fate of his native land, witness his letter of 23rd September 1794 (after the French success on the Riviera), that they must now chase the English from Corsica, a position which gives them the mastery of the Mediterranean.[2] Other signs betoken his resolve to carry out this plan at the earliest possible time. It is probable that the rising near Corte and Bocognano, in the spring of 1796, was due to his emissaries, it being always his plan to busy his enemies by stirring up revolts in their midst. Owing to Elliot's tactful acquiescence in the demands of the islanders, the danger soon passed; for Nelson, when off Genoa on 14th May, wrote: ' Corsica is, I hope (at least the Viceroy says so), in a fair way, of being made quiet, the refractory are few, and he is now fully equal to face either outward or inward enemies."[3]

The prospect soon darkened. The raid of Bonaparte's troops

[1] Elliot, " Mems.," ii, 345.   [2] " Nap. Corresp.," i, 58.
[3] " Nelson Dispatches," vii, lxxii.

against British shipping at Leghorn at the end of June, besides doing great damage to our commerce, threatened Corsica with a new danger. As is well known, the young conqueror organized at that seaport a corps of Corsican exiles for an expedition to the island. The arrival of Nelson off Leghorn, and his blockade of that port, checked the scheme; but Nelson saw that it could be frustrated only by a bold counter-stroke, the occupation of Elba. As he wrote to Elliot on 2nd July: " The way to Corsica, if our fleet is at hand, is through Elba." Elliot therefore directed him to seize that island, and he did so on 10th July. Elliot at that time reported matters as " better than quiet in Corsica."[1] This report contradicted a rumour that reached Trevor, our envoy at Turin, as to " foul play in that cursed Corsica." In fact Corsican privateers helped Nelson in capturing the enemy's vessels along the Italian coast.

Up to the middle of August, all the danger to Corsica was from the side of Leghorn. But now a cloud rose in the West, which soon overcast the whole sky. Spain was on the brink of war with us. At first, that is on 15th August Nelson feared little even if the Dons should come; for he knew their fleet to be " ill-manned and worse officered." But after three days' reflection he penned the ominous words, " If they do [come], we must give up Corsica, that is all. Our fleets will cover every sea but the Mediterranean." He hoped that the British force in those waters, when reinforced by Mann's squadron from off Cadiz, would number 22 sail-of-the-line. As for the troops in Corsica, they were " more than usually healthy and prepared for service."[2] Still, the main question was—could Corsica be held, now that the Spanish navy threatened our communications with that island? Closely linked with this was the further question—Austria having lost Italy by the defeat at Castiglione, was it worth while to keep a large fleet in that sea, to assist a Power which could not help herself? Pitt, as I have shown elsewhere, was aiming more and more at peace. Certainly he no longer relied on Austria, as of yore. Naples being also bent on an accommodation with France,[3] there was little reason for keeping a fleet in that sea, as the treaties of the summer of 1793 required. Moreover,

---

[1] "Nelson Dispatches," ii, 194-211, 238.

[2] *Ibid.*, ii, 241, 242; vii, p. ci.

[3] Naples signed an armistice with France at Pistoja on 26th June 1796 (" Nap. Corresp.," i, 687).

the Franco-Spanish combination threatened, not only the British West Indies, but also the United Kingdom on its most vulnerable side, Ireland.

Clearly, then, the supreme need of the moment was concentration of sea-power. Too long had England spread out her efforts in what may be termed an enveloping strategy against a State which had most effectively retorted by blows from an inner arc. Holland, Brittany, Hayti, Toulon, Corsica—these had been our points of attack on France. The last-named proved the most serviceable of those bases. But now the defection of Spain necessitated its abandonment. On 31st August the Duke of Portland sent off an order for the evacuation of the island and of Elba. Elliot heard the news with consternation, for nothing previously had foreshadowed so abrupt a resolve.[1] There is scarcely a shred of evidence for the assertion often made, that it was due to the discontent of the Corsicans. On the contrary, the islanders were at that time unusually quiet. Captain Mahan quotes Nelson's statement of 20th May that Corsica was not worth holding in the present temper of the inhabitants.[2] But he does not quote later letters of a more hopeful tenour. Besides, Nelson could not know the causes of the decision of the Ministry, though on 18th August he made the shrewd surmise quoted above.

If we compare the date of that decision with those of the rupture with Spain, we find them to tally very closely. During the month of August events marched quickly towards war. On or about the 26th, the Spanish ambassador pettishly left England on a flimsy excuse; and by that time Pitt and Grenville knew that the French squadron had left Cadiz under convoy of the Spanish fleet.[3] In view of this openly hostile act, what Government would not have taken steps to guard against a Spanish attack? The most vulnerable of our possessions were Hayti, Gibraltar, and Corsica. Ministers had already taken steps to strengthen the garrisons at Gibraltar and in Hayti. Portugal, menaced by Spain, also called out for British succour. These pressing claims involved retrenchment elsewhere, namely, at Corsica.

Such, then, is the cause of the evacuation of Corsica. Partisans of Moore and critics of Elliot may ascribe it to the in-

---

[1] Elliot, "Mems.," ii, 355. This corrects Mr. Frewen Lord ("Lost Possessions of England," p. 219), as to Elliot's "relief" at being recalled.
[2] Mahan, "Life of Nelson," i, 243.   [3] "F. O.," Spain, 43.

competence of the latter and "the change from enthusiastic loyalty to revolt."[1] But this charge is refuted by the facts above stated, which prove that the abandonment of Corsica resulted from the victories of Bonaparte and the perfidy of the Spanish Court. If further proofs are needed, they may be found in two facts. First, that the Pitt Ministry on 31st August decided to evacuate Elba as well as Corsica. Now, to hold Elba was a comparatively easy task; and from its excellent harbour, Porto Ferrajo, the Sea Power could threaten the coasts of Italy under French control. Nevertheless Elba was also given up. Secondly, on 20th October Ministers countermanded the evacuation of Corsica and Elba.[2] Could anything show more conclusively that the retention of Corsica depended, not on the whims of the islanders, but on the trend of military and naval events?

The reason for the strange oscillation of Pitt's plans on 20th October is to be found, not in the encouraging news of Austrian successes in Swabia (as Captain Mahan asserts) but in the recent resolve of the Cabinet to offer Corsica to the Empress Catharine. She had lately offered to send 60,000 Russians against France, if England and Austria would satisfy her pecuniary demands, which were scarcely in accord with her eager royalism. As British credit was on the brink of a collapse, Pitt viewed her proposals with suspicion, and on 19th October he and his colleagues unanimously resolved to offer to her Corsica, which she was known to covet, provided that its ports were open to the British fleet during the war, and thereafter to British commerce.[3] Alas for the proposal, Nelson and Elliot completed the evacuation of Bastia on the very next day! And by the end of the month the young commodore set sail from St. Fiorenzo Bay for Elba with the remaining troops and stores. Further, it is doubtful whether the tempting offer ever reached the ears of Catharine, for on 16th November, after a long and distressing illness, she expired. With her died the last hopes of the First Coalition, which her eager professions had nursed to life and her calculating selfishness had scandalously betrayed. Whether, in those last sad weeks, she intended to do anything more than incite England and Austria to further fruitless efforts is a problem which she carried with her into silence. Her son Paul forthwith reversed her policy, and little more was heard of Russian rule in Corsica.

[1] Sir F. D. Maurice, in Moore's "Diary," i, 31.
[2] "Auckland Journals," iii, 363.   [3] "Dropmore P.," iii, 246-9, 261.

For yet another reason the prompt withdrawal of Britain from Corsica was most opportune. By a grave error of judgement, Admiral Mann, who was ordered to reinforce Admiral Jervis, commanding the Mediterranean fleet, decided that the risks of encountering a superior Spanish force were too great, and made sail for Spithead. On his arrival he was promptly disgraced. His retreat necessitated the prompt evacuation of the Mediterranean by Jervis and Nelson.[1]

The conduct of the British Government towards Corsica was weak and dilatory. Pitt must have known of Portland's delays in answering despatches; for Windham wrote to Elliot that the Cabinet's fault was not to have thought or acted wrongly about him, but not to have thought at all.[2] Windham was at that time smarting under the Quiberon disaster and the proposals for a peace with France. But his letter convicts the Prime Minister of neglect of the other Departments of State, which in this case implied leaving Corsica at the mercy of Portland. The results of the evacuation were very great. The re-conquest of the island by the French enabled them to draw thence the timber and the naval stores on which the dockyard at Toulon largely depended. The French navy therefore speedily recovered its wonted strength in the Mediterranean; and Austria, lacking the naval support of England in the Adriatic, threw on us the responsibility for the conclusion of the separate peace to which the triumphs of Bonaparte in Styria reduced her in the month of October 1797. From the wreck of their fortunes the Hapsburgs snatched Venice and Eastern Venetia; but the Ionian Isles perforce went to France, which for a time became undisputed mistress of Italy and the Mediterranean. The young Corsican hailed in these events the dawn of a far more brilliant future. The recovery of his native island and the gain of Corfu beckoned him on to the conquest of Egypt and of India. Not without reason, then, did General Stuart on 2nd November 1796 write to Paoli that the abandonment of Corsica was an eternal disgrace to the British Government.[3]

---

[1] Mahan, "Sea Power," i, 213-5. A large number of Corsican Royalists went into exile and formed a battalion, the Corsican Rangers, which did excellent service under Colonel Hudson Lowe ("Napoleon and Sir Hudson Lowe," by R. C. Seaton, 44). For the British attempt to retake Corsica in 1814 see Jollivet, App. XIII.

[2] Elliot, "Mems.," ii, 277.   [3] B.M. Add. MSS., 22688.

PITT AND RELIEF OF THE POOR

THE English poor have rarely if ever been plunged into deeper distress than in the years 1794-7. Uncertainty of work, heavy taxes, and an alarming increase in the prices of the necessaries of life strained to breaking-point the antiquated system of poor relief. Dating from the forty-third year of Queen Elizabeth's reign, it assigned to the magistrates of each parish the responsibility for the poor of that parish; and there was little or no supervision from London of the parochial systems which grew up. Seeing that differences in the scale of relief induced pauper vagrants to seek out the most desirable place of abode, Parliament, in the reign of Charles II, passed Acts of Settlement so severe as to check even migration in search of work. Adam Smith pointed out that they killed all enterprise in the English rural poor, who were as much tied to the soil, or rather to the parish, as under the old Feudalism. To this cause we may in part ascribe the curious inequalities in wages and well-being then prevalent in English villages, some being burdened with an excess of helpless desponding drones, while others languished for want of hands.[1] Scotland and Ireland, which had no Poor Law until far into the next century, showed no such perplexing diversities.

Despite some attempts to remedy the cramping effects of the Acts of Settlement, no material change took place until 1782, when the philanthropist, Gilbert, succeeded in carrying through an Act which bears his name. With the purpose of facilitating the movement of labour, he provided that parishes should be allowed to form Unions, which, furnishing relief in common, would replace the village poor-houses by one central workhouse. Paid guardians were to be chosen by the justices of the peace, the duties of the overseers being limited to the collection of the

[1] A. Smith, "Wealth of Nations," i, ch. x, § 2; Aschrott, "English Poor Law System," 9-13; Garnier, "Annals of the British Peasantry," ch. xvi.

poor-rate. As the Act was permissive, and was taken up by only 924 parishes, it never attained to national importance, though it heralded the dawn of a national system. In one respect Gilbert's well-meant effort led to highly mischievous results. A clause of his Act enabled the guardians to provide the able-bodied poor with work near their own homes on terms which would ensure their maintenance.[1] It was soon found that this charitable proposal led to the adoption of lax schemes of out-door relief, that form of succour which needs the closest supervision.

The interest of Pitt in these questions appears in his institution of a Parliamentary Inquiry. The resulting Report, issued in 1786, is a thin production compared with its famous successor of 1834; but it shows the strangely diverse customs prevalent even in London parishes. Some had houses of industry, others had not. Some let out their paupers at 3s. 6d. or 4s. each per week to contractors at Blackfriars, Hoxton, etc. In other workhouses the paupers toiled on behalf of the rates; elsewhere, for the benefit of the master or mistress. The occupations were mostly spinning, weaving, or oakum-picking. In the country workhouses spinning or weaving was the rule; but the method of sale of the produce is not stated. In view of the future developments in Berkshire, it is worth noting that that county had no workhouse; but there were three workhouses in Reading.[2] The Report, meagre though it is, testifies to the slipshod ways of the English people, who very rarely organize well on a large scale except under the lead of a genius or the pressure of dire necessity.

A fact not very creditable to the intelligence of the race is the continuance of the oppressive Act of Settlement without any considerable change from 1662 to 1795. In the latter year Pitt undertook to mitigate one of its severities by enacting that a settler should not be expelled from his new abode until he became actually chargeable to the rates. This seems a small concession; and, from his memorable speech of 6th February 1796, it is clear that he regarded it as inadequate. Nevertheless he then helped in some measure to restore liberty of movement

[1] Nicholls, "History of the English Poor Law," ii, ch. xi; Aschrott, 19-21.

[2] Pitt MSS., 307. This packet contains several proposals and criticisms by Gilbert and copies of earlier Acts.

to the workers, and to promote the fluidity of labour so desirable in the ever-changing phases of the Industrial Revolution.[1]

Meanwhile, the magistrates of Berkshire, assisted by "several discreet persons," assembled at Speenhamland near Newbury on 6th May 1795, took a step fraught with momentous issues. Finding that the weavers of that district and the makers of broadcloth at Newbury were in sore distress owing to lack of work and the high price of bread, they resolved to systematize the custom of supplementing wages from the poor-rates, which, as we have seen, was legalized by Gilbert's Act of the year 1782. They preferred this course to the alternative of raising the wages of day labourers by magisterial enactment, a custom which, besides being almost obsolete, entailed much friction at the ensuing time of reduction of wages. Accordingly, they enacted that, when the gallon loaf of second flour cost one shilling, every poor and industrious man should receive three shillings a week for himself and half that amount for his wife and each child. When the loaf cost one shilling and fourpence, the relief was assessed at four shillings for the man and one shilling and tenpence for the wife or child. For every penny of increase in the price of the loaf, the dole rose by threepence and one penny respectively.[2]

Now, it is only fair to remember that the magistrates of mid-Berkshire were confronted by a serious crisis, and that they endeavoured to meet it by an expedient adopted from Gilbert's Act. They further sought to guard their experiment from abuse by restricting relief to the "poor and industrious man."[3] But how long was a man likely to remain industrious on those terms? All unwittingly they sapped independence at its very base; for they made a man's wage depend, not on the effectiveness of his work, but on the price of bread and the size of his family. The same provision induced the recipient to view with unconcern the rise in the price of wheat, and to hail with joy the birth of every child as an economic gain. It therefore encouraged early and improvident marriages, families of patriarchal size, and thriftless housekeeping. Not without reason did Malthus brand

[1] Parl. Hist., xxxii, 708; 35 Geo. III, cap. 101.

[2] Nicholl, ii, 131; "Mercury," 11th May, 1795; Sidney and Beatrice Webb, "Hist. of the Poor Law," § 6.

[3] See Sidney and Beatrice Webb, "County and Parish," 545-7, 594, with evidence defending the Berks Justices. Those of Dorset adopted a similar plan, but apparently only for a time.

this so-called "Speenhamland Act" as the effective cause of a race of bounty-bred and bounty-fed paupers; for it nullified all the previous attempts to withhold relief from able-bodied paupers unless they came into the workhouse, and enabled them comfortably to slide into pauperized domesticity. It demoralized not only labourers but masters. Farmers, knowing that the minimum wage would be made good out of the rates, began to reduce wages, and thereby threw an added burden on ratepayers. The same cause, then, tended to impair the energies of villagers and to increase their burdens. Is it surprising that by the year 1803 the poor-rates of Witley in Surrey rose to eighteen shillings in the £?[1] Or that some twenty-five years later, in Cholesbury, a village of Bucks, everybody but the parson was a pauper? So much lay enfolded in the kindly experiment of the Berkshire magistrates. Pitt, as we shall see, abetted their slipshod philanthropy; but it should be remembered that the Report of Sturges Bourne's Committee in 1817 and the Parliamentary Report of 1833 were the first documents which proved conclusively that the Speenhamland experiment was bringing England to the brink of financial and moral bankruptcy.

The distress of the years 1795, 1796 prompted other noteworthy expedients. In December 1795 Whitbread introduced a Bill enabling justices of the peace to fix a minimum wage of labour. On the second reading he supported his proposals by quoting the dicta of Price, that during two centuries wages had increased only threefold, or at most fourfold, while the prices of meat and of clothing were sevenfold and fifteenfold respectively. In a hundred years the poor-rates had risen from £100,000 to upwards of £3,000,000, though Whitbread judged it to be doubtful whether the population had increased. In his opinion it was needful to assess the minimum wage in all callings, even as the Lord Mayor and Council of London controlled that of the silk-weavers of the metropolis. In reply on 12th February 1796 Pitt asserted that the figures of Dr. Price were illusory, as leaving out of account the very different conditions of life at the two periods. He further objected to all attempts to draw a hard-and-fast line in regard to wages, seeing that "trade, industry, and barter will always find their own level and will be impeded by regulations which violate their natural operation and derange their proper

[1] I am indebted for this fact to Mr. H. E. Malden, M.A., editor of the Victoria County History for Surrey.

effect." There spoke the pupil of Adam Smith. He left firm ground for morass when he pleaded for the assessment of relief in proportion to the number of children, with the aim of making a large family a blessing, not a curse. He trod safely once more in adverting to the subject of Friendly Societies. In this connection we may notice that Pitt's friend, George Rose, had in 1793 introduced a measure which for the first time recognized the existence of those praiseworthy unions and assisted them by procuring relief from undue financial burdens as well as securing their members from arbitrary removals under the Acts of Settlement. Thereafter they increased rapidly in number and usefulness, a proof that the war period was far from being so barren in remedial legislation as is generally supposed. Whitbread's Bill was negatived, but Pitt now outlined a plan for assuring compulsory payment to one of the Friendly Societies.

In this proposal he had many sympathizers. Gilbert and his compeers had set the fashion for social reforms; and that generation now discerned the important truth that they were more immediately beneficial than merely political changes such as the widening of the franchise. Amidst the misery of 1795-6, when Parliamentary Reform was at a discount, social questions came uppermost; and pamphlet literature, which two years earlier bristled with electoral tirades, now beamed social betterment. One of the many plans for assuring comfort in old age may here be noticed. John Harriott put forward what must be one of the earliest schemes for Old Age Pensions. Its chief provisions may be thus summarized:

EVERY WEEKLY SUBSCRIBER OF	SHALL RECEIVE WEEKLY AT		
	65 YEARS	70 YEARS	75 YEARS
s. d.	s. d.	s. d.	s. d.
0 2	1 0	1 7	3 6
0 3	1 2	1 9	4 0
0 4	1 3	1 10	4 4
0 5	1 4	1 11	4 9
0 6	1 5	2 0	5 0
1 0	2 0	2 6	6 6

Harriott also touched on the question of compulsory subscription, but admitted it to be very difficult if not impracticable.

Nevertheless he hoped to sweep sluggards into his beneficent net by procuring parliamentary sanction for his scheme, along with the proviso that every person who did not subscribe should be termed a drone, and, on applying to the parish for relief, should be compelled to wear a badge bearing in large red letters the word "DRONE."[1] The incongruity of sex in the case of half of the applicants apparently did not trouble Harriott.

Two other proposals of Pitt in the speech of 12th February 1796 deserve notice. He suggested the founding of parochial Schools of Industry, for the training of children in some useful trade. Locke and Lord Hale had advocated such schools, and they had proved serviceable both in imparting technical skill and in enabling families to keep the wolf from the door. He also strongly recommended the publication of what he termed an Annual Poor-Law Budget, including official evidence as to the general working of the system. Both suggestions were of the utmost value; and it is most unfortunate that they were not adopted.[2]

The assembly of the new Parliament on 27th September 1796, the fear of invasion and the scarcity of money, delayed the presentation of the Poor Bill which Pitt's speech of 12th February so hopefully outlined. The year 1796, however, witnessed two noteworthy departures. Pitt lent his support to a measure which allowed magistrates to assess relief to the poor in proportion to the price of wheat, provided that the whole amount thus paid was not more than double of that already awarded. The second Act extended to all parishes the permission, already accorded to Gilbert's Unions, of granting outdoor relief to able-bodied persons. This lax custom having crept in, other parishes clamoured for the same liberty or licence; and Pitt was weak enough to accord it to "industrious poor persons" in time of temporary distress.[3] In consequence the recipients ceased to be industrious, the village was impoverished, and the custom took permanent hold until it was uprooted by the drastic reform of 1834.

Finally, on presenting his Poor Bill on 12th November 1796, Pitt had to meet Sheridan's charge that he had taken the matter out of Whitbread's hands. He easily repelled this peevish attack, showing that Whitbread had sought merely to enforce a minimum wage, while the present Bill contained constructive

---

[1] Pitt MSS., 308.   [2] Parl. Hist., xxxii, 705-12.
[3] 36 Geo. III, caps. 10 and 23.

proposals of far-reaching import. As illustrating an almost unknown side of his career, I propose to describe them somewhat fully. A sign of his singularly sanguine nature appears in the preamble of the Bill, which thus outlines its aims: "To improve the condition [of the poor], and to ensure a more comfortable maintenance and support to them and their families, to encourage habits of industry and good order, and thereby gradually to reduce the excessive amount of the rates."

The chief provisions of the Bill may be summarized as follows: A father entitled to poor relief, who is unable to support his children exceeding two in number, or a widow unable to support more than one child, shall receive not less than one shilling a week for each child above that number, until the child becomes self-supporting. If a poor and industrious person cannot maintain himself, it shall be lawful to make good from the rates the deficiency in his earnings. If by the purchase of a cow or other animal a poor person can maintain a family without the receipt of further relief, the parish shall be at liberty to advance money for such purchase, the loan being repaid on terms to be agreed on. No person shall be excluded from poor relief unless his or her property or belongings exceed £30 in value; but those who have not a legal settlement in the parish shall not benefit by the present legislation. Section 6 deserves quoting almost in full. "For the securing a competent provision in cases of sickness, infirmity, and old age, it may be expedient to establish a parochial fund, which may arise partly from subscriptions or voluntary contributions and benefactions, and partly from an aid to be given out of the poor-rates, whereby the persons subscribing may become entitled to greater allowances than can be secured to them by such savings as can be expected to be made by them out of their own earnings." Accordingly, on the decision of two local magistrates, "a parochial fund for the relief of sick, infirm, and aged subscribers may be formed for providing a stock for the relief of subscribers in sickness, infirmity, and old age by certain allowances increasing in proportion to the periods for which they have subscribed." Suggestions are then given as to the methods which may be adopted, the members of legally established Friendly Societies being entitled, on a moderate subscription, to the benefits of that fund.

The next clause is equally important. In pursuance of the aims of the Elizabethan Act of 1601, a School of Industry shall

be established in each parish or union of parishes for the training of children in some useful trade or calling.[1] The school is
to be supervised by two magistrates and by duly qualified
Visitors of the Poor, among them being beneficed clergymen
and laymen, provided that the latter are freeholders of £50 a
year or rent houses or land worth £150 a year. The parish
meeting is to decide whether the parish unites with its neighbours to found such School of Industry. If not, it must itself
establish a school, to be under the control of a Warden of the
Poor, who also supervises the relief of destitution. Persons
needing succour may be instructed or employed in such schools
or at their own homes on a plan to be agreed upon, the parish
supplying hemp, flax, silk, thread, cotton, wool, iron, leather,
etc., along with the tools and implements needful for the several
trades. Parents who do not undertake to train their children at
home may send any child of more than five years of age to such
a school; and children who cannot be maintained at home shall
be sent thither for training. During the hay and corn harvests
parents may hire out to farmers their boys of more than fourteen
years and their girls of more than twelve years for not more
than six weeks at a time. The parish pays the apprenticeship
fees of its best pupils. For the rest, the School of Industry may
be in part supported by voluntary contributions and by the
labour of the scholars. If the cost of construction exceed £100,
the Overseers of the Poor may build the school by money raised
on security of the rates.

There follows a clause which opens up a vista of beneficent
activity. After gaining the assent of the majority of parishioners,
those who control the relief of the poor may contract with the
lord of the manor for the inclosure of such parts of the " wastes,
commons, or uncultivated land as may be deemed necessary
for the better accommodation of a supply of wholesome food to
the poor at such Schools of Industry as aforesaid, or for the
purpose of building upon, or occupying, cultivating, or improving
the same for the use and benefit of such schools and the poor
persons within the parish where the same shall be or the parishes
united therewith." The remaining clauses of the Bill enable any

---

[1] Workhouses were established by the Act of 1723, and some of them provided a little elementary training. For these and similar experiments see
Dr. Cunningham, " Eng. Industry and Commerce," Part II, pp. 202, 383,
491-3.

parish to turn a House of Industry (Workhouse) into a School of Industry, and to frame contracts for the sale of its productions; they also affirm the right of beneficed clergymen to inspect the School, and to make known any complaints of the recipients of the parochial fund. The election of Guardians of the Poor by the Visitors is also regulated, the property qualification of a guardian being fixed at a rental of £200, or a freehold worth £100 a year. The Bill is to come into operation on 10th July 1797.

In the Pitt MSS. (No. 307) is a draft of these proposals, which is minutely amended by the statesman himself, notably at the clause which enables local authorities to turn a Workhouse into a School of Industry. In order to submit his measure to the judgement of practical men, he had copies of his Bill printed, with wide margins for their written comments. Several of these annotated copies survive, and reveal the drift of thought of experts, while numerous letters also touch on the same topics. It may be well to give a few typical specimens.

Ellis, Clerk of the Peace for Sussex, feared that the indoor work provided in the School of Industry would unfit boys for the work of ploughing, besides indisposing labourers to field work, especially during the winter. He urged the need of placing out boys for farm work as soon as possible, especially at the time of ploughing, sowing, and harvest. He advised the halving of the property qualification for Visitors. A magistrate of Morpeth pointed out that parents should benefit by poor-relief only in the case of legitimate children,[1] and suggested that no compulsion should be exerted to send children to the School of Industry until a magistrate has heard the objections of the parents, if any. Very pungent were the comments of Fenwick of Earsdon, also in Northumberland. In a letter written to a friend, and forwarded to Pitt, the Bill was pronounced ambitious, unworkable, and likely to cause endless litigation. It would make for confusion and waste by creating new local divisions, and too many officials; the schools and the parochial funds would be ruinous

---

[1] The evil results of laxity in relief given to bastards appears in E. Chadwick's " Report on the Poor Law in London and Berks " (1833) where he shows that in some villages (e.g., Burghfield) the bastards nearly equalled the legitimate children. These customs varied much. At Cookham, where the magistrates refused out-relief for bastards, their number greatly diminished.

to poor villages, and, where work was plentiful, the prospect of
the allowance would tempt men away from their usual employ-
ments.   The pitmen would plead infirmity so as to get a lower
wage, in the assurance that their average would be made up
out of the rates.   In place of the local Pension Fund there
should be a National Friendly Society.   Above all, the writer
scoffed at the purchase of cows by the parish, and asked how the
loan would be recovered if the pauper ate his cow.   In brief (he
says): " The Bill requires more disinterested virtue than either
the poor or the guardians are likely to possess."

Scarcely less hostile was the verdict of the Rev. R. Master, D.D.,
of Croston, near Chorley (Lancs.); for in his district, where families
of weavers were multiplying fast, one parish often contained six
new townships.   Little or no grazing land was available for the
pauper cows of the future; and if all the families claimed them
at any time of short work the parishes would become bankrupt.
Further, the multiplication of officials must entail heavy burdens,
besides doubling the duties of magistrates.   Other correspondents
expressed different opinions as to the wide powers entrusted to
the local clergy in the control of the schools and the parochial
funds, some condemning those proposals, while others approved
them.   Thus a Rev. C. N. Michell, near Ross, invoked blessings
on the head of Pitt for enabling the clergy to lessen the con-
trolling powers of brutal overseers who maltreated the poor in
very many villages.   The thrifty poor, who had brought up five
or more children, deserved a pension in their old age.   The
Vicar of Fordingbridge (Hants) also wrote, rejoicing that the
clergy would at last find their fit place in local government.[1]

Very noteworthy are the complaints of several correspondents
that Pitt did not sweep aside that source of litigation and expense,
the Acts of Settlement.   The Rev. E. Robson, Curate of White-
chapel, urged him to do so, and suggested that, in order to safe-
guard London and other large towns, where the poor lived in
outer suburbs, the destitute should be chargeable to the parish
where their employers lived. He warned Pitt that his Bill
would meet with formidable opposition, now organized by
Marylebone and St. Giles.   Henry Palmer wrote from Dublin,
asserting that the Acts of Settlement were responsible for
one-eighth of all the cases which recently came before the
Court of King's Bench, their cost being equal to that of the

[1] Pitt MSS., 307, 308.

maintenance of six paupers for six months. Besides the repeal of those Acts, he advocated the control of poor relief by five National Commissioners, supervising the work of inspectors of workhouses, one for each county. Of a similar tenour were the observations of L. T. Davies, of Brewer's Lane, Oxford, who assured Pitt that he would withhold from publication a projected work on poor relief if its proposals could be embodied in the Bill. They were in effect these. To give new vitality to the Act of 1601 by enlarging the areas and ordaining that each county and town should relieve its own poor; to regulate the wages of labourers so as to enable them to contribute towards a pension fund which would help them in case of sickness and accident, and during old age; to educate the young in "virtue and industry"; to afford occasional work to the thrifty and deserving in time of distress, and a comfortable retreat in old age; but to imprison and punish vagrants and the persistently idle and profligate. This plan, it will be seen, is far more extensive than that of Pitt; for Davies proposed to break down the parochial system of relief and the Acts of Settlement, besides setting on foot educational agencies and a provident fund of an almost national character. He also cut down or annulled the powers of magistrates, visitors and clergy; and, on the ground that there was no system about Pitt's proposed House of Industry or School of Industry, he referred him to the excellent plan lately designed by Count Rumford on the Munich model.[1]

On the other hand nothing but praise was accorded to Pitt's plan of facilitating the transfer, or cultivation of part at least of the wastes and commons, so as to provide sites for the School of Industry and food for its inmates. To all appearance, it did not include common fields, a far more difficult problem. But public opinion warmly favoured the cultivation of waste land as the best means of enriching the village and keeping down the price of provisions. Probably Pitt intended, on the advent of peace, to legislate on this great question, but the opportunity did not come; and, as I have pointed out, he did little or nothing to prevent the defeat of Sinclair's more thorough reform by the Lords.[2]

Most searching of all were the criticisms of that able jurist,

[1] Pitt MSS., 308.
[2] Rose, "William Pitt and the Great War," pp. 295-7.

Jeremy Bentham. His analytical powers, which dropped like
corrosive acid on so many venerable monuments, found free scope
in dealing with the new Poor Bill. His pamphlet on this topic
was private, but evidently went before one of the Ministers. It
did not see the light until 1838, and the editor then asserted
that Bentham's strictures largely conduced to the abandonment
of Pitt's proposals. Bentham, we may notice, had long studied
these questions, and in 1790 put forth a plan for Frugality
Banks on the lines of Savings Banks. Passing over his strictures
on the careless drafting and haphazard arrangement of the Bill,
we notice that he condemned Pitt's proposal for affording help
from the rates to those who were physically unable to earn the
usual wage. He declared the discrimination of the really
deserving from the lazy to be a most difficult task which the
Bill wholly evaded. Further, it would lead men of more than
middle age to relax their efforts in reliance on the dole from the
poor-box. His other objection, that this enactment would
entice men up to London, where wages far exceeded those in
the country, is hypercritical; for surely magistrates could be
trusted to stop excessive migration by the Act of Settlement.
Equally futile is his criticism on the proposal respecting the
allowance per child to the father or to the widow, which presumes in the local magistrates no exceptional powers of tact and
discernment.

Bentham foresaw endless trouble in the " cow-money clause."
How would the parish have any hold on the animals unless they
were lodged in a parish cow-house? How guard against fraudu-
lent sales and claims for more cows? At best the cost to the
parish must be enormous, especially in view of the diminution
in the number and size of commons. A loom would be a safer
form of investment. The whole plan was too burdensome; for,
as he adds, the true system of relief is one " which shall make
the supply of means keep pace with that of wants; " and this
the Bill would not do. Similarly, he regards the clause of the
Bill which extends out-relief to those who possess property up
to the value of £30, as more remarkable for benevolence than
wisdom. Along with the other provisions facilitating out-relief,
its tendency would be to pauperize. He also found many defects
in the clause enabling the parish to pay the fees of apprentices;
for, as there were fully 10,000 parishes, it would cost the country
£100,000 a year if each parish bound over two apprentices even

at the low sum of £5 apiece. He does not inquire how much these would cost the country if they became felons. The School of Industry then passes under his microscopic gaze; and he loftily dismisses the whole Bill as prolix, obscure, and certain to prove ruinously expensive. These criticisms in several cases hit the mark; and we can now see why Pitt dropped his Bill. Not only did it involve an enormous outlay at a time when the country was entering on the Bank crisis, but it contained many defects. Bentham, Davies and others raked the measure fore and aft, and reduced it to a waterlogged wreck before it drifted within range of the broadsides of Fox and Whitbread, double-shotted by the indignant magistrates of Marylebone and St. Giles.

In truth, Pitt entered upon the most elusive of all legislative quests with more zeal than knowledge. Perhaps no one then fully understood the extreme difficulty of helping the deserving poor without demoralizing them and overtaxing the ratepayers. The problem baffles us even now, when Political Economy and Social Science have come to maturity. Can we blame Pitt for undue hopefulness in that time of twilight? The old rural England was merging into the new industrial England; and he, who knew little more than the life of a prosperous village, sought to apply to the whole land a cure suitable to the homes of Arcady. His parochial Pension Fund was a pleasing device, workable only where the parson and squire were actuaries in embryo. His School of Industry further presumed that they possessed technical skill and organizing powers of no mean order; for, without guidance from headquarters, who can cheaply and efficiently teach diverse trades and callings to small groups of rustics? As for the pauper cow, she is clearly an idyllic creation.

In some respects Pitt's proposals offered a promising first draft for a generous experiment, which might have succeeded in time of peace. Certainly it enables us to feel the warm aspirations that throbbed under that cold exterior. And who shall say that England might not have derived more benefit from parts at least of this measure than from the rigorous regime advocated by Bentham, wherein men, women and children, clad in pauper garb, toiled in huge polygonal workhouses under Argus-eyed masters and matrons? The one scheme emanated from an enthusiast, the other embodied the frigid calculations of a doctrinaire. Nevertheless, as the final test of statesmanship is not fertility in suggestion, but sagacity in construction, and strength in accomplishment, Pitt cannot be absolved from the charge of weakness in not bringing forward an amended measure at a time more favourable than the winter of 1796-7. Probably he deferred the matter to the days of peace, to which he ever looked forward. But those days were never to come during his tenure of office.

SOME NEW LETTERS OF PITT

LEISURE is essential to the formation of the best epistolary style. The great letter-writers are they who have had time to give full play to their gifts of insight and humour. Just as the highest oratory demands a dignified amplitude of expression, so, too, in the interchange of thought between friends the mind should roam at ease, unchecked by considerations of time and space. The correspondence which the world will never let die resembles the converse of friend with friend amidst spacious lawns or down glades that open up far vistas. Haste and conventionality are the two most fatal enemies to a vital correspondence. Letters live on only if they express a frank outpouring of the heart, and those which are written against time, or to conceal thought, never live at all.

For these reasons the correspondence of responsible statesmen is rarely of interest, except during the intervals of leisure, when self-suppression ceases to be the rule of life. From the time of Cicero to that of Gladstone some have been found of individuality so marked, and interests so varied, as to enrich periods of rest with a brisk exchange of thoughts. But Pitt is scarcely among the number. His love of the Classics was no less keen than that of Fox; his friendships were as strong as those of Cicero; but he left behind no literary correspondence like that between Fox and the elder Gilbert Wakefield. True, his letters were afterwards thinned out by his literary executor, Bishop Tomline, who judged it right " to suppress many circumstances or anecdotes of a more private nature." But, from what remains, it is clear that Pitt was always more or less oppressed by his position as Prime Minister, and, even when in retirement in 1801-4, did not recover unofficial spontaneity. He early freed himself from the intolerable pomposity of the epistolary style of Chatham; but he never shook off entirely the cautious reserve congenial to Downing Street.

In one respect he fell far below the traditions of that abode. He was most careless about his papers. Lady Hester Stanhope afterwards described to Lord Stratford de Redcliffe the disorder of Pitt's room, littered over with documents, the only clearance being an occasional secretion under the cushions of a sofa. These slipshod habits were accountable for another serious defect. He often left letters unanswered, sometimes even unread. On this topic George III, in the year 1810, made some shrewd remarks to William Dacre Adams, formerly private secretary to Pitt. When Adams confessed the many delinquencies of his master in leaving letters unnoticed, the King struck in:

I have frequently said to Mr. Pitt the next time I saw him after I had written to him—"Mr. Pitt, I did not receive an answer to that letter I wrote to you the other day." He then (continued Adams) described Mr. Pitt's embarrassment and "hems" and "Sirs"—"by which it was evident he had never read my letter at all." The King talked of Mr. Pitt's style, which he admired for its point and conciseness. He then asked after Pitt's time of rising.—Adams: He was seldom stirring before 12 o'clock, Sir.—The King: Ah! he ruined his health by those late hours. I believe he was not fond of doing business after dinner.—Adams: No, Sir, he was not, I seldom went to him in the evening, unless there was something particular to be done. His rule was to finish everything before dinner.[1]

Though Pitt's letters have not the highest merits, they are of considerable interest as the outcome of a cultured mind and of a noble and patriotic nature. Therefore, while reserving for Part II those which belong to his correspondence with the King and some of his colleagues, I propose to give here some of a more miscellaneous description, selecting those which throw fresh light on his mental development or his career. The first letters display the pomposity which his father's example ingrained in him at the age of eleven. I need only add that the family abodes were Hayes, near Bromley, Kent, and Burton Pynsent in Somerset, the nearest seaside resort to the latter being Lyme Regis. The scholar referred to in the first letter is his younger brother James, who became a midshipman, and to whom Pitt's letter of 16th June 1773 was written. The play mentioned

---

[1] Note communicated to the fifth Earl Stanhope in 1863 (Chevening MSS.).

in the P.S. was "Laurentius," which the Pitt children composed and acted at Burton Pynsent in May 1772:

Hayes, July 31, 1770.

DEAR PAPA,

From the weather we have had here I flatter myself that the sun shone on your expedition, and that the views were enough enliven'd thereby to prevent the drowsy Morpheus from taking the opportunity of the heat to diffuse his poppies upon the eyes of any of the travellers (whose names I mention not lest it should come to the ears of the Attorney-General and he should file an information *ex officio* against me). I have nothing to say of the scholar, who calls himself under my direction, but that he goes on as well as his present master could wish, and I think he will do me great honour. I have this instant receiv'd the incomparable diary, which, as I cannot by any means defer answering, I must beg you to permit me to curtail this letter. I therefore only add that I most eagerly wish that the rest of your journey may prove agreeable, that you may arrive at the end of your labours in perfect health without the firing of any more wheels, and that your resting places may afford what is wanted to allay an hungry appetite and content desire of sleep.

Lyme Regis, June 16, 1773.

Abundance of thanks to my Dear Brother for the most entertaining of letters. I am in want both of matter and abilities to answer in the same stile. I can tell you, however, that I am infinitely obliged for it, and, what is worth infinitely more, Papa's annotation is *inimitably charming*. I think it really hard that from a seaport I can scarce pick up any news for a seaman. I wrote in my first that the *Sherborne* cutter was here. She is so still. We were on board last night *with the ladies*. The cabin would scarce hold the table I write upon. But it is on much the same scale as its captain, who is quite of the seaman's size. We have not navigated yet, and when I tell you some of the ladies are not much inclined to venture, you will probably say we never shall. If the midshipman was among us (which we much wish) he might perhaps be able to join the two favourite objects of the profession, the *ladies* and the sea, from which their type, Venus, sprung. I have only to add, I rejoice in your acquisition of the sweet grey mare. May she, together with fishing, disputing, etc. etc., afford every possible entertainment to you and all with you. To them and yourself, all love.

P.S. If you are in want of employment allow me to hint nothing can be done better than to take a copy of the play, which, I must not forget to say (as it may encourage you in the laborious work) Mr. Hollis's goodness still kindly remembers. Mr. Wilson desires his affectionate compliments to everybody. Pray remember me most kindly to Pam.

Hayes, August 16, 1773.

DEAR PAPA,

It is impossible to tell you what pleasure an expedition yesterday as far as Chev'ning afforded us all, and myself in particular; for, our accustomed squire being absent, I had the honour of serving as his deputy, and, mounting my *Long Sutton*, attended a noble cavalcade there. James, I think, did gallantly, having rode a great way for him. Nothing remarkable happen'd in our journey. . . . It rained so hard that we were not able to go out. However, the library afforded us good entertainment till dinner. In the evening it cleared up and we returned home in nearly the same manner. . . .

Burton Pynsent, December 30, 1773.

The violent rain, hail and wind which seem to be collecting their forces to usher in the New Year have so much chill'd my pen, that it wou'd be unreasonable to expect it shou'd convey any proportion of the warm congratulations and wishes of a happy New Year which the heart wou'd send to the dear colony at Lyme [Regis]. I must, however, attempt to say something of my feelings, tho' in strains as frozen as the congratulatory ode of a poet laureate. Of one thing, however, be assur'd, my dear father, they are to the full as sincere, or, shou'd they fail of expressing the sentiments of the breast, it will not be for a courtly reason. In short every thought is employ'd in wishing you every joy and comfort with approaching 74. May it shortly compleat the work of recovery 73 has so happily begun; if it is necessary, I will add, under the same auspices. . . .

After entering at Pembroke Hall (now College), Cambridge, early in October 1773, Pitt fell seriously ill and not until December was able to return home. He stayed there for six months, and became once more engrossed in family life. It was therefore as a valetudinarian and a stranger to the men of his year that he came back to Cambridge in July 1774, accompanied by his private tutor, the Rev. Edward Wilson. Evidently he was home-sick; for in a letter to his sister, Hester, he reproaches her for not sending news about the loved circle at Hayes, every detail of which he desires to hear; as for himself, he has nothing to chronicle. A similar tone pervades his first letters at Cambridge; and only by degrees did he appreciate the charm of the place. The dulness of nearly all his letters written there is surprising until we remember that he was a delicate boy of fourteen years, thrust into the University when as yet he knew nothing of school-life. This error of judgement of Chatham, and the illness and subsequent isolation, were irreparable misfortunes to one who was soon to be prematurely and continuously immersed in public affairs. The following new letters to his mother in the years 1774-8 speak for themselves:

Hayes, Sunday, Feb. 5, 1774.

I am commission'd by my father to inform you of his state as to gout, which is, that he has a good deal in both feet and threatening in both hands. It is not yet of the most violent sort, but enough to confine him to his bed. He received this morning a letter from Lord Camden, by which he learns that the Debate on the Address to be brought up from the Commons, cannot come on till Wednesday next, which, as it gives him a day longer than he expected, affords some hope that he may be able to attend. If he can be lifted into the House of Lords, he certainly will be present that day, but whether even this will be possible, cannot be guess'd till tomorrow. . . .

Pembroke Hall, July 13, 1774.

The first thing I undertake in my new quarters is to discharge myself of my promise by informing you that, after a dull and prosperous journey, I am once more within the walls of Pembroke. We reach'd Hockerill (?) the first night with great ease and found exceeding good beds and more excessive bills. We breakfasted this morning at Chesterford, which when I was there last, was a day's journey from this place, but is now diminish'd into a short drive, and follow'd the footsteps of many gentlemen of the turf who were flying to Newmarket. To-day, being sacred to the Grosvenor Sweepstakes, I fear I am too late to obtain a place in the coach-and-four, so that I must defer being initiated. On my arrival here, the first object that met my eyes was my friend Dr. Glynn, who was walking by the college. He has lately been very ill, but is got much better, and seems to be in his usual spirits. He was extremely flatter'd by my father's compliments. I find that the greatest part of the Fellows, as well as the master, are here. Mr. Turner and Mr. Prettyman (*sic*) I have seen for a minute, and I believe they are not going immediately. Most of the younger part of the University are gone, but my acquaintance, Mr. Hamilton, is here still, and probably will be some time longer. . . .

P.S. . . . Pray have the goodness to give my love to Mrs. Sparry and to assure her that the beds have been thoroughly air'd, and that we found Christmas fires in the rooms. Dr. Glynn enquir'd kindly after her. Mr. Wilson desires his best respects.

H

Pembroke Hall, Sept. 17, 1774.

Surrounded by all the noise and distraction that must naturally attend a canvass for the important borough of Cambridge, I sit down to offer the warmest thanks for your kind letter, which I had the pleasure of receiving yesterday. The confusion of election business in such a town as this, you will easily believe, is not favorable to letter-writing, and indeed the influence of Bacchus has already been so copious that we are almost stun'd with the effusions of gratitude pour'd from the hearts of the inspir'd freemen. The candidates in opposition to the present members, who are the causes of this jolly day, made a most glorious entry early this morning, attended by a numerous crowd, with colours flying, drums beating, etc., and drawn in their coach by the hands of the inhabitants, who had sallied forth a couple of miles to meet them for that purpose. One of the gentlemen was formerly of this college, and, I learn, is in that innumerable list of my distant cousins, whom I never had the pleasure to see.

Pembroke Hall, May 22, 1775.

. . . I am as much pleased as ever with college life, and find the University as yet pretty full. Upon the whole I feel nothing to regret but that the communication from Cambridge is not more expeditious that I might frequently have a flying glimpse of Hayes and an opportunity of enquiring after its dear inhabitants. . . .

The next letter, to his elder brother, John (Lord Pitt), affords curious proof of the lethargy of that youth, which was to cost England so dear, and of the keen interest of the others in parliamentary debates, especially in Burke's motion of 22nd March 1775 for conciliation with America, set forth in the famous " thirteen propositions ":

Hayes, March 23, 1775.

MY DEAR LORD,

Excuse the eager impatience of the Hayes politicians, Harriot in particular, to be informed of the result of yesterday's debate in the House of Commons, which occasions my troubling you with this note; and allow me to prefer a petition in the name of all the busy Speculatists (*sic*) here that, if accidentally you should have quitted your pillow before noon, and been able to procure any intelligence as to the nature and fate of Mr. Burke's intended motion, you will be graciously pleased out of your fraternal goodness to favour us with an early communication of the same; and your petitioner, as in duty bound, shall ever pray.

Signed by order of the Society,

Your ever affectionate Brother,

W. PITT.

The other letters of this period are to Lady Chatham:

Pembroke Hall, July 24, 1775.

MY DEAR MOTHER,

[He is in good health and his steed is the admiration of all Cambridge.] . . . I went yesterday with Dr. Glynn to see Wimp[o]le, my Lord Hardwicke's, which answer'd very well as an object for an excursion, and in this country has pretensions to comparative beauty, but would scarcely be thought worth looking at anywhere else. There are, I believe, one or two good pictures, some moderate, and a great many bad. . . .

Burton Pynsent, Dec. 28, 1776.

. . . As far as we are able to discover, the farm is in a pretty good condition. The shrubberies are most of them wonderfully grown, and altogether, after so long an absence, the place charmed me even more than I expected. We dine constantly with Mr. Speke, who is the same cordial friend that he always has been. He has equipped us once for a hunt, tho' almost in as ragged a stile as Butts himself. . . .

Pembroke Hall, April 3, 1777.

. . . It is not in my power to learn, much less to communicate anything like news, as the University is just at present very empty, and the few that are left in it turn their attention from eastern and western revolutions to the cause (*sic*) of a member of their own body who has blended the character of broker and usurer with that of Justice of the Peace and Doctor of Laws. This being the case, I am left to the study of politics of two thousand years ago; only glancing enough at modern times to discover that Lord Pigot and the East Indies have almost supplanted in the newspapers the Dictator and America.[1]

Hotel, King Street [London], Tuesday, Feb. 10, 1778.

[After expressing sorrow at the attack of gout of Lord Chatham, he continues]:

" I had not thought of delaying my return to Cambridge, beyond to-morrow; but Lord Mahon[2] tells me that there will probably be an interesting debate tomorrow on the subject of all the campaigns of this

---

[1] Lord Pigot, Governor of Madras, was arrested by his Council, and died in confinement. The "Dictator" is Lord North, Prime Minister in 1770-1782.

[2] Lord Mahon (afterwards Earl Stanhope) married Pitt's elder sister, Hester, in 1774.

war, which I shall hardly prevail upon myself to leave. After that I shall resume my former intention. It is not necessary for me to apply to you on the affair of money before I go; and I am always glad to pass it in silence; but I believe soon after my arrival at Cambridge it will become necessary. I shall not, I know, find demands to any considerable amount, nor stand in need of anything more than a small sum for current expenses. . . . I am now going to Lincoln's Inn, which will complete my term. As it is very near time, I am oblig'd to hurry these confus'd sentences; and the thickest of fogs, in a dark house, is an additional apology for such a scrawl. I hope however it will not make my apology at Hayes in person. Adieu, my dear mother.

The reader will have noticed that Pitt had by this time rid himself of the magniloquence of Chatham and had adopted the simple and direct style natural to him. The death of his father in May 1778 threw him on his own resources; and the struggle to maintain himself at the Bar and thereafter in the parliamentary arena further served to chasten and shorten his effusions. After becoming Prime Minister in December 1783, he wrote few private letters. I select those which illustrate his treatment of friends or critics, and afterwards others of a more general character. The following letter opened his correspondence with his future friend and admirer, the Earl of Mornington, afterwards the Marquis Wellesley. Mornington, an Irish peer, having helped on the measures of Government at Dublin, required some reward from the Lord Lieutenant, the Duke of Rutland, and hoped for the Vice-Treasurership of Ireland, then likely to fall vacant. The Duke's representations at Whitehall seeming somewhat lukewarm, Mornington wrote to Grenville to complain and to hint at the alternative plan of leaving Ireland altogether.[1] Pitt found out from Grenville the annoyance of Mornington, and wrote the following gracious letter, which, however disappointing for the time, served to win the allegiance of the Earl:

Downing St., Jany. 12, 1785.

My dear Lord,

I had some time since a letter from the Duke of Rutland urging very strongly His Grace's wish that on any vacancy of the office of Vice-Treasurer, your Lordship might succeed to it. The circumstances of his illness and a variety of pressing business since has delayed too long my answer. Your Lordship will, I trust, do me the justice to believe

[1] " Dropmore Papers," i, 241.

that the Duke of Rutland could not have proposed any arrangement which would give me more satisfaction if I could find it practicable. Under the present circumstances I do not see any immediate prospect of any such opening, and I fear if it were to take place there are necessarily expectations and pretensions here which could not leave me at liberty. I could not content myself without troubling your Lordship with this short explanation, and at the same time sincerely regret that the present occasion does not allow me a better opportunity of marking as strongly as I wish the regard and esteem with which, etc.

Equally tactful is the next letter, in which Pitt breaks to Viscount Townshend the unwelcome news that the King does not accord to him the wished-for marquisate:

> Putney Heath, May 16, 1785.
>
> My Lord,
>
> I am extremely ashamed in looking back at the date of the letter with which your Lordship honored me, to find how long, from the succession of a variety of business I have delayed obeying your commands. I have now taken an opportunity of laying before the King the letter from the Duke of Grafton which your Lordship enclosed to me; and I have His Majesty's commands to assure your Lordship that altho' particular circumstances determined His Majesty to confine the late promotion to the rank of Marquis to the two Peers who were the immediate objects of it; yet His Majesty still retains the sense he has before graciously expressed of your lordship's services as well as of the merits and just pretensions of your family. Not having anything more particular in charge from His Majesty at this moment, I have only to add the personal satisfaction I should receive in any occasion of marking the respect and regard with which, etc.

Serenity is perhaps the most prominent of Pitt's characteristics; and it appears in this letter to the Marquis of Buckingham, written during the complications on the Continent which boded ill for England. In his judgement the prospect of establishing a Sinking Fund for paying off annually a million sterling of the National Debt outweighed the perils of the diplomatic situation:

> Brighthelmstone, Nov. 8th, 1785.
>
> My dear Lord,
>
> . . . The state of our finance well justifies their rise [i.e., of the stocks]. We may, I think, fairly reckon already upon an annual surplus of £800,000 per annum at least. . . The little that is wanting to make

good the complete million may be had with ease, and even, I believe, without much more of the unpopularity which is generally the effect of productive taxes, especially in times of peace. This seems a sanguine picture, but I think will be more than realized. The storm on the Continent seems to have subsided for the present, but is not, I believe, quite dispersed. . . .

The following letter to the Foreign Minister, the Marquis of Carmarthen, shows the care of Pitt concerning the interests of India. In September 1786 amidst delicate discussions with France, he proposed to modify a treaty which Colonel Cathcart, on behalf of the Government of Bengal, had signed at Mauritius with the French plenipotentiary, de Souillac. Finding that the French Minister, Vergennes, was far from unfriendly during the Anglo-French commercial negotiations, Pitt urged that the Indian convention should be re-opened by our special envoy at Paris, William Eden, afterwards first Baron Auckland. To do so might have imperilled the commercial treaty; but Pitt decided on this bold course. As Vergennes knew nothing whatever of the disputes in the East Indies, they were adjusted in a way highly favourable to England. Pitt wrote this letter at Wimbledon, in the house of Henry Dundas, Chairman of the India Board. Colonel Cathcart, here mentioned, was not Colonel Lord Cathcart, but a commoner in the service of the Indian Government, who met his death in the year 1787 during a voyage to Pekin for the purpose of opening up better trade relations with China.[1]

Wimbledon, Saturday, Sept. 16 [1786].

MY DEAR LORD,

On discussing the points relative to Colonel Cathcart's Treaty, etc., it is the opinion of the India Board, in which I fully concur, that no time should be lost in sending an intimation to the French Court that we do not mean to hold that treaty as binding in all its details. At the same time it seems right to use such a *language* as may prepare them for a temperate and friendly discussion of the points in question. With this view the accompanying heads of a dispatch have been prepared, which, if you concur in the opinion, I should wish to have forwarded by a messenger as soon as possible. I submit to you whether it may not upon the whole be most advisable to adopt Mons‍ʳ. de Vergennes' [plan] of considering the chief object of this discussion to be com-

---

[1] "Auckland Journals," i, 154, 156, 186-8, 201, 213, 216; "Dropmore Papers," i, 484.

mercial. In this case the instructions ought, I think, to be addressed to Mr. Eden: and the business may in its progress be involved in so much detail that there will be an advantage in having it in his hands. More formal instructions and perhaps new powers may be necessary before we can regularly open a treaty on the subject. But in the mean time I apprehend these general instructions will be sufficient to lay the ground we wish. We may afterwards insist or relax on particular points, as we see occasion. I believe, however, the negotiation may be so managed as to give the French Court reasonable satisfaction, and yet regain much of what has been improperly conceded by the Bengal Government.

P.S. I have sent to Fraser a letter to Eden to accompany this dispatch if you send it.

The next note, to William Eden, bespeaks Pitt's desire to reward his eminent services at Paris, yet with due regard for the public exchequer:

Downing Street, July 28, 1787.

SIR,

As the important service in which you have been engaged in negotiating the treaty of commerce with the Court of France is now completed, and as you have received His Majesty's commands to hold yourself in readiness to proceed as his ambassador to the Court of Spain, I have His Majesty's orders to assure you in His name, previous to your departure, that, from His gracious approbation of your services, His Majesty is pleased to consider you entitled to a permanent provision of the same amount as was given to Sir Joseph Yorke and the late Lord Grantham, and that the same shall take effect at the close of your Spanish mission, provided that you do not then accept or continue to hold some office of profit from the Crown to the amount of such provision.

In the year 1787 the questions at issue between George III and the Prince of Wales were complicated by the extravagance of the latter. Having described them in Chapter XVII of "William Pitt and National Revival," I here insert without comment the following "Draft of a Message from the King to the Prince of Wales," which is in Pitt's writing and appears to have been sent without alteration:

[*Endorsed*, May 20, 1787.]

On examining the plan proposed under the inspection of the Prince of Wales, arranging his expenses in the several departments, the King observed many articles in which H[is] M[ajesty] thought there was room for considerable reduction. But, in order to avoid as far as possible entering into detail on the particulars of the estimate, H.M. directed Mr. Pitt to express thro' the Prince's officers H.M.'s wish that it should be revived through the Prince's direction. H.M. is sorry to find that this has been declined, and that at a time when the Prince is so strongly called upon to show his disposition to confine his expenses within the most reasonable bounds, he adheres to an estimate in which most of the articles are stated at a higher rate than can appear to H.M. on any calculation to be necessary. This observation applies particularly to the household expenses under the comptroller, the robes, and wardrobes, the stables and the Privy Purse. A proper regulation under these heads might, as H.M. is persuaded, enable the Prince to reduce his expenses within his income, and also to support an establishment of officers and servants such as is stated in his plan.

Under these circumstances, and at the time of calling upon Parliament for their assistance to discharge so heavy a debt, it is impossible for H.M. to propose any augmentation of income which shall bring further expense on his subjects. But, as a proof of H.M.'s paternal affection, and in order to remove any possible doubt respecting the sufficiency of the Prince's income to support amply the dignity of his situation, H.M. is ready, whenever the plan is settled for preventing arrears in future, to allow £10,000 per annum in addition to the sum now paid to the Prince out of H.M.'s Civil List—a sum which exceeds the difference between the salaries and allowance of the Prince's family at present and his proposed establishment. H.M. approves of the order of payment which the Prince proposes to establish; but, as H.M. must in his application to Parliament pledge himself for every possible security that new debts will not be contracted, H.M. desires that the Prince will give a general order for the officers at the head of each department to receive immediately at the end of each quarter the sums respectively allotted to them, and that he will direct an abstract of the total sums paid, authenticated by the proper officers and certifying what arrears, if any, are outstanding, to be laid before H.M. within one month after the expiration of every quarter. H.M. is also willing to recommend it to Parliament to make a proper provision for compleating Carlton House; but the charge on this head may probably be much reduced; and it must be more explained than in the paper sent by the Prince of Wales before any specifick sum can be named.

Pitt's cousin, the Marquis of Buckingham, a man of proud and sensitive nature, was deeply wounded, first, by the neglect of the King adequately to reward his services as Viceroy of Ireland, and afterwards at the time of the Regency Crisis of 1788-9. He ardently desired the title of duke, and Pitt sought, but in vain, to reverse the decision of the King to grant that honour to none but members of the royal family. Pitt informed his kinsman of the rebuff in the following letter, the first part of which was omitted by Earl Stanhope:[1]

Nov. 12, 1789.

My dear Lord,

It is with very sincere regret that I find myself obliged to inform you that the King's decision has proved as unfavourable as I feared it would from His Majesty's first answer which I conveyed to him, and from the rooted determination which I apprehended him to have formed on the subject. From the manner in which His Majesty expressed himself, I certainly can entertain no hope that any further representation will be like to change his opinion. It is but just to add that his not complying with your request does not seem in any degree to proceed from the want of a real and strong sense of the signal services which you rendered during the late extraordinary crisis, but from the general and, I fear, insurmountable objections which he has conceived to the measure proposed.

I hope you will forgive my adding that the step which you meditate in consequence is not only painful to me for a thousand reasons, both public and personal, but is one which seems likely to produce effects in the public impression the reverse of everything you would yourself wish.

Pitt then states that he desires an interview with the Marquis at Stowe; and it seems to have produced the desired result. His resolve to trust to an oral rather than a written communication is characteristic and often accounts for the lack of startling secrets in his correspondence. The next letter, to the Hon. James Cornwallis, Bishop of Lichfield, illustrates Pitt's power of dealing a crushing rebuke for some unjust imputation, the nature of which I have not discovered. The second note to the bishop is equally remarkable for its frank forgiveness on the withdrawal of the imputation. Pitt's friend, the Bishop of Lincoln, then held the sinecure Deanery of St. Paul's:

Downing Street, Sat' night, June 11, 1791.

My Lord,

On my return to town this afternoon I found your lordship's letter. I am willing to hope that, on further consideration, and on

---

[1] Stanhope, "Pitt," ii, 42. For the circumstances see Rose, "William Pitt and National Revival," p. 153; "Dropmore Papers," i, 537-9.

recollecting all the circumstances, there are parts of that letter which you would yourself wish never to have written. My respect for your lordship's situation, and my regard for Lord Cornwallis prevent my saying more than that, until that letter is recalled, your lordship makes any further intercourse between you and me impossible.

(Draft.) Downing Street, June 12, 1791.

My Lord,

I have this morning received the honor of your lordship's letter, dated the 11th, and have great satisfaction in being enabled to dismiss from my mind any impression occasioned by a paragraph in the former letter which I received from you. With respect to any further arrangement, I can only say that I have no reason to believe that the Bishop of Lincoln would wish to remove to Salisbury, but if he were, I should certainly have no hesitation in recommending your lordship for the Deanery of St. Paul's.

Pitt's sensitiveness as to bargaining in matters of patronage drew forth the following dignified rejoinder:

[*Endorsed*—To Sir J. Honywood.] Downing Street, 5th October 1791.

Dear Sir,

I have just received your letter of yesterday, and you must excuse me if I cannot help confessing myself surprized and hurt at its contents. You cannot, I think, wonder that under the circumstances of the application of the receivership I felt some difficulty in deciding, and wished first to converse with the Duke of Dorset, who, as Lord Lieutenant is naturally entitled to attention on such an occasion. A sense of your support and personal regard were strong inducements to me to endeavour, if I could make it practicable, to comply with your wishes; and certainly the disposition to do so could in no case be increased by intimations of the nature of those which seem to be conveyed in your last letter. I still sincerely wish that you may not have intended them in the sense in [*sic*] which they appear to me to carry, and which, even if I had been able to come to any decision, would have prevented me from entering further at present on the subject.

On the other hand, a frank recognition of the monetary value of a pocket-borough, St. Mawes, in Cornwall, finds expression in the following lines, addressed probably to its "owner," Lord Hobart:

Private.   Downing Street, Nov. 5, 1791.

MY DEAR LORD,

It was not till to-day that I have been able to find a person whom I could propose to you to take Mr. Sanders's place on the terms proposed at St. Mawes. The gentleman whom I have now heard of is a Mr. Calvert, an East Indian of good fortune and character, and a nephew of Calvert of Hertfordshire. He is ready, I understand, to go as far as three thousand pounds, and I have no reason to think that any unexceptionable person will be found who will give more. The name of the place has of course not yet been mentioned to him. If you approve of him, I think from what you said, you would be desirous that it should be particularly explained to him that Sanders is the only person who will be benefited by the transaction.

Pitt's rebuke to an official of the Treasury guilty of corrupt conduct deserves to be placed on record, though I suppress his name:

                               Downing Street, November 28, 1793.
SIR,

Some circumstances relative to you have recently come to my knowledge, which I think it right to inform you of, in order to give you an opportunity, if you wish it, of stating anything which you may think can explain your conduct. I understand that in two instances you have applied for and received pecuniary assistance from persons with whom you had no particular connection but from their being employed on commission business by Government, and who either were at the time of the application, or recently had been, subject to examination and control in your office. The gentlemen I allude to are Mr. Davison and Mr. Maitland. I shall certainly feel it a duty to take into consideration anything which you may wish to state on this subject, either in person or by letter; but I think it fair to apprise you that the circumstances, as represented to me, make me consider it as impossible that you should any longer remain in the office of trust which you now hold.

TO THE SAME

                               Downing Street, November 30, 1793.
SIR,

The circumstance which Mr. Rose[1] mentioned to me yesterday by your desire, of your being prepar'd to repay the sums, which were lent you by Mr. Davison and Mr. Maitland, does not appear to me

---

[1] The Rt. Hon. George Rose was Secretary to the Treasury.

material in judging of the transaction, and after reflecting fully on everything which you stated when I saw you, I see no reason to depart from my opinion that you cannot any longer continue in the offices which you now hold. At the same time, from a consideration of your services, I am desirous that you should retire in a way as little disagreeable to yourself as possible. On this ground I do not mean that the circumstances which have led to your quitting your situation should be known, and I have no objection to its appearing, if you wish it, to be at your own desire. I shall also be willing to recommend that you should receive an allowance of £750 per annum on y* estimate, or in such other mode as on further consideration, shall be thought most convenient.

The next letters are specimens of retorts equally courteous and crushing. The former of them is to the Duke of Grafton:

Downing Street, January 14, 1794.

My LORD,

I have been honor'd with your Grace's letter in which you have the goodness to communicate to me your sentiments on public affairs. Being for my own part fully convinc'd that the system of measures which have been pursued both at home and abroad is necessary for the safety of the country and the preservation of the constitution, I have only to express my regret at finding that my opinions are so opposite to those which your Grace entertains.

[*Endorsed*—To Lord Elcho.]   Downing Street, September 28, 1798.

My LORD,

I received yesterday from your Lordship a paper reminding me that I had omitted to notice a former letter from you on the subject of finance. You must give me leave to observe that in such cases the *right* which your Lordship is pleased to state of being listened to will always depend in my opinion more on the apparent merits of the project than on the rank of the projector. I should certainly most readily have acknowledged the zeal for the public service which dictated your first letter, if, in the midst of other business, it had not inadvertently escaped me; but I own that I have not the good fortune to enter sufficiently into your ideas, as stated in either paper, to lead me to trouble you further on the subject.

The letters of Pitt to his brother, the second Earl of Chatham, are few in number, especially after his enforced resignation of the Admiralty at the end of 1794. In the rearrangement of offices consequent on the accession of the Old Whigs in July 1794, Dundas relinquished to Portland the Secretaryship of State for Home Affairs, but took the similar office for War, with Windham as colleague. Apparently Chatham raised some question about the position of Dundas, which called forth from Pitt this reply:

Downing Street, Saturday, July 12 [1794].

MY DEAR BROTHER,

. . . Dundas retains the same Seals of Secretary of State in virtue of which he has acted ever since he has held the office. Whether there are two Secretaries of State or three, each is equally the regular channel to signify the King's pleasure whenever it may be necessary on all matters of State; and the distribution of Departments is only a matter of convenience, settled by mutual understanding, with the King's approbation but without any formal authority. The mode of payment cannot alter the nature of the office. It can concern no other Department whether Dundas receives a salary from the Civil List or holds an additional office; and, besides all this, the office is the same which he has held ever since he was Secretary of State. Under these circumstances I really cannot conceive to my own mind where the difficulty can arise. But if there be any, you will I am sure recollect that it ought to have been stated sooner. . . . There is no assignable reason why everything should not go on between Dundas in his present Department and the Admiralty, exactly in the train in which it has done hitherto. I am so convinced that on consideration you must see this as I do, that I do not like to press it further, or to say anything of the embarrassment which would otherwise arise, and which, both for my sake and for the service, you must, I am sure, wish to avoid.

Several of Pitt's letters to the Bishop of Lincoln were published by Lord Ashbourne in his valuable work; but the following, selected from the Pretyman Archives, are new. They refer to the time of ill-health and anxiety spent in retirement, when the Addington Ministry was unable to prevent the continued aggressions of Bonaparte on neighbouring States to the detriment of British interests. Pitt's pledge of support to Addington made his position one of great anxiety. After stating that he had begun the Bath waters very gently and is the better for them he announces his desire to go up to town for the opening of the session. He then continues:

Bath, November 5, 1802.

. . . The state of things is certainly full of difficulty. I had remained in perfect ignorance (except from the newspapers) of all that was passing

during the summer. From what I learnt on my way hither I was very
glad to find that the line taken by our Government up to that time was
such as appears to me right, and their intention for the future, as far as
it could then be formed, seemed the same. But I know nothing of what
has been going on since that time. My own opinion is that, altho', without some support on the Continent, we have no sufficient inducement
to declare actual war in consequence of all Bonaparte's succession of
encroachments, yet we are called upon to take such steps for our own
security as, in his present disposition, he will never acquiesce in; and
therefore how war in the end and that probably very speedily is to be
avoided, I confess I do not see. My present intention is to make as
short a stay in Town as possible and to return hither about the beginning of December to stay till Parl⁺ meets again. . . .

The next letter to Bishop Tomline belongs to the second
part of Pitt's stay at Bath in 1802, after a short break in London.
Mrs. (not Mr.) Trimmer's book advocated national education on
the system devised by Mr. Lancaster, which excluded religious
teaching of a dogmatic character:

Johnstone Street, Bath, Dec. 9, [1802].

MY DEAR BISHOP,
        . . . I read Mr. Trimmer's book on the road, and I am strongly
persuaded that Mr. Lancaster's project, if allowed to operate to any
great extent, is likely to produce great mischief, and that it is very
important to find some safe and effectual substitute. I am already much
better for my journey and shall begin the waters to-morrow.

Walmer Castle, March 18, 1803.

MY DEAR BISHOP,
        [Glad that he is enjoying Lymington. He (Pitt) may possibly
take it on his way to Bath, though life at Walmer suits him as well as
Bath, unless Farquhar orders otherwise.] The time of my coming to
town remains rather uncertain and will be regulated a good deal by
what is now very difficult to guess, the result of the present discussions
with France. If they should end in war, I think I can hardly avoid
going up to attend Parliament, tho' perhaps only for a single day. If
on the other hand there is to be peace (or what will be called peace) I
may feel it equally necessary to state my opinions, at least on the
question of finance. But while the present undecided state continues I
shall probably think it best still to remain in the country for the same
reason that I have hitherto done so. Perhaps in a few days I may be
able to form a better conjecture on these points. . . .

So little is known of Pitt's organization of the military defence of East Kent that the following undated letter from him to Lieutenant-Colonel Dillon at Walmer will be read with interest. It belongs probably to September 1804, when an invasion from Boulogne seemed highly probable:

As the harvest is now nearly over, I imagine this would be a very fitting time for proposing to assemble your battalion on permanent duty; and there seems chance enough of the occasion arriving for actual service to make it desirable that there should be as little delay as possible. Lord Carrington has gone to Deal Castle to-day, and if you can contrive to see him to-morrow, or next day, I shall be glad if you will settle with him the necessary arrangements. I think the time should not be less than ten weeks; and in that case, an extra allowance will be made of a guinea per man, which, added to the usual pay, will amount to 2s. per day for the whole period. This will enable us to give the men full compensation for at least six or seven hours a day, on an average; and will therefore allow of three or four long field days in each week, and only short drills on the remaining days, and such arrangements would, I think, answer every purpose. I should hope you might fix the commencement of permanent duty for Monday fortnight, very soon after which day I hope to come to Walmer to make some stay. I shall be at Dover on Tuesday next for a day, but have some business which will carry me from thence along the coast, and probably back to town before I reach Walmer.

The following refers to the first reports of the Austrian disaster at Ulm, which dealt Pitt's system of alliances so severe a blow. The news was confirmed on the morrow:

Downing St., Nov. 1, 1805.

My DEAR BISHOP,

I will try to make a visit to Cambridge about Christmas if I can. In the course of this month (if I can get away at all) I mean to go for a short time to Bath. We are waiting with the utmost anxiety for authentick accounts of military events on the Continent. The Reports which have hitherto reached us are probably very exaggerated, and possibly altogether false; and at all events, with the means that are still in reserve, there is no reason to be discouraged. . . .

The effort of Pitt to form a national Administration, fit to cope with Napoleon, is seen in the following lines, in which he once again asks the support of the Right Honourable J. Foster, formerly Chancellor of the Exchequer in Ireland, and one of the bitterest opponents of the Act of Union:

(*Private.*)   Downing Street, June 29, 1805.

DEAR SIR,
        I have received with very great concern the communication contained in your letter of this morning and feel most anxious, both on publick and personal grounds, that it may be still possible to induce you to reconsider your determination. I trust at least that you will still allow me to have the satisfaction of conversing fully with you on the subject before I take any steps in consequence of your letter. I would therefore beg the favour of seeing you at half-past twelve on Monday if that time will be convenient to you, and I name that day, because I have a particular engagement in the country to-day and am obliged to attend His Majesty at Windsor to-morrow.

I conclude these miscellaneous letters by notes, drawn up at or just after Christmas, 1805, to prove the falseness of the news of an armistice said to have been concluded by Russia and Austria after the defeat at Austerlitz on 2nd December. As I have shown in " William Pitt and the Great War" (pp. 548-551) the news of Austerlitz and of the armistice of 4th December was long disbelieved. Tidings of the latter event, which was regarded as far more serious than the defeat, did not reach London till 29th December. The paper is probably in Pitt's handwriting; and certainly it expresses the hopeful spirit which animated him until 13th January 1806, when he received the last fatal news. Canning, writing to him on 7th January, states that his remarks on continental affairs comforted him much:

The observation which occurs in the " Argus " and its supplement is that it contains nothing of a later date than what was transmitted by the French Minister at Vienna dated the 6th, to La Foret at Berlin and sent by him to Bourrienne at Hamburgh, where it was published the 13th. It arrived at Berlin on the 10th.

Would news of an Armistice which, sent round from Vienna the 6th reached Hamburgh the 13th and Berlin the 10th, not reach Paris, when sent directly, before the 16th?

Col. Brun, Buonaparté's aid-de-camp (*sic*) left Austerlitz the 3rd and arrived at Paris the 11th.

The Armistice took place, if true, on the 4th. If the account of it travelled as fast as the aid-de-camp, it would have been in Paris the 12th. Yet it is not stated to be known and published till the 16th.

An account of an Armistice is precisely an account for a telegraph.[1] The account of the victory of the 2nd, which must have been sent off the 3rd, arrived at Paris by telegraph the 10th, for it is published on the 11th. The account of the Armistice should have arrived at Paris by telegraph on the 11th.

In the "Argus" of the 17th an account from Stuttgard dated the 10th is given, relating to the action of the 2nd. There is no allusion to an Armistice.

Two or three American merchants arrived to-day from Amsterdam, which they left the 21st; and they state that no accounts had arrived or been published in Holland from the armies of a later date than those giving an account of the action of the 2nd.

[1] There was a line of semaphore telegraphs between Strassburg and Paris.

DID NAPOLEON INTEND TO INVADE ENGLAND?

A T the outset it will be well to distinguish between two
questions, the confusion of which often obscures the issue.
They are these—" Were Napoleon's schemes of invasion practicable?" And, "Did he believe them to be practicable?" The
former question would involve the discussion of technical topics
far too wide and complex to be treated in this essay, which deals
solely with the more personal issue just stated.

Obviously the decision depends largely on our estimate of the
character of Napoleon; but, as he was endowed both with a
daring imagination and with administrative powers of a high
order, we must watch closely the development of the great
flotilla at Boulogne and of the plans for convoying it to the
English coast, as well as the difficulties arising out of the attitude of the Continental Powers. The ventures of Napoleon
should be viewed in the light of his declaration to Talleyrand,
that the splendid results foreseen by an enthusiastic imagination
can be attained only by " the extremely cool, persevering and
accurate man."[1] It is therefore important to notice his attitude
towards the great ventures of war. Then the chief facts relating
to the Boulogne flotilla and the French naval combinations
must be examined somewhat closely. The impressions of on-
lookers and the assertions even of Napoleon himself may be set
aside as of little importance; for the success of all such enterprises depends mainly on deceiving the enemy. Falsehoods are
therefore as necessary as feints; and a letter designed to pass
under the eyes of an informer may render as good service as
a squadron. Therefore, only by keeping close watch upon
Napoleon's actions and the state of the flotilla and of the " Army
of England," shall we avoid pitfalls, and come near the truth.
Finally, from the nature of the case, the truth cannot be reached

[1] " Napoleon Corresp.," iii, 371 (10th October 1797).

with certainty. It will be only that conclusion which best explains all the ascertainable facts, due regard being also paid to the character of the Emperor.

Eager activity, contempt of danger, and resolve to carry through his purpose at all costs, figure prominently among his characteristics. In childhood he was remarkable for a sensitive pride which readily burst forth in passion and impetuous attacks; witness that curious story, told to O'Meara at St. Helena, of his behaviour when his schoolfellows teased him for his fondness of a little girl. On such occasions he would pick up stones or sticks, or use fists and feet against his tormentors, however tall or numerous. A strongly developed instinct, the warlike customs of Corsica, and his perception during the course of the French Revolution that defence spelt failure, bred in him the conviction that triumph comes only to him who greatly dares. Among his first pronouncements on the art of war is this, in the " Souper de Beaucaire " (September 1793): " He who stays in his entrenchments is beaten. Experience and theory are at one on this point."

His first plans of campaign, those of July 1795, urge the change of a tame defensive in the Maritime Alps into a swift advance; and the deeds of the campaign of 1796-7 only embody the thoughts sketched out in some obscure lodging in Paris. Italy conquered, he turns to the East, and uses the resources of the Venetian Republic along with those of Malta, for an eventual attack on Britain's Indian Empire. He alone of the army of Egypt is not daunted by Nelson's triumph at the Nile, but writes on 21st August 1798 to Rear-Admirals Villeneuve and Decrès, urging the immediate resumption of the offensive at sea. He reminds them that the British fleet must sail away to dispose of its prizes, and orders them in its absence to collect all the ships available in France and Italy and at Malta and Corfu in order to form a squadron strong enough to support his army in its further operations. The thought that the British will capture some of Villeneuve's ships, the sole relics of Brueys' fleet, and will blockade Malta, does not occur to him. Boundless confidence also appears in a sentence of his letter of the same date to Kléber—" If the English continue to overrun the Mediterranean, they will compel us to do greater things than we intended." Confidence is one of the first essentials for a great commander; and Napoleon never wrote a truer sentence than this in his letter

of 30th April 1809 to Eugène Beauharnais: "In war one sees
one's own difficulties, and does not take into account those of the
enemy; one must have confidence in oneself." Certainly Napoleon never erred through diffidence. Nearly all his mistakes
can be traced to excess of daring, the most extraordinary instance of which is his plan, drawn up at Moscow, so late as 16th
October 1812, for an immediate march on St. Petersburg in
order to wring peace from the Czar.[1]

It is true that love of grandiose schemes grew on Napoleon
with advancing years and heightened prestige. But on many
occasions before the Moscow Campaign he carried daring to
the verge of foolhardiness. The Eastern Expedition of 1798
was undertaken in defiance of England's maritime supremacy,
won by the victories of Jervis and Duncan in the previous year;
but, because she had abandoned the Mediterranean at the close
of 1796, he left her sea-power virtually out of count. The Battle
of the Nile did not undeceive him. He looked on it as a temporary check soon to be retrieved, and set about the Syrian
campaign against the Turkish army advancing by land, as
though the British, Turkish and Russian fleets did not dominate
the Mediterranean. The capture of his battering-train off Mount
Carmel by Sidney Smith thwarted the efforts of the French for
the capture of Acre. But, even so, the young crusader always
asserted that his failure to win the Empire of the East was
due to "that mud-hole which came between me and my destiny."
If we may judge by his later statements, he never realized that
Britain's sea-power doomed to sterility his utmost efforts in
that quarter. His sternly objective nature saw the most obvious
effects of naval supremacy; but its unseen yet potent influence,
of which Aboukir and Acre were but prominent manifestations,
never duly registered itself in his sense of causation.

On land his genius continued to exert an invariably triumphant activity. His victorious attacks on the tumultuary levies of
Turkey at Mount Tabor, and on the Isthmus of Aboukir, re-
established his prestige. Similarly, after his return to France and
assumption of authority as First Consul, he shattered the Second
Coalition of the Powers by a daring initiative, meeting the
Austrian invasion of Provence, not by a defensive campaign on
the River Var, but by the incisive counterstroke at their communications on the line Coni-Alessandria-Milan. Thus, his

---

[1] Fain, "Manuscrit de 1812," ii, 93.

daring moves from Toulon in 1793 to Marengo in 1800 brought brilliant results, and led him to scorn the safe tactics of lesser men. The events of the campaigns of 1805-7 are informed by the same underlying conception. Ulm, Austerlitz, Jena, Fried-land, are but the salient points of a strategy which aims at attacking the enemy at the earliest possible opportunity, and of profiting by the first slip. " March thirty miles a day, fight a battle, and then bivouac in peace "—such is his motto. The moves of the five days before Ratisbon (19th to 23rd April 1809), whereby he changes Berthier's blundering defence into a victorious advance against the Archduke Charles's exposed flank, are among his finest conceptions; and no less remarkable is his resolve after the serious reverse at Aspern-Essling to maintain an offensive attitude in order to impose on a leader whom he knows to be somewhat nervous and diffident. The device is perfectly successful, and leads to the triumphant finale at Wagram—the grandest instance in modern history of the effects of an indomitable determination, which, even after defeat, retains the initiative and compels the victor of a day to conform to a greater will and more masterly combinations than his own. These features of Napoleon's character are factors essential to a due consideration of the problem before us. He who scoffed at the word " impossible," and desired to blot it out from the French dictionary, was no braggart, but a giant in action, whose soaring imagination, unequalled power of work, inflexible will, and unique success in inspiring enthusiasm, set at defiance all precedent, and moved far onward the bounds of the possible.

The salient facts of the naval situation in the year 1803 were as follows:—During the Peace of Amiens, 1802-3, the British navy was reduced to a peace establishment. In October 1802 only 39 sail-of-the-line, 13 smaller ships, and 120 frigates were in commission; but behind these were 134 sail-of-the-line, 10 smaller ships, and 97 frigates. By great exertions these numbers were brought up respectively to 189, 37, and 197, ready for sea in November 1803, that is six months after the renewal of war. At its commencement France had ready for sea only 13 sail-of-the-line; but she had many more in the second line, or under repair, or building, so that her potential strength may be set at 60 sail-of-the-line.[1] She also counted on the support of

[1] James, " Naval History," iii, 486.

Holland, which Napoleon's forceful policy had made a mere appanage of France; but in May 1803 the Dutch navy comprised only 21 sail-of-the-line, of which six were in the Indies, and 4 needed repairs; of 12 frigates, 7 were on distant service and 3 were building. The naval resources of the Genoese or Ligurian Republic were also at the disposal of France, and Spain was a probable ally. The impatience of the First Consul in naval affairs is seen in his reiterated orders to press on construction and repairs at Brest and other ports. On 3rd June 1803 he ordered that 20 sail-of-the-line must be ready at Brest by 22nd November 1803. Despite hard work, Admiral Truguet could get ready for sea only 8 sail with 8 smaller ships at that port. Similarly, on 22nd August Napoleon ordered Ganteaume, Maritime Prefect at Toulon, to have ready for sea in four months' time 11 sail-of-the-line and all the frigates in the dockyard. Even in January 1804 Ganteaume could muster only 6 sail and 4 frigates.[1] In both cases Napoleon's orders corresponded to his wishes, not to the facts of the situation.

As to the French flotilla of corvettes (*prames*), gun-brigs (*chaloupes canonnières*), gun-vessels (*bateaux canonnières*), and luggers (*péniches*), no trustworthy data are available. It seems to have deteriorated so quickly during the Peace of Amiens that few vessels were serviceable, though, in order to satisfy Napoleon, its effective strength and numbers on paper were reckoned as the same. At Dunkirk, out of 125 gun-vessels, only 10 were fit to take the sea at Midsummer 1803; 64 could be ready in a month, 25 were beyond repair. In the middle of August, when Napoleon ordered 100 craft of the flotilla immediately to set sail from Dunkirk, only 21 were ready, a fact which caused him great annoyance.[2] The first important order, that of 22nd August 1803, assumed that a flotilla of 2,008 sail would soon be available; but this estimate far outran possibility. Great energy was shown in naval construction, towards which several towns and Departments contributed liberally. On 12th June Seine-Inférieure offered to build a 74; and Seine-et-Oise, in presenting 1,200,000 francs for naval construction, added that, as the Alps had not stopped the French arms, neither would the Straits of Dover. A similar spirit prevailed through France, leading to the offer of gifts of money or materials valued at about 25,000,000

[1] Desbrière, "Projets . . . de Débarquement . . ." iii, 240-6.
[2] *Ibid.*, iii, 93-95.

francs. In order to stimulate these patriotic offers, Napoleon kept up, and even emphasized the threat of an invasion of England, though the preparations were so inadequate as to preclude that momentous enterprise in the year 1803. The smaller boats might be hurried on to completion, but the new *prames* and *chaloupes* could not be ready before the spring of 1804; and the enormous expenditure of materials and labour on the flotilla necessarily told against the building of the sea-going fleet, which all experienced men deemed a necessary condition of success.

These and other difficulties were far from daunting Napoleon. He pushed on the new basin at Boulogne, hoping for a time that by 8th October 1803 it would be ready to receive 100 *chaloupes* and 800 or 900 smaller vessels. He even rejected the advice of Admiral Bruix as to the insufficiency of the space on the ground that more extensive works would require a longer period. Even on the present cramped scale they were months behind the stipulated time. On 26th August the First Consul proposed to make up for the smallness of the existing harbour by mooring a line of *chaloupes*, etc., in the outer road, a suggestion quite feasible for summer weather, but destined to entail serious losses in the storms of the autumn and winter. The attacks of British vessels also caused much damage, and could not be prevented even with the help of forts recently constructed on the shore and cliffs. As for the concentration at or near Boulogne of the various parts of the flotilla constructed at the Biscay, Channel, and Flemish ports, it was a sorry failure, which showed the grave danger of opposing the *chaloupes*, etc., to the sea-going vessels of Britain.[1] In the autumn of 1803 Napoleon cherished the belief that his flotilla could fight its way across the straits. Later on, after the abandonment of the whole enterprise, he informed Decrès that the idea had never been in his mind, and that his object in arming the flotilla heavily had been to dupe the British Ministry, as he had completely succeeded in doing.[2] Clearly this is a piece of bluff. His arrangements in the autumn of 1803 presume that the flotilla can, in case of need, force a passage alone. He himself was the dupe of this notion, which never was taken seriously by the British Admiralty or its

[1] *Ibid.*, iii, ch. x. At the end of January 1804 there were at Boulogne and Étaples only 281 vessels of war.

[2] "Napoleon Corresp.," xi, p. 192.

naval officers. All their desire was that he should make such an attempt.

Other schemes came to take its place. During a stay of eighteen days at Boulogne in the month of November 1803 his letters breathe an unruffled confidence. He writes to General Augereau at Brest, appointing him to command an expedition which he designed against Ireland, adding that in a reasonable time all will be ready at Boulogne to exact from England the vengeance due during six centuries. On his return to Paris he writes (23rd November) to Ganteaume at Toulon, stating that by the middle of Nivôse (6th January 1804) the Boulogne flotilla will probably number 1,300 craft, each carrying one or more cannon, and in all 100,000 men. The Dutch fleet and flotilla can take over 60,000 men. He adds—" Eight hours of night favourable to us would decide the fate of the world."

In view of the actual state of the flotilla in November 1803, which Colonel Desbrière terms " pitiable," it is difficult to take these statements seriously. They imply two naval enterprises, one against Ireland, the other against England, each of which transcended the capacity of the naval resources of France. Assuming that the squadrons of Brest, l'Orient, and Rochefort sufficed to protect the Irish expedition, could the fleets at Toulon and the Texel be relied on to co-operate with sufficient exactitude so as to convey to the English coast the French and Batavian flotillas, supposing that these last had assembled in full force at Boulogne and the Texel respectively? This seems to have been Napoleon's plan in November 1803; but, as it rested on the supposition that everything would go smoothly, we may infer that he relied on the Boulogne flotilla in the last resort to make its way across the straits with little protection by large ships. Certainly the time allowed to the Toulon fleet to come round to Boulogne was utterly inadequate. Only under the most favourable conditions, such as favouring winds and the absence of Nelson from his station near Toulon, could it be expected before the spring. Indeed, the sketches sent to Augereau and Ganteaume are so slight and so roseate in tints as scarcely to warrant the name of plans. The mention of eight hours as the time of crossing for a great flotilla, which, as was notorious, could not get out of Boulogne harbour in one tide, would alone suffice to condemn the scheme. The flotilla must proceed as far as possible *en masse*, otherwise it would be defeated in detail by the English squadron and flotilla always held ready to crush it. The words "eight hours of night" reveal what was for a time Napoleon's leading conception; the passage of the straits must be attempted only by night or in a fog. He expressly stated that after April the enterprise was impracticable, until of course the approach of autumn brought long nights again. In the sequel he began to realize the immense difficulty of keeping a great flotilla together during hours of darkness or fog, especially in straits where the tide ran strongly; but at the outset he either overlooked or ignored this important factor in the case. Accustomed in youth to the almost tideless Mediterranean, he failed to realize the difficulties of navigation in the English Channel. Certainly he never allowed the time necessary for so vast an enterprise, undertaken by vessels of various sizes, mostly keelless, and therefore certain to drift to leeward if a wind arose.[1]

Napoleon's refusal or omission to recognize these difficulties, so patent to all seamen acquainted with the Channel, has sometimes been taken as proof that the scheme of invasion by the flotilla was nothing more than an elaborate blind. In the case of ordinary men this inference would be tenable; but Napoleon was no ordinary man. His nature was eager and enthusiastic; his will unbending and masterful beyond that of any man known to authentic history; his mind, keen, incisive, capacious, found its highest joy in essaying mighty tasks, in setting myriads of men to work, and, as was seen in Syria and Russia, in defying alike his enemies and the forces of Nature herself. The mere mention of the word "impossible" provoked him to assert the superiority of his will over any and every difficulty. Moreover, like all strong-willed men, he was always prone to follow the bent of his fundamental instincts, foremost among which were a craving for certainty and a detestation of the vague and incalculable. Where he had to deal only with men, the superb range of his intellect, alike highly imaginative and sternly objective

[1] See Admiral Montagu's report on the capture of one of them, due to this defect (Rose, "Life of Napoleon," i, 485). Dumouriez in his plan of defence drawn up for the British Government in 1804, scoffed at the notion of an invasion by the flotilla alone (Rose and Broadley, "Dumouriez and the Defence of England," ch. ix). Sir Neil Campbell at Elba noted Napoleon's inability to allow for risks and delays on sea ("Sir N. Campbell's Journal," p. 339). Wheeler and Broadley, "Napoleon and the Invasion of England," ii, ch. xiv.

ensured almost unvarying success, until he failed to recognize the strength of the new spirit which came over the nations. But that same intellect played him false when he confronted the elemental forces of nature amidst sandy deserts, by stormy and tidal seas, or on the steppes of Russia.

Reviewing in a more general manner his scheme of the late autumn of 1803 we may hazard the following conjectures. Undoubtedly it answered one purpose of great moment, namely, that of stimulating army, navy, and the whole nation to the utmost exertion by holding out to view a glorious enterprise. Again it may have served, in that time of activity of his spy, Méhée de la Touche, to mislead or intimidate the British Government;[1] or, the First Consul may have looked on this threatening display of naval activity, ruinously expensive though it was, as necessary to secure and maintain the initiative in war, which he held to be the chief secret of success. Perhaps all these motives were operative; for the threats of invasions of England and Ireland were the most obvious means of assuring his own prestige and the acquiescence of France in his rule, besides condemning the Addington Government to persist in a demoralizing defensive. On the whole, perhaps, this first scheme may be dismissed as a feint, except in so far as it served to quicken the energies of France, and, in part at least, to gain the initiative even at sea, where France was at her weakest.

In one other respect the menace of invasion was serviceable. It served to detain in home waters no small portion of the British fleet, which otherwise could have operated in full force against the Colonies and commerce of the enemy, as happened after Trafalgar. True, even in the year 1803 the British fleets were far from being wholly condemned to the defensive. In the West Indies they delivered telling blows. St. Lucia, Tobago, Demerara fell to the Union Jack in the first months of the war; and elsewhere French coast towns and commerce were harried so far effectively as, perhaps, to furnish an explanation of Napoleon's change of plans in September 1804, which will appear in due course. Meanwhile, until the maritime resources of France and her allies provided him with a formidable navy, the threat of an invasion by the flotilla, whether with or without convoy, was almost the only means of securing the initiative in war on

---

[1] At St. Helena, after reading Méhée's work, he told Gourgaud that he (Napoleon) had inspired it (Gourgaud "Journal," i, 560).

which the great warrior always laid so much stress. We can therefore understand his efforts at all times to keep up the appearance of preparing a formidable blow. But it is unsafe to adduce as conclusive proof of his intentions the many stories of his angry outbursts against Berthier and others who sought to dissuade him from "leaping the ditch." In him passion was always subject to the will; and he had the best of reasons for furiously repelling all attempts that would discredit vast preparations, the utility of which must vanish with the first suspicion of their unreality.[1]

In this connection it is worth noting that on 16th November 1811, when war with Russia was considered improbable, Napoleon wrote to Decrès urging him to keep in good repair some 500 vessels of the Boulogne flotilla. He adds that the flotilla "will always be one of the most powerful means of influencing England; and every time that our squadrons begin to move and that we double or triple the flotilla, requisitioning fishermen and sailors, and embarking artillery and stores, England will expect a combination bringing squadrons to Boulogne, and will thenceforth be obliged to hold in reserve a great part of her sail-of-the-line in the Thames and the Downs, and a fairly large body of troops to cover London and her dockyards."[2]

Turning from the doubtful sphere of assertion to the domain of fact, we notice that the experience of the winter 1803-4 proved the impossibility of a crossing by night, or even, for that matter, by day, except in light airs. Bonaparte, arguing more as an artilleryman than a sailor, had overloaded his vessels in respect of cannon, crews, and cargoes, so that many alterations were needed; and the newer craft, being broader, were ill adapted to propulsion by oars, to which, as will appear, he at that time largely trusted. Therefore it may be inferred, that, whatever his words, he abandoned all thought of invasion during the months February-June 1804, when, moreover, political events of high importance detained him in Paris. Further, the Grand Army encamped at and near Boulogne was far below its nominal strength. The muster rolls of March 1804 showed heavy deficiencies, those of Ney's Corps amounting to 7,803 men against

---

[1] See the interesting evidence in Desbrière, iii, ch. xiii, and the reports of spies in England, and of a general who had commanded in Ireland, as to the feasibility of invasion (*ibid.*, iii, pp. 317-335).

[2] "Napoleon Corresp.," xxiii, p. 19. See, too, xvii, 114, 211.

an effective total of 18,882. By the summer, however, the grand total reached nearly 100,000 men.[1] The concentration of the flotilla in the harbours of Picardy continued to present great difficulties, especially from the ports of Brittany and beyond. Even the short coast voyages from Normandy or Flanders entailed frequent losses. At the end of March 1804 there were at Boulogne and the three neighbouring ports only 462 vessels of war and 474 small transports. Even so, the harbour at Boulogne was overcrowded; and in rough weather it was found impossible to keep in the roadstead a large number of vessels. In the middle of April 1804 a line of nearly 150 vessels of war was formed outside; but a storm from the north-east broke it up and compelled many of the boats to run for Etaples, while some of those anchored off Wimereux made for Boulogne. The event caused great discouragement among those who were responsible for the flotilla, seeing that the storms from the west were still more to be dreaded. The event also proved that not more than 100 vessels could regain the harbour in a single tide.[2]

On Napoleon, however, it made no impression, if we may judge by his letters. True, he had had to face the royalist plot and was now considering the addresses which begged him to establish monarchy. He could, therefore, ill give way in his naval projects; and on 21st April he ordered Decrès, Minister of Marine, to push on work on frigates, brigs, and the vessels of the flotilla, adding that the maritime Departments, hitherto out of sympathy with the Revolution, must be made to look forward to a time when France will dominate the sea as well as the land. Therefore, an additional sum of 2,000,000 francs a month must be spent on ship-building. He adds—" I am in no hurry as to the time [of action] but I ask that great preparations be made." Before the time of proclamation of the imperial title (18th May), all decisive action in the Straits was out of the question; but apart from that, the flotilla was still very widely dispersed. Even at the end of June 1804, there were at Boulogne and the neighbouring ports only 610 vessels of war; 80 were at Dunkirk; 182 at Ostend; 208 at Havre; and 254 were at ports further west as far as Rochefort, no fewer than 55 being at that port. No one who has noticed the stress laid by Napoleon on

---

[1] Desbrière, iii, 429, 430.

[2] *Ibid.*, iii, 542-5, 557-565. Up to the end of June 1804, 9 vessels had been taken by the British and 17 had been wrecked.

concentration of all available forces can believe that he seriously intended invasion until a large proportion of these scattered units was assembled; and in view of the evidence now adduced it is almost certain that he resolved to postpone the attempt at invasion. It is worth noting that the grand total of vessels of war ready at midsummer 1804, along the coast from Ostend to Rochefort was 1,334, a number barely exceeding that which he had stated to Ganteaume as ordered to be ready *at Boulogne* by 6th January 1804.[1] So far had his soaring fancy risen above the utmost possibilities of the situation.

In one respect these exertions achieved their aim. They caused widespread apprehension in England except among experienced seamen. Pitt rarely donned the flaming robe of the alarmist; but in his speech of 15th March 1804 in Parliament there were one or two flamboyant patches. He declared that more than 1,000 transports had assembled at Boulogne by December, 1803, a number more than double of that collected there in March 1804. His further statement, that we were threatened with invasion day by day, far exceeded the facts of the case. Already it was known that the flotilla could not make the passage during a high wind; and his own correspondence shows that at such times he ran up from Walmer to London in full confidence that he and his Volunteers would not be called upon to oppose a landing. His speech shows that even a Lord Warden of the Cinque Ports was ignorant of the state of things then existing at Boulogne, which precluded all chance of an invasion for several weeks. Nevertheless it was well to urge the Addington Ministry to reassure the country by strengthening the flotilla of gunboats along the threatened coast. In 1801 the Pitt Administration had formed such a flotilla; but during the present war only twenty-three gun-vessels had been ordered. True, from 500 to 700 volunteer gun-boats were ready for service, but they were not under the immediate control of the Admiralty, and had been forced on it by the enthusiasm of the people. Pitt therefore called for a national flotilla as well as for greater exertions in the construction of warships in private yards, it being proved that in time of war the royal dockyards could do little but repairs; out of twenty-four sail-of-the-line built during the last war (1793-1801) only two came from the royal yards.

As Pitt's speech was calculated to increase the prevailing

[1] Desbrière, iii, 568, where the total is wrongly given as 1,144.

alarm, Sir Edward Pellew (afterwards Lord Exmouth) declared that the measures of defence were ample. They consisted in squadrons acting along the enemy's coasts, another of heavier ships stationed in the Downs, and a third, of light vessels, for coast defence. His naval experience warranted the belief that the enemy would never pierce this triple barrier. Pitt's remonstrance, however, did good in compelling the Addington Ministry to strengthen the navy and the volunteer flotilla; but Pellew was right in deprecating too great attention to gun-vessels. So long as the navy could watch the French naval ports, close the mouth of the English Channel, observe Boulogne, and muster strongly in the Downs, there was no real danger, as the experience of past wars had amply shown. Yet, so long as a large part of the British public was in a state of nervous apprehension, Napoleon attained one of his chief ends, that of ensuring the "moral" superiority which a threatening attitude always confers. In this respect the alarmists in England played into his hands. In the autumn of 1804 Dumouriez prophesied that, if this state of things lasted, it would paralyse the energies of England. Pitt resolved to end "the benumbing influence of suspense" by striking at Napoleon in South Italy, as will soon appear.[1]

There was only one probable case in which Napoleon's flotilla could hope unaided to force a landing, namely, in the event of a protracted calm. Counting on this eventuality, he had ordered all the vessels of the flotilla, even the *prames* (corvettes) to be provided with oars, at which the sailors and troops were to be exercised on all possible occasions. On 21st May 1804 he issued orders to this effect, even for the Dutch flotilla, as though the enthusiasm and strength of the Dutch would suffice to row large vessels across the North Sea.[2] It is highly questionable whether any but the smallest vessels at Boulogne and Wimereux could be propelled across the baffling tides of the Straits of Dover; certainly the *prames* could not. But he seems to have hoped that with sufficient practice sailors and troops could row across most of the flotilla during a calm which would

---

[1] Rose and Broadley, "Dumouriez and the Defence of England against Napoleon," p. 261.

[2] "Napoleon Corresp.," ix, 369. For Napoleon's refusal of Fulton's offer to propel the flotilla by steam power see Desbrière, iii, 307-315; Wheeler and Broadley, "Napoleon and the Invasion of England," i, ch. xi.

render useless for the time the British squadron in the Downs. It was to meet this contingency that gun-vessels were needed on the Kentish coast. Even by the month of October 1803 Pitt, as Lord Warden, had ready as many as 170 between Margate and Hastings; and the number was afterwards so far increased as to leave scant hopes of success for the comparatively few light vessels that could be rowed across from the coast of Picardy. Calms rarely last more than two days in the Straits; and if Napoleon continued to rely on the unlikely conjunction of neap tides and three or four days' calm, he was imposing an altogether unwarrantable risk on his weary crews who would meet a flotilla of nearly equal strength on the shores of Kent. Whether he realized this fact there is no evidence to prove. His seamen never even essayed this feat of endurance. In fact, the British cruisers off Boulogne prevented the constant practice with the sweeps and oars which was the first condition of success.

The extreme danger of isolated action by the flotilla having been amply shown in several brushes with small British cruisers off Boulogne, Napoleon came to see that the problem of invasion turned on the destruction, or at least the evasion, of England's naval power. That fact had long been evident to British naval experts; and we may note that when Pitt came back to office in May 1804 (a few days before the assumption of the imperial title by Napoleon) no radical change took place in the balance of our naval strength. Several gun-vessels were built; but the chief care was now, as always, bestowed on the navy. In reality the chief burden of responsibility rested with Admirals Cornwallis and Gardner, successively commanding the great fleet off Brest and Ushant. So long as it held the chops of the Channel, neither the squadrons nor the flotilla in the Biscay ports could reach Boulogne. The confidence of the British Admiralty in the effectiveness of their arrangements appears in the instructions of 24th August 1804 to the Commander of the fleet observing Brest:[1]

If the enemy put to sea with the whole of their fleet, without any considerable body of troops on board, the probability is that they mean an attempt on some part of the coast of Britain, and that the object of the fleet is to cover the disembarkation of some of the numerous assemblages of troops now collected in the ports opposite to the coast of

[1] "The Barham Papers," iii, 232 (Navy Records Society, 1911).

England. This seems a very desperate attempt, and is likely to terminate in the destruction of their fleet, if they should be able, by any extraordinary unforeseen events, to elude your vigilance, and thereby to make their way up the Channel; but if the existing government of France is determined to risk everything on this long-menaced attempt against this country, we are not at liberty to calculate solely on what is rational or probable, but we must likewise keep in view such contingencies as may be barely possible, and such as passion and intemperance may give rise to. You are therefore hereby directed to continue to watch the motions of the enemy with the fleet under your command as closely as may be, consistently with the safety of the ships.

If, on the other hand, the French set sail from Brest with many troops on board, their destination might be assumed to be the West Indies, and a detachment equal in strength to that of the enemy is to be sent in pursuit and, in the event of not discovering its route, must return to the blockading fleet off Brest. If the enemy sought to overpower the British squadrons off Rochefort and Ferrol, the British commander is to proceed to a rendezvous previously arranged with the Admirals of those squadrons. Thus, no probable contingency was left out of count; and, secure in the command of the central position at the mouth of the English Channel, the blockaders of Brest could confidently await the development of Napoleon's plans.

Gradually he came to the conclusion that the crux of the problem was not at Boulogne, but off Brest. To drive away Cornwallis was essential even for the concentration of the French flotilla, 181 vessels of which were in the Biscay ports at the end of June 1804. With the aim of overpowering or driving off, the blockaders of Brest, the Emperor concocted several plans, which are of interest as showing his transference of the principles of military strategy to the more complex and shifting problems of oceanic warfare. It is impossible to describe them all. The schemes which on 7th December 1803 he outlined to Ganteaume were clearly tentative and faulty. They imply a speedy concentration of the French fleets of Toulon and Rochefort without hindrance from the blockaders, as well as the presence at Boulogne of 130,000 men and 2,000 vessels by 20th February 1804. On 13th June 1804 he bade Decrès prepare for a landing in Jersey with 10,000 men, a plan which was not pressed, and may be considered a false scent designed to deceive British or royalist spies.

Far more important is that which he outlined on 25th May 1804 to Vice-Admiral Latouche-Tréville commanding the fleet at Toulon. Not being " hermetically sealed " by Nelson, Latouche must as soon as possible evade the blockade and prepare to co-operate with Truguet's fleet so soon as it can escape from Brest. A long and undated order to Latouche also instructs him to make for Cadiz, pick up a French warship there, make a wide sweep round Finisterre so as to avoid tbe British squadron off Ferrol, chase away the blockaders of Rochefort and rally the French squadron of six sail-of-the-line in that roadstead. Then, avoiding the fleet of Cornwallis, Latouche will enter the English Channel and touch at Cherbourg, with a view to a grand junction at Boulogne.[1] Of the same tenour, but implying that more precise instructions have been given, is the Emperor's letter of 2nd July to Latouche, which enjoins the same general tactics. It ends with the expression of a hope that Latouche will arrive off Boulogne in September when the nights are long enough and the weather calm enough to favour the grand enterprise. To ensure its success, Napoleon will have there 120,000 men, and 10,000 horses ready to embark on 1,800 vessels of the flotilla. " Let us be masters of the Straits for six hours, and we shall be masters of the world."

These three documents afford cumulative and almost conclusive proof that in May-July 1804 the Emperor resolved on the invasion. True, he over-estimated the numbers of the flotilla available at Boulogne in September; for the British blockade of Havre detained there for many weeks 152 vessels on which he had reckoned; and for the like cause many others could not arrive. Worst of all was the situation of the flotilla in the Biscay ports. Of the 231 vessels ready for sea at Brest and other ports as far south as Rochefort, only 35 succeeded in reaching Cherbourg by the first week of October 1804.[2]

Nevertheless, everything seemed to promise a serious effort. In the middle of July 1804 he set out for Boulogne and there on the 19th received a magnificent reception. Along the street re-named *Rue Impériale* were erected twelve triumphal arches, named after his chief victories; and further on was a

[1] M. Desbrière thinks that this order is anterior to that of 25th May 1804, which prescribes a junction with the French fleet at Brest. It seems to me to resemble rather that of 2nd July 1805.

[2] Desbrière, iv (1), pp. 49-51, 73-4. James, " Naval History," iii, p. 227.

portico leading to a Temple of Immortality. On reaching the quay, an obelisk confronted him bearing an inscription which bade him vindicate the liberty of the seas, soon to be assured by the avenging thunderbolts flying forth from that estuary. These incidents are of more than scenic interest. Among a people sensitive to glory and to ridicule this ovation furnished an additional incentive to a triumphant activity; and it is fairly certain that during part at least of the five weeks spent on that coast, he looked forward to a landing in Kent. He urged the adoption of all possible measures for bringing up the flotilla from the western ports; everywhere he encouraged the sailors and troops to the utmost exertions; and we may not unreasonably assign to the first part of this sojourn at or near Boulogne the order for the construction of the famous medal showing him as Hercules strangling a merman. The legend is as follows: "*Descente en Angleterre: frappée à Londres,* 1804." The fact that all possible copies of this medal were afterwards destroyed affords additional proof that he had at one time cherished the confident expectation of dictating terms of peace at London.

A spirit of boundless confidence pervaded his actions at that time. On two occasions he disregarded the warnings of Admiral Bruix. On the first he insisted on sailing past a fort north of Wimereux, in defiance of British broadsides and a coming squall, thereby running into a position of grave peril, from which Bruix's disregard of the imperial orders alone rescued him. Untaught by this incident, he soon after ordered a review of the flotilla to be held in the roadstead in the teeth of a rising gale. Again Bruix remonstrated, and finally refused to execute his commands. A violent scene ensued, but Bruix refused to give way. Rear-Admiral Magon thereupon ordered preparations for the review, the result being the loss of some vessels and of about two hundred men of their crews. The indignation aroused by this insensate obstinacy was allayed by a distribution of money,[1] but it is doubtful whether the naval officers ever regained complete confidence in the Emperor's judgement. He continued to press on the preparations with feverish energy. On 20th August, while at Pont-de-Briques, near Boulogne, he ordered the two portions of the Dutch flotilla to proceed to Dunkirk, the third portion also making ready for a junction at Ostend. Eight days later he heard news destructive of his hopes for September, namely,

[1] F. Nicolay, "Napoleon at the Boulogne Camp," ch. ix.

the death of Admiral Latouche, which occurred at Toulon on 20th August. This event caused much concern. To Decrès he submitted the names of Bruix, Villèneuve, and Rosily, as those of possible successors. As Bruix was needed at Boulogne, and Rosily had insufficient experience, his choice inclined towards Villeneuve; and he ordered him to come to Paris for an interview concerning the grand aims to be set before the Toulon fleet.

For the present he seems to have given up all thought of an immediate attempt at invasion, doubtless owing to the death of Latouche and the unexpected difficulties that arose at Boulogne. Whatever the cause, he set out for a tour to Mons, Aix-la-Chapelle, and Mainz.[1] It is also significant that for some time past his language to the Czar carried defiance to the verge of insolence. Because Alexander had protested to the German Diet against the violation of its territory by the kidnapping of the Duc d'Enghien, Napoleon bade Talleyrand insert in an official note to Russia a reference to the immorality of the Czar in showing favour to a murderer of the Czar Paul, his father. Russia was also to be informed that she could no more interfere in the affairs of Europe than France in those of Persia. If Alexander made a league with Austria against France, the power of the latter State would become colossal; for she had vanquished them in the last Coalition. His attitude to Austria was scarcely less provocative. The only monarch whom he humoured was Frederick William III of Prussia, who, he suggested, should take the title of Emperor, as Francis of Austria had done. These letters, dating from 7th August to the middle of September, raise a doubt whether he was not even then shaping his policy so as to have ready to hand a continental war as an alternative to the maritime venture. His occupation of Hanover was a dire affront to Prussia; and in the middle of December 1803, Lucchesini, the Prussian ambassador at Paris, informed his Court that "a continental war would offer to the general and the statesman chances far less doubtful than the maritime enterprises against England." This was a belief widely prevalent in continental capitals; and it must have had a place in Napoleon's calculations, though, on the other hand, he may have cherished the hope that Austria and Prussia were fully

---

[1] "Napoleon Corresp.," vol. ix. Letters of 6th, 7th, 24th, 28th, 30th August, 3rd, 9th September.

occupied in digesting the broad ecclesiastical domains absorbed by them in the early part of 1803. In the case of any other man than Napoleon the inference would be irresistible that he all along desired to have a second string to his bow. But to his self-confidence, boundless as his contempt for "the old Coalition machines," the task of browbeating the two Emperors may not have seemed incompatible with that of paralyzing Great Britain either by an invasion or by the long nightmare of the dread of invasion.

In view of the elaborate preparations for the coronation of 2nd December 1804, little more than the appearance of activity was now kept up at Boulogne and neighbouring ports. Thus, while bidding Ganteaume, Truguet's successor at Brest, to terrify the British by frequent sorties from that port, he summoned to Paris several of his chief naval officers as well as those of the Boulogne flotilla; and in a letter of 10th September to Decrès he stated significantly that, whereas the flotilla had been considered as an expeditionary force, thenceforth it must be thought of as "a fixed establishment."[1] In view of these facts, and of the impossibility of bringing to Boulogne the strong detachments held captive at Havre and further west, an air of mystery hangs over the grandiose plans which he drew up at Mainz on 27th to 29th September 1804 for an expedition of 18,000 men from Brest to Ireland, reinforced by 25,000 under Marmont from Holland, while at the same time the Boulogne flotilla is to set sail in order to force a landing in Kent. What were the salient facts of the situation? At Brest there were in August only 6,606 officers and men, while the "Irish legion" had sunk to forty-eight officers and sixteen soldiers.[2] Marmont's armada must also have found immense difficulty in forcing the Straits of Dover or in rounding the north of Scotland so as to effect a junction with the expedition from Brest, which, moreover, had to evade the grip of Cornwallis. And would the Boulogne flotilla, for which Napoleon had of late ordered stringent economies, be able to time its attack on Kent so as to draw the blockading squadrons from the coasts of Holland and Brest? Finally, did Napoleon really believe his own statement that,

---

[1] "Napoleon Coresp.," ix, 9th 10th September; Desbrière, iv (1), pp. 168, 177.

[2] Desbrière, iv (1), p. 180. On 29th September Napoleon ordered 29 gun-brigs at Brest to be unmanned.

whichever of the two expeditions succeeded, the war would be gained? It is not easy to fathom the thoughts of a man who thus set at defiance the lessons of experience, treating the ocean as a chess-board and fleets as pieces to be moved at will. We shall not be far wrong in dismissing these schemes either as a sign of the megalomania now beginning to distort his judgement, or as material for the consumption of spies and intended to keep up the alarm in England. Or again, he may have wished to lead the Irish refugees in France to foment a rising in their native land, just as in 1798 he undoubtedly made use of the Irish malcontents to further his oriental designs.

At this time, too, he formed vast colonial schemes, doubtless with the aim of scattering the British navy over the oceans. On 29th September 1804 he issued orders to prepare expeditions against the British West Indies, as well as Surinam, St. Domingo, St. Helena, Goree, and Senegal. These expeditionary forces were to set out *before* that of Brest, destined for Ireland. The latter was now to land troops in Ireland and then proceed *viâ* the north of Scotland to the Texel, where 25,000 were to be on board awaiting it. Naval history furnishes no more ludicrous example of mechanical accuracy applied to complex movements on the most uncertain of elements. For a long time none of the squadrons could elude the grip of the blockaders, and not until 11th January 1805 did that of Rochefort succeed in slipping out, whereupon it effected some damage in the West Indies.

For the present, then, it is probable that Napoleon gave up all thought of an invasion by the flotilla, a scheme which British naval officers had long declared to be impossible. Lord Melville, First Lord of the Admiralty, summed up their opinions in a letter to Pitt, dated 14th October 1804, declaring that the embarkation of the Grand Army in the outer road at Boulogne must take four, five, or perhaps even six tides, during which time attacks by our cruisers would throw it into confusion. Experience had shown, added Melville, that the cruisers suffered little from the combined broadsides of the forts and the flotilla; and it would be well to assail the latter with fireships.[1] Efforts of this kind having failed, Pitt discouraged any further attempt; but it is clear that by this time only the alarmists looked on the flotilla with fear. Perhaps it was a perception of the diminu-

[1] Rose, "William Pitt and the Great War," p. 511.

tion of "the terror" in England which led Napoleon to turn to colonial enterprises.

In these he was to receive help from Spain. During several months he had compelled that Power to pay him a subsidy and to help in the repair of French warships at Cadiz and Ferrol. Evidently he was working to bring about a rupture between Spain and England, which occurred in December 1804. As, however, the Spanish navy was in bad repair, no change took place in the naval situation, British squadrons having for more than six months closely watched those two ports. Napoleon now urged Charles IV to throw all his energy into his fleet; and the Emperor's plans of 12th to 23rd December 1804 counted largely on the support of Spain; but they do not point to a forthcoming invasion of the British Isles. In another scheme, of 16th January 1805, he renounces the Irish expedition in favour of one to India, and prophesies terrible things to England from the concentration of 23,000 French troops and 3,000 Spaniards at L'Isle de France (Mauritius) and Réunion. Probably this scheme was no more than a bait for British spies, the real aim being to effect a dissemination of England's naval power over the West and East Indies, and a relaxation of its grip on Brest and Toulon. Evidently Napoleon's former trust in a crossing of the flotilla during a winter's night had disappeared, and he looked forward solely to an open attack by day during average weather under the convoy of a fleet.

It is virtually certain that he renounced all thought of a landing in England during the period September 1804 to May 1805. For the plans which he drew up on 12th and 23rd December 1804 for Villeneuve and Missiessy, commanding at Toulon and Rochefort, prescribed the destruction of British commerce in the West Indies, the succour of French garrisons, the uniting of the two squadrons at Martinique, and a return to France, without any hint of a further offensive. Apparently Napoleon had not yet distinctly formulated the scheme of an advance in force into the English Channel; but his note of 14th December to Decrès lays stress on the preparation of strong Spanish squadrons at Cadiz and Ferrol, in order to join Villeneuve, on his return, in a French port unnamed.[1] This we may regard as the germ of an idea soon to be greatly developed. But, at

---

[1] "Napoleon Corresp.," x, 63-7, 70-2, 78-81. Villeneuve's sortie on 18th January 1805 was a failure.

present, he laid stress on these colonial enterprises, which could not possibly be carried out before the end of May 1805. Obviously, then, the invasion was deferred to such time as the two squadrons should return and unite with the as yet ill-prepared squadrons of Spain. Another proof of postponement is the neglect to take ordinary precautions for the upkeep of the harbours of Boulogne and Ambleteuse, the result being that, on resuming his earlier plans in March 1805, he had to allot 700,000 francs to making good defects.[1]

Political as well as naval reasons had contributed to this delay. In November 1804 the seizure of Rumbold, British Ambassador at Hamburg, for a time portended a rupture between France and Prussia. In the following month the Czar sent one of his *confidantes*, Novossiltzoff, on a mission to London, the general aim of which became known to French agents.[2] The Emperor, desirous of sounding the situation, used a device—it can scarcely be considered more—like that which he adopted at Christmas 1799.[3] He sent to George III a proposal for peace, to which there came the reply that it could not be considered until after consultation with friendly States, especially Russia. The reply would have given pause to any other man than Napoleon; but he cared little for Russia, provided that he remained on good terms with Austria and Prussia. After his release of Rumbold in order to humour the Prussian King, the Court of Berlin resumed its normally complaisant tone; and Austria, though restive at French supremacy in Italy and Switzerland, sent assurances of a peaceful character. Therefore towards the end of February 1805 Napoleon, feeling sure of all the Continental States but Russia, defined his naval policy more clearly. On the 23rd he ordered Junot to proceed to Madrid to reproach the King and Queen and her all-powerful favourite, Godoy, with the languor displayed at the dockyards, and to hold out the bait of Portugal, in case that little State refused to comply with the French demands. Godoy was also to be allured by the offer of a large present, conditional on the speedy efficiency of the Spanish navy, which must also have ready on

---

[1] " Napoleon Corresp.," x, 222, Napoleon to Soult, 13th March 1805.

[2] Lefebvre, " Cabinets de l'Europe," ii, 33.

[3] See his admission to Roederer on 1st October 1800, that his negotiations with the Emperor Francis after Marengo were only with the aim of putting him in the wrong. Roederer, " Journal," p. 21.

board provisions for six months and prepare to join a French fleet.[1] All this portended a great blow at England; and when news soon arrived that the Spanish ships were in a more forward state than was thought to be the case,[2] the Emperor drew up his famous plan of 2nd March. In brief, it aimed at uniting the Toulon and Brest squadrons with those of Cadiz and Ferrol, making Martinique the rendezvous (it being believed that Missiessy with the Rochefort squadron was there), and after damaging British commerce to the utmost, effecting a return to Boulogne in the month of June. Such was Napoleon's statement to General Lauriston, commanding the 4,000 troops on board, which were finally to form part of the Grand Army at and near Boulogne.[3]

It is difficult to believe that these vast preparations were a mere blind; and events challenged him to strike out boldly. At that time there were few signs of the impending Coalition. So long as his pretensions met with acquiescence or faint protests from Prussia and Austria the feelings of the Czar might with safety be neglected. The addition of the Russian navy to that of England would make no serious difference; and if Spain, Holland, and Italy continued to furnish ships and naval stores, Napoleon might hope sooner or later to overbear Britain on her own element. Obviously, two courses were open to him, either to adopt a peaceful attitude on land and play a waiting game at sea; or to hurry on affairs to a decisive issue on one of those elements, a course consonant with his pride and energy, his untarnished prestige and the eager hopes of a sensitive and critical nation. Prudence counselled the former alternative; and of late, up to the end of February 1805, signs of its adoption are clearly visible in his correspondence, his neglect of the flotilla and harbours of Picardy, and his pre-occupation in schemes for harrying the colonies and commerce of the enemy. But at the beginning of March the good news from Madrid and Vienna throws him back upon the former alternative. It is characteristic that, while abating not a jot of his claims in Germany and Italy, he pushes on naval preparations apace. The Boulogne flotilla is strengthened, and orders are given to send away the slowest vessels to the depots, also to exercise the troops in embarking, disembark-

---

[1] "Napoleon Corresp.," x, 161-4. See, too, the letter of 27th February to Soult at Boulogne that vigorous operations would soon begin.

[2] Desbrière, iv (iii), 337-9.   [3] "Napoleon Corresp.," x, 182-9.

ing, and firing. All ships of war are to be provided with carron-
ades, a weapon effectively used by the British. His aide-de-
camp, Lauriston, who commands the troops on Villeneuve's
squadron, is urged to press on that Admiral and see to it that he
is not intimidated by the English.[1] Both to Villeneuve and
Lauriston Napoleon declares that their present mission is far
more important than that which he had originally designed, a
sure proof that the colonial aims of the recent past had now
widened into a far grander enterprise.

Collateral evidence points towards the resumption of the plan
of invasion of England. On 14th March the Emperor orders the
expenditure of additional sums of money, 20,000,000 francs a
year if necessary, on the most important roads, namely, those
from Paris to Boulogne, Cherbourg, and Brest. The roads of a
second order are those from Paris to Turin, Toulon, and into
Spain. Those of the third order are from Paris to Strassburg
and to Cologne *viâ* Brussels. The local roads between Étaples
and Dunkirk are also to be improved, and the Simplon road
finished in the current year. There is no mention of the roads
leading from Boulogne and Calais towards the middle Rhine.
These facts are significant in view of his care of the chief military routes, especially those likely to be used in war (witness his
despatch of Murat into Swabia to report on the roads, on 25th
August 1805). They throw doubt upon his later assertions to
the Council of State and to Metternich, that the army assembled
at Boulogne was always intended for action against Austria. If
that had been so, he would have assigned great importance to
the roads leading from Picardy into Champagne and the Rhine-
land.[2] Evidently, then, he did not expect a Coalition in the near
future; and this explains the bold and masterful way in which
he traced out the course of events both by land and sea.

Only three days after giving orders concerning the chief roads
of France, he accepted the crown of the kingdom of Italy, an act
subversive of his treaty of Lunéville with Austria (February
1801). True, he wrote to the Emperor Francis, laying stress on
his reluctance to assume this heavy burden and the urgent need
of complying with the wishes of the Italians for protection so

[1] "Napoleon Corresp.," x, letters of 10th to 16th March 1805.

[2] It may be urged that his expenditure on the roads to the three northern
ports, and his disregard of other roads was a blind. But I think this objection too subtle, where the expenditure of 20,000,000 francs was concerned.

long as Russia held Corfu, and England Malta. He even promised to lay down the crown when those islands achieved their independence. To Frederick William of Prussia he wrote in the same strain. To the Czar he sent not a word. Possibly he persuaded himself that Austria would accept this further rebuff, aggravated though it was by the gift of the Principality of Piombino, on the coast of Tuscany, to his sister Élisa (18th March). But it is difficult to follow the workings of a brain which set at defiance the lessons of experience both in diplomacy and navigation. On land he hoped to browbeat or cajole three great States while he set aside a treaty and altered the balance of power. On sea he dictated the order of events with the same confidence, as appears in his letter, written at Malmaison on 22nd March to Lauriston, ordering that the Toulon fleet must get away by 26th March. Certainly time was pressing if the combined fleets, after their voyage to the West Indies, were to appear before Boulogne in the month of June. By good fortune Villeneuve managed to slip away on 30th March. Ganteaume was held fast at Brest by Cornwallis.

Another misfortune for the Emperor was that Missiessy with the Rochefort squadron had slipped away in the middle of January, and, making sail for the West Indies, had enlightened the British Admiralty, which might otherwise have been distracted by the *guerre de course* planned by Napoleon in September. It also disconcerted Napoleon, who saw that his plan of a great naval concentration at Martinique would miscarry. At Lyons on 11th April he heard of Villeneuve's departure from Toulon twelve days before, and now refashioned the whole scheme. Assuming that Ganteaume would detain Cornwallis off Brest, and that Missiessy's expected return would hold another British squadron off Rochefort, he ordered Villeneuve, along with two more French ships now preparing for sea at Rochefort, to compass the grand object of his voyage by doubling the north of Scotland on his return voyage and so making for Dunkirk. There in the month of July he would rally the flotilla of the Dutch and Flemish ports and prepare to convoy that of Boulogne so as to avenge " the many centuries of insult." Two days later, while still at Lyons, he again altered his scheme, apparently in the belief that there was great alarm in London at the success of Missiessy's expedition and the defencelessness of the British West Indies. Elated also by news from India, where he

believed that French officers would help the Mahrattas stoutly
to contest the British supremacy, he directed Villeneuve and
Lauriston to do all the harm possible in the West Indies, and
wait there a month from the time of the arrival of those orders,
in hope of joining Ganteaume's fleet in case it escaped from
Brest. Failing that, Villeneuve was forthwith to set sail for
Ferrol, there rally fifteen French and Spanish ships, and, releas-
ing the Brest fleet, make straight for Boulogne, where all would
be in readiness for the final blow.

These constant changes of plans deserve the censure that has
been bestowed upon them.[1] But they imply a fixed resolve to
effect a landing in Kent in the month of July. In full assurance,
then, the Emperor left Lyons, after a splendid reception, and
met with equal adulation at Chambéry and in Piedmont. The
journey was a political necessity, and by no means told against
the chances of the invasion, but rather tended to reassure the
enemy respecting the Channel and divert attention to the two
Indies. On 20th April, while staying at the castle of Stupingi,
near Turin, Napoleon hears with delight that Nelson is searching the central Mediterranean for the Toulon fleet, whence he
infers that he has gone to Egypt. All his letters written in
North Italy breathe complete confidence in the result. Eagerly
he awaits news of the sailing of the Brest and Rochefort squadrons, he plans an expedition to Africa, and cherishes the hope
that 5,000 or 6,000 French troops, if sent to India, will overthrow the British Company. On the next day, 30th April, he
pictures Villeneuve reaching Martinique by 5th May (nine days
before the actual time) while Nelson is groping about the
Levant. In order to hold him there, he on 4th May orders a
feint to be made towards Egypt.

The long letters of these days to Decrès and Villeneuve are
incompatible with the theory that he did not intend the invasion
of England. It was the one aim which energized all the schemes
emanating from that fertile brain. He imagined the British
Ministers to be gabbling panic-stricken in Parliament, and engaging in spasmodic efforts to save the East and West Indies.
Craig's expedition, which set sail on 16th April for Sicily and

---

[1] Corbett, "Campaign of Trafalgar," ch. ix. French naval experts discouraged the notion that the French fleet blockaded at Brest could help
in a naval battle that might occur off that port between Cornwallis and
Villeneuve: but Napoleon held to it. Desbrière, iv (iii), 517.

Naples (Pitt's blow at the Napoleonic supremacy in the Mediterranean) appeared to him a despairing effort to prop up the
tottering fabric of the East India Company. As for the Mediterranean, he wrote to Decrès on 11th May at Milan: "I am
sure the English have not a single ship there." They were
chasing French squadrons to the Cape of Good Hope, or round
Ireland.

Plan follows plan in quick succession, until, on 25th May, he
convinces himself that after all the moves just described he will
have sixty-five sail-of-the-line united with every chance of success, a number which the English will never succeed in uniting.
On the next day a further calculation proves that they "will
never succeed in uniting forty sail-of-the-line." In order still
further to scatter their squadrons, he on the 29th proposes an
expedition to Ireland. Two days later, fathering his own
schemes on the enemy, he says the disorder of the English is
extreme and leads to nothing but orders and counter-orders.
On 22nd June he warns Decrès that feints must be made so as
to weaken the blockaders off Brest, "which is the grand point."

If such was his concentration on naval problems, leading to
the destruction of Great Britain, how are we to account for his
annexation of the Genoese Republic on 4th June? That action
has been looked on as a sign that he secretly despaired of the
invasion project, and now took a step certain to lead to a continental war, which without loss of prestige would disengage
him from the Boulogne enterprise. Much can be said in favour
of this view, which is antecedently probable and has the support
of Napoleon's later statements, whatever their worth may be.
But we must remember these facts; that he himself explained to
the Arch-Chancellor of the Genoese Republic that he annexed
it solely in order to gain full command of its naval resources;
further, that his ingrained doggedness led him to carry through
to the end every cherished enterprise, even in the teeth of the
most formidable obstacles; while also he felt strongly that Italy
was his own land, on which he could work his will in complete
disregard of the barbarians north of the Alps; finally, that his
voluminous correspondence of May-June 1805 shows no expectation of serious opposition to his last infraction of the Treaty
of Lunéville by the other signatory, Austria. That Power
had of late acquiesced in so many *faits accomplis*, that, apparently, he believed she would make no more than a formal

protest. In these months he scarcely mentions her; and, what is more significant, he makes no preparations for a land campaign. The order to improve the road from Chambéry to the Mont Cenis is the only one which bears on a possible campaign in Italy; [1] and not until 5th July does he give any order for the strengthening of her fortresses. As for Russia, she is referred to only once, and in very slighting terms, namely, in his letter of 9th May to the King of Prussia. He there states that he will not accept the mediation of the Czar Alexander with a view to peace between France and England; for the character of that potentate is feeble and uncertain, and France no more owes an explanation to Russia on the affairs of Italy than the Czar does to him on those of Turkey and Persia. He, Napoleon, loves peace, and has no ambition; but he cannot see his people disinherited from the world's commerce. Apparently, then, he recked little of Russia's opposition and expected none from Austria, so long as he had the friendship of Frederick William of Prussia, which he seeks to assure by polite assurances. On 27th July, after his return to St. Cloud, he writes to Eugène, Viceroy of Italy, making light of the rumours of hostilities from Austria. "What Austria is doing is probably from fear." But, on 31st July, he hears ominous news from Italy, and urges Talleyrand to soothe Austria. On 3rd August, while at Boulogne, he informs Talleyrand that Austria is undoubtedly arming; she must therefore be warned that such conduct favours England, against whom the French armies are embattled, from Holland to Brest; the Emperor is at Boulogne, intent on his maritime enterprises.

As is well known, the annexation of Genoa led Russia and Austria to form plans for the speedy opening of the campaign; but there is every sign that their resolve took Napoleon by surprise. Up to the 3rd August, his correspondence shows him to be bent on the concentration of the flotilla at Boulogne and the three neighbouring ports, which was for the most part successfully accomplished. [2] There are two facts which tell against the theory that he resolved to attempt the invasion; namely, that early in August 1805, the effective strength of the Grand Army at and near Boulogne was only 93,000 men and 2,700 horses,

---

[1] " Napoleon Corresp.," x, 331.

[2] Desbrière, iv (iii), ch. iv. In all there were 1,928 vessels at those ports, 223 at Calais, 157 at Dunkirk, 35 at Ostend.

whereas the flotilla and transports could carry as many as 151,940 men and 9,632 horses; also that the order of 7th August for the Imperial Guard to set out from Paris to Boulogne was countermanded on the following day. These facts are held by M. Desbrière to warrant the doubt whether Napoleon had of late seriously intended the invasion of England. But it must be remembered that 23,000 troops were held in readiness at Calais and Dunkirk; also that the roads between Paris and Boulogne, and that port and neighbouring places, had been so much improved as to admit of a quick concentration of troops; further, that a change had clearly come over Napoleon's plans on 31st July and early in August, the letter above cited proving undoubtedly that he now began to prepare a heavy blow at Austria.[1] The shrinkage in the number of troops at Boulogne and the countermanding of the march of the Guard support this explanation; and it may be taken as certain that from the first days of August Napoleon began "to make his plans in two ways." If Austria dissociated herself from Russia, peace would last on the Continent, and he would still press on with the Boulogne project. If not, the troops he had withdrawn from the coast, and the Guard at Paris, would form the nucleus of an army able speedily to act against the Hapsburgs. The words in his letter of 4th August to Decrès—"If we are masters of the Straits for twelve hours, England is no more"—were probably merely a device for keeping up activity in naval circles until he foresaw more clearly the issue of events on land.

The days (22nd, 23rd August) were days of anxious speculation at the imperial headquarters at Boulogne. On the former Napoleon heard that Villeneuve's fleet, after putting in to Ferrol to refit, had set out again. He believed him to be making for Brest, and therefore, to all appearance, framed once more the desperate resolve of forcing a landing in Kent, if Villeneuve and Ganteaume appeared in the offing. On that day he sent off six letters to Decrès, two to Ganteaume, and one to Villeneuve, all inspired by that thought. But on the morrow he heard for the first time of the arrival of a British expedition of 6,000 men at

---

[1] "Napoleon Corresp.," xi, letters of 31st July and 3rd August. The letter of 31st July to Talleyrand is the first that shows signs of alarm at Austria's preparations. On 4th August he hears that 20 British sail-of-the-line are in the Mediterranean, and this makes him anxious for the French troops in the Kingdom of Naples. See too "Napoleon Corresp.," Nos. 9117, 9118.

Malta and coupled with it the significant fact of the demand of the Court of Naples for the withdrawal of the French Army of Occupation. He took these facts and the presence of a Russian force at Corfu to imply a design of the Allies for wresting from him the command of the Mediterranean, which he regarded as a French lake. This offensive move of the British filled him with astonishment, for he had believed them to be tied to a tame and ineffective defensive.[1] The imminence of a formidable Coalition between Great Britain, Austria, Russia, and Naples was now patent; and on that day he resolved to send his favourite aide-de-camp, Duroc, a *persona grata* at Berlin, to induce that Court by the offer of Hanover to join France and redress the balance in Central Europe. Duroc's mission can scarcely be regarded as proof that Napoleon confidently expected to secure peace on the Continent; for the character of Frederick William of Prussia was so passive and vacillating as to give little hope of speedy and drastic action such as would intimidate Austria and Russia. Moreover, Napoleon's letter of the same day to Talleyrand shows that his chief aim now was to gain fifteen days on Austria. On 28th August, in his letter to General Déjean, he says that after a few battles he may return to Boulogne.[2]

This gain of time the warlike preparations on the coast of Picardy secured, with results finally fatal to Mack's army at Ulm. But there is no definite sign that the thought of using these preparations as a blind entered his head before the early part of August. While keeping up the fiction that he was awaiting the arrival of Villeneuve off Boulogne he made alternative plans for a campaign against Austria. On 24th August he instructed Talleyrand to demand that she should keep only eight regiments in her Venetian province and only one in Tyrol, demands with which no self-respecting Power could comply. His instructions of the same day to Duroc show that he would henceforth decline either to guarantee the independence of Holland and Switzerland, or to renounce the Italian crown, stipulations of the Treaty of Lunéville on which Austria had the right to insist. It is certain, therefore, that by 24th August, if not earlier, he had resolved on settling his quarrel with Austria. On the 25th he ordered Murat to proceed at once from Paris to Mainz and

---

[1] See Mr. Julian Corbett's " Campaign of Trafalgar," chs. xviii and xix on this masterly move of Pitt.

[2] " Napoleon Corresp.," xi, pp. 118, 152.

Würzburg and survey the roads leading to the Upper Danube at Ulm, Ingolstadt, and Ratisbon. This is the first sign of Napoleon's special interest in those roads, which would certainly have been surveyed had Napoleon all along intended his vast preparations on the coast of Picardy to mask his design of a sudden blow at Austria. On 13th September, after his return to St. Cloud, he gave out that this was an alternative aim which he had always kept in view. The facts of the case and his earlier correspondence alike refute this contention, which obviously was designed to exhibit his infallibility and the folly of Villeneuve.[1] It is worth noting that on that very day he first heard that the Austrians had crossed the River Inn and invaded Bavaria, a fact which disposes of the melodramatic story, that, while still at Boulogne, he broke out into furious exclamations against the imbecility and cowardice of Villeneuve, and then, while still heaving with passion, dictated to Daru the arrangements as to provisions and depots, which provided for the daily marches of the Grand Army from Boulogne to Ulm and even beyond.

The results of our inquiry may be thus summed up:

(1) The instincts and convictions of Napoleon always urged him to take the offensive, and to seek to retain it by all possible means, because, even if it did not assure success (as had nearly always been the case hitherto), it conferred the moral advantage which a bold attitude gains over a tame defensive.

(2) The risks of an invasion of England were not much greater than those which he ran in 1798-9, in virtually ignoring her maritime supremacy. He believed that a single victory would bring him to London, whereupon risings in Ireland, Scotland, and even of English democrats, would compel Great Britain to a peace.[2]

(3) At first the only means of attacking England, and thereby securing the initiative in war, was by strengthening the flotilla, in the hope of attempting an invasion, with or without the help of French and allied warships. Even the threat of such an

---

[1] "Napoleon Corresp.," ch. xi, 193 (13th September 1805).

[2] See his words to Major Vivian, quoted later; also "Napoleon's last Voyages," pp. 90-8 (edit. of 1906). Thiers in 1854 told N. Senior that, if Napoleon had landed in England, he could have marched anywhere; but he termed Napoleon's Egyptian Expedition rash beyond anything recorded in history. (N. Senior, "Conversations with Thiers, etc.," i, 198, 251.)

event would be likely to 'paralyse her action elsewhere, and thereby to some extent screen the French Colonies from the full pressure of her naval power.

(4) These reasons and the temper of the French, which is better suited to attack than defence, justified in his eyes the enormous expenditure and efforts on the flotilla and harbours, which moreover tended to rally all Frenchmen to his rule.

(5) It is practically certain that in the autumn and winter of 1803-4, in July-August 1804, and in March-July 1805, he was determined to attempt the invasion. In March-June 1804 he desisted from the scheme owing to preoccupation in home affairs and the inadequacy of the naval preparations. In the months September 1804-February 1805 the harrying of British Colonies and commerce held the first place in his thoughts; but thereafter the pacific assurances of Austria and the forward state . of the Spanish navy led him to evolve scheme after scheme for assuring the command of the Channel, which for a time he believed could become a permanent maritime ascendency.

(6) The chances of Villeneuve appearing off Boulogne late in July or early in August 1805 were fairly good. Certainly Napoleon believed them to be so; and, had the fleet appeared, the Emperor must have attempted the invasion under pain of encountering a storm of ridicule.

(7) There is no sign, apart from hearsays and his own biassed assertions of a later date, that he believed his aggressive policy in North Italy likely to entail war. From 2nd March to 31st July 1805 he resolved on the invasion of England, in the belief that the occupation of London and an Irish revolt would bring about a collapse of British power. Thenceforth he faced the alternative of war with Austria, and on and after 24th August decisively chose that alternative.

(8) His later assertions and those of Méneval, Bourrienne, and others on the subject of the projected invasion are valueless in comparison with the contemporary evidence at first hand, which has here been passed in review.[1]

(9) The fact that nearly all naval authorities pronounced his

[1] For the secondary evidence, see "Méneval Mems.," i, 406-13; the "Fouché Mems.," p. 196 (Eng. edit.); also Wheeler and Broadley, "Napoleon and the Invasion of England," vol. i, ch. x; also Napoleon's interesting conversations with Admiral Ussher, "Napoleon's Last Voyages" (edit. of 1906), pp. 88-90, 139-142.

naval schemes impracticable and highly dangerous,[1] by no means proves that he did not seriously intend to carry them out; for his character and his sense of the value of prestige bade him press them on until an alternative course of action presented itself. As we have seen this opportunity occurred in August 1805; and he strove thereafter to represent the ensuing war with Austria as brought about solely by British gold, and therefore the counterpart to his scheme of the invasion of England.

[1] See on 176 of this volume, proof that the officers of the French Imperial Guard at Elba considered the invasion of England as likely, or certain, to end in disaster.

THE TRUE SIGNIFICANCE OF TRAFALGAR [1]

NOW that the jubilation aroused by the centenary of Nelson's great triumph has subsided, it may be well to inquire what results accrued from the Battle of Trafalgar.

Perhaps in the case of few victories has the outcome been so different from that which has been assigned to it in the popular belief. The reason for this confusion of thought is not hard to discover. The years 1803-1805 had been to our countrymen years of "the great fear." Their thoughts turned, with tense expectation, towards the coasts of Kent and Picardy. On the cliffs at and near Boulogne, an army of well-nigh 120,000 veterans was encamped, led by the greatest warrior of the age, and by captains of almost equal prowess. A huge flotilla rode in the harbours of Étaples, Boulogne, Ambleteuse, Calais, and thence as far as Flushing, in readiness to transport this formidable host to the coasts of Kent or Essex, as soon as a convoying fleet should appear. On the British coasts, numbers and enthusiasm were by no means lacking. But where was the organization, where were the leaders, that could victoriously oppose the Grand Army led by Napoleon and his Marshals? Few persons shared the confidence that possessed Wordsworth during his unusually bellicose mood in the autumn of 1803.

> Nor discipline nor valour can withstand
> The shock, nor quell the inevitable rout,
> When in some great extremity breaks out
> A people, on their own beloved land
> Risen, like one man, to combat in the sight
> Of a just God for liberty and right.

The dearth of organizing power and military talent at home (Sir Arthur Wellesley did not return from India until the summer of 1805) caused grave searchings of heart; and most patriots

[1] From "The Independent Review," November 1905.

sympathized secretly with Wordsworth when, in a more subdued mood, he gazed from the Dover valley back on France, and saw—

—the coast of France how near!
Drawn almost into frightful neighbourhood.

At last, in the autumn of 1805, these fears died down; and then came the news of Trafalgar. What more natural than to connect the new sense of security that supervened, after the first painful shock at the news of the death of Nelson had passed away, with his last exploit? The impression that England's safety from invasion resulted from the Battle of Trafalgar, was strengthened when men came to read the last despatches and letters of the hero. Everything bore eloquent witness to his determination to force on a battle as decisively as possible. The evidence which Mr. Newbolt has brought together in his work, "The Year of Trafalgar," serves to illustrate anew the eagerness evinced by Nelson to close with the enemy in the shortest possible time, wholly regardless of the terrible risks in which his tactics must involve the leading ships of both of his attacking columns. Everything impelled him to strike with the utmost vigour. The weary months of waiting off Toulon, the consciousness of failing strength, the many irritations of that long baffling chase after Villeneuve to the West Indies and back, would alone have led him to seek to annihilate his elusive antagonists.

But there was another consideration, which has never received due notice. Nelson, so far as we can judge from his despatches, believed, up to the very end, that England was still in danger of invasion from the Grand Army and its flotilla at Boulogne, provided that a convoying fleet could reach that all-important point. The evidence on this topic is not conclusive; but it is fairly strong. First, it must be remembered that Napoleon remained at Boulogne until 2nd September 1805, and that, while superintending the movements of the mass of his troops away from that town towards the Rhine in order to confront the legions of Austria, he took all possible precautions to prevent the new plan from becoming known to the British cruisers in the offing. His decree of 30th August ordered that the flat-bottomed boats which were at Étaples, Wimereux, and Ambleteuse, should sail to Boulogne as soon as possible, and that Admiral Lacrosse at Boulogne should seize every opportunity to attack the British and keep them far off. This concentration of the flotilla and these harrying tactics must have led our seamen for several days to suppose that the great move against the coast of Kent was about to be made. They knew not the whereabouts of Villeneuve, and therefore kept up all the old precautions. The result was, that the departure of the bulk of the Grand Army from Boulogne, which actually began before 31st August, was not known in England for many days; and (this is the important point) Nelson and his captains seem to have had no knowledge of it when they went into battle at Trafalgar. In these days of telegraphs, this may seem incredible. But the marvel disappears if we remember that Nelson hoisted his flag on the " Victory " at Portsmouth on 14th September, and sailed from St. Helen's Roads on the next day. It is certain that, at that time, no news of the departure of the Emperor and of most of his army for the interior of France could have reached Portsmouth. There is not a word in Nelson's letters, or in the account of his interviews with Ministers in London, that reveals any perception of the real facts of the case. All that was known with certainty was, that Villeneuve had arrived at Cadiz, on 18th August. That piece of news was brought very quickly to London by Captain Blackwood of H.M.S. " Euryalus," on 2nd September; and it led to the request for Nelson's services once more.

Thus, while affairs on land were as deceptive as a mirage, the naval situation was fairly clear. The great fleet which, with that of Ganteaume at Brest, menaced the safety of Britain, was for the present unable to get through to Boulogne. Its objective might be that port, or it might be the Mediterranean. Ministers had to face the possibility of the latter alternative, with the prospect of a long and complicated pursuit, in case Villeneuve evaded Collingwood's blockading squadron and reached that sea.

But there was also the possibility that the retreat to Cadiz was a feint, and that, at the first opportunity, the great fleet would seek to resume its original mission and convoy the flotilla across. Nelson kept an open mind on the subject. On the one hand, there was the chance that the Emperor would adhere to his plans with his wonted tenacity, and would not leave Boulogne without doing something to justify his conduct in spending vast sums of money on the ships, boats, and harbours along that coast. As far as Nelson knew, there was nothing to tempt

Napoleon away from Boulogne. On 30th September, when off Cadiz, he wrote a letter to Sir John Acton, expressing the hope that "both Austria and Russia have begun" the war against Napoleon. But this was mere conjecture; and, short of that event, scarcely anything would be likely to divert Napoleon from his plan of invading England. In another letter of the same date, Nelson wrote sarcastically about a small British force destined for Naples "doing good to the common cause"; but he also stated that he had scarcely discussed anything but naval matters with Ministers in London. He evidently hoped that the Anglo-Russian expedition, then at or near Naples, would protect that coast, but was concerned to hear of three French sail-of-the-line, with as many cruisers, being ready for sea at Toulon. This portended trouble for the allied expedition at Naples; and he begged the Admiralty for more ships, above all more frigates, which he might use in the Mediterranean.

Once again, however, his thoughts swung round to the safety of England. "Some day or other," he wrote, on 8th October, "that Buonaparte, if he lives, will attempt the invasion and conquest of Great Britain." But obviously he believed that the safety of his native land rested with the fleet then watching Cadiz, and that a crushing blow dealt to Villeneuve might compel the Emperor to make peace. "We can, my dear Coll[ingwood] have no little jealousies" he wrote on the 9th. "We have only one great object in view, that of annihilating our Enemies, and getting a glorious Peace for our Country."

The secret orders from the British Admiralty, dated 21st September, which reached him on 8th October, threw little light on the perplexities of the general situation. The Admiralty enjoined on Nelson the need of covering the operations of the British expedition at Naples, when the blockade of Cadiz was provided for. In his reply of 10th October, Nelson pointed out the virtual impossibility of complying with the new instructions, until Villeneuve should be disposed of. Amidst the distracting gloom that surrounded him, one thing alone was clear, that the allied fleets then in Cadiz must be not merely conquered, but annihilated. So far as we can judge from his letters and conversations, this was all that Nelson knew of the actual state of European affairs when he went into battle, determined to "give them such a shaking as they (the enemy) never yet experienced. At least I will lay down my life in the attempt."

It is pathetic to turn from the twilight of Nelson's beliefs and surmises, to events as they then unfolded themselves. They were such as to vitiate every hope that peace would be the speedy outcome of his triumph. Judging from the very imperfect information at his command, he was justified in indulging that hope. But even before he left "dear dear Merton," on 13th September, events had occurred which altered the whole trend of history. A few days previously, the Austrian army under General Mack entered Bavaria, with the aim of compelling the Elector to join the Austro-Russian alliance and declare against Napoleon. The French Emperor, long aware of the storm gathering in the east, left Boulogne on 2nd September, to be ready to profit by any imprudence that the Hapsburgs might commit; and when Nelson was journeying across the Surrey hills to Portsmouth, Napoleon was drawing up the first draft of plans at St. Cloud which led up to the brilliant triumph at Ulm on 19-20th October.

A comparison of Napoleon's despatches with those of Nelson at the same time is of high interest. While the admiral believed that the solution of the European problem lay in his hands, Napoleon, having the advantage of a far wider and more accurate survey of events, saw that the whole interest had suddenly shifted from the sea to the land. Sea-power, for the present, he held in small account. Everything depended on his ability to defeat the new Coalition. Whereas, before the days (24-30th August) of his momentous decision to turn against Austria and Russia, nine out of ten of his despatches turned on matters connected with the hoped-for invasion of England; thenceforth, on the contrary, naval affairs fell away into the background. True, in his letter of 28th August to General Déjean he stated that after a few battles there may be peace, whereupon he will return to Boulogne. Further, in his Note of 13th September to Decrès, Minister of Marine, he ordered the maintenance of a large naval and military force at Boulogne and neighbouring ports; but, obviously, he valued the presence of 60,000 troops there, mainly because it would help to keep up the state of alarm in England, prevent her from effectively aiding her allies on land, and furnish an excuse for maintaining an army in the utmost efficiency within easy stages of the Rhine. He admitted that Villeneuve's retreat to Cadiz had unmasked his supposed secret (which the British Admiralty had already divined) that the flotilla was not meant to cross the Channel without a powerful convoy; and thenceforth it was to do little more than threaten Albion until he could resume his naval plans. As for Villeneuve, he was to use every effort to get out from Cadiz with the allied fleets and set sail for Carthagena, there to pick up eight Spanish sail-of-the-line. It is worth noting that, in these instructions of 14th September to an admittedly unlucky admiral, the Emperor did not once face the contingency that British ships might be in the way. The optimism, which pervaded all his geometrical calculations for the most uncertain of elements, here again appears in most instructive guise.

But what was to be Villeneuve's objective? The Emperor directs him to make at once for Naples, there to help a French army under General St. Cyr to capture, or drive away, the Anglo-Russian expedition. That is now the Emperor's aim. The coast of Kent has faded from his thoughts; and he turns to a smaller but still very desirable object, the capture of a hostile force in Naples, and the complete subjection of that kingdom. On 17th September, he decides to replace Villeneuve by Rosily, but always with the same objective—Naples, not London. As for the other French squadrons, they are to adopt privateering tactics. In a long despatch of that same date he directs the Minister of Marine to organize four cruising squadrons. One powerful squadron is to scour the seas between St. Helena and the Cape of Good Hope, in order to sweep up British East Indiamen, and thereafter re-fit at Martinique for a similar purpose around Barbadoes. Another is to proceed to San Domingo and Jamaica with the same aim. A third and far smaller squadron will "ravage all the coast of Africa." Finally, two frigates will act in the same way around Ireland, and then pick up prizes between Cape Clear and San Domingo. The Emperor concludes with the suggestive remark: "English commerce is everywhere. We must try to be at as many points as possible, in order to harm it."

Now, what do these details imply? They imply that, between 24th August and 17th September, Napoleon had entirely changed his plans. Formerly, his aim had been concentration on the all-important points, Boulogne and the Straits of Dover. After Villeneuve's "treason" in retiring to Cadiz, the Emperor's aim is entirely the opposite. Now it is dispersion, with a view to a war against British commerce. What brought about this *volte-*

face? Undoubtedly the outbreak of war on the Continent. Nelson, as we have seen, had discerned the importance of the diversion which such an event might produce. But, even up to the time of his death, he knew nothing as to its actual occurrence, and the consequent change in the French plans. Happily for him, he believed that his victory might "bring Buonaparte on to his marrow-bones;"[1] and no news came to trouble his mind in his last hours with doubts as to the crowning efficacy of his last great stroke.

What significance, then, are we to assign to Trafalgar? Clearly it was very different from that which British officers and the British public assigned to it. They could not assess its importance accurately, because they were ignorant of the intentions of Napoleon, and of many of the facts of the situation. We have now seen, from the Emperor's own despatches, that it was the outbreak of war with Austria and Russia, along with Villeneuve's tame retreat to Cadiz, which gave England a time of respite, while her great foe betook himself to guerilla tactics on sea. The Austrian army at Ulm acted, so to speak, as the lightning conductor for England, diverting the stroke which was to have fallen on her. At present, she really had to fear nothing more than a succession of pin-pricks at many points of her Empire; and we may here observe that such a *guerre de course* would have been very effective, had Napoleon been content with letting Villeneuve remain at Cadiz and hold Nelson to that port during the winter storms of 1805-1806. Nelson would certainly have clung to his task with the same indomitable resolve that marked his twenty months' blockade of Toulon in 1803-1805; and, with another British force held to Brest, the French naval guerilla might have been most galling. Napoleon, in fact, had the game in his own hands on sea and on land, had he been content to wait until winter had done its work on the blockaders. But he marred his chances by his impatience. His bitter reproaches to Villeneuve, and his appointment of Rosily as his successor, drove the doomed fleets out of Cadiz. The consequences are well known. Out of thirty-three French and Spanish ships that left that harbour, only eleven returned after the battle. Four escaped to the north, only to be captured off Cape Ortegal by a British squadron of the same strength (4th November). Rosily took over the five French ships that remained in Cadiz, but had to

[1] Nelson's despatch of 6th October 1805.

surrender to the Spanish patriots in June 1808, when Spain rose against Napoleon.

The brilliance of the triumph must not, however, blind us to the fact that, at the time, it made very little difference to Napoleon's plans, and to the course of the war in Europe. Far from being "beaten to his marrow-bones," the Emperor made light of " ce combat de Cadiz," when he heard of it at Znaim in Moravia (18th November). There was some reason for this haughty attitude. After capturing some 60,000 Austrians at and near Ulm (18th to 20th October), he could treat any disaster at sea as of secondary importance. Until Russia and Austria were overthrown, he could not in any case resume the Boulogne enterprise; and, meanwhile, the duties which he assigned to his navy were to chastise the Neapolitan Bourbons and harry British commerce on the high seas. Having these merely secondary objects in view, he might well regard Villeneuve's defeat as a regrettable but by no means serious incident. At that time he heard only the first details of the affair; and, with characteristic tenacity, he directed his Minister of Marine to push on all the cruising operations, just as if the battle had not occurred. Of course, the French demonstration against Naples fell through; but that was the sole immediate change which the battle made in Napoleon's naval plans.

Probably the battle also enabled the British Admiralty to push on with greater vigour the pursuit of the French squadrons designed for the destruction of our commerce. It is doubtful whether Sir John Duckworth could otherwise have procured a force sufficient to free the West Indies from the depredations of the force commanded by Leissègues. As it was, Duckworth was able to annihilate Leissègues' squadron in a brilliant engagement off San Domingo (6th February 1806). The other French squadron, detailed for service between St. Helena and the Cape ought to have fallen in with the British force which effected the conquest of Cape Town early in the year 1806. It did not, however, sight that convoy, either on the outward or the homeward voyage. Finally it sailed away to the West Indies and North America, where its strength was shattered by a terrible storm. The two smaller French squadrons also effected nothing of note. Apart, then, from Duckworth's brilliant triumph at San Domingo, the failure of the French naval guerilla seems to be traceable to chance rather than to the results of Trafalgar. This consideration, however, must not blind us to the immense advantages conferred by the command of the sea, in the reduction successively of the French and Dutch colonies in and after 1806.

It is also important to note the slow but irresistible pressure exerted by the Sea-Power upon the Land-Power after Trafalgar. Though the French Emperor rated its consequences but lightly at the time, he was, nevertheless, compelled henceforth to systematize his warfare against British commerce. So far back as the month of February 1798, he gave it as his judgement that France had only three ways of beating down the might of England; (1) by a direct attack on London; (2) by depriving her of the outlets of her trade with the Continent on the north-west of Germany; or (3) by an Eastern expedition, which would ruin her trade with India. To the last of these alternatives he bent all his energies during his Egyptian expedition of 1798-99. The first plan engaged most of his energies, from the renewal of war with England in May 1803 up to the close of August 1805. Baffled in his efforts to strike at our heart, he then, as we have seen by his instructions of the middle of September 1805 (as also in those of 27th-29th September 1804), proposed to make war on British commerce by sea. The result of the battles of Ulm, Trafalgar, and Austerlitz, now revived his earlier plan of warring against it by land. Already he had designed what he called his "coast system" for the exclusion of British goods from Hanover and the North-Sea ports of Germany. Henceforth he used all the resources of war and diplomacy, hermetically to seal up the Continent against the islanders.

There is a very suggestive passage in Napoleon's letter of 14th December 1805, to Talleyrand, instructing him to protract negotiations with the Hapsburgs, cast down as they were by the disaster of Austerlitz twelve days previously, until he had arranged matters with Prussia: "When I am sure of Prussia, Austria will do exactly what I want of her. Likewise I will make Prussia declare against England." On Prussia, then, he concentrated all the resources of his diplomacy (Austria being almost *une quantité négligeable*), obviously because Prussia controlled the north-west and north coasts of Germany. To her he offered fatally alluring terms, but only on condition that she entirely excluded British goods from her new acquisition, Hanover. Struggle as it might, the Court of Berlin could not evade this stringent obligation, which entailed war with Great

Britain, the blockade of the North-Sea coast by our cruisers, and the Berlin Decree of November 1806. Usually we date the definite commencement of Napoleon's Continental System from that *coup de théâtre* dealt from Berlin, excluding British commerce from the Continent. In reality, we ought to date it from the time of Napoleon's interviews with Prussia's envoy at Schönbrunn, soon after the staggering blow dealt to the third Coalition at Austerlitz. The fatal gift of Hanover, which that envoy and, later on, his master, accepted, implied the extension of Napoleon's anti-British system to the whole of North Germany. Are we not justified in believing that this momentous decision on the part of the French Emperor was due to later and fuller news of Trafalgar?

Therefore, while that victory had singularly little influence on the situation at Boulogne, Dover, and other French and British ports; while its immediate effects may be limited to Mediterranean affairs and to the energetic pursuit of the French squadrons told off for the harrying of British commerce; nevertheless, its ultimate results in the sphere of European policy were incalculably great. The Emperor was brought by stress of circumstances, rather than by mere ambition, as we islanders usually assert, to seek to conquer Britain on the Continent; and his eager activity led him to adopt measure after measure—Berlin Decree, Milan Decree, Treaty of Tilsit, occupation of Portugal, Fontainebleau Decree and other measures of the year 1810, Russian Expedition of 1812—which promised in turn to overwhelm England under the mass of Europe, but really buried Napoleon himself under the ruins of his Continental System. In this sense, then, Nelson's prophecy was finally fulfilled. By slow degrees, and in ways that the great seaman could not have foreseen, England's mighty enemy was brought to his knees; but only after nine years of fruitless toil, which Trafalgar imposed on him as the sole remaining method of attacking his elusive foe.

GENERAL MARBOT AND HIS MEMOIRS.[1]

FORTUNE full often plays tricks with reputations. Her wheel raises aloft the fame of many a man who, in his lifetime, was comparatively little known, and depresses that of celebrities who once enjoyed world-wide renown. In art, literature, and politics, the caprices of the giddy jade have strangely reversed the confident predictions of contemporaries, but perhaps her freaks have nowhere been more surprising than in the sphere of war. To limit ourselves to the Napoleonic period, which we now have in view, who could have believed that Augereau, the leader of the "fighting division" of the army of Italy, who, according to Bonaparte's own admission, "saved France at Castiglione," who had himself strapped to his horse at Eylau so that illness might not keep him from the fierce delight of leading his corps against the Russians on that snowy waste— that Augereau would lose his hold on the thoughts of Frenchmen and have no statue erected to his memory? What little is known of that burly Marshal, the most eager fighter and most expert swordsman of France, comes through the Memoirs of his young aide-de-camp, Marbot, a name rarely heard until near the close of those great days of France. At least, that is the source of the knowledge of ordinary people about the swaggering Marshal and a score of his compeers. It is safe to say that readers of Marbot's fascinating pages have there picked up as many lifelike details about the paladins of Napoleon as they would from reams of biographical articles and whole chapters of scientific military works. The well-known words of Horace respecting the power of the inspired bard to rescue the fame of heroes from the long night of oblivion may almost hold good for Marbot. He has made many an exploit live for us; he has lit up the characters of men who would otherwise be mere names; and there is an attractive quality in his work which promises to

[1] From the "Cornhill Magazine," July 1906.

give it an abiding hold on all who admire a spirited narrative of scenes of the camp and the field.

The question of the genuineness of the Marbot Memoirs has sometimes been disputed, but probably on insufficient grounds. The external evidence tells in their favour. They were well known to several prominent Frenchmen long before the date of publication. The Comte de Paris is known to have perused them while in manuscript form; and the *Nouvelle Dictionnaire de Biographie Universelle* (edition of 1860) refers to them as being comparatively well known at that time, some thirty years before publication. Marbot died at Paris in 1854. He seems to have been rather unpopular with leading persons in the Orleanist time (1830-1848); and readers of the high-flying passages in his Memoirs will understand why; but he was enough of a public character to have his doings and writings noticed with some precision; and this lends weight to the external evidence in favour of the genuineness of the Memoirs which bear his name. We may pronounce it to be satisfactory, if not altogether convincing.

But the chief test of the genuineness of writings lies, after all, in the internal evidence: that is, in the correspondence of the narrative with the actions, conduct, and characteristics of the person who claims to be the author. In very few cases can the external evidence set all doubts at rest. In order to trace the life-history of a manuscript, we need a great number of minute details respecting the dates of composition of its several parts and the care taken by those who were responsible for its preservation. These are very rarely forthcoming in such a way as to satisfy the sceptic, and, as a rule, he will trust to his own independent knowledge respecting the facts set forth, and to his perception of the agreement which the manuscript throughout exhibits with the known peculiarities of the reputed writer.

Now, as regards the personal flavour, if I may use the term, the Memoirs decidedly smack of Marbot. The boyish, rambling, but high-spirited recital of the earlier parts is evidently the outpouring of the fertile mind of a very youthful officer, who thinks well of the world in general, still better of France, and best of all of himself. The note of egotism sounds persistently through every page of the Memoirs. At first it is a sharply staccato note. Everything is going well with Marbot and the French army in the best of all possible worlds, that of the first decade of the nineteenth century. He has a good word for nearly everyone—with one prominent exception soon to be noted. Generals like Augereau and Masséna, who soon lost their early popularity, figure well in his pages, and many of the earlier episodes, if touched up by a skilled hand, would almost challenge comparison with certain passages in the " Three Musketeers." But in and after 1812 the style loses its exuberance: we notice the growth of a certain bitterness of tone which, while it detracts from the pleasure of reading, serves indirectly to confirm the genuineness of the narrative as a whole. To sum up this part of our inquiry, we may say that the personality revealed in the Memoirs agrees with the personality of Marbot.

When we approach the question of the correctness of the Memoirs, we come on to very different ground. Sometimes it is assumed that, if memoirs can be proved to be untrue to fact, therefore they may be, or even must be, spurious. This is by no means the case. Persons who hold this opinion would seem to base their reasoning on the assumption that correctness is the characteristic of French memoirs. Nothing could be further from the truth. Their characteristic is incorrectness—open, obvious, almost ostentatious embroidering on the plain pattern of real life. No very long time need be spent in comparing the statements of French memoirs with ascertained facts in order to convince historical students of the general truth of this assertion. Memoir writers were not at all concerned with advancing the cause of historical investigation. Fortunately for their readers, they lived in pre-scientific days. Their aim was to put together entertaining narratives for their families and friends; and the first requisite of success was to exhibit the writer in picturesque situations, or, in default of those, to show how he held the fate of nations in his hands during some tortuous intrigue. We must further remember that the French are essentially an artistic people; and to such a race, as to the ancient Greeks, the one unpardonable crime was dulness and baldness in narration. To artists possessed of creative power the temptation to touch up, adorn, and illuminate is irresistible. Hence comes the charm of French memoirs. Speaking generally, we may venture to assert of all memoirs that their attractiveness is in inverse proportion to their correctness; and, when the captious critic groans over some exaggeration or mis-statement more startling than usual, let him seek consolation in the reflection that, if the memoirs are not true to fact, they are at least true to character.

From all that we can glean about the life and character of Marbot, his Memoirs may find shelter under this last most comprehensive formula. Either fortune showered on him as a youth the most astounding favours by thrusting him forward at the very time when, and to the very place where, great events were occurring; or else the fickle goddess came in the guise of memory and enabled him in his old age to view those far-off events through the blissful mirage of romance. Which of these explanations is correct it is not always easy to say. But certainly the Memoirs show us Marbot as always participating in the most dramatic and exciting incidents. His luck in this respect eclipsed that even of the veriest fire-eaters of the sensational romance. As a child, his fondness for mimicking cats led him to thrust his head through the cat-door, and get it fixed, until the alarmed parents had recourse to bodily force and the lancet. At the siege of Genoa he was present when an English bombshell fell among his group and exploded—fortunately harming no one. By way of revenge the French gunners planted a shell in the middle of a British brig, which forthwith sank with all hands; an episode suspiciously like that which is thought to have happened off Boulogne some four years later.

Even more remarkable are Marbot's rides with despatches. Take, for instance, his crossing over the Splügen Pass in order to carry news from Masséna in Italy to Augereau's corps in the Breisgau (1805). On his journey into Italy by that same route, he had accomplished the feat on horseback, at a time when the pass "was almost impracticable." But on the return that wonderful horse was not available, for it froze hard; "horses fell at every step"; the two guides, to whom he had paid the sum of 600 francs, refused to go on; and it was only Marbot's energy and his appeal to their loyalty which made the little party struggle on to the inn at the foot of the northern slopes. Unfortunately, Marbot overdoes the description; for he states that if night had overtaken them on the mountain, they must all have perished. But did not the guides realize that same indubitable fact?

Events of the same doubtful description occur in nearly all of Marbot's great rides; so that one is constantly reminded of the fact that he hailed from the district of Quercy, which is not far from the borders of Gascony. At the end of his ride from Madrid to Bayonne, when he bore the news of the suppression of the heroic rising of the men of Madrid on 2nd May 1808, he was privileged to hear not only the confidential remarks of Napoleon himself, but even to overhear Charles IV of Spain and his Queen taunt their son (the *de facto* King of Spain, Ferdinand VII) with being the real instigator of that revolt and the author of all the troubles in the Peninsula. Certainly this aide-de-camp had marvellously good fortune. Napoleon called Masséna " the spoilt child of Victory." In similar phraseology we may dub Marbot the pet of Mercury, whether as newshearer, news-bearer, or news-teller.

In the incidents just noticed we have had to use common sense as guide; and that sage counsellor perforce pronounces each of those cases " not proven." But sometimes Marbot ventures beyond the comparatively safe domain of personal adventure, and essays to describe historical events. It may be well to examine his account of a few events on which we now have exact information.

The first is that strange and little-known episode, " The Plot of the Placards " of the year 1802. M. Augustin-Thierry has recently thrown a flood of light on that conspiracy by investigating the police archives of the French Government.[1] Availing ourselves of his guidance, we can now trace the course of that military intrigue. It originated in a knot of discontented officers of the " Army of the West," the force which had long been engaged in the thankless yet most dangerous task of curbing or hunting down the royalist bands of Brittany. (We note in passing that the number of the " Army of the West " was 15,000, and that Marbot gives it as 80,000.) Yet, for all their hardships, the " blues " of Brittany earned not a word of praise from the First Consul. With rags and arrears of pay as their lot, they fell to grumbling against Napoleon; they charged him with running away from his army in Egypt; with coquetting openly with the Pope—it was the time of the " Concordat " (1802)—with preferring the trimmers and *ci-devant* nobles of Paris to the men who had saved the cause of the Republic in the fanatically royalist West. By way of retort the First Consul ordered off battalion after battalion of these *grognards* to St. Domingo,

---

[1] " The Plot of the Placards," translated by A. G. Chater.

M

despite the desertion of the men and the protests of their commander, Bernadotte. This diplomatic chief managed to keep the most discontented body, the 82nd half-brigade, at Rennes, the capital of Brittany, and with the officers there and at other large military centres he seems to have concerted means for arranging some movement in the army which might lead up to a demonstration, or even a conspiracy, against the First Consul. Bernadotte's share in the affair is obscure, and probably will remain so; for he had the tact to proceed to Paris at the time when the preparations neared completion, and left the decisive steps to be taken by subordinates at Rennes. M. Augustin-Thierry, however, gives reasons, far different from those advanced by Marbot, for suspecting him. Probably Moreau, a Breton by birth but a staunch Republican by conviction, sympathized with the aims of the malcontents, and would have joined them had all gone well.

But all did not go well. The subordinates at Rennes were not the men to carry through a plot to a successful issue. Their first task was to see to the printing of a great number of placards inviting the French soldiery to throw off the yoke of the First Consul. The work was done so clumsily that a prominent defect in one of the capital letters led to the arrest and ruin of the unlucky printer; but the disclosure of the scheme was due mainly to the faintheartedness of a young subaltern, Auguste Rapatel, who was to have sent off by post a large batch of these placards from Paris. Imprudently he confided the secret to his mistress, a girl named Félicie, who, being in an interesting condition, stormed at him as doubly a traitor, and finally persuaded him to make a confession of the whole affair. The revelations made by other accessories to the plot, General Simon and the printer Chausseblanche, soon demolished the flimsy structure. The subordinates were severely punished; the 82nd was sent off promptly to that hotbed of yellow fever, St. Domingo; but Bernadotte and Moreau went scot free, apparently because the power of the latter and the marriage of the former with the sister-in-law of Joseph Bonaparte made it undesirable to push inquiries too far. Such is the conclusion of M. Augustin-Thierry, as well as of other French historians, MM. Welschinger and Guillon.

Now, the narrative given by Marbot of this whole affair is unusually full; it abounds in striking scenes, and it aims at implicating Bernadotte. But nearly every important fact is either mis-stated or passed over in silence. Marbot's spite against Bernadotte is such that he accuses him of having cruelly made a tool of Adolphe Marbot, aide-de-camp of that general, and elder brother of the writer; whereas Bernadotte can be proved to be innocent on that count. Further, the Memoirs contain not a word about Rapatel and his mistress, or the printer Chausseblanche; the parts assigned to Simon and others are strangely distorted, and the account of the collapse of the effort of the 82nd at Rennes is ascribed to the fact that its colonel had forgotten to shave, and, on going back to his room in order to carry out that operation, had his sword promptly seized by a loyal officer and gendarmes. So glaring are the inaccuracies in Marbot's account that M. Augustin-Thierry, who has now pieced together the puzzle in an altogether scholarly and convincing way, seeks, in an Appendix, to prove the spuriousness of the Memoirs. To this I must demur. The plot was an underground affair, in which the subordinates, Adolphe Marbot included, knew only what concerned them and them alone. Adolphe Marbot seems to have misrepresented even that part of the affair which concerned him and Bernadotte; but he doubtless added various details which the younger brother then proceeded to garnish in the manner to which we are accustomed in all parts of his racy narrative. The incident of the colonel's shaving is quite Marbotesque.

Let us now follow our author to the field of Austerlitz. There in his description of the battle he evidently drew largely on the account of those very historians the complexity and haziness of whose narratives he himself decried. We find the traditional story of the battle, and need not refer to any episode except the dramatic *finale*, when the Austro-Russian left wing was "engulfed" in the Lake of Satschan. The ice, we read, was very thick, and some five or six thousand men of the retreating host had gained the middle of the lake in safety, when Napoleon ordered the artillery of his Guard to fire at the ice. We may now quote Marbot's words: "The ice broke at countless points, and a mighty cracking was heard. The water, oozing through the fissures, soon covered the floes, and we saw thousands of Russians, with their horses, guns, and wagons, slowly settle down into the depths. It was a horribly majestic spectacle which I shall never forget. In an instant the surface of the lake was covered with everything that could swim." Very majestic!

though the effect is somewhat marred, at least for the critical reader, by the statement that the guns and wagons settled down slowly into the depths apparently some time after the surface was covered with swimmers.

But let that pass, as a little incongruity resulting from Marbot's fatal fondness for adverbial phrases. The description of the battle is at an end, so we think. But no; Marbot remembers a final incident in which he played no insignificant part. On the next day a "poor Russian non-commissioned officer" was observed about a hundred yards away from the bank by Napoleon and his Staff. Various clumsy efforts were made to reach him, until it occurred to Marbot that he would strip himself naked and swim to the floe to which the wounded man had clung all the night. A lieutenant followed his example, and by means of incredible exertions they brought the poor fellow ashore on the floe, which by the end of the time was "quite insufficient to bear his weight."

How far Marbot's account of this incident and of the catastrophe on the ice deserves to be credited may be judged by reference to the following facts. It has now been ascertained from the report of the "*fischmeister*," who was ordered after the battle to dredge the lake, that thirty cannon, 150 corpses of horses, but only three human corpses were found.[1] Further, the fact that they were all found in marshy corners of the lake, over which the fugitives had evidently tried to rush during the rout, entirely disposes of the majestic spectacle described by Marbot. Finally, we can account for the concoction of this spectacular narrative. Marbot here followed the hint first given in Napoleon's bulletin as to the terrible sensation caused by the cries of the drowning Russians as dusk settled on the field of Austerlitz. Where the master pointed the way several memoir-writers pressed on with loyal eagerness. Ségur and Lejeune, among others, rushed in; but Marbot far outstripped them all in the audacity of his invention.

As for the story of the wounded Russian brought to land on that crumbling ice-floe, it might have passed muster had not the writer described the incident as occurring in presence of the Emperor. We know that Napoleon on 3rd December 1805, had far more important matters on hand, in garnering the fruits of victory, than to have time to spare for the superintendence of

[1] "Napoleonic Studies," by J. H. Rose, pp. 383-4.

the rescue of marooned Russian officers. Marbot's vanity here led him to crown the story by adding a detail which enables the critical reader to demolish the picturesque little edifice.

It is impossible to follow Marbot's *gasconnades* in detail through these charming pages. Two other examples of his methods of handling facts must suffice. All students of the Peninsular War remember the pride and presumption with which Masséna in 1810 made a frontal attack on Wellington's almost impregnable position at Busaco. Marbot in his own account figures as the would-be saviour of the French army from that mad attempt. He describes the trick by which he spoke, within earshot of the Marshal, of the possibility of turning the British position by the flank march which ultimately had the desired effect. Masséna— says the writer—seemed to be convinced by those remarks, but afterwards unaccountably recurred to the original design, with results that were disastrous to France. The incident is plausibly told, and cannot altogether be controverted; but we know that the news of the existence of the pass on Wellington's flank was brought in by a peasant. The manner of its bringing and further details have recently been disclosed in the Memoirs of General Marquis d'Hautpoul, whose account serves to substantiate the accredited narrative, and therefore to discredit that of Marbot. The account of this episode by Marbot is all the more surprising when we remember that at many points he based his narrative on that of Napier. Among several cases which migh be cited we may notice the similarity of his account of an episode in the Battle of Fuentes d'Oñoro to that of our great historian of the Peninsular War. Napier, in describing the interval that occurred in the middle of that extraordinary *mêlée*, when Montbrun's cavalry was held at bay only by the firm demeanour of Craufurd's Light Division, writes : "The vast plain was covered with commissariat animals and camp-followers . . . all in such confused concourse that the Light Division squares appeared but as specks." With this compare Marbot's words, describing the same tumult in the allied ranks: "In the midst of it the three squares just formed by Craufurd's infantry appeared as mere specks (*points*)." Indeed, it is clear that Marbot took his account of the whole battle almost bodily from Napier. Sometimes he imitated that historian in the manner of his narrative while altering the matter in a sense congenial to French predilections. An example of this occurs in his summary of the results of Masséna's campaign in Portugal, which gives a total loss to the French army of only 10,000 men; while Napier's estimates, framed on far more trustworthy data, imply a loss three times as great.

The note of egotism is nowhere more prominent than in Marbot's description of the Battle of Waterloo. He was stationed on the French right wing, which sought to hold back the Prussian advance in the afternoon and evening; and in a letter written in the year 1830 he claims credit for having sent news to the Emperor's head-quarters that the column, which appeared some distance away to the right of that wing, was a Prussian column. He also ventures to state that he received a reply to the effect that the force in question could only be that of Grouchy sent in pursuit of the Prussians on 17th June, and that, if any Prussians were thereabouts, they could only be stragglers flying before Grouchy's advance. Marbot then states that he had to obey his previous orders and press on as far as possible in the direction of Wavre. Now, no despatch such as Marbot refers to was issued from the French headquarters; also we know that about 1.30 p.m. on the day of the battle Napoleon was altogether in doubt whether a force that began to appear some distance away on the French right was that of Grouchy or Blücher. Finally it is certain that no French regiment pressed on far towards Wavre, as Marbot leads us to suppose his did. Some squadrons of cavalry scouted in that direction, but his account is wholly inconsistent with the known facts, and only furnishes another example of his incurable vanity in trying always to pose as the hero of every incident and the potential saviour of the French army from disaster.

The conclusion of our brief inquiry would appear, then, to be as follows: that while Marbot's Memoirs may probably be regarded as genuine, yet they are of very little value as a contribution to the history of that epoch. They are vitiated by the persistent efforts of the writer to represent himself as the chief figure in events where he was little more than an insignificant accessory. But, after all, we do not go to Marbot's Memoirs for facts; and if we view them in their proper relation—namely, as illustrations of the stirring scenes of that *épopée* of France—we shall find them of no slight value, as they certainly are of enthralling interest.

AN INTERVIEW WITH NAPOLEON IN ELBA

[The following account by Major I. H. Vivian of the interview with Napoleon in Elba has long been out of print. A few copies were struck off in 1839 for private circulation, and from one of these the following account is printed. Mr. Vivian's companion was Mr. Wildman. They arrived from Leghorn on 22nd January 1815, and through Count Bertrand gained permission to visit Napoleon four days later. They travelled over Elba and were courteously entertained by Count and Countess Bertrand. The latter complained of the miserable accommodation in Elba. The narrative acquires additional interest from having been shown, while in manuscript, by Vivian's brother, Major-General Vivian, to certain of the British Ministers in London, shortly before receipt of the news of Napoleon's escape. His expressed opinion, that some day England would lose Canada, probably accounts for their anxiety to prevent his escape to the United States. After a short description of Elba and of the house of the Bertrands, the narrative proceeds as follows. The notes are by Major Vivian, except those bearing my initials.—J. H. R.]

THE evening of the 26th [January] being appointed for our presentation to the Emperor, we attired ourselves in our local Militia uniform, and having taken coffee with Count Bertrand, at a little after eight o'clock we proceeded from his apartments to the Imperial residence, amidst a flood of rain. From the entrance, which was situated in the left wing, we passed into an ante-chamber containing two windows, and the walls of which were hung with a number of good prints. Here we remained whilst the Count went to announce our arrival, and we were shortly after ushered into the presence of Napoleon, without any form or ceremony whatever. We found him standing by the fire, at the further end of a room adjoining the ante-chamber, and into which he had come, on being informed of our arrival. This room was about the size of that we had left, and was fitted up with old yellow furniture, brought, as we understood, from the palace of his sister, at Piombino. On our entrance, he advanced towards us, and we took our station with our backs against a table that stood between the windows. Whilst he was advancing he began the conversation:[1]

[1] The notes of this conversation were written immediately after it had taken place, and, therefore, their accuracy may be entirely relied on. Where

" Quel uniforme est celui que vous portez? "—" Celui de la Milice."

" De quel comté? "—" De Cornouailles."

" C'est un pays bien montagneux? "—" Oui, assez."

" De quelle hauteur sont les montagnes, comme celles-ci? "— " Elles sont plus hautes, d'une forme différente, et moins isolées."

" Sont-elles aussi hautes que celles de la Principauté de Galles?" —" Pas tout-à-fait."

" Combien de toises de hauteur ont-elles; 6 à 800 toises? "— " Elles ne sont pas si hautes; peut-être de 3 à 400 toises."

" Quelle est la capitale de Cornouailles? "—" Truro est une des villes principales."

" Comment! Truro, tout près de Falmouth? "

" Combien de temps par an étiez-vous assemblés? "—" Un mois chaque année."

" Qui vous payoit,—le Gouvernement? "—" Oui, le Gouvernement nous payoit, mais le Prince Régent nous habilloit."

" Quel rang avez-vous—Colonel? "—" Non—Major."

" Ah! Major."—" Nous sommes la Milice des Mineurs de Cornouailles."

" Ah! il y a des mines d'étain dans ce pays-là? "—" Oui, et aussi de cuivre."

" Le Prince Régent a-t-il des droits sur les mines? "—" Oui, sur l'étain, mais non pas sur le cuivre."

" Combien reçoit-il par an de ces droits? "—" De neuf à dix mille livres sterling."

Then turning to my friend, Mr. Wildman, he said:

" Et vous? "—" Je suis aussi de la Milice."

" De quel comté? "—" De Kent."

" Ah! nous étions voisins."

He then addressed himself to me, and asked respecting the route I had taken, and when I had left England?—I replied that I had left England nearly twelve months before; that I had passed by Paris and Bordeaux, to Toulouse, in order to visit a brother, a General Officer, who had been severely wounded there. He made no remark upon this, but observed—

" Then you passed by the Garonne and Montauban; a very pretty little town, with excellent wine.—You drink a good deal in England."—(*Vous buvez beaucoup en Angleterre.*)

He had before, I understood, made the same observation to some other English travellers, who had been introduced to him.

the exact expressions used by Napoleon, on any topic that appeared particularly interesting, were accurately remembered, they are given in French. In the first part of the conversation the form of the dialogue is preserved, which will serve to give a tolerably correct notion of Bonaparte's mode of conveying his ideas.

I told him, that formerly much more had been drunk in England than at present: and that the custom of sitting very long after dinner had, in a great measure, been done away; but that as we still sat after the ladies had left the table, we had more time and greater inducement to drink than other nations.

" Where did you cross the Rhone—at Lyons? "

" No, at Avignon."

" Ah! you passed then the Pont de Gard.—Is the bridge at Avignon finished? "—" No; over one branch of the river only."

" Ah! but you passed over the Durance, where I had made a long wooden bridge.—You visited Nice? "—" Yes."

" Did you go to Genoa? "—" No; I wished to do so, but the wind was not favourable."

" The road I was making is not yet finished, is it? " [1]—" No; we crossed the Maritime Alps, to Turin."

" Ah! by the *Col de Tende*? "—" Yes,—a very bad passage, and very badly kept."

" That is not of my making; it was made by the King of Sardinia.—I passed it twenty-five years ago; but it is only over the *Col de Tende* that it is so bad.—I did a little to the excavation, and had some idea of making a good road over it, but I did not care much about it.—I was desirous of reigning also over Italy—(*Comme je voulois dominer aussi sur l'Italie.*)—My principal object was to connect that country with France, as much as possible, by means of good roads on the side of Mont Cenis and the Simplon."

I told him that I had passed the Simplon, and complimented him on the greatness of the undertaking, and the excellence of the execution;—upon which he observed, that there was a grand road he had been making from Wesel to Hamburg, not yet finished, which had cost a considerable sum of money.— I remarked that we, travellers, at every step recognized his works. With this observation he appeared to be pleased. He then asked if the road over the Simplon was kept in good repair. I told him, that as yet, it was in good order; but that it was feared it would be neglected; that the Valais and the neighbouring countries could not support the expense of maintaining it. He said:

" That must be done by a toll, which would answer very well."

He asked if I had passed by Milan—" a fine city "—and then inquired particularly if the bridges he had laid out between Turin and Milan were finished. I told him that the bridge over the Tessino was not completed, but that the pillars were all above water.

---

[1] He had been making a road by the coast, from Nice to Genoa.

"Those over the Sesia, at Vercelli, and over the Dora, are they finished?"—"Yes."

From the subject of roads he touched upon that of canals, and asked if the canal from Pavia to Milan was finished.—I replied that I believed not; and I asked him if he had not a project of uniting the Rhine and the Danube.—He replied that it was very easy to do so; that it was an affair of only twenty millions of francs; that he had united the Rhine and the Rhone, the German Ocean and the Mediterranean. On his asking from whence I last came, and my answering, from Vienna, he exclaimed,—

"A poor little city (*une pauvre petite ville*) with large suburbs, unpaved; and the ramparts?" (*et les remparts?*)

I told him they were precisely in the situation in which he had left them.—He said—

"Yes, Bertrand performed the kind office for them very effectually."

I observed, that at Frankfort and at Manheim, where he had demolished the fortifications, they were laid out with taste.— "Yes," said he, "in fine promenades." (*Oui, des belles promenades.*)

His next subject was politics;—he asked me how Congress went on. I told him that there were plenty of fêtes, but that little progress was said to be made in business; and I mentioned to him the bon mot of the Prince de Ligne, who said—"*Le Congrès danse, mais ne marche pas,*" at which he smiled. I added, that Poland was understood to be a stumbling-block; that it was said the Emperor of Russia wanted to form a kingdom of it, but that the other powers, it was supposed, feared Russia's becoming too formidable. He remarked that it was a power that went on increasing; a very rising power. He then said that the treaty of peace between himself and the Allies should have been signed at Frankfort; separating Germany entirely from France, and taking Holland, Italy, and Spain from him; but that he never could have consented to leave France less in territory, than it was when he ascended the throne. I asked him why he did not make peace at Dresden, when those terms were offered to him: he said that the Allies were not sincere,[1] and that besides *les choses* at that time were different; that had peace been then made, England would have been saved some thousands of men and much money; that he considered it very bad policy of England to appropriate Belgium to herself;[2] that it would be a constant source of expense, and would

---

[1] A French officer to whom I put the same question, said that there were some articles besides those which were generally understood to have been proposed.

[2] By the Treaty of Vienna, Belgium went to the Kingdom of Holland.— J. H. R.

probably draw her into a war; for that any other Continental Power would be sure of France as an ally, by offering Belgium as a bribe. " Supposing," said he, " for instance, Russia were to say to France, ' do you take Belgium, and let me have Poland.'—In short," added he, " England cannot maintain herself as a power of the first rank on the Continent; Belgium must be lost on the first *coup de canon*. The English Government should have covered and fortified Holland, but Antwerp is the object; for a battle fought and lost before Brussels, which is close to the gates of Paris, would open the road to Holland.[1] England, with her immense colonies, instead of being obliged to keep up a large army to cover Belgium, should withdraw within her Island, and act when and where she chose." He spoke of the Dutch troops, and appeared to have but a poor opinion of them;—their marine, he said, was much reduced. He expressed himself with much contempt of the Austrian soldiers, who " would not fight without a belly full."—Referring to the campaign in France, he said that he should have beaten the Allies, had he not been betrayed; for that the peasants were taking arms in their rear. I asked him by whom he had been betrayed; whether by Talleyrand, whom I had heard accused.—He answered so as to give me to understand he had been a party; but he principally blamed Marmont and Augereau.[2] The latter, he told me, had a fine army, superior to the Austrians, and was to have joined him (Bonaparte) in his last movement; but that he had made his terms with the Allies a fortnight before, and that he had narrowly escaped being massacred by his soldiers for his conduct.—I observed to him, that when I had passed through Paris, I had heard there was an opinion amongst the lower orders, that he and Paris had been sold—"*que l'Empereur et Paris étoient vendus.*"

Blücher, he said, was a brave man, but not a great general; and added, that he had lost two armies.[3] The Prussians had fought well.—Of Schwartzenberg, as an officer, he expressed himself favourably.—Upon my asking him if he did not consider the Duke of Wellington a good general, he replied, " *Oui.*"—I was not satisfied with this, but repeated the question in stronger terms, asking if he was not a very good—an excellent general.

[1] It is remarkable, that within five months from the time of this conversation, the battle of Waterloo was fought, and the road to Paris not that to Holland, opened.—The expression of this opinion at this time by Bonaparte, and his subsequent conduct in conformity with it, proves, clearly, the sincerity with which he was speaking.

[2] Augereau commanded the army operating near Lyons, but it was inferior to that of the Austrians.—J. H. R.

[3] A gross exaggeration. Napoleon probably referred to Blücher's surrender near Lübeck in November 1806, and his defeat at Vauchamps in February 1814.—J. H. R.

He answered, "*Oui, oui!*" with emphasis, but not another word.
—Touching on the Corunna campaign, he said, Moore was a
good general, and had saved that army. The Spaniards, as
soldiers, he held very cheap. In the mountains they had done
something, their character was obstinacy (*opiniâtreté*)—they
wanted valour. I mentioned the gallant defence they had made
at Saragossa. This, he said, was *opiniâtreté*;—they were 50,000
men within the walls, attacked by 15,000. I observed that, at
least, the Portuguese had proved themselves very good troops.
This he admitted. "But then," added he, "they were officered
by British, and of this the national pride (*fierté*) of the Spaniards
would not admit;—besides, the Spaniards are bigots in religion,
and you know that you are heretics," (*vous savez que vous êtes
des hérétiques*), said he, laughing. The French soldiers, he asserted, were *peu constans*; that they wanted *ténacité*; that if they
had a little more *ténacité*, any thing might be done with them;—
that Cæsar had well defined their character in that respect, and
that it had not changed;[1] that he (Bonaparte) knew it well,
and had acted upon it in the campaign in France: that the
soldiers could not bear such a check (*secousse*).—He inquired
if the English soldiers, when drunk, were not ungovernable;
observing that the French, at such times, were loving (*doux et
tendres*).

Speaking of Switzerland, he said there appeared much to be
settled in that country; that he had given them a constitution
which it should seem they wished to change. I remarked that
the Canton of Berne wanted to recover what had been separated
from it.—"Yes," replied he, "the large to domineer over the
small; there is no yoke (*joug*) so severe as that of a people."—
The fate of Italy he lamented much, divided as it was into
small states. Italy, he said, should have been preserved as a
Kingdom. I agreed with him entirely in regretting the fate of
Italy, but asked, who was to be king, and who was to nominate.
"Oh! it matters little," said he, "who it is—some Italian—or
by whom appointed;" and he instanced Murat.[2] "A sovereign,"
added he, "is made for his people, and not a people for their

---

[1] That passage in Cæsar that is here referred to is doubtless that in
Book 3, Sec. 20, of Clark's Edition. "Nam ut ad bella suscipienda Gallorum
alacer et promptus est animus, sic mollis ac minime resistens ad calamitates
preferendas mens eorum est."

Livy's trait of the French soldier is equally remarkable, B. 10, Ch. 28.
"Gallorum quidem etiam corpora intolerantissima laboris atque æstus fluere :
primaque eorum prælia plusquam virorum, postrema minus quam fœmin-
arum esse."

[2] By his instancing the case of Murat, and what followed, I understood he
meant to say, that Murat was a proof, that Kings so appointed would care
but little for those by whom they were appointed, when their interest required another line of conduct; and that Murat, although owing every thing
to him, had not hesitated to join his enemies.

sovereign."—The Italians, he observed, were a people of strong passions (*passionnés*), and had a great deal of excellent stuff (*étoffe*) in them as soldiers,—much of the old Roman left.—He spoke of the bad policy of the Austrian cabinet towards Italy, and that of the Austrian officers towards the inhabitants, in not associating with them as the French had done.—He added, that he had done much to reform the Italian people; that he had found them effeminate, and living for the women and with them, all day long;—that it was a fine country. Upon this I remarked, that by transporting to Paris the best of the paintings, etc., he had taken considerably from the interest of Italy. To this he made no reply, but spoke of Bologna [1] as a *bonne et jolie ville.*—In speaking, I think, of Turin, he mentioned a fine street called *Via Napoléon*; he knew not what they called it now.

To the Pope, as the head of the church and as a sovereign, he seemed to have a great aversion; he said that he was always sacrificing his conscience to some miserable little piece of policy; that the existence of a Pope was a great misfortune for Europe (*un grand malheur pour l'Europe*); that we were very much indebted to our King Henry VIII for getting rid of him; that he had attempted to do the same, but could not succeed; that the government of priests was detestable, and that every sovereign should be at the head of his own church, as in England, Prussia, etc.; that, as a man, the Pope was a very good sort of person (*un bien bon homme*); that he had entertained him very well at Fontainbleau, and made him very comfortable there; that he (the Pope) was ignorant in the extreme; and that amongst all his Cardinals (for he had seen them all at Paris), there was not one he would allow to fill a fourth rank in his (Bonaparte's) council. Ecclesiastical States, he added, should on no account be allowed;—the empire of the church was not of this world.

Speaking of the Americans, he said, they wanted a ten years' war to make them a nation; that at present they had no noblesse, which they would acquire by a war; that they were now a nation of merchants (*une nation de marchands*), as was shewn in the case of the sale of Jefferson's library to the highest bidder; [2] that had we (the English) made peace with them before, we should have gone to Congress with more weight; that America had carried on the war with spirit after France had fallen (*après que la France eut succombée*) and that the war,

---

[1] I had heard that from another English party admitted to an audience, he had inquired after his *bonne ville de Bologna*, as if he had a particular attachment to it.

[2] I did not understand the allusion, but he laughed when he made the observation.

after all, was about nothing—a few feet more or less of lake. He then said something of a great project he had with respect to Mexico, of which I could not catch the meaning; and observed, that we should one day or other lose Canada; adding— "Of what great consequence is it to England, with her numerous colonies?" He said, that when America became more powerful, she would probably rival us in our marine; that he had made the attempt to do this, but had failed. With respect to the Right of Search, which I called a droit, he said it was no droit, but a mere *théorie*; that when we were very strong we should exercise it, but if, on the contrary, we had Russia, Sweden, and Denmark against us, we probably should not insist on it. He gave it as his opinion, that England and France should be allied. On my signifying, by a shake of my head, the improbability of such an event, he said, "Why not?—the world is large enough—France does not want to meddle too much with commerce. There was a man, Fox, who could have effected it, but unfortunately he is dead." (*Mais pourquoi pas? le monde est assez grand—la France n'a pas besoin de se mêler trop du commerce. Il y avoit un homme, Fox, qui auroit pu le faire, mais malheureusement il est mort.*) He then asked where we were going from Elba, and on my answering, "To Rome and Naples," he replied, "Ah! then you will see there a magnificent Lazzarone;" [1] adding, "From Naples, I suppose, you return to England by sea." Upon my saying that it was my intention to return by Italy and the Mont Cenis, as I had seen all the other Passes of the Alps, having come from Vienna by the Tyrol, he observed, "No, there is still that over the Julian Alps." On saying this he made us a low bow, wished us a *très bon voyage*, and retired.

We found Count Bertrand waiting for us in the ante-room, who, looking at his watch, exclaimed, "*Parbleu!* you have had a long audience."—Upon which I could not help expressing how agreeably it had passed; and I can truly say that I never passed an hour, or indeed an hour and a quarter—for our interview lasted from half-past eight o'clock until a quarter before ten, more agreeably. We stood during the whole time, I may say almost *nez à nez*; for I had my back against the table, and he had advanced close to me, looking full in my face.—After the first few minutes I felt most perfectly at my ease, and the conversation never flagged;—his strain and manner were as familiar and good-natured as possible; so very much so, that I felt no hesitation whatever in putting any question to him.— He had on a green coat, cut off in front, faced with the same colour, and trimmed with red at the skirts, and wore the stars

---

[1] Alluding to Murat.

of two orders.—Under his left arm he held his hat, and in his hand a plain snuff-box, from which he every now and then took a pinch; but as he occasionally sneezed, it appeared to me that he was not addicted to snuff-taking. His hair was without powder, and quite straight;—his shape, inclined to corpulence.

Bonaparte's manner was so unreserved, and he communicated his ideas with so much apparent candour, that, after the interview, I regretted much it had not occurred to me to touch upon a point on which there has always existed much diversity of opinion;—whether he had ever seriously contemplated the invasion of England. However, I took an opportunity on the following day of introducing the subject to Count Bertrand, during a conversation I had with him.—He reasoned for a considerable time, as if it had really been Bonaparte's intention to make the attempt;—the Emperor, he said, had forty sail of the line collected in the Mediterranean and at Cadiz; it was intended that the ships in these different ports should form a junction, and then proceed to the Channel, where the fleet would have been joined by ten sail of the line kept in readiness for that purpose. This force, he remarked, would probably have given them the command of the Channel for a fortnight or three weeks, which time would, it was calculated, have elapsed before Nelson could have discovered their real destination, and reached the scene of action. When the combined fleet had once obtained the command of the Channel, a force of 100,000 men, or more, could have been assembled on the French coast in forty-eight hours, and might have been passed over before the arrival of the British fleet.[1] The invading army, it was conceived, would have been sufficiently strong to overpower any opposition that could have been made to its progress before it had reached London, and taken possession of the seat of government. I replied, that supposing all these plans had succeeded according to their wishes, their 'army must inevitably have been destroyed, as they could not have obtained reinforcements.—He observed, that they could have kept possession of some small ports, and could have smuggled men over;—for as the run is so short, this could not have been wholly prevented by any precautions on the part of the English.—I said, that the opinion in England was, that the threat of an invasion was a mere pretext for bringing a large force together in order to be prepared to pounce upon one or other of the Continental Powers, as in fact the Emperor had done in the case of Austria.—He replied, " *Cela est possible.*"—Here the conversation ended. My own opinion is, that Bonaparte at first seriously contemplated

---

[1] See my former Essay, pp. 114-146.—J. H. R.

the invasion of this country; but that afterwards he became better informed as to the little probability there was of success. Had circumstances proved favourable, at an early period, to the project of his fleet obtaining a temporary superiority in the Channel, the attempt would probably have been made. Some of the officers of the Imperial Guard, with whom I conversed at Elba, were decidedly of opinion that, had the invasion of England been attempted, the enterprise would have failed.

At one time, in conversation with Bertrand, I expostulated on the injustice of Napoleon's conduct towards the English who were in France when he last resolved to go to war with Great Britain, and whom he detained so soon as war was declared, in violation of the usage of civilized nations. The Count said, that my countrymen had been detained as a measure of retaliation for the capture of French vessels by the English, immediately on the issuing of the declaration of war against France, without allowing fixed periods for the return of vessels from different parts of the world;—in place of which, we seized all we could lay hands upon. The probability is that Bonaparte ordered the detention of the English under the influence of a temporary irritation, and that he was afterwards unwilling to revoke the mandate he had issued.

With respect to the most material of the charges that have been urged against Bonaparte, I understood from Captain Adye, who had opportunities of conversing with travellers that had been introduced to the Ex-Emperor prior to my arrival, that he had given the following explanations respecting the points on which he has been most strongly censured,—putting the Turkish prisoners to death, and poisoning his own soldiers in Egypt; the seizure and execution of the Duke d'Enghien, and the case of Captain Wright:—

The Turks who were shot by his order, he said, had been taken prisoners on a former occasion, and had been liberated on their parole, not to serve against the French, unless they were exchanged. Having, in violation of this engagement, been subsequently taken in arms, they were subject to military execution by the laws of war; but that he should not have put them to death, had he not been in absolute want of bread for the use of the army, and therefore wholly unable to provide for so many additional mouths. The expressions Bonaparte used on this occasion, as repeated to me, were,—"*Il n'y avoit point de pain; ou les Turcs ou les François devoient se briser contre la muraille, je ne balançai pas.*" With regard to poisoning his own soldiers, he said, that it had never been intended to treat more than two or three in that manner; that these men were ill of the plague, which rendered their removal dangerous to the whole army, and their recovery almost hopeless, and that he had recommended to the surgeon to free them from their miseries by administering opium in their food. With this recommendation the surgeon refused to comply, and they were consequently left behind, and were butchered by the Turks who followed the French army.[1]

Respecting the execution, or rather, the atrocious murder (for I cannot apply any milder term) of the Duc d'Enghien, I was informed he had observed, that the Duke was the most restless of all the members of his family; that he was a conspirator against the acknowledged government of his country, and that he had been tried by a regular military tribunal, found guilty, and shot,—not during the night, or at an early hour in the morning, as had been stated, but at noonday.[2] When the case of the unfortunate Captain Wright was mentioned to him, he is said to have replied, that he had no recollection of him; but that he thought he had heard of an Englishman who had made away with himself in prison. I understood that whilst conversing on these subjects, Bonaparte had observed, that it had frequently been proposed to him to take off the Bourbons by assassination, and that even smugglers had been found who were ready to undertake this atrocious project; but that he had always spurned the idea. This fact was also stated to me by Count Bertrand; who observed, that it had been asserted the Emperor had always been surrounded by his guards, in order to secure him from personal violence; but that directly the contrary was the fact. The Emperor, he said, had never adopted any such precautions; he (Count Bertrand) had had the command of the guard at the Thuilleries, and, including the gardens, the duty was performed by (as well as I recollect) 117 men.

With respect to the habits of Napoleon, I heard, in the course of conversation, that he dined at six or seven o'clock; went to bed early, and generally rose in the middle of the night and read for three or four hours, after which he again lay down, and rose about eight or nine o'clock. He slept little, and in the summer suffered much from heat.

I remarked to Madame Bertrand that I had heard the Emperor was writing the history of his own life. She replied, that it was not so, and that he amused himself with reading.

I understood that Bonaparte was distressed for money, as the pension, for the payment of which the Allied Powers had pledged themselves, had been withheld by the French Government, who had engaged to remit it every six months.—It was said that he had declared he never would apply for it; but I was informed that Madame Mère (his mother) was loud in her complaints respecting the non-payment of the allowance which she was to

---

[1] On these two topics, see my "Life of Napoleon," i, 204, 212.—J. H. R.
[2] The Duke was not a conspirator and was shot at night.—J. H. R.

receive. Madame Bertrand assured me that the Emperor had not a farthing in the English funds, or in those of any foreign country, though the contrary had been so confidently reported; that she fully believed he had never entertained the idea of making such an investment, as in fact he had never conceived it possible that he should lose his throne. She also stated, that he had brought scarcely anything with him from France, having left behind him his jewels and his private property, observing, that in losing the Empire (*en perdant l'Empire*) he had lost everything;—and that the service of plate he had with him was merely that which he had used in his campaigns, and in travelling.[1]

It is something singular that both the Count and the Countess Bertrand had an idea, at the time I was at Elba, that the Emperor was to be removed to St. Helena; and they were very anxious in their inquiries respecting the proceedings of the Congress then sitting at Vienna.[2] From the events that have since taken place, it should really seem that such a plan was then in agitation, although, as I told Madame Bertrand, it was not even whispered at Vienna. In case his removal to St. Helena had, at that time, been really intended, it was believed that Napoleon would have resisted it to the utmost, and submitted only to force. He certainly was occupied in keeping up the forts at Elba; but resistance on his part would have been vain, had it been determined to carry the measure into execution; as the place might easily have been starved, and during the summer months there is even a scarcity of water on the Island. The force he had at Elba consisted of about 600 of the Imperial Guard, who were fine old soldiers; some Corsicans, whom he had enlisted; about 120 Polish Lancers, and five or six Mamelukes. I confess I am induced to believe, that the fear of being sent to St. Helena, and the pecuniary difficulties under which he laboured,[3] in a very great degree, occasioned his making that apparently almost hopeless, and certainly most desperate, but, eventually, most successful attempt to regain the throne of France, which shortly afterwards astonished all Europe. I know that much has been said and written to shew, that it was a concerted measure, with the numerous, and, assuredly, very active friends he had in France; but I cannot satisfy myself that this was the case.[4] On

<hr />

[1] The next paragraphs were evidently added after the original account was drawn up.—J. H. R.

[2] This report originated in the newspapers, and was not mentioned at the Congress.—J. H. R.

[3] Peyrusse in his "Mémorial" shows that Napoleon took a large sum of money from Elba to France.—J. H. R.

[4] The evidence of Fleury de Chaboulon ("Mems.," i, 105-40) and Lafayette ("Mems.," v, 355), shows Vivian to be wrong here.—J. H. R.

the contrary, I cannot but consider it as an attempt made without any general previous understanding with a party in France; although the possibility of it might have been contemplated by some few persons; but still, with a full conviction on the part of Napoleon, that the army would gladly embrace an opportunity of replacing him on the throne. The extraordinary and rapid march from Antibes to Paris, without the loss of a single life, was a circumstance so completely beyond all calculation, as to afford a decisive proof of the enthusiasm which so generally existed throughout France, in favour of Bonaparte. From this enthusiasm, which was scarcely to be created by any plot, together with the various observations I had an opportunity of making from a number of little circumstances and occurrences which took place whilst I was at Elba, as well as from what I afterwards learned at Paris and in different parts of France, I am persuaded that although, on the part of Napoleon, the measure might have been contemplated, the moment at which it was to be undertaken was undecided; and that, undertaken almost in desperation, it succeeded solely through the ardour excited amongst the French army and the people, by the reappearance of him who had so often led them to victory.

An opinion prevailed on the Continent, immediately after the escape of Bonaparte from Elba, that the British Government had connived at his departure; and in England I have heard that Colonel Campbell was censured for not having exercised a proper degree of vigilance, in observing the movements of Napoleon. Although this idea has been successfully refuted, both in and out of Parliament, I may observe, that nothing could be more absurd than to suppose that it was in Colonel Campbell's power to have prevented the escape of the Ex-Emperor. It is true that Colonel Campbell was not on the island at the time of Napoleon's departure: but it was by no means intended that he should have remained there constantly; and even if he had been on the island, he had no means of preventing the embarkation of the troops: he was possessed of no authority whatever; Bonaparte held the island in full sovereignty, having his army (composed of infantry, cavalry, and artillery), his navy, his treasury—he imposed taxes; in short, no monarch could be more absolute;—and to his credit be it related, that small as were his means, he in one particular instance shewed an example to other more powerful monarchs well worthy of imitation: he declared war with the African pirates, and forbade their entering his ports. As Sovereign of Elba, he took possession of the Island of Pianosa, and intended to establish a colony there;—an attempt which had formerly been made, but which had failed, as the colony had been carried into slavery by the African marauders. This island, which had been used only for breeding horses,

Napoleon meant to cultivate, in order to supply Elba with corn. It may be said, in reply to the foregoing observations, that we had a sloop of war on the station, to watch the movements of Bonaparte. This, however, was not exactly the case. The Partridge was stationed at Leghorn, not at Elba, and her cruising ground extended from Genoa to Civita Vecchia. Captain Adye himself expressed his regret to me that he could not run down with us to Civita Vecchia, (which was many leagues to the south of Elba, and consequently out of the line for intercepting any communication with France,) as Colonel Campbell might want to return. The French Government had also a squadron in that part of the Mediterranean, for the purpose, as was supposed, of preventing Bonaparte from obtaining recruits from Corsica. I saw this squadron off the island, during my stay at Porto Ferrajo; it consisted of two frigates, two corvettes, and two brigs. I confess it appears to me that there was, in the first instance, a great mistake in selecting the Island of Elba as the residence of Napoleon, or rather, which I believe was the case, in allowing him to have selected it;[1] its position gave him a facility of communicating both with Italy and France, of which his character might have afforded certain assurance he would have taken advantage; and it was truly short-sighted policy, and very slight knowledge of human nature, which could have led any one to suppose that a man who had for so long a period exercised such a degree of power in both these countries, would not have retained in each a most powerful number of friends, both civil and military.

Having had our audience with Napoleon, we were anxious to proceed on our route, it being our wish to reach the Eternal City before the conclusion of the Carnival. Accordingly, on the 27th of January, we hired a felucca to take us to Civita Vecchia: but the wind unfortunately proved adverse during the three following days, and our Padrone did not shew any great anxiety to move. During our prolonged stay, we had an opportunity, through the kind offices of Count Bertrand, of being presented to Madame Mère, Bonaparte's mother, and to his sister, the Princess Pauline. Madame resided in a house near that occupied by her son; the apartments which we saw were comfortably fitted up; the servants wore the Imperial liveries, green and gold, and two *Dames d'Honneur* were in attendance. From her appearance it was evident that she had been a fine woman. The Princess, who occupied the large room in the centre of Bonaparte's residence, possessed a fine figure; her smile was fascinating, and her manners peculiarly pleasing. She received us with great affability; spoke much of the Empress and the young Prince,

---

[1] Elba was the choice of the Czar, Alexander I.—J. H. R.

whom we had seen at Vienna; observed that it was cruel not to allow her to join the Emperor; spoke with great affection of her brother, *l'Empereur*; said that he, with *Maman* and herself, formed a little society; and played at cards in the evening; that the Emperor shewed himself a perfect. *philosophe*, not bestowing a thought on what he had been, and frequently not reading the newspapers for some days after he received them;—she observed, "*qu'il travailloit beaucoup*; and even there, as he had done elsewhere, was exerting himself to benefit and ornament the country." (Alluding to a new road he was making round the edge of the bay, the sides of which were planted with trees, and to a new garden he was forming at the back of the residence above the cliffs.) In the course of our conversation, the Princess complained of the gross misrepresentations which were put forth in the public journals, respecting her brother; their denial of the benefits he had conferred on France, and the infamous slanders which had been propagated, especially through the Paris papers, as to his being deficient in personal courage. She expressed herself in very indignant terms on these points, and appeared to feel acutely what she conceived the unmerited calumnies that had been heaped upon a man who had done so much for the French people. She said, that at Rome we should see her brother Louis, an "*excellent homme*," and Lucien, "*qui avoit beaucoup d'esprit*," and desired us to say "*bien de choses*," for her, to her sister at Naples.

Our prolonged stay on this island gave us an opportunity of seeing more of the Princess, and availing ourselves of an invitation to a ball which she gave on the 29th, in a temporary room built in the garden at the back of the residence, to which we went with a large party, composed principally of her *Dames d'Honneur* and officers of Napoleon's Guard, whom we had met at dinner at the house of a French family then resident at Porto Ferrajo. We spent a very pleasant evening, and were highly gratified by the attentions of all who were present; and on taking leave, the Princess kindly offered us letters of introduction to her brother Lucien, at Rome, and to her sister Caroline, Queen of Naples.

On the evening of the 31st of January we took our departure from Porto Ferrajo in an open boat. After about an hour's sail, we cleared the island, and in two hours more reached Piombino. The width of the channel between this part of the Italian coast and the island of Elba is about three leagues. We were detained for an hour on the shingles whilst our bill of health was scrutinized, and on arriving at the inn our passports were taken to the Austrian Commandant. During the time we remained on the shingles, the post-boat from Elba arrived. A soldier who appeared to belong to it, in a conversation I had with him, informed me that several of the Imperial Guard had quitted Elba and returned to France: the reason he assigned was, that they (the soldiers) found so little amusement on the island. It is, however, very possible that this means of communication with the old army kept alive the remembrance of Napoleon, and contributed most materially to his subsequent success.

Piombino was formerly the residence of Napoleon's sister Elize, the Princess Bacciochi. A building that had originally been a convent, situated on a promontory, between the town and the sea, had been converted into a palace, with suitable gardens and approaches. From Piombino we proceeded to Civita Vecchia, and from thence to Rome and Naples.

Shortly after our arrival at Naples, where Murat held his Court in all the pomp of regal splendour, we heard of the departure of Napoleon from Elba; and in less than five months from the time of my interview, was fought the memorable battle of Waterloo, which hurled from his throne, a second time, that most wonderful man, who in his conversation with me had contemplated, but with the anticipation of far different results, the very battle he had now lost, and to the brilliant result of which the distinguished valour of the British arms so gloriously contributed.

"NAPOLEON'S CONCEPTION OF THE BATTLE OF WATERLOO."

J'ai trop compté sur le gain de la bataille à Waterloo.—NAPOLEON TO
GOURGAUD, 8th September 1817 (" Gourgaud's Journal," ii, 295).

THE Battle of Waterloo derives its unique characteristics
from the misconceptions of the three great commanders
who took part in it. Napoleon believed that the order which he
gave to Marshal Grouchy near Ligny on the morning of 17th
June to pursue the Prussians, with a view to preventing their
junction with Wellington, must bring him on their flank or rear
during the battle. Blücher's letter, written at Wavre about midnight of 17th-18th June, definitely offering to Wellington that
three Prussian army corps should march at dawn towards Mont
St. Jean, led the British commander to expect their arrival on
his left about 10 a.m.; while Gneisenau, Chief of Staff to Blücher,
so distrusted Wellington as to arrange the march in a way which
brought the Prussian vanguard within sight of the battle-field
about 1.30; and not until about 4.30 did the leading corps, that
of Bülow, threaten Planchenoit and the rear of Napoleon's right
flank. Blücher's Staff, though perhaps not the Marshal himself,
suspected the Duke of a plan to draw off from Mont St. Jean,
leaving the Prussians to bear Napoleon's onset. Hence their
circumspection, which made the battle so long and sanguinary.
The French Emperor, on the other hand, unaware of the danger
threatening him on the East, believed that he would easily drive
Wellington's motley host from Mont St. Jean and that the
battle would be " the affair of a breakfast."

It may be well to examine more in detail the hopes and convictions of the Emperor before the conflict, which owes its
interest largely to the psychological problems outlined above.
Firstly, it is well to remember the mental peculiarity which had
long led him to exaggerate his own fighting power, and under-
estimate that of the enemy. It is the opinion of General Bonnal

the French historian of the Danube campaign of 1809, that owing to this defect the Emperor lost good opportunities of destroying the Archduke's Charles's army near Ratisbon. The serious reverse encountered at Aspern-Essling was due to the same cause. Napoleon's despatches relating to the war in Spain reveal a strange inability to grasp the difficulties of his marshals and the tenacious character of the British and Spanish defence.[1] The same defect was even more patent in 1812. The recently published Memoirs of Count Rambuteau show that, before the war began, the Czar Alexander warned Count Narbonne of his resolve to sweep the threatened districts bare of inhabitants and supplies, leaving the invaders to the Russian winter. Narbonne, on his return to Paris, warned Napoleon of this design;[2] but he nevertheless marched on to Moscow in September. At St. Helena he criticised his inaction in that city and stated to General Gourgaud that he ought to have advanced further still, in order to overthrow the Russian forces that had retreated beyond the old capital.[3] Not even the terrible losses during the advance to Moscow taught Napoleon prudence. For him the retreat which began on 18th-19th October was merely a change of quarters to the neighbourhood of Smolensk, whence he resolved to march on St. Petersburg in 1813. On 26th October, after the serious check at Malo-jaroslavitz, he wrote to Berthier minimizing that incident, and stating that the return northwards to the devastated line of his own advance—the final cause of disaster—was due to the cold and the necessity of saving the wounded! As for the Cossacks, they were not dangerous.[4]

Examples of this habit of mind might be multiplied. But it will be more suitable to notice the way in which he regarded the campaign of 1815. From the standpoint of public opinion (then a matter of the highest moment), it was designed to effect the liberation of the Belgians from the Dutch yoke, and crush the attempt of the Allies to appropriate the northern fortresses of France.[5] Strategically, it was an effort to surprise the Allies in their cantonments and drive them along the Charleroi-Brussels

---

[1] See his impossible orders to Berthier respecting General Drouet, who was to reinforce Masséna ("Nap. Corresp.," xxi, 250, 280, 3rd and 20th November 1810. For other examples see Prof. Oman, "Peninsular War," iv, 93, 204, 205.

[2] "Mems. of Count Rambuteau" (Eng. edit.), 68.

[3] "Gourgaud's Journal," ii, 13.

[4] "Nap. Corresp.," xxiv, 265, 292.   [5] Ibid., xxviii, 247.

and Charleroi-Namur roads towards their natural bases of operation, Antwerp for Wellington, Liège and Aix-la-Chapelle for
Blücher. This general conception resembles that of the beginning of Napoleon's first campaign, when he drove the Austrians and
Sardinians asunder; and it is probable that the parallel exerted
on his mind a delusively inspiriting influence.

At first all went as well as in 1796. On the 15th June, attacking the Prussian vanguard at and near Charleroi, he drove it
back with loss towards Ligny on the Namur road, while the
whereabouts of Wellington's main force was still unknown.
On the next day he decisively beat the Prussians at Ligny. He
regarded their losses as "enormous." Certainly they were heavy;
for Blücher had ranged his men along an exposed slope on
which the French cannon played to full effect. Gourgaud, writing at St. Helena under Napoleon's inspiration, says that the
losses of the enemy were five times as great as those of the
French; and that the Prussian generals themselves admitted a
loss of 25,000 men.[1] Evidently Gourgaud, and therefore probably
Napoleon, placed it higher; for, as the French official losses were
6,950 men, Gourgaud's ratio would award 34,750 to the enemy.[2]
Napoleon, in a slightly later estimate made at St. Helena, fixed
the Prussian loss as 25,000 killed and wounded, and 20,000
stragglers. Whether we take the Emperor's figures, or Gourgaud's, obviously the French Staff believed the Prussian army to be
nearly destroyed. The famous partisan leader, Lützow, who was
captured at Ligny, flattered French pride by giving assurances
to that effect, adding, too, that Blücher had a second time compromised the Prussian monarchy. About 8 a.m. on 17th June
Soult, the Emperor's Chief of Staff, wrote to Ney a long despatch,
containing these details, ordering him to occupy Quatre Bras
on the Brussels road, if he had not yet done so, and stating
that that operation, as well as supplying ammunition, etc., and
rallying detachments and stragglers, must be the work of the
day.[3]

This explains the comparative inaction of Napoleon on the
morning after the battle. He had heard nothing from Ney as

---

[1] This was false. The official estimate was about 18,000 killed and wounded.
The French loss was between 11,000 and 12,000.

[2] Gourgaud, "Campagne de 1815," p. 65. This work was inspired by
Napoleon; see Gourgaud, "Journal," ii, 90, 107, 295, 319.

[3] Ropes, "Waterloo," pp. 203, 384, 385.

to the fighting at Quatre Bras, but, having ordered him to occupy that important post and push Wellington back towards Brussels, he doubtless assumed, as was his wont, that the Duke was in retreat northwards along the Charleroi-Brussels *chaussée*. That he anticipated little resistance from Wellington on the 16th appears in the order, issued at Charleroi early on that day to Ney, that, "if there were any scuffle (*échauffourée*) with the English, it should fall preferably on the line regiments rather than on the Guard."[1] The words imply that Ney had the game in his hands. The Emperor did not know that Ney's rear corps was so far behind as to be of no use during the "scuffle," which ended in Ney retreating to Frasnes. Napoleon remained in ignorance of the issue of this affair until near noon of the 17th, a remissness of duty in Ney which led to the Emperor losing his chance of catching Wellington in a trap, the British leader having also failed to hear of the disaster at Ligny owing to a mishap to the officer sent to his head-quarters. As it happened, the one mischance counterbalanced the other.

Napoleon certainly believed the Prussians to be in retreat eastwards towards Namur and Liège; for, firstly, their lines had been unduly extended in that direction during the battle; secondly, that was the side on which their reinforcements were expected; and thirdly, it was the natural move for a beaten army to fall back along its line of communications, in this case, towards Namur, Liège, and the Prussian territory around Aix-la-Chapelle. Therefore, early on 17th June, Soult ordered a reconnaissance of French cavalry along the Namur road, but none along the northern road leading to Wavre. For the rest, the Emperor pictured the Belgians as everywhere welcoming the French and incommoding the Allies.[2] Thus, in the sphere of *morale*, all the omens were in his favour; while in that of strategy he seemed to have entirely succeeded, by driving back the Allies on divergent lines of retreat. It is significant that in his St. Helena narrative he describes the situation on the night of the 15th, that is, before the battles of Ligny and Quatre Bras, as highly favourable to the tricolour. "The two hostile armies were surprised; their communications were already greatly compromised. All the Emperor's manœuvres had succeeded as he wished. Thenceforth he could attack in detail the enemy's forces. For them to avoid

---

[1] "Nap. Corresp.," xxviii, 290. [2] *Ibid.*, xxviii, 288.

this mishap, the greatest of all, the only thing remaining was to retreat and to reunite at Brussels or even beyond." [1]

By the morning of the 17th he dismissed from his mind all thought of the Allies reuniting at Brussels or beyond; for Prussian prisoners had been brought in by Pajol's horsemen from the Namur or eastern road; and, as we have seen, no French cavalry was as yet sent out to scout along the north road to Wavre. But, after commenting angrily on the doings of the Chambers of Deputies, Napoleon faced the alternative, that Blücher might have taken another road. Accordingly, about 11.30 he called Marshal Grouchy and ordered him to find out the line of the Prussian retreat, adding that he himself was going to fight the English if they should make a stand on the south of the Forest of Soignes. Grouchy pointed out the difficulty and vagueness of the task allotted to him thus late in the day, but Napoleon held him to it, and dictated to Bertrand (in the absence of Soult) the written order for Grouchy with about 33,000 men to proceed eastwards to Gembloux, explore in the directions of Namur and Maestricht, and find out the line of march and the intentions of the enemy. " It is important," he added, " to find out what the enemy is intending to do; whether they are separating themselves from the English, or whether they are intending still to unite, to cover Brussels and [or?] Liége, by trying the fate of another battle." [2] Obviously this important order was hastily drawn up. The original of the phrase last quoted is " Bruxelles et Liége," which is impossible on geographical grounds. The words must have puzzled Grouchy. He had accepted the duty with reluctance, his troops being wearied out, besides expecting a day of rest. In these circumstances a carelessly drafted order was a mishap of no small importance, as tending to increase the mental cloudiness of the man charged with its execution. On the score of seniority Napoleon selected Grouchy to command the army operating along the Charleroi-Ligny route. He made that choice at Charleroi early on the 16th, when he appointed Ney to lead the army of the left towards Brussels. Neither Ney nor Grouchy was equal to the strategic

[1] " Nap. Corresp.," xxx, 168. Kelly, " The Battle of Wavre," p. 36, shows that more energy on the French side on 15th June would have accomplished their aim.

[2] Charras, i, 241 ; Ropes, 209. Gourgaud's account (p. 67) of the instructions given to Grouchy is utterly vague and misleading.

problems which speedily arose; but the Emperor expected to guide each leader as occasion demanded; for he added "I will proceed to the one or the other wing according to circumstances;" and he then assigned to the Prussians only 40,000 men.[1] The Battle of Ligny showed them to have more than double that number on the field. Nevertheless Napoleon persisted in allotting to Grouchy a difficult task which was likely to remove him beyond reach of the counsel that Ney, and doubtless Grouchy too, had been led to expect. Ney had held independent commands; Grouchy, never, and to entrust to him the pursuit of an enemy whose position and line of march were unknown, savoured of rashness. At St. Helena Napoleon admitted the error, stating that he ought to have recalled Suchet from Lyons and put him in Grouchy's place. Ney, too, he said, made an unpardonable mistake in not occupying Quatre-Bras betimes on the 16th. Soult would have done better there. Thus, during his exile the Emperor saw the defective allocation of duties, which went far to wreck the campaign. He even remarked that on the 17th he should have left only Pajol's cavalry division to follow and observe the Prussians, while he himself threw his whole weight on Wellington.[2] The criticism is highly significant; for it implies that the Prussians were so crushed at Ligny that they were *hors de combat* during the time needful for the overthrow of Wellington.

This leads us to inquire as to the amount of information which Napoleon had respecting the powerful corps which Bülow was bringing to Blücher at Wavre from the direction of Liège. The Prussian Staff had counted on Bülow's arrival at Ligny; and the loss of the battle was due to this miscalculation more than to the non-arrival of succours from Wellington, which the Duke had offered subject to the condition that he himself was not attacked at Quatre Bras. Bülow heard of the defeat at Ligny about midnight, and on the 17th led his corps, exceeding 31,000 men, by cross roads to a position east of Wavre. His arrival brought the Prussian total up to more than 90,000 men, or practically the same as at Ligny. The prompt arrival of the reserves of ammunition along the new line of operations reflects high credit on Blücher's Staff.[3]

---

[1] "Nap. Corresp.," xxviii, 290-2.   [2] Gourgaud, "Journal," i, 197, 502.

Kelly ("Battle of Wavre," pp. 71, 101, 102), who places the number of Prussian deserters after Ligny at about 8,000; Ropes (p. 159) estimates them

Now, Napoleon seems to have known nothing about this formidable concentration at Wavre, which brought about an entirely new situation. He ought to have allowed for something of the kind; for the Prussian forces had been known to be widely spread out in cantonments, and the zeal of Blücher and his Chief of Staff, Gneisenau, was notorious. At St. Helena the Emperor called Blücher a hot-head, who, if he had had only two battalions, would have flown to help Wellington.[1] The statement is of course an after-thought, irreconcilable with the other, that only Pajol's cavalry should have pursued the Prussians. But, setting the one over against the other, we conclude that Napoleon had lost his reckoning. As happened nearly always in and after 1812, he believed that events would take the course which his will prescribed. Not until about 10 a.m. of 18th June did any misgivings occur to him; but then at his headquarters at le Caillou, a little south of la Belle Alliance, he sent off to Grouchy a despatch stating that all the reports represented three bodies of Prussians as having made for Wavre. He therefore ordered the marshal to march thither " in order to approach us, to put yourself within the sphere of our operations, and to keep up your communications with us, pushing before you those bodies of Prussians which have taken this direction, and which may have stopped at Wavre, where you ought to arrive as soon as possible." These perfectly clear instructions were followed by the following, that he, Grouchy, must pick up the Prussian stragglers on his right, that is, further east, and must keep up his communications with Napoleon. Now, Grouchy had only 33,600 men. Yet he was expected to sweep up stragglers to the east of the Gembloux-Wavre road, and drive the Prussians from Wavre, besides keeping in touch with Napoleon seven miles or more to his west. The Emperor often expected the impossible from his generals; but, if he expected Grouchy to perform all these duties, he can scarcely have credited to Blücher a force larger than 30,000 men. Still less did he foresee the Prussian flank march towards Waterloo, which Blücher was intending with three army corps. Thus, Napoleon began the battle with

at 10,000 or 12,000. It is therefore difficult to fix precisely the numbers available for 18th June. Pflugk-Hartung, "Das erste Corps bei Belle Alliance," gives 6,083 as missing from that corps, Ziethen's, on the 18th.

[1] Gourgaud, "Journal," i, 502.

Wellington under a complete misconception as to the strength and the aims of the Prussians.

To Wellington, on the other hand, Napoleon assigned between 80,000 and 90,000 men; for the Duke had had time to concentrate by falling back on his supports. Reasoning on his own maxim —" Bring together all available troops for a battle: one battalion sometimes decides the day "—the Emperor could not credit the Duke with the error which mars his Waterloo campaign, that of leaving 18,000 troops at Hal, about seven miles to the westward. It is therefore all the more remarkable that he expected to beat Wellington before noon; but here again, he relied on the defection of the Belgians. He also had a poor opinion of Wellington's generalship. At Elba, when Major Vivian asked him whether he did not consider Wellington a good general, he answered curtly " Yes," but in a way which signified a negative; and to Soult and Ney at his headquarters before the battle, he said brusquely, " I tell you that Wellington is a bad general, that the English are bad troops, and that this will be the affair of a *déjeuner*." Even at St. Helena, after the experience at Waterloo, he never vouchsafed a word of praise to Wellington, though he paid a tribute to the excellence of British troops. Warden, or his *alter ego*, once asked the Emperor his opinion of Wellington; but he refused to give it. To Gourgaud, however, he once said that the Duke was " an ordinary man, prudent, and fortunate, but not a great genius." Before Waterloo, General Reille informed the Emperor that the British infantry was good but not so good as the French, who would win the day by their cavalry. This information probably accounts for the use of the French cavalry in great masses, as will appear in due course. As for the Prussians, Napoleon had a poor opinion of them after Jena.[1]

Such was the Emperor's state of mind between 10 and 11 a.m. He did not reconnoitre. He trusted to his superiority in guns, and the compactness of his army, to shiver in pieces one in which five different languages were spoken. Further, he did not pay heed to the slope of the ground northwards from the ridge of Mont St. Jean, which enabled Wellington to conceal his second line and reserves. At St. Helena the Emperor declared that he could see every one of Wellington's moves;[2] but this was

---

[1] Gourgaud, " Journal," ii, 84, 367; C. Shorter, " Napoleon and his Fellow Travellers," 278.

[2] " Nap. Corresp.," xxxi, 187.

an impossibility. The concealment of part of the Duke's army, added to the strength of the buildings at Hougomont, la Haye Sainte, and Papelotte, ought to have made Napoleon cautious. In such a case a prudent leader makes reconnaissances in force so as to compel the defenders to show themselves. Nothing of the kind was done.

There is no need to recount the details of the fighting. We are concerned solely with the views of the Emperor. Early in the afternoon, before the advance of d'Erlon's corps, he was perplexed by the appearance of a body of troops far on the east, and believed them to be Grouchy's. The incident was not unlike that at Ligny, when for a time d'Erlon's errant corps was taken to be a hostile force ; and the sole sign of caution in the Emperor on the 18th is his pause for a short time in order to ascertain whether the new comers were friends or foes. Finding from a Prussian prisoner that they were the vanguard of Bülow's corps, he added a postscript to a despatch just drawn up for Grouchy, bidding that marshal march thither and take Bülow in the rear. That despatch was in answer to one just received from Grouchy that he was marching upon Wavre in order to hinder the Prussians from retiring on Brussels, where they seemed to be intending to unite with Wellington. The Emperor, after sending off his reply to Grouchy, was by no means disconcerted at seeing the Prussians in the distance. Why? Obviously because he believed them to be only Bülow's corps.[1] The prisoner had spoken only of the march of one corps, which in point of fact did not equal Grouchy's force. As for the other Prussians, Napoleon still clung to his assumption that they could not possibly fight so soon after the severe defeat of Ligny. As we have seen, he estimated their total losses at 45,000 men; and it was natural for him to assume that the survivors could not receive fresh supplies of ammunition by the night of the 17th and be ready to attack him on the 18th.

That, however, was the case. Thus, the decisive fact of the situation was that three Prussian corps were advancing against Napoleon, when he expected only one, that one, in his conception, being doomed to be shivered between the hammer and the anvil. In his St. Helena narrative Napoleon reckoned

[1] Gourgaud (pp. 104, 105) refers only to Bülow's corps; and Napoleon's own comments show that he thought he had to deal solely with him.

Blücher's effectives after the battle of Ligny at only 40,000 men, and stated that they, "beaten and discouraged," could not over-bear 28,000 Frenchmen under Grouchy, "well placed and victorious." In this calculation, the Emperor reckoned Bülow as entirely separate from Blücher, and he assigned only 28,000 men to Grouchy on the gratuitous assumption that that marshal "must have" detached about 6,000 or 7,000 men to operate against Bülow's rear.[1] If, as seems probable, this represents the impressions implanted in that tenacious brain by the successive incidents of the battle, the cause of disaster is obvious.

Gourgaud[2] states that, before launching d'Erlon's corps forward at Wellington's left, Napoleon hesitated whether to make the chief attack by the Nivelles road against his right. Possibly this is correct; and, if so, it would explain the slight halt before d'Erlon's advance. But, on the whole, the story may be dismissed as an afterthought; for, during more than an hour, the French had been attacking the wood and outbuildings of Hougomont with little effect. That solid outpost barred the way; and success on that side would only have driven Wellington nearer to the Prussians. Moreover, with the exception of Marengo, Napoleon did not change his plans during a battle. He therefore persevered with his original plan of shaking Wellington's array by a sustained artillery fire, while solid columns wrested from him la Haye Sainte and cut through his left centre, thereby driving the chief mass of the Allies away from the Prussians. It was a costly but speedy means of assuring a decisive triumph.

The repulse of d'Erlon's columns east of la Haye Sainte, and of the French cuirassiers above that farmstead, did not alter the Emperor's resolve. He wheeled round part of his right wing to withstand the advance of Bülow towards the village of Planchenoit, the capture of which would have endangered the French rear

---

[1] "Nap. Corresp., xxxi, 190. Section ix, on page 196, is a far more correct description of Blücher's forces and movements. It seems to me a later compilation than that on p. 190, which probably represents Napoleon's notions of 18th June.

I cannot accept the views of O'Connor Morris ("Campaign of 1815," ch. viii) that Napoleon had ordered Grouchy to detach 7,000 men against Bülow's rear. There is no proof of this; and surely it was an assumption. O'Connor Morris seems to me to assign too much importance to Napoleon's "Commentaries," vol. v; they are admittedly very incorrect and biassed. The same may be said of the *Dictées* to Montholon.

[2] Gourgaud, p. 105.

and communications. Therefore between 4.30 and 5.30, as the Prussian attack developed, the Emperor sent into that village Duhesme's division of the Young Guard, thus depleting his reserve of about 4,300 excellent troops. The move of Bülow was on a point so far away from Wellington as to betoken the advance of other Prussians who would fill up the interval; and perhaps an inkling of this truth led the Emperor then to concentrate his attention on this part of the field. Bülow's attack was at a vital point; and until it was repulsed, Napoleon could not but leave to Ney the conduct of the battle against Wellington.[1] Besides, the more Bülow pressed on against Planchenoit, the worse would be his position when Grouchy fell upon his rear. Gourgaud states that when Napoleon saw that Bülow was not followed by Grouchy, he ordered Ney to "hold" la Haye Sainte. He also says that up to 6 p.m. the Staff had no news of Grouchy; and, again, that by 7.30, the sound of Grouchy's cannon was heard two and a half leagues away.[2]

It is clear, then, that Napoleon and his Staff officers paid much heed to developments on their right flank, doubtless with the hope of crushing the Prussian corps or capturing it outright. By about 6 p.m. Bülow's men were beaten back from Planchenoit by three additional battalions of the Imperial Guard; and the Emperor thereafter gave his attention to Wellington. In the interval, the Emperor's knowledge of events in his front was but partial, a fact which explains the haziness of his and Gourgaud's accounts of this part of the battle. Thus, Napoleon states that after a long and creditable defence, Hougomont was taken owing to the fire of eight howitzers which he concentrated upon it; whereas Hougomont was held by detachments of British Guards, a Nassau battalion, and a few Hanoverians to the end of the day. He also asserts that, after three hours' fighting, the French took la Haye Sainte *from Scottish regiments.*[3] Gourgaud dates its capture at 4 p.m. But Major Baring, the commander of the detachment of the King's German Legion, which staunchly held that post, states positively that he and the few survivors were not driven out from the farm itself until 6.30.[4]

The other chief point in dispute is the responsibility for the

[1] Ropes, "Campaign of Waterloo," p. 309.
[2] Gourgaud, 85.   [3] "Nap. Corresp.," xxxi, 188, 191.
[4] Ropes (p. 307), following Gourgaud, places the time at about 4 p.m., but, I am convinced, wrongly.

succession of the cavalry charges whereby Ney hoped to shatter Wellington's right centre. Had they been properly supported by infantry, success was highly probable; but that support was not forthcoming. Napoleon afterwards blamed Ney severely for beginning the cavalry charges too early. However, he believed that they had carried the enemy's position, and therefore finally ordered Kellermann's cuirassiers to support their comrades and "pursue the English army."[1] Again, then, it is clear that the Emperor failed to discern Wellington's second line and reserves, or to notice the movements by which the Duke reinforced his line at the points threatened by the French cavalry. Gourgaud also states that Napoleon himself ordered Kellermann's cuirassiers to reinforce the French cavalry, which then seemed to be in possession of the plateau of Mont St. Jean.[2] Thus, Napoleon, during the attack of Bülow on Planchenoit, must have believed that one more cavalry charge against Wellington's right centre would decide the battle. The mistake was irreparable; for it incapacitated the French cavalry from holding the Allies at bay after the repulse of the Guard.

The repulse of Bülow at Planchenoit about 6 p.m. enabled Napoleon to concentrate his thought on the battle against Wellington and thus to put a new face on affairs at his front. General Foy's division and that of Bachelu in Reille's corps pressed hard Wellington's right centre; the capture of la Haye Sainte at 6.30 also enabled d'Erlon's corps to advance and pour a destructive fire into the centre. On the left the Nassauers were driven from the village of Smohain, so that Wellington lost touch with the Prussian corps of Ziethen which slowly advanced towards the British left.[3] Carelessly though Napoleon had fought the battle hitherto, he came near to winning it between 6.30 and 7 p.m.; and, had not the greater part of Reille's corps been wasted in ineffective endeavours to storm Hougomont, the French line regiments, aided by the Imperial Guard, would probably have carried the tricolour to victory.

Napoleon believed that the fate of a battle was determined by

---

[1] "Nap. Corresp.," xxxi, 194, where it is stated that the 12,000 French horsemen overthrew the superior cavalry forces of Wellington, cut up several squares, captured 60 cannon and 6 flags, and held the plateau up to 7 p.m.!

[2] Gourgaud (pp. 86, 87) says the French cavalry broke up several squares!

[3] For the cause of Ziethen's slow advance see Rose, "Napoleonic Studies," 296, 297.

decisive encouragement imparted at the critical moment. In his judgment the crisis arrived shortly after 7 p.m., when Wellington was with the utmost difficulty holding his own, and the advance of Pirch's and Ziethen's corps had not told on the French right. The Emperor therefore ordered all the available battalions of the Guard forward to attack the allied right centre,[1] while Reille and d'Erlon redoubled their efforts. Napoleon sent his aide-de-camp, Labédoyère along the lines with the encouraging message that Grouchy was advancing; and, nerved by this belief, the French, after eight hours of desperate fighting, made a final effort.[2] The repulse of the Imperial Guard need not be described here. It occurred about the same time that the French holding the hamlets of la Haye and Smohain gave way before the attack of Ziethen and the British left. Napoleon severely blamed Durutte's division of d'Erlon's corps which bore the brunt of this double onset; but the censure is unjust. He had encouraged all his line by the report that Grouchy was at hand; and, instead of Grouchy came Ziethen's Prussians. This explains the cries of *à la trahison* and *sauve qui peut*, which now spread from division to division of d'Erlon's corps. What was intended to encourage proved to be the cause of dismay and despair.

It is noteworthy that both Napoleon and Gourgaud give no account whatever of the repulse of the Guard, excepting that the former ascribes its retirement to the need of facing about towards la Haye Sainte in order to restore order on that side.[3] A lamer excuse for the retreat of the Guard cannot be conceived; and it conflicts with the next statement, that the battle was lost owing to the sudden charge of 2,000 British horsemen, who penetrated between the Guard and Reille's corps. Gourgaud places their number at 3,000, and says that they pierced the line between Reille's corps and la Haye Sainte.[4] Both accounts are wrong. Vivian and Vandeleur were posted nearly behind Maitland's Guards, who repulsed the first column of the Imperial Guard; and their brigades followed the two columns retiring in confusion towards la Belle Alliance. Vivian, with the 10th and 18th Hussars, supported by several squadrons of the King's German

---

[1] "Nap. Corresp.," xxxi, 198, where he says the advance was in order to support "la cavalerie décontenancée," which a little earlier he had described as holding the plateau of Mont St. Jean up to 7 p.m.

[2] *Ibid.*, xxxi, 198; Gourgaud, 90.   [3] *Ibid.*

[4] *Ibid.*, xxxi, 198, 199; Gourgaud, 92.

Legion, executed most effective charges on the last reserves of French cavalry capable of offering any resistance; and his onset, together with the spirited advance of Adam's infantry brigade, including Colborne's 52nd regiment, rendered all attempt at rallying impossible even in the heart of the enemy's position. The British and German horsemen not only overthrew the wrecks of the French cavalry, but also hustled back the last square of the Imperial Guard which made a stand. Napoleon saw these effective charges and did full justice to them, stating that they decided the fate of the battle.[1] This is largely correct; for, with the support of Adam's brigade and other troops they drove back in one confused mass the two columns of the Imperial Guard, the supporting cavalry, and Reille's corps. The retreat of some 30,000 men towards the *chaussée* near la Belle Alliance would alone have occasioned a rout.

But that rout became a stampede owing to the convergence of d'Erlon's corps from the French right wing on the same road. The panic which laid hold of Durutte's division has already been explained; and it seems to have spread to the other divisions about the time when the bearskins of the Imperial Guard were seen to be tailing back into the hollow. To complete the confusion, Bülow pressed on Napoleon's right rear; and, had his horsemen been sufficiently numerous and fresh, the battle must have ended in a massacre, and the capture and execution of the Emperor himself.

Singularly enough, Napoleon never fully understood why he was beaten. The sentence quoted at the head of this essay shows that on one occasion he discerned the fundamental cause; but for the most part he sought refuge in the platitude, that Waterloo was a fatality: *journée incomprehensible; concours de fatalités—Grouchy, Ney, d'Erlon.*"[2] He once declared to Gourgaud that, even with 20,000 fewer men, he ought to have won the day.[3] He had a poor opinion of Soult as Chief of Staff.[4] Several times he blamed Ney severely for sending in the cavalry too soon and for other follies. He thought little of Friant, who led the charge of the Guard, and longed that Bessières could have been there.[5] Once he said that he ought to have beaten Wellington on 17th June.[6] He also admitted that British bravery was

---

[1] "Nap. Corresp.," xxxi, 199; Gourgaud, "Journal," i, 197.
[2] Las Cases, "Mémorial," iv, 304.   [3] Gourgaud, "Journal," i, 79.
[4] *Ibid.*, ii, 84.   [5] *Ibid.*, i, 150, 197, 503.   [6] *Ibid.*, i, 174.

superb, and added: "It was by their discipline especially that the English triumphed. They could advance thirty paces, halt, fire, retire, fire, advance thirty paces, keeping the greatest order."[1] It is significant that at St. Helena he never mentioned his having been in bad health during the Waterloo campaign, a fact which disposes of the many statements that he was a mere wreck of his former self.

The most curious feature of the whole question is the inability of Napoleon to understand that he himself was responsible for losing the campaign. As has now appeared, he underrated the fighting power of the allied armies and the abilities of their commanders. He overrated the importance of his successes over the Prussians on 15th-16th June; on the 17th he was too late in moving against Wellington at Quatre Bras, and in ordering a pursuit of Blücher. His instructions of 17th June to Grouchy did not allow for the case of a junction of Bülow's powerful corps with Blücher, though that event, which was far from improbable, would raise the Prussian army to a strength far beyond the power of Grouchy to cope with. A striking proof of Napoleon's assurance of triumph at Mont St. Jean came to light after the battle. In his carriage, which was captured at Genappe, were found proclamations dated "Notre Palais de Laeken" (near Brussels).[2] It was in that spirit that he fought the Battle of Waterloo. There is little or no sign of hesitation on which M. Houssaye has laid stress.[3] On the contrary, every move up to about 4.30 betokened absolute confidence in the result. Between 4.30 and 6 p.m. he paid much attention to the advance of the Prussians on Planchenoit, but not from apprehension so much as from a resolve to hold them at arm's length until Grouchy could come up and crush them. Confidence appears in his allowing the greater part of Reille's corps to waste its energies for hours on the walls of Hougomont; in his acquiescing in the advance of d'Erlon's corps in the solid masses which entailed disaster; in his ordering Kellermann's cuirassiers to make the final cavalry charge which left the French with no reserves

---

[1] Gourgaud, "Journal," ii, 84.

[2] Sir A. S. Frazer, "Letters," 567.

[3] Houssaye, "Waterloo," 480, 484. Napoleon's words uttered to Las Cases ("Mémorial," vii, 179 *et seq.*), about his feeling that Fortune deserted him at Waterloo, are clearly an afterthought. Napoleon's actions prove the contrary.

of horsemen; and in the onset of all but one of the remaining battalions of the Imperial Guard. His motto had always been, *risquer le tout pour le tout*, and the supreme example of that daring which rapidly raised him to power is the battle which brought about his headlong fall.

PART II

CORRESPONDENCE

PART II

CORRESPONDENCE

(A.) THE KING AND PITT

[N.B. The following letters have not hitherto been published. Others between the King and Pitt are in the Appendix of Earl Stanhope's "Life of Pitt"; but limits of space render it impossible to present summaries of them. The following letters are all from the King to Pitt, unless otherwise stated. Letters, or parts of them, given in *précis* are enclosed in brackets. The following abbreviations have been used:

Y. M. = Your Majesty.
Y. E. = Your Excellency.
H. I. M. = His Imperial Majesty.]

"Queen's House, March 20, 1783.
" Mr. Pitt, I desire you will come here immediately."

"Queen's House, Dec. 24, 1783.
" Mr. Pitt ought to know that Ld. Dartmouth and Mr. Greville have resigned their staves, and Lord Jersey the Board of Pensioners; Lord De Ferrars naturally should have his former office; I wish much, if it does not prevent other necessary arrangements, that Lord Walsingham may get some employment and that Lord Aylesford may be advanced; his vacancy in the bedchamber I should willingly confer of (*sic*) any peer who might be thought proper on this occasion. The Constable of the Tower would suit any peer and more properly a military one; might it not please Lord Effingham who must naturally have some office, and one of that nature would be more pleasing to him than any attendance at Court?"

"Windsor, Dec. 28, 1783.
" . . . As to Ireland, I like the idea thrown out on Friday by Mr. Pitt of the propriety that would attend Lord Cornwallis's holding that office; though I doubt his accepting it, I do not

think that a reason Mr. Pitt should not attempt it; Lord Sydney is a good channel to find out whether it would succeed." [1]

"Windsor, Dec. 30th, 1783.

" Mr. Pitt will give notice to Lord Effingham that he is also to be presented to-morrow as Warden of the Mint; and if Ld. Chesterfield likes the Spanish Embassy, I shall approve of his appointment. I shall be glad to hear to-morrow Mr. Pitt's ideas with regard to the Lord Lieutenancy of Ireland. . . ."

"Queen's House, Jany 1, 1784.

" As the forms of this day will probably last too long for my afterwards seeing Mr. Pitt in private, I take this method of acquainting him that the Duke of Newcastle is in town, and as right in his ideas on the present crisis as can be wished, and that he will take every method to oblige his friends to an active support of My Cause; nothing would, I find, hurt him so much as any offer to his son. If Mr. Pitt would send him a note offering to wait upon him, it would be very acceptable. Mr. Brudenell has, I find, secured his two nephews; some civility to him would be very proper: I have good hopes of Sir Henry Gough."

"Windsor, Jan. 11, 1784.

" It is with infinite satisfaction I find by Mr. Pitt's letter this morning that the proposition for arranging the East India affairs has been carried in the Court of Proprietors by so very large a majority, which certainly must have the effect of rendering the plan much more palatable to Parliament than if it had not had that sanction. The Duke of Northumberland is highly pleased. Mr. Pitt ought this day to learn from him the title he proposes taking, that the warrant may be prepared with the two others."

"Queen's House, Jan. 15, 1784.

" Though the length of the debate shows the House of Commons is not yet come to that temper which the seriousness of the times ought to effect, the not dividing against the admittance of the new East India Bill gives some hopes it may meet with more support than the leaders pretend: I should hope Mr. Yorke's notice may be of utility and bring those not quite deaf to decency to a different conduct."

"Queen's House, Jan. 17, 1784.

" The majority having fallen to 21, Mr. Drake and Sir Wm. Dolben and others joining and speaking in the minority, besides

---

[1] Lord Cornwallis (1738-1805) did not accept the Irish Viceroyalty. Lord Sydney (1723-1800) was Home Secretary.

the strength of the resolution, which is a mark of violence not unnatural to men finding they are losing ground, makes me look on this last debate as a favorable one, and I trust a few days will shew that the majority is in favour of decorum instead of siding with anarchy."

" Queen's House, Jan. 24, 1784.

" Mr. Pitt's note is but this instant arrived; by the Minutes of the House of Commons I see that the messenger of the Great Seal or his deputy have orders to attend at twelve this day: this cannot be for any common affair, yet I should suppose Mr. Pitt, if he had known it, would have mentioned it. I own I cannot see any reason if the thing is practicable that a dissolution should not be effected, if not, I fear the constitution of this country cannot subsist.

" P.S. I shall not stir from home, that no delays may be occasioned from my absence even for a couple of hours."

" Queen's House, Feb. 3, 1784.

" It appears very evident to me that the motion of Mr. Grosvenor which I can easily believe was well meant, very materially affected the division on the second; for, as it carried no very fixed complexion, both sides of the House could explain at pleasure. The second is nothing but the one past (*sic*) some days ago in other words. If the House should really carry an address this day, it will highly become the House of Lords to throw off their lethargy and also vote an address that shall show they feel that each branch of the Legislature has its fixed bounds and that the executive power is vested in the Crown and not to be infringed by the Commons."

Feb. 4, 1784.

" The whole conduct of Opposition confirms the opinion I gave very early of its dangerous intentions of going step by step as far as the House of Commons can be led, avoiding if possible any avowed illegality of conduct, but not looking to the spirit either of the constitution or of justice. The directing the resolution of Monday to be brought to me without having proved any charge against Administration, or indeed pretending to any, must make every man of reflection grieve that the House can be carried such lengths. . . ."

[For the rest see Stanhope, vol. i, App., p. vi.]

" Queen's House, Feb. 7, 1784.

" The Draught (*sic*) Mr. Pitt in conjunction with the other ministers has drawn up in answer to the one in Lord Howe's hand is conformable to every idea I have ever harboured on the subject of any communication for effecting the formation of an Administration on the widest basis, and as such meets with my fullest approbation."

"Queen's House, Feb. 11, 1784.

" I am glad the House proceeded on the estimate of the Ordnance, which, not being a favourite service, would more easily have been postponed than any other. I therefore trust that it is a sign the public services will by the more reasonable men in that House not be suffered to be longer put off. I am not surprised the language of Mr. Fox on union[1] should have been less offensive this day, the temper of London and Westminster must make such an appearance necessary; but whilst resignation is coupled with it, no expectation can be grounded on it nor any propriety in asking any further questions from Opposition on that head. The only line that can be followed is for Administration uniformly to hold the discourse that I am ever open to any proposition that can effect the forming of an Administration on a wide basis; that one formed out of only a part of my subjects I will never listen to; and that there is no man so little a friend to his country in my service as to value his own particular situation in competition with so salutary a measure."

"Queen's House, Feb. 17, 1784.

" As by Mr. Pitt's letter I am to conclude that Windsor is the most acceptable stall to Mr. Wilson, I authorize his acquainting Doctor Buller that he may be presented to-morrow as Dean of Exeter and Mr. Wilson as Canon of Windsor."[2]

"Queen's House, Feb. 18, 1784.

" . . . It seems very strange that Opposition can infatuate so many persons to neglect so long perceiving that it is impossible for me to be so wanting to my own character as not to stand firm, and consequently that if the Commons do not keep within their proper line, that confusion at least for a time must ensue."

"Queen's House, Feb. 21, 1784.

" Mr. Pitt, at any other period of my reign or on similar proceedings from any other House of Commons but the present, would have received from me expressions of surprise, which is certainly not the case at present. If it is not inconvenient to

[1] *I.e.*, a union of the parties, as recommended by the Committee at the St. Alban's Tavern, for which see Rose, "William Pitt and National Revival," 164-6.

[2] The Rev. Edward Wilson had been Pitt's private tutor.

Mr. Pitt to call here at half-past two this day, I should willingly hear his account of the debate; but should he wish first to confer with the other Ministers on the words of an answer and on the steps which the times may authorize and the safety of the constitution require, previous to seeing me, I shall in that case propose to see him as early to-morrow morning as it may suit him. As the Opposition seem so fond of bringing King William forward on all occasions, I should think his exact words in 1701, with such additional ones as the moment may call for, would not be improper to be uttered from the Chair of State when the whole House bring up this strange, and I may add as an ungrounded position, this unconstitutional address."

"Queen's House, Feb. 26, 1784.

" I should not deal with that openness towards Mr. Pitt which his conduct deserves, if I did not state my hopes that the Duke of Portland will not come into what I may deem reasonable (*sic*): a subject requiring from his sovereign exact words, agreeable to which he can alone enter into negotiation, is very revolting; but as the other Ministers seem to advise that this last trial should be made, I will not object to it, provided, in addition to the words proposed, Mr. Powys shall explain specifically to that Duke that his being called upon is to give him no right to anything above an equal share to others in the new Administration, not to be the head of it, whatever employment he may hold."

"Windsor, March 2nd, 1784.

" I am more sorry than surprised that so small a majority in the House [of] Commons have let passion so far get the better of reason as to move a second address to me, and the latter part of it in so dictatorial a style; the answer to the former having been so ample, a short reference to that sums up all that is requisite, unless the Cabinet should think it right for the Lords, either from themselves or from having the two addresses and answers communicated to them from me, ought to take notice of a conduct which really if it could succeed, would entirely overturn the balance of the constitution; but, thank Heaven, I am not of materials to act so disgracefully. I must now turn to the pleasant part of the debate, the declaration that all negotiation is broken off;[1] this I look upon as most fortunate, as it could never have ended advantageously for this country, must have proved inconvenient to those employed in it, and the idea of its subsisting certainly operating to make every man less eager, from a doubt whether his efforts might not be frustrated

---

[1] *I.e.*, for the union of parties.

by the introduction of his opponents. I suppose Mr. Pitt will
settle this day with the other Ministers the short answer to this
warm command."

"Queen's House, March 28, 1784.

" Having learnt this day that the Duke of Grafton has met
with the repulse of his candidate, Genl. Conway, at St. Edmonds-
bury, and that the Duke, to prevent the introduction of a
stranger, has been obliged to put up in his stead Capt. Geo.
Fitzroy, I think it may be agreeable to Mr. Pitt to know of a
certain friend instead of a determined enemy. I yesterday signed
the appointments of the Comptroller of the Household and the
Master of the Rolls; I wish Mr. Pitt would settle with the
Chancellor[1] that the appointments of Attorney-General and
Solicitor, as well as the Chief Justice of Chester, be sent for my
signing as the time for elections is hourly approaching. The
accounts of York show the majority was very decided; but by
the account of Ld. Percy the management wretched, and the
Sheriff frightened by Ld. Surrey into signing not being able to
decide as to the majority. By a letter Ld. Salisbury has received
from Mr. Wilberforce I find that gentleman is to be the joint
candidate with Mr. Duncombe."

"Queen's House, March 28, 1784.

" . . . No candidates have yet started at Coventry against the
late members, which is the more extraordinary, as I am told two
new men might certainly, at not more than £2,000 each, succeed,
the town is so desirous of a change of representatives."

"Windsor, March 30, 1784.

" . . . I am happy to find two candidates are likely to be
found to oppose the late representatives of Coventry. I understood Sir Jas. Pennyman declares Beverley is so offended with
Major Anderson that any fresh man would probably succeed
there. If Lieut.-Gen. Robertson is so desirous of a seat in Parliament, he ought to be encouraged to go on some of these
hazardous exploits. There has been a ridiculous attempt here of
Ld. Penryn (*sic*); but a few hours convinced him that he had
no chance against the late member. Mrs. Keppel has this day
sent to her few tenants that a candidate will still arrive before
the election, which is settled for nine to-morrow morning; but
should one appear, it cannot be of further mischief than obliging
the late representatives to have a poll."

[1] The Lord Chancellor, Lord Thurlow (1732-1806).

" Windsor, April 6, 1784.

" The introduction of Mr. Wyndham (*sic*) into the House of Commons is one of the few unexpected disasters, for undoubtedly as yet the elections have proved beyond the hopes of the most sanguine friends.[1] I find there is little doubt of the success of the new candidates for this county, and the report is current here this evening that Sir Robert Clayton has declined for Surrey. Coventry seems promising. I was in hopes some news might have come of the poll for the city of York. By what I have heard the people of Tamworth are so dissatisfied with Lord Townshend that any candidate that should have stood forth would have succeeded."

" Queen's House, April 8, 1784.

" I rejoice very sincerely at the success in the county election of York and also in that of the city of York. Mr. Pitt will certainly not require an hint that attention should be had that a proper candidate be found for Hull."

" Windsor, April 12, 1784.

" The returns of the elections just received from Mr. Pitt have the same agreeable appearance which attended the former ones. I find Ld. Verney declines coming into any agreement and has produced the list of supporters he is to meet with which appears so favourable that it is supposed Mr. Aubrey will relinquish."

" Windsor, April 13, 1784.

" Though the advance made by Mr. Fox this day can only have been by bad votes, yet similar measures must be adopted rather than let him get returned for Westminster. Nothing can be more material than the account of Mr. Coke having declined in Norfolk, as it is as strong a proof as the decision in Yorkshire of the genuine sense of the people."

" Windsor, April 17, 1784.

" The success at Coventry is a most agreeable event; from what I had heard this morning to be the opinion of one of the Conways who left that place three days since, I had every reason to expect this favourable conclusion. I am sorry to see, though indeed slowly, that Mr. Fox gains upon Sir Cecil Wray. . . ."

" Windsor, May 1, 1784.

" The poll for Westminster of this day still continues favourable to Mr. Fox; but I have heard that the Quackers (*sic*),

[1] Mr. Wyndham (or Windham) (1750-1810), a Whig, was elected for Norwich in place of a Tory.

though in general unwilling to take part in elections, have no disinclination on the present state of the poll to come forward, if properly applied to, and that their number amounts to near three hundred, which would place Lord Hood and Sir Cecil Wray in a very decided situation. I understand Lord Salisbury has sent to Mr. Barklay to desire he will call on his brethren. I think it right to acquaint Mr. Pitt that the High Bailiff is decided in his intention of granting a scrutiny if asked for, and gives that reason to his friends for not objecting more decidedly to many of the votes that are now produced."

"Queen's House, May 14, 1784.

"I am much pleased with the general turn of the Speech, which Mr. Pitt will of course at a meeting communicate to the Cabinet, and should any alterations occur, he will of course communicate it to me. . . ."

"Windsor, May 25, 1784.

"Mr. Pitt's account of the Opposition on the first question of this new Parliament having divided but 136, and on the address but 114, gives the most flattering appearance that business may be carried on with decency instead of that violence which disgraced the late Parliament and nearly overturned the constitution. . . ."

"Queen's House, June 2nd, 1784.

"I had no doubt every degree of cavil would be ransacked to protract the progress of the Westminster Election, and therefore am not surprized though sorry, the House of Commons has been prevented from getting through that business, though sitting till six this morning. I am glad the opening has been made on the part of the High Bailiff with becoming strength, and think the division in the course of the day shews the sense of the House on the unwarrantable conduct of Opposition."

"Windsor, June 15, 1784.

"Had the motion of yesterday owed its existence to any other person than the mover, it could never have been laid before the House of Commons; for it would have been but natural to sound whether support would be given previous to producing it in that assembly. I fear so long a vindication must have been prefaced by a long speech, so that Mr. Pitt was not sooner rid of the motion than the length of common debates. I hope now it will be possible to proceed with the necessary business of Parliament without more delay."

"Windsor, July 3, 1784.

"So much heat having been occasioned by the very dangerous Bill for regulating the affairs of the East India Company abroad, it is scarcely possible any step shall be taken concerning that subject that shall not bring on some debate in the House of Commons. I trust Mr. Pitt will get through the various parts that may be necessary to be discussed this session, with that success which ought ever to attend those who have no other view but that of doing justice. I am not surprised Major Cathcart met with applause on his first appearance yesterday as a speaker, having ever heard him looked on as a sensible young man. I am certain he cannot have said anything in favour of the troops in India remaining in the hands of the Company, but must have enforced that they ought to be those of the nation but paid by the Company. Then a total stop could be put to the shameful mode of increasing the number of officers every hour to answer the views of particular persons: then the half pay might be gradually diminished by obliging those on it to fill up vacancies or be struck off of it; besides putting the military in that country on a respectable foot (*sic*), which officers belonging to a company cannot pretend to."

"St. James's, July 28, 1784.

"It is impossible to frame a more proper letter than Mr. Pitt has in answer to the Duke of Rutland, as it in a masterly manner contains all the difficulties in the present stage of the business of forming a decided opinion; indeed, great as the enormity is, as it amounts as yet only to words, the punishment, if any could be obtained, would not be adequate to the tendency of it. Consequently I fully concur in the sentiments of this well drawn up letter." [1]

"Windsor, July 29, 1784.

"By Mr. Pitt's I find the East India (*sic*) is passed without a division, and the rest of the business of the day also concluded. I trust now little more trouble will be given in finishing the business of this session, as Mr. Fox's speech yesterday was, I suppose, his last words on the occasion, and that he will retire to his new purchased villa."

"Windsor, Aug. 23, 1784.

"I am sensible of Mr. Pitt's attention in transmitting the letter he has received from Mr. Orde, which undoubtedly must

---

[1] For the letters of Pitt and Rutland see "Corresp. between Pitt and the Duke of Rutland," pp. 24-36, and Lord Ashbourne, "Pitt," p. 81. They refer to the publication by the Earl of Bristol (who was also Bishop of Derry) of a pamphlet advocating the Catholic claims.

P

be more explicit than any official one that may have accompanied it to the Secretary of State. I hope the zeal of the servants of the Crown in Ireland will not overbalance their prudence; for should they find that no immediate mischief is likely to arise from not instantly seizing on the conspirators, the letting them continue to assemble, having exact intelligence of what passes at their meetings will be a means of being informed of all those concerned, and consequently when it is thought necessary to bring this plot to light, the whole scheme may be overturned; whilst, if published too soon, only the parties in Dublin will probably come to light; and though it may stop the evil for some time it will in some time again break out.' Indeed I look upon a discovery previous to the session of Parliament in Ireland, and the less time before it, as a most happy circumstance, it will take off the minds of persons from delicate subjects that can only involve that Kingdom into insurmountable difficulties."

"Windsor, Aug. 29, 1784.

"Mr. Pitt has judged very properly in communicating the private letter he has received from Mr. Orde.² I agree with the opinion that the informers greatly exaggerate, but that would not authorize any relaxation of attention to so very serious a subject. The opinions that have been sent from hence concur in recommending the postponing any publication; therefore I need not say more on that head, which certainly is the only judicious conduct that can be pursued. The publications are undoubtedly the most barefaced treason, which it would be difficult for the most *patriotic jury* to deny; but the taking any step on them I think ought also to be postponed."

"Sept. 10, 1784.

". . . Lord Southampton dropped that the Prince [of Wales's] debts are supposed to amount to £100,000, which in one year and without gaming, seems hardly credible.³ I shall certainly give no answer, should such an application be made, that can engage me to anything. I must see the whole before I can guess whether anything can be done, and then not without the fullest communication with Mr. Pitt."

¹ Thomas Orde (1748-1807) was Chief Secretary to the Lord Lieutenant, and became Baron Bolton in 1797. The affair referred to a plot supposed to be furthered by France. For Pitt's letter to Orde embodying the King's instructions, see Lord Ashbourne, "Pitt," pp. 82-3.

² *Ibid.*, pp. 83, 84.

³ Hon. George Fitzroy, 2nd Lord Southampton (1761-1810), was Groom of the Bedchamber to the Prince of Wales. For the Prince's debts, see Rose, "William Pitt and National Revival," p. 394.

"Queen's House, Jan. 28, 1785.

" I am the better able to give my sentiments to Mr. Pitt on the two letters he has sent for my perusal, the one from the Duke of Rutland, the other from Mr. Foster, as I yesterday read the public letter the Duke wrote on this delicate subject to Lord Sydney.[1] It is impossible for the most heated Irish patriot to deny that every attention to the trade of that kingdom has been given in the deliberations that have been held to make a final settlement between the two kingdoms. The justice of Ireland contributing to the general expense of the Empire, when by this measure she is to be greatly enriched, and whatever she gains appears to be at the expense of Britain, cannot, nor does not, seem to be denied: the plea now made use of is expediency: this I take it is now taken up as the only plausible ground, but I do not doubt has weight with the Castle as the ease of the Session may be affected by it; but on this side of the water the expediency, not the value to be accrued, is the main object of expecting this contribution; trifling and contemptible as the Opposition appeared on the first day of the Session, Lord North has certainly taken ground to oppose the plan unless Britain has some assistance from it, and will undoubtedly get the merchants of this kingdom to cry out on the occasion, and when they make a noise they are but too generally echoed by the manufacturers and the populace; therefore I cannot but encourage Mr. Pitt in the idea of not receding, and am clearly of opinion that it is expedient Britain should understand, that if she suffers on the one hand by this arrangement, on the other a pecuniary assistance is to be acquired towards the general defence of the Empire."

"Queen's House, March 1, 1785.

" The account Mr. Pitt gives me of the manner in which the confidential conversation he has had with Mr. Cooke[2] strikes him of the probability the Irish Parliament will in effect, though perhaps not in appearance, come into the precise mode required, is very satisfactory; and I cannot help adding that I cannot conceive why the Duke of Rutland's dispatches have not yet come to me, so that, had not Mr. Pitt not had the attention of writing this evening, I should have till to-morrow morning probably have remained ignorant of any letters having come from Ireland."

[1] The Right Hon. John Foster (1740-1828) was Chancellor of the Irish Exchequer, but in September 1785 became Speaker of the Irish House of Commons.

[2] Edward Cooke (1755-1820) was Under Secretary of State in Ireland.

[On 13th March 1785 the King sends to Pitt a draft of his reply to the Prince of Wales on the subject of his debts, and requests that any alterations made by Pitt may be clearly marked. On 28th March the King approves Pitt's alterations.]

"Queen's House, April 12, 1785.

" Having entirely approved of the draft of a message to the Prince of Wales, I have this evening sent it through the usual channel of Lord Southampton. Nothing could have given me greater satisfaction than the intimation in the note I received yesterday from Mr. Pitt of the great increase of the produce of the old taxes as well as the success [of] those established the last year; and I cannot help flattering myself Mr. Pitt will think this gives a reasonable ground for this year establishing a Commission to buy stock at the market price with the surplus that may arise of money unappropriated in the Exchequer, that by degrees the National Debt may be diminished and the credit of the country again restored; the more I reflect on the subject the more I think what I have said on this business to Mr. Pitt will answer both those salutary purposes."

[On 6th May 1785 the King congratulates Pitt on the success of his measures, and censures Opposition for referring the accounts of the East India Company for investigation to a committee of the House of Commons; this is mere meddling with private concerns, and will destroy commercial confidence.]

"Windsor, May 31, 1785.

" It seems to me that nothing can be more abandoned than the conduct of the opposers of the Irish Resolutions yesterday, after having by so decided a majority been frustrated in the attempt to have them postponed for three months, to continue an inflammatory debate till half hour past four this morning merely with a view to disunite the two kingdoms, without having any prospect of preventing the measure: this proceeding deserves every sort of execration, and I should hope that the Irish Parliament is too well acquainted with the true interests of that kingdom not to see through the drift of the opposition in this country, who have changed ground so frequently during the tedious disquisitions this difficult subject has occasioned in the House of Commons."

"Windsor, July 22, 1785.

Considering that at first there seemed some difficulty of getting rid of some etiquette between the two Houses of Parliament on account of some of the alterations made by the Lords in the Irish Resolutions, I could not but see with infinite pleasure by Mr. Pitt's note that the expedient had been adopted

in the House of Commons yesterday of throwing those amend-
ments into fresh Resolutions and immediately communicating
them to the Lords; but I doubt there (*sic*) being returned in
time on Monday for the address to be moved that day and the
leave for bringing in a Bill in consequence of them, unless
Lord Stormont should fall ill or lose his propensity of publick
haranguing. By what I heard the Lord President say on Thursday I rather imagined that on consideration the farther steps
on the Bill would be postponed, as the difficulty of a call of the
House seemed unavoidable, if proposed by Opposition, from
whence every kind of delay and embarrassment must naturally
be expected."

"Windsor, Aug. 7, 1785.

" I have this instant received Mr. Pitt's letter enclosing the
one brought him by Count Woronzow's secretary and the paper
that accompanied it, which is a copy of the one given on Friday
to Lord Carmarthen. Count Woronzow also visited Lord Sydney
and insisted a Council was to be held next day to give him an
answer whether I would break the treaty I have in my Electoral
capacity finally concluded with the King of Prussia and the
Elector of Saxony to prevent all measures contrary to the Ger-
manic Constitution.[1] If no one has such dangerous views, this
association cannot give umbrage; but the time certainly required this precaution. My only difficulty in giving an answer
to the Empress of Russia is that her declaration bears so strongly
the shape of a command that it requires a strong one. The
having succeeded in that kind of conduct with the Court of
Denmark has encouraged her adopting it on this occasion ; but,
as what I owe in my Electoral capacity to the future stability
of the Empire has alone actuated my conduct and makes me
feel that Russia has no right to interfere. An experience of
twenty years has taught me not to expect any return for the
great assistance she has received from this country. Mr. Pitt
shall receive from me when prepared copies of the answers that
have been ——(?) to the Imperial Minister and the Russian at
Hamburg, which will fully apprise him of the business. . . ."

"St. James's, Aug. 10, 1785.

" On arriving in town I have received the three papers I proposed transmitting to Mr. Pitt. I cannot say that the time

[1] For these topics see J. H. Rose, " William Pitt and National Revival,"
pp. 311, 312. Lord Carmarthen (1751-1799) became 5th Duke of Leeds in
March 1789. He was Foreign Secretary in 1783-1791. Count Simon Woronzow (Vorontzoff) (1744-1832) was Russian Ambassador in London from
1784 to 1800.

which has elapsed since last I wrote has diminished my surprise or cooled my feelings on the haughty step the Empress of Russia has taken; but I trust I have too much regard to my own dignity to wish any heat should appear in the answer that may next week be given to Count Woronzow, though she must know that when steps are taken from principle they are not to be retrograded."

[On 6th May 1786 the King approves Pitt's draft of a letter to the Prince of Wales on the subject of his debts.]

"Windsor, July 3, 1786.

[The King's family causes increasing expenditure.]

"Now three of my six daughters appear at Court and consequently the expense of their dress, masters and attendants yearly exceeds £8,000, which the Queen cannot be called upon to pay. She assures me every oeconomy is in the most rigid manner attended to; that for the present she does not ask for any additional attendants, but that she may receive £2,000 per quarter to discharge the regular expenses. . . . The Queen has desired me to acquaint Mr. Pitt that she actually exceeds her income £2,000 per quarter on account of the expenses of her six daughters, consequently the estimate relating to my children for this year must be:

	£
To the Queen, the increased expenses of the six princesses	8,000
Prince Frederick, Bishop of Osnabruck and Duke of York	5,000
Prince William.	3,500
„ Edward	2,500
„ Ernest	
„ Augustus }	3,500
„ Adolphus	
	£22,500

In 1737 the princesses Amelia, Caroline, Mary and Louisa had £19,271 1s. 1d.; so that the Queen will maintain six daughters for less than four were 49 years ago, when every article of life was cheaper than now. . . ."

"Queen's House, Sept. 22, 1786.

"The accounts from Holland yesterday have much affected me, as the great activity of Sir James Harris,[1] and his inclination

[1] For the policy of Sir James Harris (1746-1820), British Ambassador at The Hague, created Lord Malmesbury in 1788, see Rose, "William Pitt and National Revival," chs. xiii, xv, xvi.

to commit this country must draw us into difficulties, if great
caution and some temper is not shown in the answer to him.
I therefore wish to see Mr. Pitt at St. James's a little before
one this day, for it would be unjustifiable, when this country,
if she remains some years in peace, will regain her former wealth
and consideration, by being too meddling, should be drawn into
a fresh war which must bring on ruin, be it ever so prosperous."

"Windsor, Jan. 8, 1787.

"The dispatch Sir James Harris by the last mail notified
should soon be conveyed by Mr. Bouverie is arrived this day.
I therefore think it right not to delay till I see Mr. Pitt on
Wednesday communicating to him the letter I received this
morning from Lord Carmarthen and the copy of my answer;
but a very material additional difficulty occurs in the dispatch
of this day. Sir James sets the annual money that must at
present be issued for encouraging the party in the United States[1]
at twelve thousand per annum, and keeps a door open to demand
further sums. Where is this sum to be obtained, if the hazard it
may occasion of involving us in a war is risqued? Certainly it
cannot come from the Civil List. I have two younger sons
already of age who must be maintained at a much larger expense when they return to England, a third within two years
of manhood, and my daughters growing up; these considerations must, I think, make Mr. Pitt think twice before he enters
into a plan which the Foreign Secretary of State seems very
eagerly to encourage."

"Windsor, Feb. 17, 1787.

"The account just received, by Mr. Pitt's attention, of the fate
of Mr. Fox's motion respecting Portugal,[2] and the having by
eleven last night concluded the several resolutions on the Commercial Treaty with France, which secures the report on Monday, gives me the highest satisfaction, and the more so as it is
by the assiduity and temper shewn by Mr. Pitt that this great
business has been so rapidly and prosperously concluded."

"Windsor, April 21, 1787.

". . . Mr. Pitt's manner of stating the Budget afterwards left
no room for the Opposition to alledge any point worthy of the
attention of the House; and one cannot but with comfort reflect
that this country is now annually buying off one million of its

[1] *I.e.*, the United Provinces of the Netherlands.
[2] For keeping Portugal in a position commercially superior to that proposed for France in the Anglo-French treaty of September 1786, which came
into effect on 10th May, 1787.

debts, whilst France exceeds its peace establishment near six millions and seems not likely soon to adopt any plan either for diminishing its debts or even for reducing its expences within the bounds of its income."

"Windsor, May 6, 1787.

"I have just received Mr. Pitt's box and must begin with approving of his conduct in his interview this day with the Prince of Wales, but at the same time lamenting, if any person was present even at the first part of it, that so long a fellow as Mr. Sheridan should be the man pointed out as the Prince's adviser. Mr. Pitt knows my sentiments too well to expect I can consent to an increase of income: that can only be when the Prince of Wales is willing to marry: besides that has ever been the subject of dispute between us, and on that condition I should not think my honour considered in any apparent reconciliation. My idea is that, if the Prince of Wales will fairly state his debts, that there shall be a willingness to exonerate him from them; but that it must be done by installments not to affect the public too much; that if he will promise not only in future not to call for further relief either from me or the public, but that, being cleared of debt and consequently having his whole present income, will re-appoint his servants and give them injunctions and authority to keep his expences within his income, a reasonable sum may be allowed for finishing Carlton House with oeconomy, not on the former extravagant ideas. My mind is so agitated by the whole of this business that I cannot at present draw up the answer to the paper so neatly as I should wish, therefore desire Mr. Pitt will do it on these heads, and if he will send it me to-morrow, I will copy it, sign it and return it without loss of time. Lest Mr. Pitt should not have kept a copy of the paper signed by the Prince of Wales, I return the original that he may have it before him when he draws up the answer, but desire it may be returned to me with the draught (*sic*). I shall return the notes that have passed to-morrow, it being too late for me to take copies of them this night."

"Queen's House, May 11, 1787.

"However I may be desirous if the Prince of Wales will enable me to see him extricated of it, I must not act in a manner that either for example as a father, or that what I owe to my subjects, I would feel myself much to blame; I therefore desire Mr. Pitt will to-morrow consult those of the Ministers he has already apprised of the steps taken in this delicate business, and acquaint me then by a line what steps had best be taken to bring the business to some final conclusion, it must be either by Mr. Pitt inquiring whether there is no further lights to be gained, undoubtedly the state sent to him to-day is the most unsatisfactory, for it shows that every article of extravagance has been adopted; or he must lay them before me and the answer be framed accordingly. These are the thoughts that occur on a hasty perusal of these papers; indeed where there is so much obstinacy it is difficult to expect much good."

"Windsor, May 12, 1787.

"I approve of the proposed message to the Prince of Wales, and have therefore exactly copied it, but have not kept a copy, to save time. . . . It will be difficult for the Prince of Wales now to break off the negotiation, if he does it will be on the worst ground possible."

"Windsor, Wednesday, May 20, 1787.

"It would be disguising the truth very grossly if I did not mention to Mr. Pitt being very much dissatisfied with the Prince of Wales's having declined to re-examine his very exorbitant plan of an estimate for his future expenditure; but as Mr. Pitt seems to wish the £10,000 should be offered provided the other articles are complied [with], I have on that consideration alone copied the message. If Mr. Pitt can have an answer from the Prince of Wales early enough for the message to the House of Commons to be here at latest by nine to-morrow morning, I will then instantly sign it and return it. . . ."

[In letters of 21st and 24th May he further expresses his approbation of Pitt's conduct in this affair.]

"Windsor, Aug. 5, 1787.

"I have read with great satisfaction the two letters from Mr. Grenville, they are written in a clear and manly style, and shew him perfectly fit for the inquiry he is sent to procure.[1] I do not see any objection to the memorial proposed to be delivered to the States General, but cannot say I like the Princess of Orange's letter; what she means of any coolness between me and the Duke of Brunswick I am ignorant of any, for we never were nor never can be very cordial. . . ."

[On 6th August 1787 the King states his satisfaction that the Duke of Brunswick will command the Prussian forces in Holland, and his hope that full satisfaction will be procured for the insult to the Prussian Royal House.]

[1] In the Dutch Netherlands. William Windham Grenville (1759-1834) was Joint Paymaster of the Forces. He was created Lord Grenville in 1790.

"Windsor, Aug. 26, 1787.

" . . . I cannot help just expressing that the last letter from Sir James Harris confirms my opinion that he possesses *full intrigue* enough for a negociator, but that his nerves are so easily shaken that it is happy he never was placed in a military line."

"Windsor, Sept. 3, 1787.

" . . . Sir James Harris calling out for ships is most absurd, as well as any hint of the same kind from the Duke of Brunswick. If we keep France quiet, we enable the King of Prussia to have nothing to attend to but the Province of Holland. If we assisted with ships, France would have a right to oppose it and also to send troops; but this is so obvious, that I am ashamed almost to hint it."

"Windsor, Sept. 16, 1787.

" On returning to the Secretary of State's office the dispatch from Mr. Eden of the 13th, I cannot help accompanying it with a few lines to Mr. Pitt; though the language of Mr de Montmorin is so very *offensive* that I can scarcely mention it with *temper*. I disapprove of it and consequently cannot recommend it being *retorted*. We have held a fair conduct during the whole business, and France has been double to the greatest excess. I think they feel they cannot do much, and therefore from spleen indulge themselves in this unjustifiable language, which any one but Mr. Eden would have declined hearing, and still more reporting. I trust temper may still bring things into the line of negotiation; and while we are desirous of that, France should with politeness be told that we must stand by the United States [1] against the faction in the Province of Holland if France now persists in the idea now communicated of supporting it with arms. I suppose our ships, if Mr de Barthélemy's language shows France means to act without hearing further from us, ought to appear off the Dutch coast for a few days, which might decide measures previous to the arrival of any material force from France. Ought not some one instantly to go to France who might know better how to deal with Mr de Montmorin than Mr. Eden?" [2]

"Windsor, Sept. 21, 1787.

" It is impossible that any political event can give me more satisfaction than the account just received from the agent at Helvoetsluys, as I think it gives a fair prospect of this country escaping a war, and at the same time shew (*sic*) France that,

---

[1] *I.e.*, the United Provinces. For these events see Rose, " William Pitt and National Revival," ch. xv.

[2] Mr. Grenville was sent.

though England has no grasping ideas, that yet she is not of a temper tamely to let her rival succeed in her ambitious projects. I think Mr. Grenville's good judgment will make the negociation prosper, which will add to his own character as well as to that of his relation."

[On 8th October 1787 the King expresses regret that Amsterdam has not yet been reduced. He hopes that the States General will engage enough German troops to enable the Prussians to retire out of Holland. "The moment is certainly anxious, but I trust it will end prosperously." On 12th October 1787 he expresses concern at the reported plans of France against India; he will order four regiments for the Indian service to secure us against our "insiduous neighbours." On 11th December 1787 King again regrets Mr. Eden's weakness in listening to the threats of France, and wishes for a change at the Paris embassy. We need to be on our guard against France.]

[The following draft of an undated letter from Pitt to the King probably is of July—August 1788. Pitt's letter of 1st September 1788 to Grenville, is very similar to this. I have not found the King's reply. For the questions at issue, see Rose, *op. cit.*, pp. 491-9.]

"Mr. Pitt has had the honor of receiving Y. M.'s commands, and is extremely sorry to be under the necessity of troubling Y. M. in business of so much importance at the present moment. The accounts received from Berlin and the North seem to press for an early decision, and would make Mr. Pitt desirous to have the opportunity of personally submitting to Y. M. the ideas that occur to him before any answer is prepared to the Court of Berlin or any other steps proposed. He is almost afraid to mention the circumstance at present from the fear that it may be inconvenient before Y. M. is entirely recovered from the effects of your late indisposition. Y. M.'s servants in the Cabinet most of whom will probably be in town to-morrow morning are then to meet on this business. As far as Mr. Pitt can at present form an opinion upon it, it is that every attention should be used to prevent a war; that an explanation with Spain or possibly France may tend to that object; that both Denmark and Russia should be distinctly apprised of Y. M.'s having no other view but preserving the Balance of Power in the North, and of restoring peace on impartial and equitable terms; that at the same time the King of Prussia should be made acquainted with these sentiments, but be assured nevertheless of full support if it becomes necessary in consequence of the measures he has taken and of new events; and that provisional measures should be taken for that purpose in the way least likely to occasion expense or alarm. On these grounds there seems in the present situation of Europe great reason to expect that an object very important in itself might be secured with very little inconvenience or hazard."

[On 19th October 1788, the King censures the excess of zeal shown in the despatches of the ambassadors, Ewart and Elliott; but he hopes that, if the Emperor makes a separate peace with the Turks, a general pacification may result.]

PITT TO THE QUEEN (ON THE REGENCY)

"Downing Street, Dec. 31, 1788.

"Mr. Pitt humbly presumes to entreat Her Majesty's permission most respectfully to submit to Her M. the heads of the plan which Her M.'s confidential servants think it their duty to propose to Parliament for the administration of the Government during the present emergency. Those parts of it which relate to the power to be given to H.R.H. the Prince of Wales, and the limitations of that power will probably be proposed in the committee of the House of Commons on the state of the nation, to-morrow. A separate resolution will, it is conceived, be necessary on a subsequent day respecting the essential object of the care of His M.'s royal person, which important trust cannot with propriety or to the general satisfaction be executed under any direction but that of Her M. For that purpose it may be necessary that certain powers should be vested in Her M. by Parliament for the management of His M.'s household, and the direction of those attendant on the King's Person. It has occurred that there might possibly be a convenience, if it should meet with Her M.'s approbation, that a council should also be appointed in such way as Her M. may think proper, to act under Her M., and give this assistance and advice when Her M. may be pleased to require it. On these points it would be a great satisfaction to Mr. Pitt to be honoured with Her M.'s gracious commands; and, if it should not trespass improperly on Her M.'s goodness, Mr. Pitt would humbly request Her M.'s permission to pay his duty to Her M. at any time which Her M. may be graciously pleased to command."

[On 1st May 1789 the King expresses annoyance at the sudden return of his third son from the West Indies station—a proof that his own wishes will never be attended to. The Prince must now have the same allowance as the Duke of York. "I have but too much reason to expect no great comfort but an additional member to the opposite faction in my own family." He would like the Queen and his daughters secured in case he himself dies. His whole nervous system has sustained a great shock by the late illness.]

[On 14th, 16th, 17th January 1790 the King urgently requests Pitt's presence. On 19th January he requests that a frigate shall convey Prince Edward to Gibraltar. On 3rd March 1790 he expresses joy at the rejection of Fox's measure for the Repeal of the Corporation and Test Acts.]

"St. James's, March 28, 1790.

[The King regrets that the papers of the Cte. d'Artois and M. de Calonne contain so little real news about France.]

"Mr. Pitt's answer should be very civil, and may be very explicit as to no money, or other means, having been used to keep up the confusion in France, and M. de Calonne ought to convey those assurances wherever he thinks they may be of use.[1] In the present posture of affairs with Spain, I do not see we can take any step towards that Court, but, should that storm blow over, there cannot be any objection to assure her of our resolution not to prevent (*sic*) the French Constitution from being re-established on terms conformable to the sentiments of the Comte d'Artois."

"Queen's House, May 5, 1790.

"The proposed draft of the message to Parliament on the depredations and claims of the Court of Spain seems very well calculated for the unpleasant occasion; for it is a concise and fair narrative of what has as yet passed between the two Courts."[2]

[On 12th June 1790 the King states that members who have posts and offices for life do not always support Government as they should. On 18th June he compliments Pitt on his return for Cambridge University. On 30th March 1791 he expresses joy that the proposal to add to the Navy has been passed so handsomely.]

"Windsor, April 30, 1791.

"The placing Lord Grenville in the Foreign Department, where most ability as well as diligence is required, Mr. Pitt, by what I hinted must be certain would meet with my thorough approbation; as to Lord Cornwallis, I do not think he will accept of the Home Department when he returns from India, he having uniformly declared a disinclination to civil employment and keeping entirely to the military; but I do not mean by this that it is not worth while to place them [the seals?] in hands that they may without difficulty be given to his if agreeable when he returns. I therefore consent to Mr. Dundas's holding that Department; I suppose Mr. Pitt has weighed the proper method of granting a salary to Mr. Dundas when he holds only the

[1] Calonne was acting in England as the agent of the French Princes.
[2] For the dispute with Spain, see Rose, *op. cit.*, ch. xxv.

Indian Department. Lord Hawkesbury should certainly be called to the Cabinet when the arrangement takes place."[1]

"Queen's House, May 17, 1791.

"I return the messages to the two Houses of Parliament which I have signed, and lament extremely that the deficiency of the Civil List should arise from the payments to the younger branches of my family, as that expense must inevitably increase, and indeed is at this hour kept down by four sons being in foreign countries; besides, the debts incurred by Edward have never yet been satisfied, and I have at this hour a letter from the D. of York, which I will communicate to-morrow to Mr. Pitt, which shows he and William think with the strictest oeconomy they cannot keep within the sum allotted them, to which I have not yet returned any answer."

[On 6th June 1791 the King states he has received a memorial from the Prince of Wales about his debts. It is missing.]

"Windsor, January 29, 1792.

"The copy of the statement respecting the public revenue and commerce which I have just received from Mr. Pitt, I have cursorily cast eyes over, but sufficiently to think it will be an useful publication, and must prove a very agreeable information to those who wish the prosperity of this country; it seems to me drawn up in a shape to suit the attention of the present age, whose inclination does not like much discussion, and rather to have the matter entirely digested than any part left for the diligence of the reader to collect."

"Windsor, Feb. 18, 1792.

"The Resolutions moved yesterday by Mr. Pitt, and his account of their having passed unanimously (as they ought) gives me much satisfaction, as also the impudent line taken by Mr. Sheridan and Mr. Fox of shewing their disinclination, and not daring to oppose what every impartial man must esteem the most laudable plan that has been brought forward since the establishment of the Public Debt, as, at the same time that it gives ease to the poor, it looks forward to the assistance of posterity."

"Weymouth, Aug. 20, 1792.

"I cannot but think Mr. Pitt has judged right in seeing Lord Loughborough, as that will convince however [whoever?] were

[1] Henry Dundas (1742-1811), President of the Board of Control and Treasurer of the Navy. Lord Hawkesbury (1729-1808) did not then enter the Cabinet.

parties to the proposal brought by the Duke of Leeds that the scheme can never succeed; that the Duke of Portland was equally concerned with the former appeared clearly from his letter. . . ."

"Weymouth, Sept. 16, 1792.

[The King has received a letter from Pitt respecting the Prince of Wales's, which he thoroughly approves.]

[On 22nd January 1793 the King states that the division in the House of Commons will show its opinion on the great question then agitating Europe (peace or war). In a second letter of 22nd January 1793 he states that he has given eventual orders for a Hanoverian corps to be ready to start for Holland.]

"Queen's House, Jan. 24, 1793.

" As there will be no levee at St. James's to-morrow I desire Mr. Pitt will acquaint Mr. Dundas that the Privy Council for the additional sea-force is to be held here to-morrow at two, and that Lord Chatham may be apprized of it, as I wish then to see him."

[On 24th January 1793 the King sends a note as to the Hanoverian corps proposed for service in Holland: it is hoped half the corps may in eight weeks after Colonel Sporken's arrival there be in a state to march. In all there are 13,155 privates.]

"Queen's House, Feb. 20, 1793.

" I have given the necessary orders for the brigade of Foot Guards being prepared for embarkation, and hope, if Lord Chatham can furnish 44-gun ships to carry them from Gravesend to Flushing, that they may leave London on Monday. . . ."

"Queen's House, March 29, 1793.

" I return to Mr. Pitt the packet he received yesterday from the Duke of York, whose conduct since called forth into his present arduous situation has completely answered my most sanguine expectation, and I am most happy at perceiving his judgement and prudence are as conspicuous as his activity and intrepidity; these are not the sentiments alone of an affectionate father, but grounded on the basis of the propriety of his conduct. It is easy to see that the Prince of Coburg, though deserving every commendation for the activity and ability of his military conduct, is not void of negotiating qualities, and that, though it is impossible he should not be apprized that no concert as yet exists between this country and the two great German Courts on the best mode of repelling the French, yet he keeps calling both on the Duke of York and the Dutch as if he was empowered to call for unlimited assistance, and also states his own situation as much more perilous than can be the real fact.

"I think so far we may with safety concur as to authorize the moving of the English forces and the Hannoverians to Bergen-op-Zoom, and by that movement making a demonstration on the right of the Austrians, from whence they may advance to Antwerp; but, if it can be effected, the most advantageous step that can be taken and most conducive to shorten both the sea and land operations of France would be the English and combined forces, with some addition from the Dutch, getting possession of Dunkirk, as this would enable battering trains of artillery to be embarked in Holland and landed in the most advantageous situation for the Austrians to carry on regular sieges; this seems to me the real assistance that this country and Holland can give to the two German Powers, and to which extent I am ready to concur, but not to giving them the command of the combined army to be employed agreeably to their own plans or views."

"Windsor, April 9, 1793.

"I have just received Mr. Pitt's note accompanying the messages to the two Houses of Parliament, recommending the vote of credit, which I have signed. I cannot omit congratulating Mr. Pitt on the repeated providential events which, if the cause is well supported on the side of Flanders, must end most prosperously. My last letters from the Duke of York are equally as proper as the former, and show me he fully possesses my idea, that he is a separate corps to co-operate with the Austrians, not become a part of the Prince of Coburg's army. I therefore trust our accounts of the interview at Antwerp will be highly satisfactory.[1]

"Queen's House, June 7, 1793.

"By the note I have just received from Mr. Pitt I find the remains of his gout will not permit him to come out this day. I trust it has been of so regular a kind that he will find it only an effort of nature to secure him from some other illness that might have [been] less pleasant. . . . I am certain Mr. Pitt must agree with me in thinking that if anything was wanting to render the Opposition contemptible, the step on Tuesday of declaring Mr. Fox, at their meeting at the Crown and Anchor, insolvent, and opening a subscription to raise him an annuity compleats the career of this session."

---

[1] The Duke of York and Lord Auckland were conferring with the Prince of Coburg, Count Metternich, and the envoys of Prussia at Antwerp on the proposed military operations (8th April).

" I am glad to find the directions I have given for preventing anything unpleasant, or the chance of it, at Walmer Castle will encourage Mr. Pitt, when the situation of public business will permit, to go there, as it is really necessary for his health that he should have some relaxation.[1] By the letter I received on Friday from the siege of Valenciennes, I have reason to expect in the course of very few days that further plans for the campaign will be communicated by the Prince of Coburg; though they were touched upon, I thought it best to give no opinion till the Prince should have stated them on paper and consesequently till they can be thoroughly considered. The good news of the surrender of Condé will certainly accelerate the capture of Valenciennes."

"Windsor, Sept. 14, 1793.

" The misfortune of our situation is that we have too many objects to attend to, and our force consequently must be too small at each place; yet it seems to me that the Hessian infantry are the only corps we can soon get at to send to Toulon; but I fear Mr. Pitt overrates Lieut.-Gen. Beaulieu's corps; for it consists only of six regiments of infantry and six of cavalry, and that he is too sanguine in supposing the fresh Hessian corps can arrive early in October in Flanders, while I fear it cannot reach that destination before the beginning of November. I am clear the seven battalions intended for the West Indies are much better in Flanders until the arrival of the fresh corps of Hessians, and upon the whole authorize Mr. Pitt to have the dispatches written agreeable to the plans he has sent me this evening."

"Windsor, Nov. 17, 1793.

" Having conversed the last evening with Field-Marshal Freytag, whether any good German troops could be obtained in addition to those at present in British pay, he has suggested those of the Elector of Saxony, which he thinks might amount to 12,000. I do not chuse to take any step without knowing whether Mr. Pitt thinks the measure advisable; if he is of that opinion, I will through the Hannoverian Minister find out whether the measure would be likely to succeed, previous to directing Mr. Elliott to make any proposal to the Elector.

" Mr. Dundas sent me this morning Mr. Pitt's sentiments on the unfavourable situation of Toulon. I quite agree that the West India expedition, as far as offensive measures of consequence, must be deferred until the next autumn, provided 3,000

---

[1] The King had ordered the strengthening of the fosse at Walmer Castle and the stationing of a picket there.

be sent to strengthen the forces in that part of the world, and the rest of the force to be sent to Toulon, to defend that position; but the attempting more in that quarter I do not think advisable unless a plan of operations can be formed which would enable General Devins[1] with the Austrians and Neapolitans to make a diversion on some other point, and the Spaniards to take a similar line of conduct; then our army on the center might be of utility; but on the whole, as to active service I incline much more to Flanders as being more easily supplied from hence, and also, if enabled to move forward, being more able to advance to Paris."

"Queen's House, Dec. 5, 1793.

"Mr. Pitt's note is just arrived. I am sorry there is any idea of still farther lessening the force on the side of Flanders: if it must be done, I agree to its being of British troops, but can by no means consent that any of my Hannoverians shall be employed but in Flanders. I send this directly, that any arrangement may be effected, without expecting from me what I on many accounts will never consent to."

"Windsor, April 1, 1794.

[News of arrival of the Emperor at headquarters of Prince of Coburg on 15th March. Lord Elgin is to meet him, and is to be instructed exactly what to state, as the Emperor "is apt not to be too clear in his relations."]

"The account of Marshal Mellendorf's (*sic*) intention not to detach more troops till he hears farther from Berlin is also highly material; I own, the idea of drawing all the Prussian troops together and acting independent of the Imperialists, I look upon as a most fortunate measure if our treaty is concluded.[2] Rival Powers never act well together; separate, the successes of each will stimulate and be advantageous to the cause."

"Windsor, April 28, 1794.

"I have signed with great pleasure the messages to the two Houses of Parliament which Mr. Pitt has sent to me to communicate the treaty with Prussia and Convention with the States-General, although perhaps a little more firmness in Ld. Malmesbury's manner of treating might have in some particulars rendered the terms more advantageous; but as the main object is so essential, I think it best not to look out for any objections."

[1] General Devins commanded the Allies operating in the Maritime Alps.
[2] The treaty which Lord Malmesbury was negotiating with Prussia. For these events see Rose, "William Pitt and the Great War," pp. 198-208.

"Windsor, May 18, 1794.

[The King censures the conduct of the faction in the House of Commons for opposing the suspension of Habeas Corpus; but]

"it will put the personal behaviour of persons (*sic*) in so conspicuous a light that good may come of it. Should the same spirit be shown by those of that party in the House of Lords, I should not be surprised if the suspension of Habeas Corpus does not come till Wednesday for my assent."

"Windsor, July 10, 1794.

"I am much pleased at finding by Mr. Pitt's letter that Mr. Sec.y. Dundas's conduct is so proper; I wish the Duke of Portland had not occasion'd this difficulty, as I think the mode of dividing the offices as proposed by me was much better. . . ." [1]

"Windsor, August 5, 1794.

"I am much pleased at Mr. Pitt's having [sent?] a copy of the proposed distribution of the British forces, and his ideas on the necessity of using every reasonable exertion to increase our present numbers. I shall certainly duly consider it, and by this assistance be able to discuss the subject fully with Lord Amherst to-morrow, that no time may be lost in forming such a plan as may be the least open to objections, at the same time most likely to obtain the desired effect without material inconvenience."

PITT TO THE KING

[August 24, 1794?]

"On a full consideration of the state of the negotiation with Austria, and of the urgent circumstances of the present crisis, Y. M.'s servants have been unanimously led to an opinion, the general grounds of which Mr. Pitt humbly begs permission to submit to Y. M. in the accompanying paper. [2]

"On an occasion of so much importance he relies on Y. M.'s accustomed goodness and indulgence to excuse his troubling Y. M. so much at large with the sentiments which have, on the fullest reflection, presented themselves to his mind, and he trusts Y. M. will be sensible that the opinion which he ventures to lay before Y. M. can arise from no other possible sentiments but those of zeal and anxiety for Y. M.'s service in so important

[1] See Rose, "William Pitt and the Great War," pp. 191, 270.

[2] This paper I have not found; but probably it is of the same purport as Pitt's letter of August 24, 1794 to the Marquis Cornwallis (see *ibid.*, pp. 214-5, and "Cornwallis Corresp.," ii, 259). Windham was Secretary-at-War.

and critical a period. If he receives Y. M.'s permission, he would be desirous of transmitting to the Duke of York a copy of the paper itself; and he has a full persuasion that, if he should not appear to H.R.H. mistaken in his opinion, of the advantage which w^d. result to Y. M.'s service from the arrangement suggested, that consideration will ensure it H.R.H.'s cordial approbation. Should Y. M. not disapprove of the outlines of the measure, supposing it to prove satisfactory to H.R.H., Mr. Pitt would immediately take the liberty of writing to him on the subject. And, as some personal and confidential conversation on the points in question might be satisfactory to H.R.H. and in every respect desirable, Mr. Windham (whom H.R.H. has honoured with habits of intercourse) has offered, if Y. M. approves of it, to go directly to H.R.H.'s headquarters for that purpose.

"Mr. Pitt is fully sensible of the delicacy and importance of the subject, but he has felt it an indispensable duty to submit to Y. M. all that has occurred to him upon it, feeling thoroughly persuaded (on the best consideration he can give to the question) that the present circumstances admit of no other expedient which will give a reasonable hope of conducting our present arduous struggle to a safe and honourable issue."

"Weymouth, Sept. 5, 1794.

I have received Mr. Pitt's note enclosing the letter he has received from Mr. Burke: misfortunes are the great softeners of the human mind, and has (*sic*) in the instance of this distressed man made him own what his warmth of temper would not have allowed in other circumstances, viz., that he may have erred. One quality I take him to be very susceptible of, that is gratitude, which I think covers many failings and make me therefore happy at being able to relieve him: his chusing the pension to be settled on his wife I thoroughly approve of, and it will with the better grace enable the other pension to be settled on him."

"Weymouth, Sept. 10, 1794.

"I have this morning received Mr. Pitt's note, accompanied by the letters to him from the Duke of York and Mr. Wyndham; as to the first it does honour to the head and heart of my son in the most trying situation he could have been placed, and must make me willing to embrace either of the propositions, either the leaving the command to Genl. Clairfait assisted by L^t.-Genl. Beaulieu, if he succeeds in regaining Austrian Flanders, or in (*sic*) the appointment of the Archduke Charles with proper assistants, as then my son will retain the command of the troops in British pay. The letter of Mr. Wyndham Mr. Pitt will see, by what I have already suggested, meets with my thorough approbation except in one article—his supposing so absurd an idea could have arisen here as the giving the Marquis Cornwallis a local commission of Field Marshal, prior to knowing whether the Emperor will accept him as Commander-in-Chief of the allied army."

"Weymouth, Sept. 19, 1794.

"My opinion perfectly coincides with the opinion transmitted by Mr. Pitt on the letter he has received from the Prince de Condé; the advance solicited must be advanced, and I agree in thinking that this opening of a correspondence with him should be kept up, if possible, to get him out of the possession of the Austrians. He is certainly the best man we could employ at the head of the royalists; but I fear we must have with the British troops employed there some one less fond of making appeals to the public in newspapers than the Irish Earl,[1] now nominally intended for that service: the Secretary-at-War's hint is strongly confirmed by what we have since seen."

"Windsor, Oct. 12, 1794.

"Mr. Pitt's letter has been this instant received, but as the state of public affairs, I may say, fills up every crevice of my mind, I am able instantly to answer its contents: I entirely agree with him in opinion that, even should the Dutch be roused to suitable exertions, no great hope of success can be expected unless they will consent to be directed in the mode of employing those efforts suitably. I know I can answer for the zeal and good sense of my son, the Duke of York, that, to obtain so desirable an event, he will gladly consent that the Duke of Brunswick should be invited to come and take the supreme command of the allied army in the same manner the late Prince Ferdinand of Brunswick stood in the last German war, which gave no interference in the interior arrangements of the separate troops that composed his army: thus my son's commission for commanding the British and Hannoverian troops would not be infringed on, and the Hereditary Prince of Orange would still be at the head of the Dutch. Should the Duke of Brunswick decline, I do not see any other mode of forming a Council of War than the offering the Prince of Orange himself to be at the head of it, which (though the natural place of the Stadtholder in time of danger) he will decline; then I must insist on my son holding that situation with such men as Genl. Walmoden, Sir W[m]. Erskine, Lieut[t].-Genl. Abercrombie, and such other foreign, as well

---

[1] The Earl of Moira (1754-1836), who was designed for service on the coast of Brittany or La Vendée.

as national officers, as it may be thought right to place such trust in, with perhaps the assistance of some civil man for conducting the arrangements with the Dutch. It occurred to me that Mr. Wyndham might be one of the properest persons for such a commission."

THE KING TO THE EARL OF MANSFIELD.

"Windsor, Nov. 13, 1794.

". . . I have reason to imagine that it would be very pleasing to the Earl Fitzwilliam to be appointed Lord Lieutenant of Ireland; and considering the very handsome manner in which he has come forward in the present unfavourable times, I cannot but with pleasure gratify him in this wish, provided I can arrange a suitable and honourable situation for the Earl of Westmoreland: it has, therefore, occurred to me to place the Earl of Mansfield as President of the Council if he will assist in forming such arrangement by resigning his Scotch employment."

[The King then proposed to grant the reversion of a Scotch office to one of the Earl's sons. To this Lord Mansfield assented on 13th November.]

"Windsor, Nov. 14, 1794.

[The King refers to the Earl of Mansfield's consent, and adds:]

"This will enable Mr. Pitt to fix the Lord Lieutenancy of Ireland with Earl Fitzwilliam, to write in consequence to the Earl of Westmoreland my intention of appointing him Master of the Horse when he arrives in England, and settling with the Earl of Mansfield the reversionary office in Scotland for Mr. George Murray."[1]

[*Draft.*]   PITT TO THE KING.[2]

"Hollwood, Sunday, Nov. 23, 1794.

"Mr. Pitt trusts Y. M. will do him the justice to believe that he can never have a more painful task to execute than when he finds himself under the necessity of submitting any opinion to Y. M. which is likely to create the smallest uneasiness and anxiety in Y. M.'s mind. On the present occasion he is aware

[1] Son of the Earl of Mansfield. For these matters see the foregoing essay—"Pitt and Earl Fitzwilliam."

[2] The draft of this important letter was overlooked by Stanhope (II App., p. xxi). For the question see Rose, "William Pitt and the Great War," p. 215.

that the subject to which he wishes to solicit Y. M.'s attention, is one of the greatest delicacy, and the most interesting to Y. M.'s feelings. But it appears to him to be at the same time too nearly connected with Y. M.'s service to make it possible for him to suppress his sentiments upon it without proving himself unworthy of the confidence with which Y. M. has so long condescended to honour him and without sacrificing his duty to Y. M. and the Public.

"It is hardly necessary to state how much the interests of Y. M.'s dominions and of all Europe depend upon the issue of the present crisis in the situation of the United Provinces. It is obvious, too, that, supposing the negotiation between the Dutch Government and France to proceed, the chief hope of their obtaining the terms which have been held out to them, or any others, consistent even with their temporary safety must depend on effectual steps being taken during the negotiation to shew that, in case of its failure, they are prepared to defend themselves with vigour. On the other hand, if the negotiation is broken off, the utmost exertions are evidently indispensable both with a view to their immediate safety, and to any plan of operations in the next campaign. Nothing, therefore, can be of more pressing necessity than to take every measure which can be likely to encourage such exertions.

"The languor and indifference of a great part of the [Dutch] nation, and the disaffection of others towards the subsisting Government are obstacles which, perhaps, cannot be entirely overcome. But their effect is certainly heightened by other causes. It is too evident how little harmony subsists between Y. M.'s troops and those of the Republic. The inhabitants at large, instead of looking at the former as their protectors, have conceived an impression of their want of discipline and order which represented to make their approach as much dreaded in many places as that of the enemy. These sentiments are not confined to the lower orders of the people, but are entertained in a greater or less degree by persons of the first weight and consideration.

It cannot be disguised (however painful it is to be under the necessity of stating it) that these impressions with respect to the army affect in some degree the public opinion with respect to the commander. It is indeed impossible that the zeal and meritorious exertions of the Duke of York should be disputed by anyone who has the opportunity of being accurately informed of his personal conduct. But the general impression is formed on other grounds; and even those who know in how many respects he is entitled to praise, are not without apprehension that the want of experience and of habits of detail may have made it impossible for him to discharge all the complicated duties of his situation, and effectually to prevent or remedy the abuses and evils which have crept into the service. In addition to these circumstances, which relate to the interior management of the army, it is also evident that the relative situation of the Duke of York and of the Prince of Orange too naturally leads to occasions of jealousy and misunderstanding. There exists nowhere a sufficient confidence in the general direction of military operations. This circumstance would of itself be sufficient to check and discourage effectual exertions, and the Duke of York is left to contend with these disadvantages, in a situation which would of itself be difficult and arduous to the most experienced general possessing the most unlimited confidence of those with whom he is to act.

"Under these circumstances Mr. Pitt is reluctantly compelled to submit to Y. M. his deliberate opinion that the continuance of the Duke of York in the command can be attended only with the most disadvantageous consequences to H.R.H. himself; and that, considering the prejudices which he has to encounter, there is little prospect of his having the benefit of that hearty co-operation on the part of the Dutch which is so necessary at the present crisis. On these grounds alone Mr. Pitt would humbly implore Y.M. to put an end to the Duke of York's command for the sake of H.R.H. as well as that of the country.

"But it is not in Holland only that the public impression is to be considered. It is impossible to say how far this impression, if it is not removed, may operate in Parliament and in the Public (*sic*) to the disadvantage of Y. M.'s Government, and possibly to the obstruction of the vigorous prosecution of the war. At all events Mr. Pitt ought not to conceal from Y. M. that it will be impossible to prevent this subject from being brought into Parliamentary discussion; and he need not observe how much that circumstance would augment the difficulty either of H.R.H. retaining or of his relinquishing the command. Mr. Pitt has, in one respect, the less regret in finding himself obliged to state these considerations at the present moment, from a persuasion that, even if they were out of the question, the course of the war would of itself probably prevent the Duke of York's command from being of very long duration, at least to its present extent.

"It seems every day more and more evident that the period is approaching when a junction may be attempted with the royalists in the maritime provinces of France, and that the only chance of any decisive success from active operations will arise from directing the principal exertions of Y. M.'s arms to that quarter. If this opinion should, upon due consideration, appear to be well founded, Mr. Pitt knows that Y. M. feels too much the importance of all the interests which are at stake, to suffer any considerations of a personal nature to interfere with so essential an object; and he cannot doubt that the Duke of York's magnanimity and his zeal for Y. M.'s service, would make him enter warmly into the same feelings.

"Mr. Pitt trusts the importance of the occasion will be an apology for his trespassing so long on Y. M.'s indulgence. He is aware of the repugnance which Y. M. may naturally feel in the first moment to a measure which nothing but a sense of indispensible duty and the most anxious concern for Y. M.'s service would have led him to propose. If, on considering the reasons which he has taken the liberty of urging, Y. M. should be pleased to approve of the Duke of York's withdrawal from the command, it will remain to consider in what manner the measure may be adopted with the greatest attention to the wishes and feelings of the Duke of York. If the armies on each side should soon take up their winter quarters, or if events should lead to dividing Y. M.'s force according to the plan lately transmitted by H.R.H., either of those circumstances might naturally furnish an opening for H.R.H. coming home on leave of absence; in which case the command of the Hanoverians would probably devolve upon Gen¹. Walmoden, and it might perhaps not be difficult to manage that the British should be placed under the command of Gen¹. Abercrombie, who seems to stand higher than any other officer in general opinion.

"Mr. Pitt would have performed but in part the painful duty which he has undertaken if he omitted to state that in this country many persons, the most attached to Y. M.'s Government, and the most eager for the vigorous prosecution of the war, cannot suppress their anxiety on this subject. It seems generally felt that, when the Duke of York was originally appointed to the command, it was under circumstances in which he would naturally act in conjunction with officers of the first military reputation, with whom the chief direction of operations would naturally rest. But by the course of events he is now placed in a situation where the chief burden rests upon himself, and where his conduct alone may decide on the fate of Holland, and perhaps on the success of the war. Such a risk appears to be too great to remain committed to talents, however distinguished, which have not the benefit of long experience, and which cannot therefore be expected at such a time to command general confidence."

[The King's reply of 24th November is quoted in part by Stanhope ("Pitt," vol. ii, App., pp. xxi, xxii). It states that the King is much hurt by Pitt's letter, as the Duke of York saved Holland in 1793, and the present situation was due to "the conduct of Austria, the faithlessness of Prussia, and the cowardice of the Dutch." Nevertheless, he will not veto the proposal for the recall of the Duke of York, which is brought about by the "torrent of abuse" poured on him. These sentences follow.]

"... Having no longer a son at the head of the army on the Continent, I shall certainly not confer the command of the Hannoverians on any other general than Gen¹ Walmoden; and if there is any intention of drawing from the army on the Continent troops to embark for France, Mr. Pitt must remember I from the beginning of the war declared my Hannoverians could not be employed on that service. They must therefore either remain to defend Germany against the French, if this country will keep up an army on that side, or be allowed to return home. I owe from this hour I despair of any effectual measure against France; for if our attention is only taken up to the North and West, or that only on the East the appearance, not an efficient army, is kept up, I fear no good will follow such an half measure."

PITT TO THE KING

"Nov. 26, 1794.

"Mr. Pitt did not trouble Y. M. this morning on the subject on which he had so lately submitted his opinion to Y. M., conceiving from the answer which Y. M. honoured him with that Y. M. did not wish to enter into any particular description of it. Mr. Dundas now submits to Y. M. a draft of a despatch to the Duke of York conformable to that opinion. On the subject itself it is impossible for Mr. Pitt to add anything to what he has already stated except to express the satisfaction he derives from observing that Y. M. does justice to the motives which led to the representation which he humbly submitted to Y. M."

"Queen's House, Nov. 27, 1794.

"There could have been no advantage in discussing with Mr. Pitt yesterday the subject of his letter, as I had, though reluctantly, assented to his proposal. I have written to my son simply that the present complication of affairs required his presence here, but thought it more advisable not to enter any farther as to the end this business may take."

[Draft.]   PITT TO THE KING

"December 8, 1794.

"Mr. Pitt is persuaded that Y. M. will not be surprised if the present situation of affairs has made [him] look with additional anxiety to all the departments of Y. M.'s Government. This consideration leads him to submit to Y. M. that he certainly cannot mention without the sacrifice of personal feelings very near his heart, but which must give way to an indispensible duty. He has also the satisfaction to feel (after much anxiety) that what he has to propose may with Y. M.'s approbation be arranged without further difficulty or uneasiness. A variety of circumstances has made it impossible for him on full reflection not to feel (however reluctantly) that the intercourse between the Admiralty and the other Departments of Government, and even with himself, cannot be satisfactorily or usefully carried on on its present footing, and that, notwithstanding the objections to any change in an active Department in time of war, some new arrangement is become indispensibly necessary. The experience of Y. M.'s goodness both to Lord Chatham as well as to himself would prevent his having any scruple in stating to Y. M. the considerations which have led him to this opinion and of which he is sure Y. M. will feel the force. They are such as do not diminish the personal affection likely to subsist between persons who have felt it so long. He makes it his humble and most earnest request to Y. M. to permit him to propose that Lord Spencer and Lord Chatham should exchange their present situations.[1] He has ascertained that Lord Spencer will not decline coming to the Admiralty if it is thought advantageous to the public service. Lord Chatham would probably not feel it satisfactory to him to accept the Privy Seal unless Y. M. has the condescension and goodness to intimate a wish that he should receive it as a mark of Y. M.'s gracious approbation of his past conduct; and if it is not presuming too much on Y. M.'s indulgence, Mr. Pitt would beg leave to suggest that a letter from Y. M. to Lord Chatham, mentioning the arrangement as having been suggested by Mr. Pitt for the convenience of Government, and expressing a wish that he should take the Privy Seal on those grounds, would remove every difficulty; and if Y. M. should find it convenient to send the letter to-morrow, Mr. Pitt would be enabled to receive Y. M.'s commands on Wednesday and the arrangement might take effect the next week."

"Windsor, Dec. 9, 1794.

" Mr. Pitt will not be surprised that I did not expect his application for a change of Departments between the Earls of Spencer and Chatham, as I had flattered myself the intercourse between the Admiralty and the other Departments of Government had of late been on a more pleasant footing, and had not been apprized that some fresh difficulties on that head have arisen. No one is more convinced of the politeness and

[1] Lord Chatham became First Lord of the Admiralty in 1788: Lord Spencer became Lord Privy Seal in July 1794.

prudence of the Earl of Chatham, and would more unwillingly countenance what may be disagreeable to him; but, as Mr. Pitt assures me that he is willing to come into the proposed arrangement, provided he is encouraged in it by me, and as I have a very high opinion of the Earl of Spencer being the person most proper to succeed him, I will instantly write to the Earl of Chatham in a manner to make him cordially accept the proposed change."

[On 23rd December 1794 the King urges the need of the King's Speech being such as to show the determined resolve of this country to prosecute a war, "that every tye of Religion, Morality and Society not only authorizes but demands." This is especially needful after the conduct of the King of Prussia and "of the tame Dutch." On 24th December the King warmly approves Pitt's draft of the King's Speech— "the language runs so easy that I much wish it may not be altered." The exertions of the yeomanry and volunteers should be noticed.]

"Windsor, Jan. 14, 1795.

[Need of great caution for plans of campaign if the rest of Holland is to be saved. Danger to the army if moved to the right.]

" I think the only step to be taken is to permit the whole remains of the army to move to the left and retire to Germany, from whence they can return to Holland if, with Austria, a sufficient army can be formed to drive the French in the spring from thence."

[If not, the British troops might then embark for home *viâ* Emden or the Weser.]

"Queen's House, Jan. 29, 1795.

[First part as in Stanhope, ii, App., p. xxii. There occurs the sentence at end:]

" I wish also to mention the great change that seems coming forward in Ireland without the smallest attention to what was understood on the departure of Lord Fitzwilliam."

[On 3rd March 1795 the King doubts whether in the present temper of Parliament any subsidy could be obtained for the King of Prussia. As to Austrian troops, they should, if possible, act on the Dutch frontier and be commanded by Prince Hohenlohe. Clerfait was far too cautious, as the Duke of York had often observed. He adds a P.S.:]

" I am glad the Lord Lieutenant [1] has taken the determination of retiring; for his conduct from the commencement of his arrival in Ireland has been subversive of every principle of good

[1] Earl Fitzwilliam.

government, and, I believe, unwarrantable by the sound laws
both passed in this country and even by Yelverton's law passed
some few years past in Ireland."

[On 8th March 1795 the King strongly approves Pitt's sentiments
about the West of Germany, also the minute for Cabinet meeting. He
hopes that the Duke of Brunswick will command the proposed Prussian
army and the British and subsidized forces there, though the interior
direction of the latter would rest with the senior general of each of the
nations as heretofore.

On 29th March 1795 the King states he is staggered by the dis-
creditable conduct of the King of Prussia. There seems a prospect that
the French will overrun all N. Germany. On 5th April 1795 he says
that Hanover will be left open unless the Prussians can be led to stand
forth, and they must be induced to do so if possible. On the 17th he
terms the Treaty of Basle "a highly blameable measure."

On 19th May 1795 the King informs Pitt of his interview with the
Prince of Wales; he had assured him that the whole plan for managing
the Prince of Wales's debts originated with Pitt, who would certainly
not now retract on that matter and yield "to the insiduous and demo-
cratical proposition of Mr. Fox." The proposed alienation of the
Duchy of Cornwall would be resisted by Pitt.

On 29th May 1795 the King expresses a hope that Pitt will carry
through the measure respecting the Prince of Wales's debts as nearly as
possible in the form first proposed; "but any regulation to prevent
future debt is wise and proper." On 30th May he urges Pitt to take all
possible steps to secure a favourable division on Monday next on that
question.]

"Windsor, June 6, 1795.

"I have received Mr. Pitt's on the propositions and advance-
ment of the business in the House of Commons for arranging
the debts of the Prince of Wales and his future establishment;
but I am sorry with reason to observe that at times there appears too much the narrow principles of a commercial country
than the elevated sentiments of a great State, and at this hour
in great affluence."

THE KING TO DUNDAS

"Weymouth, Sept. 9, 1795.

"Mr. Secretary Dundas cannot be surprised at my having
read the Minute of Cabinet of the 7th this morning with some
degree of pain: the proposition of withdrawing the British
cavalry from Germany plainly shows that this Kingdom no
farther concerns itself in the fate of the Empire,, which I suppose will naturally drive the Emperor into such measures as
may end the contest there with France. It certainly puts my
Electoral Dominions into a most perilous situation, and must of

necessity make me in my electoral capacity submit to the Prussian neutrality and then I cannot, with safety to the original possessions of my forefathers, consent to leave any of my Hannoverian infantry in British pay, as the object is to employ them out of Germany, where it will be my duty to keep as many national troops as I can to withstand as long as possible the evils that must attend the present unhappy proposition."

[On 13th September 1795, owing to the threat of the French that they will attack Hanover unless the corps of *émigrés* there is dissolved, the King orders Dundas that it shall be removed, but gives no order regarding the British cavalry there. On 30th October 1795 he writes: ". . . England is but now in a situation, if the war is prosecuted with vigour, to place France in the predicament of suing for peace. The times may be difficult but with energy cannot fail of success."]

"Windsor, Nov. 11, 1795.

"The House of Commons having by so handsome a majority approved of bringing in a Bill for more effectually preventing seditious meetings and assemblies cannot but give me the greatest pleasure as the most convincing proof of attachment to our happy constitution."

"Queen's House, Jan. 27, 1796.

"It is but natural that I should feel much interested that every measure of magnitude should be well weighed previous to any decision being adopted. I have therefore put on paper the objections that seem to me most conclusive against any step being taken to open a negotiation of peace with France, of which I have taken a copy, which I desire to deposit in the hands of Mr. Pitt."

Enclosure. "Queen's House, Jan. 27, 1796.

"The allusion in the Speech at the opening of this Session of Parliament to a desire of making peace which was renewed in Dec' by the messages to both Houses of Parliament, though well calculated to stave off any evil impression which Opposition might create in the minds of some over tender friends of Government in the House of Commons, were perhaps useful steps at home, though certainly of a nature to cause some uneasiness to our Allies on the Continent and to damp the risings in the interior of France. I think myself compelled by the magnitude of the subject to state my sentiments, on the supposition that the idea of negotiation may again be brought forward, without waiting the issue of the great armament which has been sent to the West Indies under the command of Sir Ralph Abercromby. This I do with the greater ease at the present moment,

when I am persuaded none of my Ministers can seriously look
on this as the proper time for entering on the consideration of
that subject, and consequently that my ideas may [be] of more
use, they having as yet not fully weighed the objections which
appear to me well grounded for rendering the present period
particularly improper for attempting to set any negotiation on
foot. The great force which has been collected and sent to the
West Indies, to which I have already alluded; the additions to
be sent on the first change of wind and in the month of March
ought to have sufficient time allowed for it to be seen what
success may be obtained in that part of the globe. I perhaps am
too sanguine, but I really expect it may secure the possession of
St. Domingo, without which acquisition I cannot think our possessions in the islands secure, and that peace can be but of short
duration.

"The further successes in the E. Indies, which cannot but be
expected, are additional reasons not to hamper ourselves with
a negotiation. We are trying to persuade both the Courts of
Vienna and Petersburg to come forward and commence an
early campaign. How fruitless must be the attempt if we open
any negotiation for peace; we cannot honourably move without
first giving them notice, which will be a solid cause for their
waiting the issue of the measure prior to making preparations
which cannot be effected without expense.

"In addition to these weighty reasons, the present state of
France points out that no better agent can be employed to effect
our purposes than time: the ill success of the forced loan, and
further discrediting the Assignats must soon overwhelm the
new modelled Government; the conduct of the Republican
armies both within France as well as those employed in Germany and Italy will then appear, as well as the increasing discontent in the country. Every one of these disasters can alone
be averted by our proposing Peace, which would give a moment-
ary weight to the Executive Government of France, and put a
stop to the various engines that seem now to threaten the down-
fall of that horrid fabric, established on the avowed foundation
of the dereliction of all religious, moral, and social principles. I
wished to have stated my sentiments in fewer words, but the
subject would not admit of it."

[For Pitt's reply see Stanhope, ii, *ad fin.*]

[On 19th February 1795 the King forwards to Pitt a copy of his reply
to the Prince of Wales, expressing regret that he has been disturbed by
his creditors; for he is "interested in whatsoever regards you and the
dear little infant." The King advises the Prince to select a man of rank
and legal knowledge (*e.g.*, Lord Thurlow) to examine the whole subject.]

"Queen's House, Feb. 27, 1796.

"It is a fixed opinion with me that when Opposition bring forward questions of a personal and embarrassing kind, that they ought not to be got rid of by a previous question, but by a direct rejection or the taking of the business out of their hands by substituting an approbation of the measure objected." [He therefore is glad of the recent division.]

"Windsor, April 9, 1796.

"It is with pleasure I find by Mr. Pitt's Note that the motion for a committee to inquire into the expenditure on account of barracks has been rejected by a majority of 97 to 23. I cannot conclude without expressing the relief to my mind occasioned by the exorbitant demands of the enemy, which must close all ideas of peace till brought to more rational ones; the Note itself, I thought, went to the strangest excess, but the papers I have just read from Mr. Wickham, explaining that Savoy and the West India Islands have now been declared in the National Assembly as indivisible from the rest of the Republic, convince me that my suspicions were not exaggerated. This, when known, must rouse the tamest in this country. What a moment for Opposition! But, thank God, there is not wisdom enough to be found there to make that step be adopted which would in some degree wipe out the former ill conduct. I am not afraid to pronounce Opposition will remain Jacobins."

[On 19th April 1796 the King warmly approves Pitt's financial statement, which will show the vast resources of the country.]

"Windsor, Sept. 21, 1796.

"I desire Mr. Pitt will give notice for holding a Privy Council in the Great Room at St. James's this day, when I shall with the utmost pleasure nominate the Earl of Chatham President, and give such orders as are necessary, particularly the embargo on Spanish ships, which ought most certainly not to be delayed. The real confusion of the French in their retreat seems to give every reason to believe the Dutch account, that the French army is nearly destroyed, tho' I should doubt whether Jourdan could collect his broken army to make any stand on the 8th against the Austrians."

[On 2nd March 1797 the King gently reproves Pitt for too much compliance with Opposition, and allowing a measure to be changed.]

"My nature is quite different. I never assent till I am convinced what is proposed is right, and then I keep; then I never allow that to be destroyed by afterthoughts, which on all sub-jects tend to weaken, never to strengthen, the original pro-posal." [1]

"Queen's House, March 24, 1797.

"It is highly unprincipled to be suggesting such motions as the one produced in the House of Lords by Lord Moira and re-echoed by Mr. Fox yesterday in the House of Commons; and tho' the majorities on both occasions have been very creditable, every well-wisher to the Empire must feel hurt that the minorities were so large."

"Queen's House, May 2, [1797].

"I am happy to find by Mr. Pitt's note of last night that the Austrian loan received the sanction of the Committee of Supply by 193 to 50, though I fear the period is too late to enable Austria to withstand the unreasonable demands of France. The letter from Vienna of the last part clearly shows that Buona Parte has no power to offer terms, consequently that his plan was, either that Vienna should offer to submit to whatever the Directory might propose, or to trust to a disturbance in Vienna, which might effect the same object."

"Windsor, May 24, 1797.

"Every friend of the British constitution must rejoice at the decided majority the last evening for resisting the motion of Mr. Fox for the repeal of the two Bills respecting Treason and Sedition, and not less to find so many country gentlemen zealously step forward on every occasion to give a support that shows they feel the blessings they enjoy."

"Queen's House, May 27, 1797.

"After what has been repeated for some days, I had supposed that the division against Mr. Fox's motion for a Reform of Par-liament would have been as large as stated, but the minority less; but his art has succeeded in keeping his party together; and, of course, some speculative men, as on former occasions, have joined him in this vote, many of whom probably were solely biassed from desire of a little apparent consequence; but I am certain every freeholder in the kingdom, as well as the inhabitants of boroughs, must feel their consequence hurt by the proposal."

[1] It is not easy to say to what the King refers. In the debate of March 1 on the Bank Crisis, Pitt successfully resisted the motion of Fox for an "un-limited" inquiry into the relations of Government to the Bank (see Parl. Hist., xxxii, 1524-1562).

[*Copy*.]   PITT TO THE KING.

"Downing St., Friday, June 16, 1797.

" Mr. Pitt feels it his duty to submit to Y[our] M[ajesty] the
minute of Cabinet transmitted herewith and the draft of an
official note to which it refers. It is matter of no small concern
to him that the minute is, as Y. M. will observe, accompanied by a
dissent from Lord Grenville. It appeared, however, after repeated
and long discussion to the majority of Y. M.'s servants, that it
was not possible to adopt any line more conformable to what
Lord Grenville will probably state to Y. M. to have been his
sentiments on the occasion. Mr. Pitt has the firmest conviction
that, after the steps already adopted (and, as he thinks, necessarily and properly) of sending to Paris any measure which
might cut short the negotiation on the mere ground of form, and
did not afford the fullest opening for coming to an explanation
on points of substance, would preclude at once whatever chance
there may be of peace, and the best means of such exertions as
can alone meet the other alternative. He therefore hopes that
under the present circumstances Y. M. will approve of the note
being immediately despatched, and he knows that Y. M. will
feel that, the line of negociation having once been taken, ought
not to be hastily departed from."

"Weymouth, Saturday, Sept. 9, 1797.

"Provided Mr. Pitt, by encouraging through Lord Malmesbury that a sum of £450,000 shall be paid, if such a peace is
signed by France as is agreeable to the exact terms that have
been sent from hence, and that the Dutch agree to the whole of
our demands, and that no idea be admitted of the restitution
of the ships taken at Toulon, which must mortify the feelings
of every Englishman, I do not object to the measure, if Mr.
Pitt thinks that, the East Indies bearing a part of the expense,
he can lay the rest to the account of secret services of the war." [1]

"Windsor, Sept. 23, 1797.

[The first part of the letter, not quoted by Stanhope, is as follows:]

" The contents of Mr. Pitt's letter, had they related to any
other country than France, could not have made much effect;
but I am so thoroughly convinced of the venality of that nation,
and the strange methods used by its Directors in carrying on
negociations, that I agree with him in thinking, strange as the
proposal appears, that it may be not without foundation. . . ."

[1] This refers to the secret offer of Melvill and others to bribe the French
Directory. See Rose, " William Pitt and the Great War," pp. 324, 325.

[On 11th January 1798 the King writes at length respecting the
effort to frame a Quadruple Alliance with Russia, Prussia, and Austria.
He suggests that the Prince of Orange and General Stampfort are the
best means of influencing the Prussian Court. Lord Minto should be
sent to Vienna for that purpose.]

" and England be, with the consent of Prussia, the kind of
guarantee of the sentiments of those Courts to each other: I
think, tho' the task is arduous, the fate of every country depends
so much on not an hour being lost, that I think it ought with
vigour to be attempted."

" Windsor, April 21, 1798.

" I am much pleased with Mr. Pitt's account of the conduct of
the House of Commons yesterday, and not less so that, when
Mr. Sheridan supported the address of the necessity of exertion
and unanimity at the present crisis, he so far threw off the mask
as not to abandon his former opinions, and consequently greatly
destroy (*sic*) any merit his present conduct might otherwise
deserve by also objecting to the suspension of the Habeas Corpus
Act. . . ."

" Windsor, June 3, 1798.

" . . . I sincerely lament the necessity of sending this additional force to Ireland, as it must be very likely that we shall
have them returned in the course of the present season for
active service, and that this must completely put an end to any
measures of that kind during their absence. The draft Mr. Secretary Dundas sent to the Duke of Portland ought to impress the
Lord Lieutenant of Ireland with the necessity of not detaining
them unnecessarily; but I trust, whilst there, that as the sword
is drawn it [will] not be returned into the sheath until the whole
country has submitted without condition; the making any compromise would be perfect destruction. . . ."

" Windsor, June 13, 1798.

" Mr. Pitt has in my opinion saved Ireland by engaging
Mr. Pelham in the present state of that kingdom to return there
as soon as his health will permit, which should be known there
at least when the Marquess Cornwallis arrives. That gentleman's
knowledge of the country must be of great utility to the new
Lord Lieutenant, who must not lose the present moment of
terror for frightening the supporters of the Castle into an union
with this country; and no further indulgences must be granted
to the Roman Catholics, as no country can be governed where
there is more than one established religion; the others may be
tolerated, but that cannot extend further [than] to leave to perform their religious duties according to the tenets of their Church,

for which indulgence they cannot have any share in the government of the State."

"Queen's House, Feb. 20, 1800.

"Nothing but the desire of giving trouble could have conduced an opposition to the continuance of the suspension of the Habeas Corpus Act, which undoubtedly is at present a most salutary measure, and, it cannot but be admitted, has, as it ought to be, been exercised with the greatest moderation."

"Windsor, April 22, 1800.

"It is with infinite satisfaction I learn from Mr. Pitt's note that the three first articles of Union with Ireland was agreed to in a committee, on a division of 236 to 31; and from the House of Lords I understand an equal progress has been made and the division 82 to 3. Therefore I think the sense of Parliament now so clearly shown, that I hope no great trouble will arise in getting through this most salutary measure. . . ."

[On 10th May 1800 the King approves of Mr. Ryder being Treasurer to the Navy, and Mr. Canning Joint Paymaster. On 13th May he expresses annoyance at Prince Augustus having come back "by stealth." He had seen the Prince and arranged matters for the future.]

"Queen's House, Nov. 12, 1800.

". . . I suppose a committee on the high price of provisions will be immediately assembled, and that it will as much as possible be kept to effectuating a regular line of conduct in the corn trade rather than a trying of experiments, which on so delicate a subject are always hazardous, but [will] encourage the importation of corn on the lowest bounty that can answer this purpose, diminish the consumption of bread, unless the wheat be mixed with barley, rye, or oats, and propose the use of rice and potatoes in lieu of it for some days in the week. This latter proposition I own I should prefer to the stale bread introduced the last year."

PITT TO THE KING

"Downing St., Tuesday, Feb. 3, 1801.

"In addition to the letter with which Mr. Pitt has felt it his duty to trouble Y. M. in consequence of that with which Y. M. honored him on Sunday, he ventures, in full reliance on the gracious indulgence and goodness which Y. M. has condescended to express, humbly to solicit Y. M.'s attention to an object which he confesses he has peculiarly at heart. He should have taken the liberty of doing so some days sooner, if very soon after

forming that intention the circumstances had not intervened, on
which he has recently been under the painful necessity of submitting his sentiments to Y. M., but which were not at that time
in his contemplation. The object itself relates to the situation
of Mr. Long, who has now been ten years in the laborious situation of one of the secretaries of the Treasury, and has discharged
its duties not only to Mr. Pitt's entire satisfaction, but, he believes, he may truly add to that of every description of persons
with whom he has had intercourse, and with great advantage to
the public service. Neither Mr. Long's private fortune, nor any
which he has reason to expect, is such as would leave him, in
the event of his at any time retiring from office, with a provision at all adequate to the situation he has so long filled.
Under these circumstances Mr. Pitt had flattered himself that
Y. M. would not disapprove of his requesting the grant of a
contingent pension (with the remainder of one half of it to
Mrs. Long) to the amount of £1,500 per annum, which is not
more than was granted to a former secretary of the Treasury
above thirty years ago, and is very inferior to the value of patent
offices by which others of his predecessors have frequently been
provided for, but which no longer remain disposable. Mr. Pitt
only entreats Y. M.'s permission to add that, altho' he had
meant to submit this request under different circumstances, it is
certainly since become doubly interesting to him, and that he
should most sensibly feel Y. M.'s gracious compliance as a strong
addition to the many marks he has received of Y. M.'s kindness
and goodness to himself.'

"Queen's Palace (*sic*), May 13, 1804.

"The King is very much pleased with the manner in which
Mr. Pitt has managed his conversation with the Marquess of
Bath. H. M. certainly thinks it most advisable that he should
decline office, and if there is a possibility of taking the Duke
of Portland's report in that sense, the King will see it eagerly.
Nothing could have more surprised and flattered the Earl of
Dartmouth than the finding himself unexpected (*sic*) invested
with the key and staff of Chamberlain. To the King's utter surprise Lord Hobart seems to think the office of Captain of the
Yeomen of the Guard not a situation splendid enough for the
Secretary of State of the Colonies, but will take time to weigh
his objections till the Earl of Aylesford's acceptance of the staff
of Lord Steward or of Master of the Horse can be known, and
the Gold Stick in the possession of the Earl of Dartmouth, that

---

¹ Pitt had sent in his resignation. Charles Long, afterwards Lord Farn-
borough, retired with a pension of £2,200. (Bagot, "Canning and his
Friends," i, 127.)

I may confer it on some other person. Should Lord Hobart decline it, the King wishes to know whether he can assist Mr. Pitt's arrangements; if not, the King thinks the services of the Earl of Macclesfield and his having been dismissed by the Prince of Wales give him a prior claim to that employment. The Council will meet to-morrow at three o'clock."

"Queen's Palace, June 5, 1804.

"The King is most thoroughly gratified by Mr. Pitt's very clear account of the debate yesterday on the Defence Bill, and that Opposition judged it most prudent to defer a division till in a later stage of the Bill; but the holding back on this occasion must add strength to the Administration, and he trusts no exertion will be wanting to collect as large a force as possible for Monday. A little aid from Messrs. Rose and Long might be advantageous, as they must understand the collecting and watching the door of the House of Commons better than new men in that necessary manœuvre, which is not obtained without some experience."

THE KING TO LORD MELVILLE

"Kew, July 10, 1804.

"The King sees with infinite satisfaction the unremitting exertions of Lord Melville's active mind in the papers he has sent this morning, the consequence of which are (*sic*) most ably stated in the Mem^m. which accompanies them. H.M. rests secure in the opinion that this same spirit of examination must in very few months put that degree of energy in every branch of the naval service, and that effected with good humour which will render it the more efficacious."

[He hopes Ld. Melville will visit the dockyards that summer; and he (the King) will meet him (from Weymouth) at Portsmouth and Plymouth.]

"On board of the 'Royal Sovereign,' Oct. 6, 1804.

"The King has no doubt but that Lord Melville, at the same time he encourages making every reasonable attempt to destroy the gunboats of the enemy now collected at Boulogne, will attend to the very bad effect which naturally arises if they are unsuccessful, as it gives an idea not advantageous to the sagacity of the planners or of the executors of these designs.[1] H. M. easily sees the propriety of Lord Melville's remaining within reach of the Admiralty at this critical moment."

[1] See Rose, "William Pitt and the Great War," p. 511.

"Windsor, Dec. 25, 1804.

" The King is most highly pleased at Mr. Pitt's account of the result of his two conversations with Mr. Addington, whose good heart is the best security that old affections will be cordially and lastingly restored. H. M. will not to anyone mention the smallest hint of the arrangement to which Mr. Pitt alludes, but intrench himself in the pleasure he feels at the reunion of Mr. Pitt and Mr. Addington. If any arrangement can be made to include the Earl of Buckinghamshire,[1] provided not in an executive office, it would be desirable. In that line Yorke, Bathurst, Bond, and Vansittart are the useful men connected with Mr. Addington."

"Windsor, Jan. 9, 1805.

" The King desires Mr. Pitt will give directions that a patent be prepared creating Mr. Addington Viscount Raleigh, of Combe Raleigh[2] in the county of Devon, for which Mr. Addington may be presented on Friday previous to the Privy Council to be held that day, when he may also be named President of the Council. Lord Mulgrave may receive the seals of the Foreign Department, the Earl of Buckinghamshire be appointed to the Post Office; and, as the Duke of Portland with great propriety declines office, perhaps Mr. Bathurst may be placed either in the office of Chancellor of the Duchy of Lancaster, or, if that has ever been held by a peer, some one removed there to open a Privy Council Office for him. The King hopes on Friday to see the sketch of the speech for opening the session."

"Windsor, Jan. 9, 1805.

" The King is rather astonished that the French Usurper has addressed himself to him; and, if he judged it necessary, that he could not find a less objectionable manner. Mr. Pitt has put the mode of answering it in the only possible shape that could with any propriety be devised; and, as such, the King approves of the proposed unsigned answer. No time ought to be lost in transmitting a copy of it to the Court of Russia, to whom also the Convention with Sweden should be communicated. On the French proposal it might be right to express to the Emperor of Russia that this proposal ought to stimulate the entering into a thorough concert to attack France with vigour."

"Kew, May 1, 1805.

" The King sincerely rejoices at the House of Commons having rejected the motion of Mr. Whitbread yesterday for ex-

---

[1] See Rose, "William Pitt and the Great War," p. 517.
[2] The title was finally taken from Sidmouth.

punging the names of Lord Castlereagh, the Master of the Rolls, and some others, out of the list of the secret committee. H. M. is sorry Mr. Pitt has so much fatigue, and also grudges the waste of time that might be more advantageously employed in forwarding the public business; but he trusts that temper will soon effect that desirable object."

"Kew, June 13, 1805.

" The King finds with the greatest satisfaction that Mr. Whitbread's original motion for impeaching Lord Melville has been rejected by 272 to 192, but regrets that the criminal prosecution has been carried by 238 to 229, as he thinks it an unnecessary severity. If he only viewed Mr. Pitt's political situation, he should think the division must give him ease, as the world must see that the House of Commons put their face so strongly against any incorrect conduct in matters of account that even the private friendship of Ministers to any individual cannot screen him in a matter so essential to the public."

"Windsor, June 15, 1805.

"The King is highly pleased that Mr. Whitbread's very improper motion was got rid of, and one stating the truth carried without a division. The House of Commons has certainly shown more rancour in ordering a criminal prosecution, having previously censured Lord Melville without calling on him for any justification of his conduct, which certainly is not agreeable to any idea of the laws of this country; but on the present occasion the line pursued is one more to its credit."

"Kew, Oct. 16, 1805.

" The King will with pleasure receive Mr. Pitt at three o'clock this day."

(B.) PITT TO THE DUKE OF PORTLAND

[N.B. All the following letters are from Pitt to the Duke of Portland, who became Secretary of State for Home Affairs in July 1794.]

"Downing St., May 9, 1792.

"Having the satisfaction of thinking that Your Grace and many persons of weight and consideration with whom you are connected are disposed to manifest your concurrence in such measures as may on due consideration be thought necessary under the present circumstances for checking any attempts dangerous to public order and tranquillity, I have received His Majesty's permission to state to Your Grace the ideas which have occurred to His Majesty's servants and to request the communication of your sentiments upon them. If it is not disagreeable to Your Grace, I should be happy to have the honor of waiting upon you for that purpose in the course of to-morrow either between two and four, or at any hour in the evening."

"Tuesday, April 8, 1794.

"Mr. Pitt presents his compliments to the Duke of Portland. Having had the satisfaction of hearing that the object of enabling His Majesty to form French corps meets with His Grace's approbation, he takes the liberty of troubling him with the draft of the proposed Bill which is intended to be presented to day; and should any suggestions occur to His Grace, Mr. Pitt would be happy to be honored with a communication of them, at any time before the Bill is in the Committee, which will probably be Monday or Tuesday next, Downing Street."

"Downing Street, Friday, May 23d, 1794.

"Mr. Pitt presents his compliments to the Duke of Portland, and takes the liberty of expressing a wish to have the honor of conversing with His Grace at any time that may be most convenient to him on the present state of public affairs. Mr. Pitt will be disengaged at any hour that His Grace may name either this evening or in the course of to-morrow or Sunday."

[Private.]

"Downing Street, Wednesday, July 2nd, 1794.

"Since I had the honor of conversing with Your Grace yesterday a mode has occurred to me, by which if it should be thought right to adopt it, the situation of Lord Lieutenant of Ireland might be opened whenever it is agreeable to Lord Fitzwilliam to accept it; and in the mean time the arrangement for Sir George Yonge, on his quitting the War Office, might take place immediately.[1] On Lord Fitzwilliam ceasing to be Lord President, if Lord Hawkesbury were to be appointed to that office, Lord Westmorland might succeed Lord Hawkesbury as Chancellor of the Duchy of Lancaster. My motive for suggesting this idea is that it seems to furnish a facility for effecting the arrangement in the manner most consonant to Your Grace's wishes. It would at the same time, if you approve it, be in all respects convenient, as the office of Chancellor of the Duchy is exactly of the description which I should wish to propose to Lord Westmorland, and the exchange would certainly be very acceptable to Lord Hawkesbury. I have not however hinted the idea to Lord Hawkesbury and must therefore beg Your Grace to have the goodness to consider it as a private suggestion, to yourself or to those to whom you may wish confidentially to communicate it."

"Downing Street, Thursday, July 3d, [1794].

Mr. Pitt presents his compliments to the Duke of Portland. He is very sorry that it did not occur to him to mention to His Grace yesterday that he is under the necessity of being absent from town to-morrow to attend a meeting of the Cinque Ports at Romney, which he cannot well defer. Mr. Pitt means to be in town by nine on Saturday morning. As the King is prepared to see the Duke of Portland after the Levee to-morrow, and will be disposed to accede to any mode of arranging the different offices which have been in question, which may be most satisfactory, Mr. Pitt hopes his necessary absence for this short interval, will be attended with no inconvenience. Mr. Pitt will wait for the Duke of Portland's answer before he sets out, and can defer doing so till any hour this evening, if His Grace has any particular commands for him."

"Wimbledon, Sunday, July 6th, 1794.

"I have had an opportunity of conversing with Lord Grenville and Mr. Dundas on the subject of the unexpected difficulty which has arisen in the arrangement which they as well as myself are earnestly desirous of seeing accomplished. I must

[1] Sir George Yonge took the Mint. For these changes see the foregoing Essay, "Pitt and Earl Fitzwilliam."

begin by saying that Mr. Dundas, as far as he is concerned, makes a point that no consideration merely personal to him should stand in the way; but I must add that I remain myself fully convinced that to place the War Department in any new hands must in point of effect, and of public impression, be attended with great inconvenience; and I feel this sentiment so strongly, that, even with all the anxiety which I have to promote an arrangement which I consider as of great public importance, it is impossible for me to recommend it. With respect to the proposed division of the branches of business now included under the Home Department, I am satisfied from observation for some time past, that the different details arising out of an extensive war, and those which relate to the internal state of the kingdom, are both of them so important, and require separately so much time and constant attention, as to render such a division if not indispensible, at least highly desireable for the public service.[1] It would have afforded me great satisfaction if Your Grace had thought it right to undertake that part of the business, which relates to internal affairs. As however I understood from Your Grace that your objection applies to accepting a Department in a less extensive state than it has hitherto been, I flatter myself the difficulty may possibly be removed by an expedient which Lord Grenville enables me to suggest. He has expressed to me his readiness, if it can afford any accommodation, to quit the Foreign Office and to accept the Home Department in the way in which it is proposed to be modelled, in order to leave the Foreign Office open to Your Grace if it should be agreeable to you to accept it.

" This circumstance will, I hope, appear to Your Grace an additional proof of the eagerness we feel to do whatever is practicable in order to remove the present embarrassment, and also of the light in which we view the Department in question. As the House of Commons meets to-morrow, and it is very desireable, if possible, to be able to fix the time of Prorogation, I shall be very glad if Your Grace should be enabled to favor me with your answer on this subject, or to name any time at which you can allow me the honor of seeing you to-morrow morning."

" Walmer Castle, Septr. 3d, 1794.

" Before I left town Mr. Douglas, who is at Brighthelmstone, sent me, together with some Treasury papers, the two enclosed letters from the Lord Lieutenant to be transmitted to Your Grace.[2] I find by some mistake, that instead of being sent to your office they were put in a box which I brought hither.

---

[1] See Rose, " William Pitt and the Great War," pp. 270-2.
[2] These are missing. The Lord Lieutenant was Lord Westmorland.

The delay will I hope not have been material. I have received a letter from Mr. Burke, by which I am very happy to find, that he is extremely gratified by the proposal of the pension at present to Mrs. Burke, and the intended recommendation to Parliament to make a further provision for him. I have sent his letter, as he seemed to intend I should, to the King. Mr. Windham will, I imagine, have reached the Duke of York yesterday or to-day, but with the wind as it is at present, it may be some time before we hear from him."

"Downing Street, Monday, Sept. 22d [1794].

" I send Your Grace the Mem^m which Mr. V. Dillon left with me this morning. You will see by it that he is brother to the late Arthur Dillon, and he told me that he is the only brother now left of Ld Dillon. He explained to me that by appointing his officers he meant only recommending them under the rules observed in other corps. The terms seem to me very reasonable. The additional battalion which he proposes to raise as well as that now at St. Domingo, would naturally make part of the Irish Brigade."

[*Endorsed* 25 Septr. 1794]

"Downing Street, Thursday.

" I send Your Grace a letter which I have received this morning from Windham, and one which came on Tuesday evening and which I omitted to shew you. I am sorry to add the dispatch from the Duke of York contains the account of the Prince of Coburg having retreated (in consequence of the enemy's having forced some of the ports to his left on the Ourte) and having crossed the Roer. The enemy will probably invest Maestricht, in which there seems to be left a moderate garrison with three months' provisions, but some doubt is expressed as to the quantity of ammunition. I should wish to converse with Your Grace on this subject any time to-day. There are one or two smaller points near home, on which it would be useful that Ld. Amherst[1] should meet us for five minutes, if you will have the goodness to fix when and where it will suit you best.

"P.S. I send the Duke of York's dispatch."

"Hollwood, Sunday, July 5th, 1795.

". . . . The Reports from Paris give great reason to believe that a naval action has taken place in the Mediterranean, but

---

[1] Lord Amherst was Commander-in-Chief of the British army. He was soon replaced by the Duke of York.

are wholly silent as to the event. There are also accounts from Col. Crauford, which look as if the Austrians were preparing to act in earnest on the side of Franche Compté (*sic*), and to make a proper use of the Prince of Condé's army."

[*Endorsed* ℞ 6 August 1795]

"Horse Guards, Thursday.

"It has occurred to me that if (as seems clear) we must relinquish operations on a great scale on the coast, there would be infinite advantage in prevailing on Lord Moira to go to St. Domingo.[1] By this means, the change of plan would be concealed till the moment of executing it, and the enemy kept in uneasiness at home might be prevented from detaching to the islands. This would avoid all the inconvenience that must otherwise arise from Lord Moira's relinquishing his command. The only difficulty that I see arises from Williamson's situation.[2] I own however that for so great an object, I think there ought to be no ceremony in bringing him away, with the intention of making it up to him either by command in the East Indies (where there will be an opening) or by any other arrangement. If Your Grace sees this in the same light, I should be inclined to lose no time, in making the proposal to Lord Moira, who is now here. It is on that account I give you this trouble now, instead of waiting till we meet.

"P.S. Ld. Cornwallis, to whom I have mentioned this idea, strongly concurs in it."

Private.

"Downing Street, Aug. 22d, 1795.

"It has occurred to some of us that it would be a handsome and liberal measure, not to let Lord Moira quit his command without some mark of the King's favor, as a compensation for time, labour and expence which he has devoted to a service, in the completion of which he has been disappointed by events, but by no faults of his own. On this ground, and taking care to set aside all consideration of his political conduct, it might be thought right to offer him the Earldom of Huntingdon;[3] and I should be inclined to write to the King to suggest the idea, but I wished first to know your Grace's sentiments upon [it]."

---

[1] Lord Moira commanded a force destined for the coast of Brittany or la Vendée.

[2] General Williamson held a command in the West Indies.

[3] Lord Moira refused all offers of this kind.

[On 20th September 1795 Pitt writes with respect to the marquisate for Lord Bute, which the King wished to waive.]

Private.

"Downing Street, Sept. 20th, 1795.

"Since my return from Weymouth, such of us as are in town have had a good deal of consultation, on the state of things as affected by the recent conduct of Hanover, and by the prospect which opens in France. Most of us are strongly inclined to think that with a view to prevent the Emperor being alarmed into a separate peace, or at least being deserted by most of the princes of the Empire, as well as in order to satisfy the public mind here at the meeting of Parliament, it would be very useful to come immediately to such an explanation with Austria, as may put it in our power, if things soon assume a settled shape in France, to make use of any opening for ascertaining on what terms the new government may be disposed to treat, and may on the other hand establish in time a full concert for the prosecution of the war, if necessary, next year. Every thing that is passing seems to make it more and more evident that no higher language can be used at the meeting of Parliament (on the supposition of the new government [1] being by that time tolerably established), than that we shall be prepared to treat whenever we see a prospect of obtaining secure, honorable, and advantageous terms.

"It may perhaps be well doubted whether the moment will be ripe for obtaining those terms till we have had the benefit of our successes in the West Indies; and I am persuaded we should be fully supported in a determination not to think of accepting terms that are not reasonably advantageous; but on the other hand it is possible, that if our expedition is once sailed, we may be in a posture without waiting for its effects, in which the enemy, considering the extreme pressure upon them, might be inclined immediately to give us all the sacrifices we should require; it is also to be considered that by waiting for the actual success in the West Indies, we may run some hazard of losing the benefit of the co-operation of Austria at least on the Rhine, and that our relative situation may thus upon the whole become less favourable instead of more so. We should perhaps therefore hardly justify the not taking some steps between this and the meeting of Parliament, to try the ground, more especially if any overture should come from France, which the enclosed papers and the general desire for peace which seems to prevail there, render not impossible.[2] These considerations by no means

---

[1] That of the Directory.

[2] These papers are missing at Welbeck. They are probably the letters of M. Monneron referred to later in this letter.

lead to taking any decisive step in the present moment, which is indeed at all events impracticable, till things are brought more to a point in France. But they seem to make it necessary to open ourselves confidentially on the subject to Austria without loss of time. On this idea Lord Grenville has prepared a dispatch which he sends Your Grace, and which I trust you will not disapprove of. It will, I think, tend to give us as much chance as we ought to have of peace at any early moment, and still more to give us if necessary the means of the further prosecution of the war. Our meeting to-day consisted of the Chancellor, Lord Spencer, Lord Grenville, Mr. Dundas, Mr. Windham, and myself. You will naturally imagine that Mr. Windham is averse to any idea of even the possibility of negotiation; but I think all the rest of us fully agreed in the propriety of going thus far, but we did not like to decide on the measure without knowing Your Grace's opinion. Lord Mansfield was present when the subject was discussed yesterday, but was prevented from coming to us to-day, from the effects of an overturn by which I am afraid he has suffered a good deal, as he seemed yesterday in much pain. As probably on that account he entered less on the subject, I am not quite sure of his opinion, but I do not think he felt any material objection to the measure. Lord Grenville will probably state to you that if this step is taken we think it would be very desirable to prevail upon Pelham to go to Vienna, as being much more likely than Sir M. Eden, to bring the business to a good issue.

"With respect to the letters from M. Monneron, we have thought that we could not refuse to allow him to come on the ground he states, as far as Dover, but we do not mean, at least in the first instance, to let him come to town. There can be little doubt that he means some overture on the subject of peace. If he contrives to bring forward any such proposal, the natural answer seems to be that, till we see the issue of what is now passing in France, there seems no ground for negotiation. This will have the desireable effect of precluding any intercourse with the Convention as now formed, but will not discourage the new government from making a fresh overture, if they meet under as pacifick a disposition as may be expected. Pelham at all events cannot go before the time when Your Grace would be returned to town, and we meant to fix another meeting according to the day that will suit you best, to resume this subject; but we wish much that the present dispatch should go in the mean time, as the interval to the 29th Octr. is not a long one."[1]

---

[1] Pitt and Grenville proposed to send Pelham to Vienna to sound the disposition of that Court. The Duke of Portland disliked Pitt's proposal (see "Dropmore Papers," iii, 135, 136).

(C.) LORD GRENVILLE TO PITT

[Several of the following letters are answers to those of Pitt, for which see "Dropmore Papers," vols. iii-vi.]

"Walmer, Oct. 4, 1793.

"I have considered the draft of instructions to the Toulon commissioners with as much attention as I could give to it. I have made some marginal notes—the most material is˜that which relates to the exceptions to be made respecting such frontier towns or districts as may become objects of indemnity —I think it is absolutely necessary to say something on this point. You will consider that this paper is not meant for publication, but is a direction given to the King's Commissioners to regulate their conduct. Now if Perpignan, for instance, were to comply with the conditions required, the comm[issione]rs, as the instructions now stand, would have no discretion, but must immediately give to that town such assurances as would be directly inconsistent with the ideas wh. Lord St. Helens has been directed to hold out to Spain.[1] I suppose this instruction would be considered only as applicable to the south of France, and that this limitation removes all difficulties about Flanders and Alsace, but it surely exists with great force as applicable to the places I have mentioned in my marginal note on that passage.

"The consideration of this point naturally leads to that of our situation at Toulon as with respect to Spain. The place is now held jointly by the British and Spanish forces, and in the letter from Langara to the Spanish Minister at Turin (I think) wh. Jackson transmits, you will see some mention is made of an agreement with Lord Hood for perfect equality in all that relates to Toulon. I do not know that Lord Hood has ever sent home any account of such agreement, but if it exists you will see how delicate our situation is in this respect. I do not mention this as a reason for delaying the steps now taking, or even for altering the principles of the instructions, but it seems to render further communication to Madrid indispensable, and that immediately, and also to require something to be said in the

[1] Alleyne Fitzherbert (1753-1839) created Lord St. Helens in 1791, was British ambassador at Madrid.

instructions respecting the mode and extent of their co-operation either with the Spanish officers, or with any person having from the K. of Spain an authority similar to theirs.[1]

"Another point respecting which nothing is said in the instructions, but which cannot well be passed over, is the question respecting the recognizing the authority of any regent claiming to exercise the powers of the French monarchy. If the constitution of 1791 was re-established, purely and simply, this difficulty wd. not exist for the present, because as far as I recollect, the regency is, under that constitution, elective according to a form then laid down; and the impossibility of complying with that form necessarily would make a sort of interregnum during wh. no person could claim to exercise that authority. But if hereditary monarchy only is restored, and that in the person of a minor and captive king,[2] this seems to imply the necessity of some immediate consideration of the mode of exercising his authority. This point is still more likely to come in question whenever steps are taken for forming anything like a Royalist army which subject is also omitted in the instructions, and is one which must, I think, be adverted to. We can never hope I think to go forward with advantage in that part of France without some such support from the country itself, and the forming such an army would in another point of view be of infinite use in employing active and turbulent spirits who have been too busy for five years to make it possible for them now to sit still.

"There is one point only left which I think of any very considerable importance, but it is the most difficult of all. In the instructions you particularly point at re-assembling the States General under the antient form. That Govt. can never be well established in France except thro' the medium of some deliberating Assembly is I think sufficiently evident, tho' I know there are persons who think differently, and wish a settled constitution to be given in the King's name, including some such Assembly, and giving to that body, with the consent of the Crown, the power of immediate change as fully as it is possessed here by the King and Parliament. But the mode of organizing, as they call it, such deliberating Assembly, is perhaps of all points the most difficult, and one on which I think we should rather ask information than hazard a present opinion.

"You see how many points are at once decided, by saying that this Assembly shall be an Assembly of the States General— and how many more, and those involving the very first seeds of

---

[1] For the disputes at Toulon, see Rose, "William Pitt and the Great War," ch. vi.

[2] Louis XVII, then captive at the Temple.

dissention, by saying that it shall be the States Gen[l]. in their *antient form*. I was led to feel the more difficulty on these points from having put Mounier[1] to talk upon them in one of our conversations. If you had heard all he said upon some of the points I have alluded to, and how pertinaciously he adhered to all his particular opinions about them, you would I think have been struck, as I was, to see how little these theorists have profited by experience, and how much danger there is in committing ourselves hastily to any distinct line respecting these discussions.

"The double representation, the indiscriminate election from amongst all the Orders, the deliberation *par ordre*, the veto to be exercised by each Order or only by a majority of the three, the King's veto, with fifty other points must all be thrown at sea again, and I think we must *voir venir* respecting them rather than attempt to make previous decisions. And all these difficulties would, I think, in speculation rather lead one to wish for some Assembly of Notables, or some Convention expressly differing from all legislative bodies than to go back to all the antient uncertainties. But this is mere speculation, and I expect that all I think we can now do is to collect opinions on this subject.

"This observation applies both to the article of the instructions which relates expressly to the States General, and also to that which speaks of the King's declaration in June 1789, which besides the points of what we should call constitutional liberty, involved also some regulations about the mode of deliberating in the States General, and those regulations, if I recollect right, were so absurd and incoherent as to be quite impracticable.

"The point about the Provincial States seems to me to be properly guarded by the condition of general concurrence. I recollect no other point except what I have marked in the margin of the paper itself. If there is time I should much wish to see it again before it goes, with your ideas on these loose suggestions.

"The draft to Sir Jas. Murray[2] did not come this morning. I conclude it is different from a draft I saw yesterday, which came in circulation, and which I thought much too loose to stand as the only paper on the subject—particularly because it nowhere expressly stated, which I think the material point, that we call upon them to submit a plan to us, formed in concert with the Prince Coburg founded solely on the consideration of

---

[1] Mounier, leader of the moderate Reformers, in 1789, was doing work for us in Switzerland ("Dropmore Papers," ii, 427, 449).

[2] Sir J. Murray acted as Quartermaster-General to the Duke of York in Flanders.

the best military use to be made of the existing force, leaving to us to modify that if necessary by political considerations.

"P.S. I have said nothing about the employment of their ships at Toulon, tho' I continue to think that a very material point. We have here an immense body of their naval officers, and there were in the emigrant army of last year one or two corps composed of nothing else. It would afford employment for these people who are a burthen and would besides be productive of innumerable other advantages. It would, I think, be easy to keep a proper check upon them. If you still feel difficulties on this subject which do not strike me, there can surely be none in giving to the Commrs. a general power to do in this respect as they shall find most expedient. I trust also that you will advert to Mulgrave's personal situation which I touched upon yesterday. He surely deserves much independent of our wish to put him forward."

[Pitt in his reply of 5th October (see "Dropmore Papers," ii, 438, 439) approves of Grenville's suggestions, and proposes to issue a declaration at Toulon. He would prefer to specify "monarchy as the only system in the re-establishment of which we are disposed to concur:" but he would not decline to treat "with any other form of regular Government, if, in the end, any other should be solidly established."]

"Walmer Castle, Oct. 8, 1793.

"You will receive with this letter what I have written to Lord Yarmouth and Eden in answer to their late dispatches. The King of Prussia's conduct announces such determined treachery that the bringing forward the Bavarian project, to secure him, is clearly out of the question: and the only question with respect to that seems to be whether Lord Y[armouth] or M. Thugut are most accurate in point of fact, as to the means wh. Bavaria might have, with pecuniary assistance, of furnishing a useful body of troops. To this point Switzerland seems to offer better hopes, and we should neither run the risk of offending Austria, nor involve ourselves in fresh guarantys, by rather looking there than to Bavaria for mere subsidiary troops. By encouraging Thugut's journey here, wh. I much prefer to Mercy's, all the other points may probably be well arranged, the mode he proposes for securing our mutual co-operation merits attention but is *primâ facie* liable to the objection of subjecting to us to a possible obligation of furnishing means to a limited extent for pursuing objects which we may not approve.[1]

[1] Neither Thugut, Austrian Chancellor, nor Count Mercy came to London. See Rose, "William Pitt and the Great War," p. 205.

" What resolution do you take in consequence of Eden's letter No. 56 about sending the Hessians? What Thugut says is certainly true, that 5,000 more Austrians might be cheaper, easier, and sooner sent than the Hessians.—But can we depend as much upon them, either for their actual arrival or for their subsequent operations? This is doubtful, and yet the chance is tempting. When Eden says in his letter 57, that Thugut *repeated* that, independent of the Milanese troops, Devins's Corps[1] was at H. My's. disposal does he mean those as the additional troops referred to in 56; if so this will not answer our purpose, we having counted on those as well as the Hessians."

Monday, 4 o'clock [probably Oct. 12, 1794].

" You will find the letters from Morris in the packet which I send herewith, worth reading. But my particular motive for sending this packet to you arises from the letters to Berlin which you will find in it. I was ignorant that you and Dundas had seen Jacobi at all, and I am well enough acquainted with his stile (*sic*) of representing conversations to place no reliance in his statement. But I have seen it with the most serious concern from a thorough conviction that nothing could have so effectually tended to frustrate all our hopes in that quarter as the arrival of that letter at Berlin. I have once or twice mentioned at the Cabinet my ideas on that subject. They are not lightly taken up, and I feel as confident as one can be of any speculative opinion, that experience will confirm them. I should be very glad to talk them over fully with you, because the subject is of no light importance, and the worst thing that can happen is that you and Dundas should be *acting* on one line, and I on another, for this must defeat both chances.[2] It would be very desirable that before we have another Cabinet on the subject we should have discussed this point a little amongst ourselves. I am going to-morrow morning to Dropmore, but I could either see you at eleven to-morrow, or at any hour on Thursday that would suit you, or the thing may wait to the end of the week. . . ."

Dover, 1st March 1795.

" . . . With respect to the latter part of your note I am sure I need not say that both on public and on private grounds the most anxious wish of my heart must be, in taking a step which I think unavoidable, to do it in such a manner as may be least

---

[1] This was a corps helping to defend Piedmont.
[2] See Rose, " William Pitt and the Great War," pp. 212, 213.

injurious to the interests and credit of the Government and least embarrassing to you.[1] If it takes this shape, which I will fairly say with your decided opinion on the subject I think it ought, I shall most willingly converse with you about the particular mode and time of my doing what certainly I cannot do without great regret. I see objections to what you propose, but perhaps they may be got over, perhaps other suggestions may occur, and at all events they must be very strong objections indeed which can prevent my complying with your wishes on such a point as this at a moment like the present."

"Dropmore, Feb. 5, 1797.

"The news from Italy,[2] deplorable as it is, does not seem to lead to the adoption of any new measures, at least not till we hear again from Vienna and know the effect which these misfortunes have produced there. I think it may however be very useful to send a messenger on Tuesday merely for the purpose of giving general assurances that this event does not alter our dispositions to take in concert the most effectual measures for supporting the war, there being no probability that the tone of the Directory will be lowered or their dispositions rendered more pacific by this unexpected success. It seems particularly important to give immediate assurances that we continue disposed to make the same pecuniary sacrifices for what Austria can still do, as we were ready to make in order to enable her to have done much more. I will prepare dispatches to this effect to-day and if you see no objection they may go on Tuesday; unless anything else occurs to you there seems no necessity for any Cabinet on this subject, as this step would only be the following up the measures already determined on.

"I wish the succours to Puysaye and Frotté were increased to double their amount—that is to give each separately the men now allotted for their joint account. If Windham is left to make the distribution of the present allowance it is to be feared his opinions and wishes may make the division favourable to Puisaye. Have I any chance of seeing you here? Ld. Spencer seems to think the project about Cadiz too hazardous; his reasoning certainly has weight, but I do not think it quite conclusive, and surely in this state of things much may and ought to be hazarded."

---

[1] This refers to Grenville's resolve to resign if Pitt carried through a proposed treaty with Prussia. For Grenville's opposition to this see "Dropmore Papers," iii, 26-30. The proposal was dropped and Grenville remained in office.

[2] Battle of Rivoli, January 14, 1797.

[*Endorsed* Lord Grenville.]

[July—August 1797 ?]

" I return you the projet you sent me, because I conclude you wish to read it again before we meet.[1]

" It is hardly necessary to say that it does not meet my ideas on any one of the 3 points; of 1, the manner of submitting to their demand of definitive articles, which submission is I think made more humiliating by the labour used to argue in favour of preliminaries. 2. The explicit renunciation of all interference in the peace of the Continent, or share in the Congress—to wh. are now added words of reflection in that mode of treating which seem to be nearly copied from Barthelemi's note to Wickham— or 3, the pains taken to shew, that our objections to separate treaty rest only on Portugal—and the manner in which the interests of the allies of France seem to be more and more carefully provided for than those of our ally Portugal. I sincerely wish that on consideration the draft I sent you may appear more reconcileable to your ideas than this is to mine, for without that, painful as it is to me to say it, I see no hope of our bringing our ideas to meet on a subject of so much importance as this must be felt to be."

Cleveland Row, Aug. 1, 1799.

" . . . I would go, not to Walmer, but to Bengal, if I thought my doing so could prevent so fatal a measure as the letter I just receive from you announces. I do not know where to begin, or how to describe to you what I feel, in writing to you on the *first of August*,[2] with a fine west wind blowing in at my windows, and being now to consider whether I can be with you three days hence, to deliberate whether our expedition shall sail, or wait for the arrival of an embarkation from Revel which at the very earliest was not to sail from thence till the 27th of July. Were all the generals on earth assembled, and unanimous in that opinion, I am sure nothing they could say would weigh a feather in my mind. Our secret must transpire in the interval. We shall lose the most favourable moment that ever was offered. We give time as if they paid us for it, to the Batavian Government to prepare their defence. We give to the Prussian Government out of our hands the very means they are seeking for to thwart all our projects. Being now far beforehand with them, we make them as much beforehand with us. We run the risk of irrecoverably offending the Emperor of Russia by failing in the execution of a

[1] See "Dropmore Papers," pp. 322, 323, for Grenville's opposition to the peace negotiations with France.

[2] The anniversary of the Battle of the Nile. This letter refers to delays in the expedition to the Texel.

plan deliberately announced to him, and earnestly pressed on his acceptance. Being necessarily too late in the season, we wantonly incur a further and uncertain delay. We put out of our hands the possibility of acting for the Netherlands this year. And all this we do for no assignable reason that I can frame to my own mind.

"It is now more than three months that these plans have been in agitation. During all that time no doubt has been stated, till now, that 10,000 men were amply sufficient to make their landing good in any one point of the coast. Instead of unforeseen difficulties every thing has turned out more in our favour than we could hope. If ten or rather twelve thousand men are not sufficient for the first enterprize why will twenty? *They* would not be sufficient to undertake on military rules the conquest of Holland—no, nor twenty thousand men added to them. We ought surely to have known our own mind before we proposed these plans at Petersbg. as certain of success, which we must now write that we abandon as hopeless. Is the country stronger or better defended? it is less so. The French army, you are told, instead of being reinforced is daily diminished—the Government we act against instead of being united and confident, see that their existence hangs on a thread—France abandons them to Prussia—they cannot be ignorant of the fact, and if they are it is our business that they should not remain so. Their fleet was in mutiny at the mere report of the approach of an English force—the whole machine is breaking up, and we instead of profiting of all this are catching from the D. of Brunswick the contagion of all his military doubts and fears.

"It is a great responsibility that a man takes upon himself who gives a decided opinion to undertake without delay a military enterprize the issue of which is to decide upon the lives of the persons engaged in it, on the reputation of our arms, and on our ultimate success in Holland. I see it in all its extent, and, with my eyes open to it, I do most earnestly conjure you, as you value your own character and peace of mind, not to give way on this occasion. If the Russians arrive soon, they will arrive in time to support us. If they are delayed we shall lose by waiting for them what we never can recover—I mean time, and ,with it reputation and solid advantage. . . ."

"Dropmore, Aug. 2, 1799.

"You will judge by my letter of this morning how happy I am made by that which I have just received from you.[1] I only wish that I had staid in town a few hours longer, for I should have saved myself a most melancholy ride, and perhaps I might

---

[1] Probably that of August 2 in the "Dropmore Papers," v, 224, *q.v.*

have found something to do to help the thing forward. I have anticipated your wish about the Prince of Orange's address. It is not only written but printed—and Hammond will send you down by to-morrow's mail the printed copies both of that and of the declaration, in order that Abercomby may take them with him. The former is Fagel's writing and I think very good. . . .

" I am much of your opinion about the Netherlands, and will endeavour to put that idea into shape—but you must of course expect to see Prussia cringing to us again. I hope you will not relent. I thought Irish and French officers not near so good for the Netherlands as a good Scotchman. But if the thing succeeds there will be room for more. I will write to you again about "Monsieur."[1] I incline to put him off for four or five days longer, as I foresee several unreasonable demands which I should like to have your aid in resisting—and I shall not be sorry to have a few days more to prepare a sort of note which I wish to put into his hands, to explain what we can do for him, and what we expect of him. Adieu—I shall sleep better to-night than I had hoped."

"Dropmore, Sept. 12, 1799.

" I will do my best to execute your plans, tho' certainly not *con amore*. What we are now doing approaches nearer to Εὐρυβατον Πρᾶγμα than any transaction of English politics in my remembrance. I am heartily glad my brother is out of the scrape.[2]

" The scheme, besides its injustice, must fail of success, for you will see by Whitworth's last dispt (when they are returned from Weymouth) that while Thugut is looking to get *all* Piedmont, the Emperor of Russia makes it a positive condition of continuing his succour, that the K. of Sardinia shall be restored to *all* his dominions. What, then, is Whitworth to have a discretionary power to do at Petersburgh? To negotiate for Austria, who will not negotiate there at all, a treaty on grounds which are the direct opposite to the intentions of Russia—and this, in the hope of binding Austria by engagements to do what nothing but her interest of the moment will ever make her do, and what she is now compelled by the course of events to do without our owing her even thanks for it.

" I do not like to urge an opinion so strongly against a plan

[1] " Monsieur," [the Comte d'Artois] was to go to Dropmore to meet Pitt.
[2] Mr. Thomas Grenville had now left Berlin and was at Hamburg, on his way to Holland to which country he was deputed as commissioner (" Dropmore Papers," v. 393). For the differences of Pitt and Grenville on Austrian schemes, see Rose, *op. cit.*, p. 378.

which you seem to have so much at heart; and certainly your opinion makes me distrust my own. But hitherto all I have ventured to foretell on this subject has been confirmed by the court, and I cannot conceal from you my fear that by what we are now doing we shall lose our ground at Petersbg. and certainly gain none at Vienna; and which is still worse, shall descend from the high ground of probity, and morality on which we now stand in Europe.

"I do not want to volunteer a Quixote opposition to the views of Austria, but I do want to be able to say in this case, with as clear a heart as in those of Poland and Venice, that this Government is too great to need such villainies and too proud to share in them.[1] Let Austria settle them as she can with the court of Petersburgh, but do not afford her the pretence that England has seduced and abetted her in them.

"I trust I shall see you before it can be necessary to write anything more on this subject. My ideas of instruction to Maitland[2] are, that he should go no further than to raise with every effort he can make, an insurrection against France, but that he should say distinctly to the leaders, that their fate does and must depend on the result of the war, and the arrangements of the great Powers, and that England will not give a guaranty in that respect which it may be unable to maintain. But that the best mode of providing for their interests is, that they shall arm themselves, and put themselves in a condition to have *voix au chapitre*, and that in that we are willing to help them.

"P.S. Panin is appointed Vice Chancellor in the room of Kotschoubey. I am afraid he will not long keep that situation, but it puts Vienna out of the question for him. I will write to Whitworth about our further plans of attack, but we must use great diligence indeed, both here and in Holland, before we can hope to be ready in time for this autumn. If we do not get some one or more of the towns of the Generality[3] I fear 20,000 men will be much too little for the defence of Holland, for a week's frost would enable the enemy by drawing together two of those garrisons to penetrate your line in any one point, with a larger force than you have on the whole line. I have not yet received Monsieur's answer—when do you come to town? I hope you will have your militia measure ready, so as not to be obliged to keep people in town at this time of the year."

[1] *I.e.*, the entire annexation of Piedmont.

[2] General Maitland commanding in the West Indies, came to an agreement with the negro chiefs. See Rose, "William Pitt and the Great War," pp. 247-8.

[3] The term "Generality" denotes the Dutch provinces outside that of Holland.

GRENVILLE TO DUNDAS

"Dropmore, Apr. 10, 1800.

" If I had felt at all sure that I should find you at Wimbledon you would have seen me there instead of this letter. It would be useless now to tell you how much I differ from the opinion you have formed, or to discuss the grounds of your determination, because, however strongly impressed with the conviction which I have already stated to you, I am not vain enough to wish that my single opinion should prevail against what appears to be the sense of all the King's Ministers. I heartily wish I could alter my own opinion, but certainly there is nothing in Stuart's notes which can produce that effect.[1]

" I never imagined that an army could act without cavalry, baggage, horses, and waggons, and have on the contrary repeatedly pressed both on Mr. Pitt and you the necessity of sending a Commissary there long before Stuart, in order to prepare these articles, and those of provisions. In answer to your question whether there is any reason to think that Austria will allow us to purchase these articles in her territory and export them from hence in the manner Stuart points out I have no hesitation in saying that I am convinced she will not only do that, but more and better—for that we may if we please, obtain the same arrangement there as Wickham has obtained on the Rhine, and be allowed to purchase these articles (paying only a little dearer for them from the Austrian magazines themselves).

" If I had known or suspected a doubt upon that subject this might easily have been made a condition of the arrangement which Lord Minto is enabled to conclude, nor is it too late to make it so still. But in truth this is not the sort of difficulty we have to apprehend from Thugut, who, if he does not conclude a separate peace, will certainly facilitate to us all means of acting that do not commit the Austrian army; because by so doing he will forward his own objects.[2]

" I undertake therefore confidently that if this be the only difficulty it might already have been removed, and may still be so before your second division can arrive; and this merely by writing to Lord Minto. Provided always that a separate peace is not made, in which case of course we should not want to act in the Mediterranean.

" But I desire you to observe that the obtaining this in Italy

[1] General Stuart was to be sent to concert plans for a British expedition to the coast of Provence or Liguria. This letter is in reply to Dundas's of 9th April in " Dropmore Papers," vi, 193.

[2] Thugut was Austrian Chancellor; Lord Minto, British Ambassador at Vienna; General Melas commanded the Austrian army in North Italy.

will not in the least be forwarded by Stuart's seeing Wickham
at General Kray's head quarters on the Rhine. He must therefore proceed, not there, but to Melas's head quarters at Genoa, or
in the neighbourhood; and when he has got them [there?] he will
find Melas uninstructed on the subject, having no authority to
consent to such an arrangement on his own part, still less to
give any orders to the Austrian Ministers, and (Political) Com-
missaries, in the different parts of Lombardy and Tuscany. A
reference must then be made to Vienna, and by the present plan
we are to wait the answer either directly from Vienna, or what is
more probable if details are to be treated of and settled, cir-
cuitously again by Genoa before our troops sail.

"My last letters from Mr. Jackson at Turin, which is rather
nearer, are of the 8th March—supposing therefore that Stuart
travels as fast as a messenger, he will not be there till the
second week in May, nor receive his first answer from Vienna
till the beginning of June; nor shall we hear from him in consequence of it, till the beginning of July, when we are to
deliberate upon it whether we shall send troops to the Mediterranean who would be to arrive there at soonest the middle of
August, and then at last to begin a co-operation with Royalists
whose fate will have been decided one way or other many weeks
before.

"I enter into this detail, not for the purpose of combating,
however I lament it, your decision not to send more than 5,000
troops now to the Mediterranean, but to intreat you not to
deceive yourself with false hopes by believing that if the plan is
delayed now, you can resume its execution in the autumn. But
rather to turn your mind with its own natural and manly
exertion, to some other real and effective plan of operation which
you can execute, and for which the total abandonment of this
plan will afford you, as I trust, abundant means. The worst that
we can do by ourselves and the country, is to waste the whole
campaign in inactivity, and to withdraw from the war the powerful aid of our military cooperation in the only campaign in which
we can give it.

"Your attack on Bellisle will not occupy, even during the
operation, more than 10,000 men, nor afterwards more than
2 or 3,000. If after sending 15,000 to the Med^n. you would have
had 27,000 disposable, you will, by sending only 5,000, have
37,000, a force sufficient not only to take Walcheren, but to
act from thence with effect *under a proper direction.* Or what I
should prefer, a force amply sufficient to act on Pichegru's plan
against Bordeaux, and to raise those provinces, where the
Royalist standard has not yet been reared. Do this, or anything else that you prefer, but for God's sake, for your own
honour, and for the cause in which we are engaged, do not let us,

after having by immense exertions collected a fine army, leave it unemployed, gaping after messengers from Genoa, Augsburg, and Vienna, till the moment for acting is irrecoverably past by. For this can lead to nothing but disgrace. . . ." [1]

GRENVILLE TO DUNDAS

"Dropmore, April 11, 1800.

" I have sent the dispatch to Wickham in the form you re-commend, because I know no quality in business worse than obstinacy, but I must be at the same time for the discharge of my own conscience tell you that, if I understand your plan as you have now shaped it, the whole is utterly impracticable. I have no wish to dispute either Sir Ch. Stuart's military opinions or yours, but I must be a driveller if I do not after nine years' experience know the Court of Vienna better than either of you. It is impossible to hope that your ideas can be executed in any other form than by Stuart going himself to Vienna—and I cannot but say to you as I would to him that I know that if he did go there, instead of persuading Thugut, he would quarrel with him in the first half hour.

" As to imagining that Thugut will give to Melas (much more that he will give to Kray, who has nothing to do with it) any authority to enter at his own discretion with plans of co-operation with Stuart which require Austrian troops to be put under an English general, I do not say the thing is *impossible* because nothing is so after what we have seen, but I am sure the chances are at least a thousand to one against it. And if pro-mised, the execution will still be liable to a repetition of all we experienced at Toulon, Dunkirk, Condé, etc., etc.

" This letter however is not for the purpose of fatiguing you with remonstrances against that to which I have already ex-pressed my utter and complete dissent, but in order to remark to you that you have given me no answer about the Condé corps, the destination of which is nevertheless an essential part of your plan, in whatever shape; and what is still more em-barrassing you desire me to write to Ld. Minto to ask, and obtain if possible, a categorical answer about supplies, baggage waggons, forage, etc., and even about an Austrian force to be put under our orders, but you do not tell me what explanation he is to give of our plans, views, numbers, objects, or time of operation.

" It would save much time and trouble if you would put down upon paper, according to your own ideas, drafts of dispatches (1) to Wickham about the Condé army, and (2) to Ld. Minto

---

[1] For Dundas's reply see " Dropmore Papers," vi, 194.

about Stuart's expedition. Do not think I have any indisposition to execute fairly whatever is determined upon, but as I really do not understand your plan and think it (as far as I do understand it) in contradiction to the most obvious calculations of time, it is much better that your ideas should be stated in the manner you wish them to be, and according to your own conception of them, rather than according to the imperfect view I have of them.

" I *have* sent off one messenger to Wickham with your alteration of my draft but another must follow in two days with a letter about the Condé army and other things, etc. Ld. Minto's servant returns also to him in two or three days."

GRENVILLE TO PITT

"Dropmore, Apr. 11, 1800.

" I have just received the inclosed, from which I can only collect that Dundas is (I trust without reason) offended at me or both of my two letters to him, in which I have stated with freedom, but certainly without intending the smallest personal offence, my opinion of the present decision respecting the Mediterranean operations. It is an easy answer for him to give me, that the Condé army must do as it can, and wait at Leghorn the chapter of events. But I doubt whether Parlt., who are to pay this army, or the country who expect service from them, will be quite as well satisfied with such an answer as Dundas seems in giving it [*sic*]. And he also forgets that Ld. Minto has positively engaged to Thugut that they shall *not* remain at Leghorn.

" Now all this confusion can be settled only by our coming to a distinct understanding and resolution about the Mediterranean expedition. I was, and am of opinion, that the sending there a large force (15 or 20,000 men) was the most effectual way of bringing our means to tell against the enemy. The objections urged against this measure appeared to me to be of no weight, and least of all those grounded on the necessity of having horses and baggage waggons, which (I would pledge my life for it) the Austrians would willingly let us purchase in Italy, and would still more readily sell us from their own magazines.

" But I do not deny that the propriety of this destination of our force is a point on which able men may sincerely differ, and I have no desire to force my plans upon other people in opposition to the opinions of the majority of those who have a right to decide the question. But if the plan is not to be executed I am clear it ought to be distinctly, and at once, abandoned, that we may have the use of our force elsewhere. And that nothing can be more idle than to keep our means locked up by the discussion of plans of cooperation which never can be brought to bear.

"Dundas says *now* that his opinion *is* clearly that we ought to have more than 5,000 men in the Mediterranean in addition to the garrison of Minorca. Now it so happens that I so far at least agree with him, as to think clearly that if we do not *now*, and without an hour's delay, send our remaining force, at least 10, if not 15,000 men more, there, we ought not to think of sending any more at a later season of the year.

"Why then with these opinions should we enter upon the farce of an illusory negotiation at Vienna? Why should we send Stuart to Wickham who can tell him nothing? And above all why should we let the Condé army march to Leghorn, instead of sending it either to reinforce the Swiss levies, or to cooperate with Willot in Piedmont?[1] I have kept no copies of my letters to Dundas, so little did I think of giving offence. Ask him for them if you think it worth while, or leave it alone, but let us at least have some fixed plan agreed upon amongst ourselves, which we may all be endeavouring to forward to the utmost, instead of drawing different ways.

"If I can in no other way obtain an opinion on the subject, summon a Cabinet to consider of the answer to be given to Wickham and Ld. Minto about the Condé army,—for I cannot take upon myself in such a business to guess at the opinions of my colleagues. But before we summon our numerous Cabinet, it is much better that those who are to execute should understand each other upon the subject.

"If you have not seen Ld. Minto's dispatch and Wickham's on the subject of the Condé army, ask Dundas for them. I sent them to him, and he has not returned them to me.

"Let me know what you wish me to say or do on this subject, and on that of the dispatch which Sir Ch. Stuart wants to have written to Ld. Minto. If we are to ask for cooperation from Austria, we must explain our ideas to them at least in general, and how can I explain those ideas without knowing what they are? But, with the present opinions, it is surely better to give the thing up, for sanguine as I was in the hope of brilliant and useful operations there, I am not such a novice as to expect that success, in opposition to the opinions of the Commander in Chief, the War Department, and the War Office."

[Enclosure. An unsigned letter dated Somerset Place, 11th April 1800, to "My dear Lord," on the same subject.]

[1] For General Willot's plans for the Mediterranean coast, see "Wickham Papers," ii, 402-8.

GRENVILLE TO PITT

"Dropmore, June 2, 1800.

" I got your letter here only this morning and some arrangements about horses will make it very inconvenient to me to be
in town by the hour you mention, but I shall certainly be in
Cleveland Row to dinner and can either see you in the evening
if you can call there, or I can call upon you at any time you
please to-morrow morning.[1]

" The delay is of less importance because I trust you will be
satisfied on consideration that, whatever decision you adopt
respecting the bulk of your force, all the late events make it
more important than ever that the Bellisle Expedition should
go on. If you send 12,000 men to the Mediterranean, you can
have no other equally good employment for the remainder of
your force as that of Bellisle, nor is it possible that anything can
so much distract Bonaparte's plans and operations in Germany
and Italy as the necessity of giving his attention to Bellisle and
the Vendée. If on the other hand you persevere in the present
determinations, the capture of Bellisle is more than ever an
indispensable preliminary to the execution of all plans on
that side.

" In either case I think by abandoning this undertaking you
will renounce the only chance of making your force tell at all,
during the real crisis of the campaign. Whereas if we take Bellisle in a fortnight or three weeks from this time (and much more
if we had taken it as we were promised a fortnight ago) your
whole force whether really destined for the Vendée or the Med^n.
would from the moment of its embarkation (and even in some
degree before it was embarked) tell exclusively on that point for
the next three weeks or month after that operation was known
at Paris, and by Bonaparte—for he must then conclude that
every thing we embark is destined for that point.

" With regard to the real destination which we shall give to
the mass of our force, that is too large a question to be discussed
by letter. If we *had* at this moment 12,000 or 15,000 men in the
Med^n. there is no doubt that they would decide the campaign.
But to *send* them there now is a very different question. Yet
even this I should think better than keeping them here under
the colour of an expedition which is not really intended, and
actively pursued. These points, with all the various considerations, of persons as well as things, to which they lead, we shall
better talk over than discuss by letter.

" Have you considered what orders to give Lord Keith about

[1] In answer to Pitt's of 1st June, see " Dropmore Papers," vi, 242.

Kléber? My own mind strongly inclines to make use of the opportunity which the French have afforded us, and to keep the Egyptian army in a position where it certainly does us less harm than it would do any where else." [1]

GRENVILLE TO PITT

"Feb. 1, 1801.

" I return your letter, which appears to me to be perfectly well drawn.[2] Ld. Spencer was with me when I received it, and I concluded you did not wish me to conceal it from him. I fully concur in every part of it, except that I do not see in what manner, or by what shape of argument you hope to prevent the discussion of the subject, as *all* that has passed upon it is so publickly and universally known, and is even I believe stated in the newspapers. This we may talk over together for I must of course wish to make my own line as nearly consonant to yours as it is possible for me, without actually doing what I think dishonourable.

I shall also be very anxious to know what language you mean to hold to the numerous individuals who have a right to some confidential communication from us on such an occasion, and whom the public discourse on the subject will naturally lead to wish to know what has really passed."

[On 5th February 1801 Grenville wrote to the King requesting permission to resign office. On 19th October 1801 he wrote to the King deferentially offering advice as to the tone of "unnecessary and degrading concession" shown by the Addington Government in its negotiations with France and Russia.]

GRENVILLE TO PITT

" Dropmore, Nov. 28, 1803.

" Among the subjects which ought to be attended to by Parliament in our present situation, and which appear to be totally neglected by Government, there is one of peculiar importance, to which my thoughts have lately been much turned, and on which, if you had been in town at the opening of the Session I should have been very desirous of conversing with you, from an opinion that, independently of your superior knowledge of the

---

[1] This refers to Kléber's capitulation of El Arish with the Turks (January 24, 1800), which the British Government declined to recognize. See "Dropmore Papers," vi, 161, 186, 221; Mahan, "Sea Power," i, 331-4.

[2] Pitt's letter to the King on the subject of Catholic Emancipation, which Pitt submitted to him. See "Dropmore Papers," vi, 434.

subject itself, there are other circumstances which point you out as the only person who can now propose anything relating to it with much prospect of advantage.

" If a landing should be effected, in spite of such resistance as we may oppose to the enemy on the coast, our troops must of course fall back on the first maintainable position on which they can be collected; while our fleet endeavours to destroy the enemy's transports and cut off his communication with his own coasts. In such a state the destruction of the enemy may be a work of time, especially as under such circumstances it may possibly be more advantageous for us to harass and circumscribe his army, than to risk a general action in the hope of his immediate defeat.

" Now let me ask you, for you must I am sure have considered the question, what is in this state of things to be the situation of the whole monied transactions of the country, and of the whole mass of that paper credit by which they are carried on, and under circumstances of peace, (or even of *security* tho' in war,) very beneficially carried on? Suppose the enemy advancing towards the capital or even pointing that way at whatever distance? The Bank pays all demands that can be made upon it *in paper.* But how will bankers, merchants, or even considerable tradesmen answer the demands on them? If in their own paper, who will receive it, not being by law a legal tender? Even if in Bank paper, what security can there be that it will not suffer a depreciation, (and if any who shall say how large a depreciation?) when the issue is to be proportioned to the new demand which a run on the Bank would occasion, and no longer restricted by such limitations as the ordinary course of their affairs has produced? Will it be that the exigency of such a crisis shall justify the bankers in combining to refuse all payments? By law, which law would neither be suspended nor superseded by invasion, every such refusal is an act of bankruptcy. Their credit, however, might, in case of our ultimate success, be restored by Parliament. But in the interval what will the effect have been? Who is there in the country that could command one hundred pounds, if his banker's shop in London were shut up by the alarm of an attack on London, or by the effect of any general combination among the bankers?

" The difficulties of this subject might easily be pursued into much more detail, but when your own mind begins to canvass it, you will readily enough follow it farther than my suggestions would lead you.

" If you ask me for the remedy, I should answer first, that wherever it may lay, it certainly cannot be found in inert or hopeless despair. The ideas which have offered themselves to my mind would lead to two courses, to be combined with each other. The first would be, a previously concerted plan which, stupendous as the undertaking may seem, I do not believe impracticable, to remove in case of emergency, the credit, and the most important part of the capital of the City of London to some situation less threatened with immediate danger, and to enable those who *must*, if the enemy approaches, shut their houses in London, to open them again at Manchester, Liverpool, or York. The other, still more gigantic, but perhaps something easier in the execution, would be to make among the whole monied and mercantile interest of the metropolis, (and I do not see why it might not even be carried farther,) a joint and reciprocal guaranty of paper to be issued by each other, to a limited extent, known to the persons entering into such guaranty, and which could not be exceeded without immediate detection, and (I should say) bankruptcy, if not punishment.

"That these notions are crude and hitherto quite shapeless, I very readily admit. Perhaps you may think that no farther consideration could make them useful. If so there is no other harm done than that you will have had the honour of reading a long and useless letter. If anything can be done in this matter, the next consideration would be how? with what communication prepared and digested, in what manner brought forward, and how enforced upon the attention of the public? If there were any near prospect of our meeting we could have few more interesting topics of conversation. If not, let me know what occurs to you upon this view of it."

(D.) PITT AND WINDHAM

WINDHAM TO PITT

[For earlier letters, see "Quarterly Review" for 1912. The following refers to the Quiberon expedition (for which see *ante*), and the help offered to the Vendéan chief, Charette, to make a move on its behalf.]

"Hill St., Friday evg. [July] 3rd, [1795].

"I have been most unfortunate in missing you to-day, having called upon you both just before your arrival and just after your departure. . . . The remittance of the money which I spoke to you about, through Paris, and which I mentioned to Lord Grenville yesterday at St. James's, should be made without loss of time. It is one of those things in which four and twenty hours may make the most important difference, and the matter becomes more pressing, as an opportunity occurs of sending off a letter to Paris to-morrow morning. The manner in which I have at length proposed to arrange it is this. An engagement, signed on the part of the Government, shall be left sealed up with the banker here, by which we shall promise to pay all sums (within a certain amount) for which receipts shall be produced from Charette or whoever shall succeed him in case of his death. A sum shall then be deposited as a sort of earnest, and as a proof that the whole is not a dream on the part of the person here; for which we must be content to run the risk (in my opinion not a considerable one) which in the way first proposed we were to have been exposed to throughout. It is this sum and this engagement that I want to have by 10 or 11 o'clock to-morrow morning; in order that the letter, announcing these to have been severally deposited, and putting the whole proceeding in train, may be sent off by the opportunity above mentioned. The propriety of the proceeding seems to me so clear, and the importance of despatch so great, that, if I do not get your answer in time, I shall from my own means deposit a sum to as large an account as I can, trusting to you to bear me harmless, and shall feel a great inclination to engage for the Government, as far as I can, that, to the amount of £20,000 they will pay all sums vouched for in the manner above stated. Some step, sufficient to set the business a going, must be taken, so as not to lose the opportunity of writing by the means that will offer to-morrow.

"Another matter, equally requiring despatch, and making part of the same business, occurs in the case of the vessel now on her way down the river, for the purpose of conveying Sérent's and Ld. Grenville's letter (*sic*). As the business of procuring a vessel had been put at first in the hands of Huskisson and Nepean, and they had told me that nothing was done in it, I was not aware, till Ld. Grenville spoke to me about it yesterday, that the measure was so far advanced. I was sorry to find from Ld. Grenville that all that his letter contained was a general assurance of goodwill, and a request that the person would tell us what he wanted. Perhaps this is all that is to be said; but in that case it may be doubted how far it is worth while to send the letter. In fact, we know what he [Charette] wants. He wants a body of regular troops; he wants powder; and he wants money. The troops we have not to send. The powder is already on its way to him. The only thing that remains is the money; and this I could wish to make part of the cargo of the vessel now going out. I have for this purpose commissioned Sérent to procure, if possible, a thousand or two louis, to be sent down to-morrow, to meet the vessel in the Downs. He has told me the person whom he employs to go out; and I have no scruple of trusting him. I want only your authority, therefore, to answer for the sum, and your concurrence for sending it out by the present conveyance.[1] The enabling Charette to act, and to act speedily, is of the greatest and most pressing importance. There are most fearful accounts of the marching of the enemies' troops from all the northern frontiers for the professed purpose of opposing the risings in the interior.

"This consideration would lead me to another subject, the necessity of accelerating our preparations here, and the difficulties that rise in the way in consequence of the strange situation in which we are placed with respect to Ld. Moira.[2] He was beginning to tell me at St. James', when I was obliged to quit him to put myself in the way of the King, that there was a difference in the statements of his situation made to him by

---

[1] This probably refers to the mission of Baron de Nantiat, who sailed from England on 4th July for Nantes to meet Charette in la Vendée. See "Dropmore Papers," iii, 105-124. The Comte de Sérent was agent in England for the French Princes.

[2] Lord Moira commanded the force that was soon to proceed to strengthen that which had sailed for Quiberon. He deemed the force insufficient. See "Dropmore Papers," iii, 90.

you and the D. of Y[ork] which he wished to have cleared up. In the meantime he is keeping aloof and reserving himself for a declaration that he takes the command merely as a person ordered, and protesting to a certain degree against the service on which he is to be employed. One deficiency which he complains of, I think ought instantly to be provided for—I mean that of cavalry. As we shall have few infantry to send, and that (*sic*) so large a force may probably be wanted, we must, at least, endeavour to make it up in cavalry, which ought to be prepared for embarkation with all possible expedition, since it is but too likely that, even should a landing be made good (which every hour of delay renders more doubtful), they may be so much pressed as to make it extremely important that a strong force should be ready to come to their aid. At present, I fear, little or no provision is made for this, and therefore I am anxious to mention it."

PITT TO WINDHAM

"Hollwood, Saturday, July 4, 1795.

"I enclose a paper which I have signed containing an engagement in the name of the Lords of the Treasury which I hope will answer your purpose.[1] If any thing more formal is necessary it may be supplied afterwards. I have left of necessity a blank for the name of the banker to whom the money is to be paid here, which you will have the goodness to fill up. I must also trouble you to have a copy made of the paper. I do not know whether it will be possible at so short a warning to procure any money for the deposit you wish, but I have written to Mr. Carthew, my secretary, to try all means at the Treasury and let you know the result. From what you mention respecting the money to be sent by Sérent, I conclude there is no difficulty in his procuring the sum wanted, and I will take care it shall be immediately reimbursed.

"I will take an early opportunity of seeing Lord Moira to clear up what he supposes to be a difference in the Duke of York's statement and mine: and I very much hope it will end in his declining to undertake the command, as I have reason to believe that if anything material is to be done, Lord Cornwallis would undertake it."

[On 31st July 1796 Pitt invites Windham to meet him and Dundas at Hertford Bridge on the Southampton road to meet and confer with Moira as to the Vendéan expedition.]

[1] The money to be sent to the French Royalists, referred to in the previous letter.

PITT TO WINDHAM

"Saty. Aug. 8, [1795].

". . . The orders for selecting the regts. for Noirmoutier were concerted last night with the Duke of York who undertook that they should go to-day. But the instructions cannot be sent before Monday, as there must be a Cabinet for that purpose."

[On 2nd September 1795 Pitt refers to difficulties in the way of coining French money for use with the French Royalists.]

WINDHAM TO PITT

"Oct. 16, 1795.

" Though I have long seen and lamented the little disposition that there is, to give to the Royalist cause the sort of support, which I should think necessary; of which I cannot but consider the late decision of the Cabinet, as a new and unfortunate proof;[1] yet there is one species of assistance, which I thought it was agreed to continue without abatement, during the continuance of the war. I mean that of arms, ammunition, and money. Are we however doing any such thing? Independent of the decision, which I have just been regretting, and which will have the effect I fear, of lessening in an immense proportion, the facility of our communication with Charette, there are no less than seven large enrolments of people that may not be improperly called armies, the lowest being 8,000, and the highest 20 or 25 thousand, some of which are in a situation to be supplied from the money sent from Monsieur, even if Monsieur shd. [not?] find the means of landing and taking the money with him. These have long represented their capacity and disposition to act, and to make important diversions in favour of Charette, if they could be assisted by means, and those not very considerable ones, of assembling and putting their people in motion. The greatest part of these are under the conduct of people perfectly well known to us, and on whom entire reliance can be placed for a due application of any sums entrusted to them. Some of these persons are here; and for the others, there [are?] agents ready, on whom an equal reliance might be placed.

" It becomes absolutely necessary to come to some resolution on this point. For, as it is, these persons are acting under a per-

---

[1] This refers to the decision of the Cabinet on the Wednesday previous to withdraw the British troops from l'Ile d'Yeu, and to leave the Comte d'Artois ["Monsieur"] and the *émigrés* free to return. See Pitt's letter of 16th October to Grenville (" Dropmore Papers," iii, 140).

suasion, that no assistance which this country can give them of
the sort above described, and of which it could be sure of the
application, would be withheld. To say the truth, I feel myself
in a very unpleasant situation; for having uniformly contributed
to give this persuasion, in some instances more directly, in others
less so, if a contrary determination is taken, or if this is not certain of being acted upon, I must of necessity take the earliest
steps to undeceive them; that I may not be instrumental in
leading them into an error, so fatal as that of expecting, which
they are not likely to receive. My own case however in this respect is little different to that of any other member of the Government, except inasmuch as I may have had with many of the
parties more personal communication; for nothing that I have
conveyed to them, differs from that which is to be found in effect
in various publick instruments, both written and printed. We
are all therefore interested in coming to some explicit determination upon the subject; and interested likewise, that this should
be done speedily, in order that no more precious time should be
lost, of which there has been already a great deal; if the intention has been to give to the force still subsisting in Brittany all
the effect, of which I think be capable [*sic*]. . . ."

PITT TO WINDHAM

"Walmer Castle, Octr. 18, 1795.

"I received your letter this morning, and tho' I cannot but
feel the impossibility under the present circumstances of risking
any further operations with our own troops on the coast of
France, I entirely agree with you in the expediency of sending
liberal supplies of money, wherever we have reasonable ground
to hope that they will not be misapplied. I have accordingly
given directions for procuring as expeditiously as possible a
further sum of £100,000 in dollars. The precaution you suggest
of sending stores etc. for our own troops with a view to their
possible detention, is certainly highly proper; and directions
have been sent for providing the most necessary articles. I shall
certainly be in town on Tuesday."

WINDHAM TO PITT

"Park St., March 14, 1796.

[The number of arms in store or expected is *in total* 116,000; the
army being fully supplied, this whole number is disposable for foreign
service. Crewe, at the Office of Ordnance, represents the number disposable as only 22,000]—

—"a quantity which, though possibly sufficient for such clandes-
tine conveyance as has hitherto been carried on from Jersey,

and such imperfect and languid attempts as we have hitherto made upon other parts of the coast is utterly inadequate to what the country cd. dispose of, or to what we shd. wish to send, shd. the Royalists by any chance get possession of a port or a post on the coast. In fact, Puisaye has uniformly said, and repeats the offer in his last letters, that, for any such supply of arms and powder, as will repay him for the effort, he can come down to the coast and retain possession of it for a week possibly or ten days; and I am actually endeavouring to arrange with the Prince de Bouillon a plan for that purpose—besides the attempt which I hope we shall continually be making to throw in supplies to the Morbihan and to Charette; even tho' we have abandoned (unwisely as I think) the having a fleet nearly stationary at Quiberon. I think therefore you will be of opinion that, however it may be expedient to stop the further manufacture of Trade Arms, it will clearly not be right to refuse a contract for the purchase of 60,000 stand, many of them second hand, I believe, but in good state from the Continent. The question depends very much upon the portion of the 116,000 which will be ready to be produced, if called for, for any service in the interior. But for God's sake do not let us be in the situation of finding an opportunity for sending into France what quantity of arms we please, either for the support of the Royalists in conjunction with us, or for their support separately, and of not having the arms to send."

[On 30th March 1796 Windham issues instructions to officers about to proceed to Brittany, bidding them repair to the headquarters of the Royalist armies, find out their strength, taking as guide the paper delivered by Lord Gr[sic] to the D. of Har[court?]. They are to act as British officers, and seek to mitigate the horrors of that civil war.

On 27th April 1796 Windham states at length to Pitt the difficulties hindering his action in helping the French Royalists, and his conviction that that work, involving close and minute attention to the news that came over, would be transacted better as part of the official duties of the War Department; but neither Dundas nor Huskisson singly would have the time duly to attend to it. Unless care is at once taken, the force under Scépeaux will go the same way as those under Stofflet, Sapinaud, and Charette.

On 10th July 1796 Windham informs Pitt of the way in which he was distributing 6,000 louis d'or between the French Royalist leaders, Frotté and Puisaye. Of the £30,000 per month promised to the French Royalists, only £1,000 or £2,000 has been sent, a deficiency due to the "unfortunate ill opinion that has been entertained of that service." Frotté, when in England, had been promised at least £1,000 a month. Arguing in favour of a vigorous support of the Royalists, Windham says:]

" The sum, as an article of national expense, will be nothing, and the effects of it may go to everything that is most important. When the whole force of the Republic shall be turned to the destruction of this country, as I cannot but think it will before we shall attain the blessings of peace, we shall then know what the difference is between having all this side of France smooth and open to their operations, and perhaps even willing to co-operate with them, or of having it, as it has been hitherto, filled with bodies of people fighting with them at every step and ready to rise upon them in a mass in case of any misfortune that should befal them."

[Again, on 10th July 1796 Windham informs Pitt that of the £30,000 per month promised the Royalists, only about £15,000 or £16,000 has been sent. At present the Prince de Bouillon has not a sou in hand to send over. He adds:]

"The question is, not now of retaining the Royalists as a means of effecting a counter-Revolution or of rescuing a part of the country from the usurpers, but as a great rampart and barrier interposed for the defence of this country. Four great provinces filled with insurrection on the western side of France were no bad outworks for the protection of Great Britain. . . . I cannot wish to leave a bad name in a country distinguished by the most glorious struggle that has ever been made in support of virtue and order against vice and crime."

PITT TO WINDHAM

"Dropmore, Sunday, Aug. 28, 1796.

"I received this morning your letter of yesterday, and agree very much with you that a communication such as you mention ought to be made to M. de Puisaye. As his letter of authority and instructions, I believe, came from Mr. Dundas, the recal ought naturally to be from the same quarter, and I have just written to him on the subject. I have also mentioned to him that it seems to me adviseable to take any reasonable chance even with some risk, of sending a moderate sum of money, and have desired him if he concurs in this, to direct application to be made for an issue of secret service, which is the only fund from which the money can be furnished, or to the account of which it can be placed without much inconvenience. I rather fear we may find some embarrassment with respect to part of what has been furnished already, which however we must arrange as well as we can. I mention it now only as the reason for wishing the issue to be made in the first instance in this channel."

[On 5th January 1797 Windham recounts the sums sent to the French Royalists, and states that of what was sent to the Isle d'Yeu, about £18,000 came back. The *émigrés* discharged from the *cadres* recently dissolved were in a wretched state, and should be succoured. On 18th March 1797 he mentions a report that Pitt will soon]

" reduce all the foreign corps except a certain number of them that are serving in the West Indies. I don't know what sort of a war you are going to carry on, except that it cannot be one in which troops are wanted of the first quality and capable of being employed offensively."

[For the accounts of sums spent for the Royalists, see Windham's letter of 2nd September 1797 in " Dropmore Papers," iii, 362-8.]

WINDHAM TO PITT

" Fulham, Oct. 10, 1797.

" I send you because I am bound to do so, an extract of a letter from M. de Puysaye; tho' with no very sanguine expectation that you will be disposed to give to the contents, the same attention that I should. You are of opinion, at least so I should collect, that amidst the endless changes of things in France, some government may be found willing to listen to our vows for peace, and grant us terms not utterly destructive, in the first instance of the independence or commerce of the country—such an event may certainly happen; and if we go lower and lower in our terms, at least within certain limits, the probability may very likely be increased.[1] Yet you must admit, that such an event may not happen, and in fact unless our terms should fall faster than our means, is hardly more likely at any future period, than at present. My own idea of the probability is that this will not happen. But that we shall go on, and on, in this tiding [2] system, till at last we shall be utterly aground, and lye without resistance at the mercy of the enemy, to be disposed of as they think fit. It seems to me that what are called safe and prudent counsels, are often the most replete with danger, and lead to risks the most dreadful of any, that men can resort to. —When we threw the desperate cast of risking the last army of the country, in a conflict with the yellow fever, we did it under the notion of playing a safe game, and not committing ourselves in such perilous enterprizes, as those of attempting to co-operate with the Royalists of France. It is not necessary to point out the consequences—we are in the whimsical situation of being condemned to a period of indefinite war, without any means of annoying the enemy. Let us take care that by the same line of

[1] The Fructidorian Directory had haughtily rejected Pitt's terms.
[2] Cf. W.'s phrase to Malmesbury (" Malmesbury Diaries," iii, 590).

prudent conduct, we do not find ourselves in a similar, and worse situation a year or two hence.

"What I have to say, upon the immediate subject of the letter, is, that the names there mentioned, are not persons that I now hear of for the first time. They have been known to me long since, as persons with whom Puysay was in correspondence for the object in question, and by whom probably, bating the risks that must always attend such enterprizes, it wd. long ago have been delivered into our hands, if the fatal determination had not been taken to recall our fleet at any price, from the station at Quiberon, a station which I have good authority in believing the best that could be taken, even independent of any views to the internal state of France.

"At all events, let me beg your attention, before the business of Parliament shall call it off, to the several points mentioned in my letter of a month or two. If you think it wise and fitting, wholly to abandon the Royalists, at least let us do it, in a way not to leave upon our name the reproach of false dealing in pecuniary concerns. At least, let us pay the debts, which are strictly and all but legally due, if not those which are equitably so. With respect to cooperation with the interiour, I shall agree with you perhaps, that unless this is done upon system it can hardly be done with effect, or be done at all; and that such a change of system cannot be made without great effort. But are we not in a situation in which nothing but great efforts can save the country, and are we not acting like persons who prefer to die of a mortification, rather than to submit to the immediate pain and hazard of an operation?"

Private. PITT TO WINDHAM

"Downing Street, Feb. 13th, 1798.

"It seems hard to break in upon the enviable repose of the secession established at Bath, by any thing like politics. But I cannot help troubling you with a piece of intelligence, which if you should have any thoughts of coming back in the course of the year to the House of Commons or the Cabinet, you ought to be previously acquainted with. You will not be surprised to hear that it has been thought necessary not longer to delay filling up the vacancy in the Privy Seal, lest Mr. Harrison should discover that, we could go on as well without any such office. On the whole, I have seen no better arrangement than that it should be given to Lord Westmoreland, Lord Chesterfield succeeding him as Master of the Horse, and Lord Auckland coming to the Post Office. I perhaps guess that towards some of the parties in this arrangement, you are not likely to feel any particular partiality, but I hope you will not see any material objection to it. You will be glad to hear at the same time that Lord Fitzwilliam accepts the Lieutenancy of the West Riding. More difficulties have been created, and much more negociation in consequence than seemed at all to belong to so simple a transaction, but it is finally settled."

Private. PITT TO WINDHAM

"Hollwood, Tuesday, June 12th, 1798.

"In consequence of repeated representations from Lord Camden, recently and very strongly renewed, it has been thought right to propose to Lord Cornwallis to undertake the situation both of Lord Lieutenant and Commander-in-Chief, which his zeal for the Public Service has induced him to accept; and the appointment will take place immediately. I hope the arrangement will appear to you likely to be attended with good consequences."

PITT TO WINDHAM

"Friday, 11 A.M. [July 12, 1798].

"I am just going to a Conference on our secret expedition which will be an excuse for deferring the Minorca coals till to-morrow, and I have no thoughts of absconding this evening."

PITT TO WINDHAM

"Downing Street, May 4, 1799.

"In consequence of the intelligence yesterday confirming the probability that the French may be gone southward five ships of the line have been ordered to proceed immediately from Cawsand Bay [1] to join Lord St. Vincent. Six or seven more will be in readiness at a moment's warning, either for the same destination, or any other which fresh intelligence may point out. With this force at our disposal, it seems to be thought better not to send any provisional instruction to Lord Bridport, especially as I find the opinion at the Admiralty is that he is not likely to receive certain accounts from the southward as soon as we are; and the bare knowledge of their having at first steered that way would not be sufficient to justify his leaving Ireland and the Channel open. Every precaution has been taken to put Ld. St. Vincent and all our squadrons in the Mediterranean on their

[1] In Plymouth Sound. This refers to the voyage of Admiral Bruix to the Mediterranean to join the Spanish fleet. St. Vincent was blockading Cadiz

guard, and to apprise them of the reinforcement sent and of that in readiness."

[On 22nd May 1799 Windham deprecates any plan of getting an indemnity from France as she was before 1791. We cannot restore monarchy without the help of the French Royalists, and the announcements of indemnities will be fatal to that. It is useless to announce that that plan will be adopted after the expiration of a certain time. It is also useless to suppress our opinions as to the restoration of monarchy. On 2nd July 1799 Windham recommends that Barthélemy shall be sent back to the Continent in a neutral vessel.]

WINDHAM TO GRENVILLE

"Park Street, 16 July, 1799.

"The change of things, which has brought us back to the same hopes as at the beginning of the war seems to have brought us likewise to the same errors. We are proceeding equally without regard to those Allies, who if not in the first instance must in the last be the most necessary of all; and are letting loose upon the royalists in the interior, all those whom the successors of the Allies have set aside from combatting upon the frontier. The garrisons of Turin and other places are now about to do the same thing, that the garrisons of Mayence and Valenciennes did at the beginning of the contest. They are to be employed in garrisoning Brest and keeping in order the royalists of those provinces. Surely it is necessary that something should be done with a view to this evil. My idea is, that in the case of any future prisoners, taken upon capitulation, one of the conditions should be, that they should not serve (either against the allies) or against any party in France acting in the name of Louis XVIII. It is perfectly possible and most likely that such a condition will produce no effect, in the use that will be made of any prisoners so surrendered; and that not a man the less will be employed against the royalists. But the same may be said probably in the case of any conditions made in favour of the Allies. The chief advantage will be in the impression made upon the royalists; and in its furnishing the most safe and possibly the most efficacious of all modes of manifesting to the well-affected in France, the sentiments with which the Allies are actuated. . . .

"It appears by accounts from all quarters, that a considerable tendency to insurrection is showing itself throughout the whole extent of the royalist provinces, it is certain indeed that it must be so. The disposition has never ceased to exist, and having only been kept down, by the strong hand of military force, is sure to rise the moment that pressure is removed. Do we mean to leave this spirit wholly unassisted, and while we are seeking and relying upon insurrection every where else, to reject it in the quarter where we are sure to find it in its highest degree of intensity, and where it can alone prove directly and completely effectual? If we do not, it is high time that means should be taken to co-operate with these dispositions; and that we should not be to seek at the moment, when some successful operation on the part of the royalists may call upon us for immediate assistance."

WINDHAM TO PITT

"24 July, 1799.

"If the design is really and seriously entertained of directing the war to the coast of France, as soon as the Allies shall have entered on the other side, it is very necessary that some preparatory measures for that purpose should be begun without loss of time. I stated once in conversation with you, what I urged more at large in a letter to Lord Grenville, that the notion of keeping back the exertions of the royalists, by leaving them without assistance or countenance was a very mistaken one; and that the only way of preventing the insurrection from breaking out prematurely, and of acquiring over the royalists any useful ascendancy, was to rescue them from their present state of distress and abandonment, and to give them reason to think that at a proper period you meant to espouse their cause. It is plain at least, that a contrary system has not proved effectual; as the insurrection seems to be breaking out very generally at this moment.

"The Duke of Harcourt by the desire of 'Monsieur' has made an application to send into France most of the chiefs who have been resident for some time here; with a view to their exerting their influence towards stopping the insurrection that has already in many parts begun. . . .

"From all that appears respecting the state of things in France, as well as the probable progress of the allied armies, it would have been well that the present armament had in the first instance been sent to the coast of France rather than to Holland. I cannot but think that the moment for us to act on the coast of France is the moment when the Allies shall enter on the other side. I do not on reflection see much ground for the notion that if the insurrection of the Royalists shd. break out before the beginning of the next campaign, they will be liable to be crushed during the time that the armies of the Allies must remain to a certain degree inactive. In the first place the insurrection of the Royalists will in a great measure break out in spite of everything that can be done to prevent it: it is impossible to suppose that the armies of the Allies can be advancing towards Lyons, and the Royalist provinces not be thrown into a state in which their intentions will be clearly manifested, and the Directory be excited to employ against them whatever means shall be in their power. . . ."

[For Pitt's letter of 30th August 1799 to Windham see Rose, "William Pitt and the Great War," p. 379.]

[On 7th September 1799 Windham writes to Pitt on the means to be used for the conveyance of arms into Brittany. He adds:]

" Whether anything can be done, in case Austria should persist in her present foolish and scandalous policy, or should wholly fly off, is a matter of very difficult consideration, and on which I am far from being sanguine; much as I have been inclined to count on the resources to be derived from the discontents of France, and on the alliance to be form'd, with the well affected party there. Something however must be tried in that way, as the only resource in fact that will be left us, for I hope we should even then be far from hearing again, and still further from listening to, any cry for peace.

" Ld. Grenville seems to speak very candidly and moderately upon his favourite plan of operations in Flanders; I hope you and Mr. Dundas are in the same dispositions. My own idea would clearly be, whatever were the success of our operations; to desist as soon as we had driven the enemy across the [River] Waal, or to acquiesce in what we have already got, shd. the Dutch not fairly declare themselves. The new government would then, I conceive, be safe, supposing France incapable of detaching an army against it; and except on that supposition, I don't conceive it could be safe; though we could succeed in getting possession of the frontier fortresses. It does not appear to me that there is in point of fact, anything between these two cases. I cannot but deprecate any proceedings that should pledge us to engage further, either in Holland, or Flanders; and in consequence feel fearful of the effect of measures, such as were started, when I was with you at Walmer; of sending officers from hence to co-operate with the insurgents in Brabant. I stated this danger soon after to Ld. Grenville. . . ."

[On 3rd October 1799 Windham strongly deprecates the despatch of cavalry to the Duke of York in Holland.]

WINDHAM TO PITT

" Park Str., 30 Octr. 99.

" . . . For God's sake let us at length exert ourselves to support these people [the French Royalists] who, very contrary to other promised insurgents, rise first, and trust to support afterwards. We have refused them assistance for years upon the plea that assistance was useless, for they were not in force ever to venture to shew themselves. They now do shew themselves, and what shall be said, if we refuse or neglect to support them. I tremble for the event, but do not let it be said to be our fault. —Delay is destruction.—The crisis is such, that we must count by hours. Remember that the first great effort of the Royalists for co-operation with this country, in their march to Granville, was lost by a delay of not more than three days; and the arrival of the reinforcement at Quiberon, by which the whole of that disaster might have been prevented, by a period still less.[1] There are demurs about arms, because we cannot afford to send them any but foreign arms. I wish you to consider, in what hands twenty thousand stand of arms can at this moment be so important, as in those, who are to determine whether the Royalist war is to subsist or not in the western provinces of France."

PITT TO WINDHAM

" Downing Street, Friday, Nov. 1st.

" I have seen Crewe from the Ordnance. We have settled to send immediately twenty thousand arms from the Tower in addition to seven thousand in store at Portsmouth: and there is a good prospect of collecting speedily some thousand more both of foreign arms and of those returned from the Militia."

[On 5th November 1799 Windham writes to Pitt urging immediate succour in money to the Royalists ready to rise in Normandy: "It is perfectly idle to be paying at the rate of £120,000 per month for a Russian army in Switzerland, and to scruple any sum which can be made effectual for the purpose of creating an army in France." The next letter refers to offers which might come from the French Government installed in power by the *coup d'état* of Brumaire.]

WINDHAM TO PITT

" Park St., Nov. 18th, 1799.

" It is certainly very right that upon a question such as that which may soon arise, no decision should be taken hastily, nor without allowing a careful consideration to objections the most repugnant to our wishes and first impressions. But after all that

---

[1] Windham's charge is incorrect. The succours under Sombreuil reached Quiberon in time, but were refused admission to the fort on the isthmus by Hervilly, the commander; and the loss of that fort through treachery caused the disaster.

is done, I cannot see any difficulty in rejecting flatly and [at] once any overtures that may be made in the present moment. It seems to me that there would be ridicule as well as danger, in adopting any other course. For some time to come, I should say for a long time, a governt. such as the present, dropt from the clouds, or rather starting from underneath the ground, is in no state to offer anything. It cannot answer for its own existence for the next four and twenty hours. Its propositions for some time to come should be treated, in my opinion, as something scarcely deserving a serious answer, and such I am persuaded will be the publick opinion, if we do not leave it to be formed, not by chance, but by something a great deal worse, by the language of those whose business it is to mislead it. . . .

"I am sorry to find that the placing the Russians at Jersey has already had the effect which I apprehended, and has occasioned the marching into that neighbourhood of part of the army of Holland."

PITT TO WINDHAM

"Bromley Hill, Sunday, Dec. 22d, 1799.

"I most entirely agree with you that the delay of ten days (or even much more) in sending one ship with troops to Ireland, can be of no importance compared with risking the delay of a month in sending 10,000 arms to the Royalists under their present circumstances; and I hope you will find no difficulty in settling that the ship in question shall be transferred to the latter service. I shall return to town to-morrow, and expect M. de la Rosière at one with some farther information; after which I shall be extremely glad to talk over the business with you, if you find it convenient to call. The more I consider it, the more I feel impatient to arrange a plan for giving as speedily as the season will admit, effectual succour in troops as well as arms and money."

Private   SAME TO SAME

"Downing Street, Wednesday, Jan. 15th [1800].

"It turns out that there is a 2d letter from the P. of Bouillon of the 8th, saying positively that the 17th is the day fixed by Monsr. Bourmont. At any rate therefore our reinforcement can scarce be in time, and frigates there are none at this moment disposable. Enclosed however is a note of the arrangement we have made, and we may take the chance of any delay on the coast which may still render it useful. We shall I think have no tryal for our voices sooner than Monday the 27th, as the papers

U

will probably not be laid till Wednesday, and cannot be considered for some days. This delay will I hope give you ample time to get rid of your hoarseness, and the west wind is come to your aid. If anything more is wanting, my experience would recommend common spermacetti mixture as infallible; Canning gives the same account of malt tea."

SAME TO SAME

"Downing Street, Monday, Jan. 20th [1800].

"The answer[1] has been drawn quick conformably to the ideas we talked of, and was generally approved by the Cabinet to-day. I think it completely keeps up to the tone of the former paper, and without weakening in any respect the substance, recapitulates the leading ideas in a way to obviate all possible misconstruction, and to help very much the impression here. I am very glad you did not venture out to-day, and hope you will be repaid for your prudence."

Private   ### SAME TO SAME

"Downing Street, Thursday, April 24th, 1800.

"The King having approved of Mr. Dundas being appointed to the office of Keeper of the Privy Seal of Scotland, he will in consequence resign that of Treasurer of the Navy. I do not know whether you would on the whole prefer the latter situation to that which you now hold; but as it is certainly in some respects more desirable, and is from practise equally fit to be held with a seat in the Cabinet, I have thought it right to lay the circumstance before you for your decision, in preference to any other arrangement which may come under consideration. . . ."

WINDHAM TO PITT

"Friday, April 25, 1800.

"I lose no time in thanking you for the consideration which has led to the offer contained in your letter. Though the situation would in many respects be more eligible than that which I now hold, yet under all the circumstances I cannot hesitate in declining it, including certainly as an insuperable objection, any condition that would seem to deliver the office to me in a state less complete and respectable, than that in which it has been before held."

[1] *I.e.*, the answer to Bonaparte's offer of peace (see Rose's "William Pitt and the Great War," p. 384).

SAME TO SAME

Thursday, May 8th [1800].

" I have been just told at St. James', from what seemed to be good authority, that, in some of the arrangements proposed for disposing of the Treasurership of the Navy, the reserve respecting the House, has been no longer insisted upon. I must recall to your recollection, that the refusal in my answer applied solely to the offer, as coupled with that condition ; and was accompanied with no declaration as to the judgement I should form upon an offer of the situation free from any qualification."

PITT TO WINDHAM

" Downing Street, Friday, May 9th, 1800.

" The information which I find had reached you on the subject of the arrangement relative to the house at Somerset Place was erroneous, no change having been made in the proposed allotment, which I before communicated to you. If any had arisen, I would not have omitted, after the sentiment stated in your letter, to have apprised you of it before the office of Treasurer of the Navy had been offered to any other person."

(E.) BURKE TO WINDHAM

[For earlier letters see "Quarterly Review" for 1912.]

[N.B. The first two letters refer to the brief Viceroyalty in Ireland of Earl Fitzwilliam (December 1794 to February 1795), who went as the nominee of the Portland Whigs after their accession to the Pitt Cabinet in July 1794. It is now known by a memorandum of Lord Grenville ("Dropmore Papers," iii, pp. 35-8) that Ministers had prescribed the policy to be followed at Dublin, and that Fitzwilliam departed from that agreement. (See *ante* for a discussion of this subject.) He was therefore recalled, to the indignation of Burke, whose letters show lack of knowledge of the essential facts of the case. Mrs. Crewe was a prominent figure in the Whig *salons*. The former of these letters is probably to her; the latter almost certainly.]

[March, 1795 ?]

". . . I did not think it possible that, after my great domestic blow,[1] I should ever have felt pain or anxiety from any other cause. But I did not calculate rightly. For a year past, and longer, I have done perhaps as much as ever man did to bring and to keep people together. But I have been unfortunate. All the means of conciliation I have used have become so many causes of contention. In that contention, I am certain, I have had no intentional share—as certain as that I have had my full share in the punishment. A great man[2] may say that this, too, is poetic justice; and it may be so. I am little disposed to attack others, and not much more so to defend myself. I have lived, and now I have nothing to do but to die. The gentleman you mention to have seen at Ld. P.'s has always had a very great share in my esteem.[3] He did me the honour to call at Nerot's Hotel in my absence. I pity him very much. I am quite sure he always acts on principle: but it is a most unfortunate thing when, without either personal breach or party hostility, an opinion of duty leads a man to execute a sentence of punishment on a man of good character, with whom he has lived on terms of amity, how deserved soever the punishment may be. But every man will judge best for himself. It was in a manner

---

[1] The death of his only son, Richard, on 2nd August, 1794.
[2] Pitt (?).   [3] Windham.

but the other day before I knew that Ld. Mn. would go, that I spoke of Pelham as the properest man in the world to go secretary to the illustrious culprit who is now coming hither under an accusation;[1] and, such are the revolutions of the world that he now takes the secretary's place forfeited under that accusation. The world is much above my understanding. As to the proceedings about the [Prince of Wales's] marriage, I wish everything had looked more auspiciously. What delays the bride? An hundred ardent vows are uttered for an eastern gale. Is Pichegru's passport necessary?[2] Cannot a Prince get so much as a wife without the leave of democracy? I suppose this dreadful case stuns all the great men into the most serious recollection, and the Prince is retired to Kempshott to meditate on this great change. Has he seen the Stadholder? Dionysius is at Corinth. Well! They all amaze me. Princes, dukes, marquises, Chancellors of the Exchequer, Secretaries of State! My heart is sick: my stomach turns; my head grows dizzy. The world seems to me to reel and stagger. The crimes of Democracy and the madness and folly of Aristocracy alike frighten and confound me. The only refuge is in God, who sees thro' all these mazes. Adieu, God bless you ever."

"Saturday [March—April, 1795?].

". . . I feel to the bottom of my heart for the distresses that touch you so much to the quick for our worthy friend at Burlington House [the Duke of Portland]. I read the part of your letter that regards him at Lord F[itzwilliam]'s, where I received it. He was exceedingly affected: so was Lady Fitzwilliam. But how either of the parties can do anything towards the alleviation of their common sufferings I know not. Lord F. assured me that he felt with the utmost tenderness for what his old friend must suffer: that his heart towards him was exactly in its old place; that the change in their relation was a cause of great grief to him, but not in the smallest degree, of resentment; that the task he had to go through was one imposed upon him by the most tyrannical necessity; and that if, for private regards and feelings (which the world would construe into something a great deal worse) he was to abandon his cause, he must not only forfeit his own honour, but the honour and character of his friends, who had so nobly supported his Government, and indeed of the whole kingdom of Ireland, that had shown uncommon marks of confidence in him. That if he were to compromise on these points, no Englishman after him would be trusted by the honourable and disinterested part of that country. These things he re-

---

[1] Earl Fitzwilliam.

[2] Pichegru had conquered Holland, and his troops were entering North Germany. The Princess Caroline of Brunswick therefore had to return.

iterated with great sensibility but with great temper over and over again, as indeed he had done at several other times. It is a woful situation of things, which time and events (that do more to bring matters to rights than all our endeavours) can alone rectifye. I must think that they who saw, step by step, this excellent man led to his own suicide, for such it is truly in a public light, must be inexpressibly hard-hearted not to have taken some measures to prevent him from inflicting that unheard of punishment, on his friend in the first instance, but in the end much more surely and much more severely, upon himself.

"God bless you and forward all your wishes and labours for the wretched.[1] They are in the great hotels, in the pompous colonnades, in the spacious Courts, in the town gardens, in the titled heads, and the hearts covered with purple honours, in great fortunes and in high offices—in what-not outward show of happiness, as well as in the cottages of starving fugitives, which your kindness led you the other day to visit—with this woful difference, that to the unhappy of the latter you may bring some relief—not to the former. Their sufferings are out of reach of your charity.

"The Kings are all gone out of town. May Heaven give us better days. Adieu. Adieu.

"Put down Lady F. for a subscriber."

[The remaining letters, with one exception, are from Burke to his old friend William Windham, Secretary at War conjointly with Dundas in the Pitt Ministry, who, along with Burke, warmly espoused the cause of the French Royalists, and desired that all our military efforts should be used in their assistance in Brittany and la Vendée. As has been shown in the essay—"Was Pitt responsible for the Quiberon Disaster?"— Windham had been largely concerned with the preparations for that expedition. In a letter, probably of 27th June 1795, Burke assured Windham of his joy at the first successes at Quiberon, and of his hope that he might be mistaken in the character and capacity of the French leader, the Comte de Puisaye. On hearing of the disaster at Quiberon Burke wrote in a state of distress, which was aggravated by the news of the death of Colonel Havilland, husband of a young lady who was staying with Mr. and Mrs. Burke at Beaconsfield:]

"30th July, [1795].

"I am at the dregs of the vessel, and I must drink what is in it. How I shall break this dreadful affair to the poor worthy creature, now the only remains of my family, I cannot conceive. She is delicate in the extreme, and far gone with child. If I could conceal it from her by any arts of my own, her mother-in-law would not conceal it. In other respects the times are woful

---

[1] *I.e.*, the French *émigrés* in England.

indeed. I suppose the utmost I hear is but too true. Adieu!
Thanks for your most friendly attentions. Nothing could be
more accommodating than Dundas. He is always so. But the
thing is not with him."

"Nov. 17, 1795.

[Burke comments on recent debates, in which Lord Grenville behaved
handsomely, the Duke of Bedford ill, and Windham splendidly. He
thanks him and criticises Sheridan for his abusing "the privilege of
his new kindred with the Duke of Portland."]

". . . The number of those gentlemen *in the* House is not
large, but their style seems to bespeak confidence in numbers
elsewhere, within the kingdom or in the neighbouring Republic.
It was said, I know not by what Spartan to an ambassador, I
know not of what small commonwealth: 'Friend! your speech
supposes an army.' Their speeches certainly do. If I knew
nothing but from the paper, I should think they contrived to
keep the *haut de pavée.* Mr. Pitt seems to have begun his speech
in a perfectly proper manner; but it looks as if he were beat
down by clamour and had abandoned the ground he had so
advantageously taken. This I am sure of, that it is perfectly
ridiculous, after all that has happened, to affect to consider the
present traitorous machinations, or any other of the evils of our
time, to a mob. If that were all, tho' in that case I should not
despise the danger, I should think it infinitely less than I do.
The body of the people is untainted in all ranks, and is by far
the most sound in the humblest of all. But there is no rank or
class into which the evil of Jacobinism has not penetrated; and
that disseminated contagion is infinitely more mischievous than
if it had seized upon the *whole* of any *one* description; for then
the *whole* of some *other* would be enabled to act with union,
energy, and vigour against it. But it will happen with us, I fear,
as it has happened in France, where the *crasis* of the blood was
everywhere broke, curdled and in a manner dissolved, and this
led to the general dissolution. As to the Bills [1] you have in hand,
they are good so far as they go. *Valeant quantum valere possunt.*
You must make many more of them, and after all the whole
body will be ineffectual. Do you not trust too much in *laws*
and take *men* too little into your account? Your magistrates
will not be able to balance or even to stand before the great men,
who, by and by, will attend those meetings which your Bills
permit and in vain endeavour to regulate. They raise all the
clamour of the strongest measure and are imbecillity itself. They
will produce other Bills, the children not of their strength, but
of their weakness, and will multiply like those feeble animals

---

[1] The Bills limiting public meetings.

who increase in proportion to their insignificance. 'With the French Republic at your door, your Constitution *cannot* exist.' It is too weak to protect itself. With every trial you will make new discoveries of its impotence; and what is worse, of the debility of the materials that compose it. If you attempt to change it you will shake the country on which it stands to its very center, and let in the very evil you mean to prevent. All I have to advise at present is, that you will follow your Bills for the safety of the King's person, etc., with an Act of Association, like that in Queen Elizabeth's and in King William's reign, contriving, if possible, to discriminate by some effectual test, and, what is more effectual, by the judicious choice of some committees of weight enough to call upon the other Associators (always under the sanction of Govt. for their acts and their existence too) to assist them with their whole *posse*.[1] This will be absolutely necessary towards making a regular party for the constitution. But still remember I say all this, *protestando*, that, with a fraternity with the regicide system of France, neither anything I can propose or that can come from wisdom ten thousand times beyond mine, can ever adjourn our ruin for a very short period."

[He then advises caution on the affair of *provisions*.]

" Wednesday, Nov. 29, 1795.

" . . . It is coming fast to that point which you and I have long foreseen. As we have foreseen it, it would be a shame indeed if we were not prepared for it, both in the collectedness of our own minds and in every precaution which in our situation belongs to us. After what has happened in France it would be a shame indeed if Mr. Foxe's guillotine (I mean the travelling guillotine for me, the permanent for you) should come to our doors, without our having a previous struggle for our necks, and for what ought to be far more precious to us. . . . If it comes to a requisition, Beaconsfield will furnish 30 heavy horsemen and 20 light. By this scantling judge of England."

[He then refers to the fury of the Jacobin attack in the House of Commons, as reported in the "Sun." When a little earlier they charged Ministers with a plot against the King in order to further their plans, why did not the Ministry refuse to go on till that foul charge was cleared up?]

---

[1] The Associations were loyal. The Societies and Clubs, as a rule, malcontent.

"Jany. 17, 1796.

[Burke sends Windham the pamphlet—the twin brother of the one he has been considering.]

" The moment of peace is yet, I hope, so far distant that chance may still do much to save us from so dreadful a catastrophe. I mean, of course, peace with a Jacobinical republic. Yet everything has a dreadful tendency that way: and the great impediment is wanting—a conviction of the extent of the danger which from that moment will begin to operate against the country. It really does not appear to me that from the moment such a peace is made, the shame and degradation of this country will be any longer supportable. What would happen if a regicide ambassador were to set up house here, with his wife ' removable upon four days' notice '? "

" Beaconsfield, March 6, 1796.

" What I was given to understand, but what I could not believe, nor could you, has happened. The House of Commons is condemned in costs and damages by the East India Company. We have charged Hastings with robbery of the people of India. Instead of punishing him, we reward him with a second robbery. No account demanded of him. No reason asked why, with an immense salary, when he might have been honestly rich, he is, as he says, miserably poor? Why no account of the bribes? The Lords may say—they will not convict him of them. But they have not said, nor can they say, that he has accounted for the money: then their judgment has the infamy to say that bribery and forgery of bonds to cover it, is a proper way of getting a revenue. But no account! No account of any kind! My dear sir, I must not have it said that we have compromised the matter by a pension to the accuser and another to the accused. The House of Lords may say we have made a false charge. So may the bystanders. Are we to say it ourselves?

" I hope to have my petition ready by the end of the week. Your poor friend, Mrs. Burke, is still very ill, and cannot quit her room or her couch. I have suspended the work on the peace.[1] It is not fit that any good should happen to this enormous mass of corruption, peculation, oppression, robbery, prevarication in judgment, and direct perversion of judgment. God's ways are unsearchable. But I think the bolt will fall; and it is fit that it should fall on me among the rest. Adieu. Adieu."

[1] " Thoughts on a Regicide Peace " was published late in the summer of 1796.

"Bath, August 1, 1796.

[Burke deplores the present state of things.]

"If you, in the full force of a youthful manhood, in an high situation, with such virtues, talents, and acquirements as God has disposed to very few living (if to any), can do nothing; if from your meridian lustre the public can reflect no light, what can be done by the expiring snuff of my farthing candle? No: there is no one thing which we can propose that to those who shut their eyes to the evil (and therefore cannot conceive what remedies are to be proportioned to it) that would not be thought monstrous, wild, and extravagant? Are we of the stuff of those who, with Hannibal in the bowels of Italy, would think of transporting the gross of our [their?] strength to Africk and to Spain? I go no further. All must depend on individuals, a very few individuals, now, as always it has done. If the Duumvirate [1] who direct all (you will pardon me if I do not call you a minister) have not the courage to look our situation in the face themselves, and to state it to Parliament too, if they do not cease to consider what is to be said to their adversaries there, as an eloquent Bar defence, grounded on the principles of those adversaries, rather than what ought to be done against the grand adversary—then, I say, there is not for us a ray of hope. Their talents are great indeed; but if they are thus directed, better half with a just direction, than the whole, than twice the whole, in the present course."

[On 27th August 1796 he congratulates Windham on having saved from dissolution the remains of the regiments of French *émigrés* in British pay. The following letters refer to the negotiations for peace with France conducted by Lord Malmesbury at Paris.]

"Bath, Sept. 11, 1796.

"We seem to me to be descending to the center of ruin with so accelerated a motion thro' the thin medium of pusillanimity, disgrace, and humiliation, that it seems to be an attempt to fight with the established laws of nature to stop the course which things are taking. But on this we shall talk more when we meet. . . ."

"Tuesday, Nov. 1, 1796.

". . . The more I think of it the more I feel astonished that the Ministry can think of putting the whole affairs of Europe blindfold into the hands of Lord Malmesbury: it is at this time they are mad enough to evacuate Corsica; and is it now that

[1] Pitt and Dundas.

they are to look for a fleet to confront that of Spain.[1] My head and heart are ready to split at once. Adieu."

"Friday, Nov. 11, 1796.

". . . This City business is curious enough. It is but a foretaste of what Mr. Pitt is to expect from his mistaken politicks at home and abroad. His favourite commissary,[2] who left us for Lord North and Lord North for him, contrives a triumph for Mr. Fox over him, when he is led before the triumphal car of his enemy covered over with obloquy and mud! Oh! But the newspaper says, these mobs that drew the one and threw stones at the other, were hired mobs. Possibly it may be so. But I am sure such hirelings would have fared but ill, if a general sentiment, more mitigated indeed and decent, did not go with those who committed outrages. The whole democratick corps was there. Why was that? Ought wooden-head to have been left to his own indiscretion?

"Indeed Mr. Pitt will daily feel the effects of his leaving himself without a cause, and without any independent and honourable support. He cannot hinder the world from feeling (?) that, when he assumes Mr. Foxe's principles, that Mr. Fox had the advantage of an earlier profession, and proposed peace when peace might clearly be had with more advantage than it can be made at present. The people, God knows, reason but little. But surely our shameful flight from the Mediterranean must be felt as the most disgraceful event, and possibly the most fatal that has ever occurred in our history. He would not suffer a spirit to be raised in favour of himself and his measures. He will find a spirit raised against him and them which he will endeavour in vain to resist. He will, by and bye, be as ill treated in his person in London, as he is by his substitute in Paris. Well! God send you all well out of this ugly scrape."

"Nov. 25, 1796.

[Burke dislikes the proposed appointment of General Stuart to help in the defence of Portugal; for his proceedings in Corsica prove him unfit for the work. He will quarrel with the *émigré* corps there.]

"We have abandoned Italy politically, commercially, morally. Spain is become our enemy. Our negotiation at Paris will serve no purpose but to discover the limits of what it is we propose

[1] The evacuation of Corsica and Elba was mainly in order to concentrate our naval forces in home waters in view of the recent declaration of war by Spain.

[2] *I.e.*, Dundas. Burke next refers to the riotous reception accorded to Pitt in the City, in consequence of the recent serious increase of taxation.

for the Emperor—for the accommodation of the regicides (much abler politicians than we are) in their scheme of opening a separate treaty with him; and now our last hold on the Continent Genl. Stuart is to secure it to us. It is all over. No experience of the fatal effects of jobbs (*sic*) will hinder jobbers from jobbing to the last. . . ."

BURKE TO WOODFORD

"Beaconsfield, Dec. 9, 1796.
". . . I have read the debate on the budget. I think Mr. Pitt was less lofty and loud in his triumph than I expected. As to Fox, he seemed in a perfect paroxism (*sic*) of rage and fury."

[He then refers at length to the proposal for an effort to induce the Emperor to liberate Lafayette, which he strongly deprecates.]

"With what face can Mr. Fox desire a national interference with the Emperor for this man at the very moment when he is opposing, as all along he has opposed, the grant of any loan or subsidy or assistance whatsoever to this our Ally, and who in the moment of this proposition, instead of an attempt to soothe or soften him, speaks an insulting language, such as was never heard before, in this time, and before this time never would have been tolerated in relation to an Ally of this country. . . . In the name of God what is the meaning of this project of Mr. Pitt concerning the further relief of the poor.[1] What relief do they want, except that which it will be difficult indeed to give, to make them more frugal or more industrious? I see he's running for popular plates with Mr. Fox. . . . Lord Malmesbury fills me with despair, or rather those who have sent him. Are they quite mad to found this treaty on a basis of exchanges and mutual cessions? Why did Mr. Pitt conceal the succours he gave the Emperor? Policy required they should be as publick as possible. Why not state that he intends to give him a further subsidy?"

BURKE TO WINDHAM

"Sunday Dec. 18, 1796.[2]
[Burke again refers to Fox's motion on behalf of Lafayette.]

"The whole drift of this motion is subservient to the general plan of making every Power in alliance with this country odious. . . . As I should have expected, even from the report of your

[1] For this subject see *ante* the essay, "Pitt and Relief of the Poor."
[2] For Windham's reply to this letter see Burke's "Correspondence," iv, 401.

speech in the 'Sun,' the impression it made on the House was great and decisive. Laurence[1] told me that this impression did honour both to the speaker and to the feelings of the House, which he states to have been on both sides just what they ought to have been. Nothing can exceed the ability of that speech; and it was necessary it should be so, as no overabundant zeal was shown for the general cause of sovereign Powers by those who had spoken before you. . . . The fact is, that the minority here must consider *the mere fact of rebellion* to be the most transcendant of all merit. Be it so with them, if they please. But is that a plea that is likely to be prevalent with sovereigns? . . . God save me from falling into the merciful hands of those who think the business of Foulon and Bertier (*sic*) no act of cruelty. God save you from their humanity and compassion. This has been a very bad day for me, but I have begun to work. I see I must fortify myself on the point of the nation's ability to prosecute the war. I would not wish, however, to call much attention to the collection of materials I wish you [to] procure for me. I think they may easily be had at the Excise and Customs. . . ."

"Beaconsfield, 25 Dec. 1796.[2]

"I received your kind letter. The return of Lord Malmesbury is just in all its circumstances what it ought to be, and indeed, just what might be expected. This mongrel has been whipped back to the kennel yelping and with his tail between his legs. This will be a great triumph of Ministry, of Opposition, and of the nation at large. The Opposition only will be true to its principles. Woeful fidelity and consistency when such are the principles. The rest will certainly fail on the tryal. Indeed they have so much relyed on the certainty of peace and have provided, if for any war, only a war at home, that I do not see how they can carry on any other with energy and effect. However, anything is better than a Jacobin peace. In every other posture of things there are at least chances. I am quite sure that notwithstanding all that Ld. Malmesbury has suffered, both as a negotiator and a gentleman, that, in order to justify himself in his first step, kicked in as he has been and kicked out, he will still in the House of Lords hold out some sort of hopes. He will endeavour to keep open to himself a rode (*sic*) to some such infamous employment in future. You know better than I do, who know nothing of the subject, what is to be done with the *Interior* of France, but of this I am sure, if nothing can be

---

[1] Dr. French Laurence, M.P., an intimate friend of Burke.

[2] In reply to Windham's letter of 24th December announcing the failure of Lord Malmesbury's mission (Burke, "Correspondence," iv, 412).

done there, nothing can be done with effect anywhere. Unfortunately we have disabled ourselves of our best means by sending the French Royalists to Portugal, but that is no fault of yours, who advized that measure in order to save these unhappy corps from being broke as criminals with every sort of disgrace, or sent with equal disgrace and with every sort of other ill consequence to the West Indies. God Almighty bless you and support you in the endeavours which yet you will make use of for the salvation of your country and of betrayed Europe. . . ."

"Jany. 5th, 1797.

[Burke still hopes to procure the accounts for his projected work, but not so as to reveal his purpose.]

"The use that I intend to make of these accounts, if they come up to my ideas, as I think they will, is to finish my demonstration—that no class of the Poeple (*sic*) hath as yet felt the war in any sort of privation. . . .

"If Ireland was the object of the Brest armament (and it now looks not improbable) what handsome provision has been made for its defence! No depôt of force in any central point, no pre-concerted arrangement. Agamemnon General in the South, with Cooks for his Aid-de-Camps (*sic*), and so corpulent that I am told he cannot go on horseback. Had Hoche landed in Bantry Bay or in any bay more commodious for his purposes, as many there are on that coast, nothing could have hindered him from making himself master of Cork, of putting that place under contribution of money and provisions, and, having routed the weak force in that part, from marching forward and beating all the rest in detail. The apparent want of intelligence of the enemy's design was truly deplorable, but if intelligence was received and credited, that the enemy's design pointed at Ireland, how did it happen that no fleet was off Ireland to oppose the enemy on his approach, or, on failure, to intercept him on his return? While the Jacobin fleet was at anchor in Bantry Bay, Lord Bridport was at Portsmouth, and Colpoys, after going God knows where, returns himself into harbour. The French leave Bantry on the 27th of Decr., and Ld. Bridport sails from Portsmouth to look for them on the 3rd of this month: if he meets any of them it is a miracle, and it must be owing to the terrible condition which they are in. So much for intelligence, foresight, and precaution.

"'For my own part I never believed that the French could have thought of Ireland, equipped as they were in such a tempestuous season.'[1] . . . But the fate of that expedition is, I trust, now

---

[1] Burke adds here that he thought the French aimed at Nova Scotia.

decided by an arm stronger than ours, and by a wisdom capable of counteracting our folly. Yet, my dear friend, I do tremble lest the boldness of these men in risquing everything, and our negligence or misfortune in not providing for anything, may not always find the Heavens so propitious. I confess, I tremble at the danger whilst I am rejoicing at the escape. However, I sincerely congratulate you upon it. I consider you so much as a friend, to whom I am used to disburthen myself, that I forget I am writing to a Minister with whom I ought to have management[1] when I discuss anything relative to the conduct of his colleagues. The want of a steady intelligence, both from Paris and from Brest, is a thing I cannot comprehend, because I am sure it might have been obtained. God bless you. I am very faint and perhaps peevish, but ever most truly yours."

"Bath, 12 Feb., 1797.

[Burke has been reading Erskine's pamphlet, which is less full of vanity than he expected but contained]—

"all the old matter hashed up. France would have been very good if she had not been provoked by the wickedness of Great Britain and other Powers, who are confederates, not against her ambition, but against her Liberty; that she was right in every point and at all times and with all nations; that the cure for all disorders consists in your making your representation at home as like hers as possible, in making peace with her by giving her all that you offer and all that she demands. . . .

"I am to observe once for all that these gentlemen put the case of France and America exactly upon a par, and always have done so. I leave them to rejoice in that discovery, and in my inconsistency and the antidote they have found in one part of my writings against the poison that exists in another. You will observe that this *alliance* with France and a change in the Constitution are things that always go hand in hand, and, I think, consistently enough. The only point upon which he is strong, but on which I don't think he makes the most is Mr. Pitt having refused to make proffers of peace whilst our affairs were in a prosperous condition. . . . Mr. Pitt unfortunately is in the condition of '*Paulo pugnante.*' He cannot make peace, and he will not make war. '*Deus dabit his quoque finem*'—which I believe I will not live to see. I wish [I] may live to make my final protest against the proceedings of both factions. . . ."

---

[1] The French word *ménagements* (*i.e.*, considerate treatment) is the sense.

"Bath, April 26, 1797.[1]

". . . To do anything without raising a spirit (I mean a national spirit), with all the energy and much of the conduct of a party spirit, I hold to be a thing absolutely impossible; and I hold it to be impossible to raise that spirit whilst the Minister who ought to excite it and direct it, and to employ it for the purposes of his own existence, as well as of that of his master and of his country, is the very person who oppresses it, and who, with double the expense and double the apparatus of every sort with which our most vigorous wars were ever carried on, is resolved to make no war at all. Our only hope is in a submission to the enemy by taking up the principles of that enemy at home, and by submitting to any terms which the directing body of that enemy abroad shall think fit to prescribe. If they demand Portsmouth as a cautionary town, it will be yielded to them; and as to our navy, that has already perished, with its discipline, for ever. I have my thoughts upon a modification, without a departure from the terms of our late unhappy submission; but they are of no moment because no attention will be paid to them. What cure for all this? What but in that spirit

> 'which might create a soul
> Under the ribs of Death.'[2]

"But to this end it is absolutely necessary that no terms within or without doors should be kept with the French party in our Parliament, who must be treated as public enemies, else they and the Head of the Republic abroad will infallibly overpower all the feeble force of a flying resistance."

[Burke then refers to an estimable pamphlet, "Reasons against National Despondency," as ably written, but too tenderly towards Ministers. We must, he adds, undertake "an active war in the territory of France," despite the recent disbanding of some cavalry regiments.]

"Bath, 16 May, 1797.

". . . There is an end of us. The Revolution is accomplished even before the Jacobin peace."

[He prophesies the end of all discipline in the Navy owing to the weak tolerance shown to the mutineers by Lord Howe in his mission to ascertain grievances. He then refers despairingly to Irish affairs and the despatch of 8,000 soldiers to support the Junto there.]

"'to which both kingdoms are sacrificed.' . . . I see they are making a run through the most contemptible wretch on

---

[1] In answer to Windham's letter of 25th April (Burke, "Correspondence," iv, 439).
[2] Milton, "Comus," 561, 562.

earth, Lord Dillon, and another, not much less so, a Mr. Day, at my friend Dr. Hussey, upon account of his zeal in strengthening his flock according to his principles against the religious persecution which, under pretence of military discipline, has been exercised against the Roman Catholic soldiery.[1]

[He then refers to the Fitzwilliam affair and says Pitt's plan is to destroy all those who will not further "a Jacobin indifference to all religion." The common people in Ireland are Roman Catholics and will have no other religion. He had pointed this out to Dundas, who listened patiently, but took no heed "to the purpose I had so much at heart, the peace of Ireland, its consolidation with this kingdom, and a direction of our common force against our common enemy."]

[Burke died on 9th July 1797 at Beaconsfield.]

[1] See Burke's letter of 12th May to Dr. Hussey in Burke's "Correspondence," iv, 447.

(F.) PITT TO LORD HARROWBY

[The Earl of Harrowby was Minister for Foreign Affairs in the Pitt Cabinet of 1804. In January 1805 he resigned owing to ill-health, but in July 1805 became Chancellor of the Duchy of Lancaster, and undertook an important mission to the Court of Berlin, for which see Rose, "Despatches relating to the Third Coalition." The first letter refers to the expected rupture with Spain.]

"Walmer Castle, Friday, Sept. 23rd, 1804.

" I entirely concur with you in thinking that permission ought to be given to the Spanish ships now in our ports to compleat their lading with our manufactures and produce and proceed to Spain, and also that vessels with cargoes of grain for Spain from foreign ports should be allowed protection from our cruisers under the restrictions you propose. I see nothing that can be said to Souza[1] in the smallest degree different from what you propose. We certainly can say nothing positive as to what assistance we can give, and nothing that implies we can give any, without knowing what exertions they would make for themselves.

" The account you give of the information brought from Ferrol by Mr. Brickdale (? Bircdale) seems to give some probability to the idea that nothing more may be intended by the Spanish preparations than to send troops to Bilboa. It seems therefore quite right to give such an authority as you propose to Frere, if he is satisfied with the Spanish explanation and receives assurances that the arming any ships to act as ships of war is suspended, to direct Cochrane to suffer any ships armed *en flûte* and fitted as transports to pass unmolested; but in that case Cochrane must of course also take means on the spot to ascertain that such really is the description of the vessels.[2] Might it not also be right to send similar directions from hence immediately to Cochrane? I put this question doubtfully, because we certainly are justified in stopping any ships till such explanation as we are entitled to expect is given by the Spanish

[1] The Portuguese Ambassador in London.
[2] Cochrane was watching five French sail-of-the-line which took refuge in Ferrol in July 1803.

306

Court; but perhaps if it turns out that the orders were really given under an unexpected and pressing necessity on account of the insurrections, we might overlook the omission of previous communication to us. I return the papers from the Spanish merchants. I shall be happy to see you and Leveson on Sunday.

"P.S. On the subject of the note about Wright,[1] I still think there is no room for any civil words, and that it is better not to say anything in writing of our intention to release any French officer in return."

"Walmer Castle, Wednesday, Sept. 12, 1804.

"I return the draft which I received from you by the post this morning, and concur entirely in the propriety of sending them immediately. I have obeyed your orders by endeavouring to *entière* (?), but have found nothing to suggest beyond a few trifling verbal alterations. If you can without much inconvenience to yourself go to Weymouth about Monday, as you propose, it would I think on every account be very desirable. I propose being in town on Saturday, and we shall probably either meet in Downing Street on that day, or at Putney on Sunday morning."

[See "Stanhope Miscellanies" (1863), 26, *et seq.*, for Pitt's letters of 18th September and 19th November, 1804.]

"Downing Street, Nov. 20th, 1804.

"I hope I shall have not have judged wrong in acting quite contrary to your orders, but I think what Woronzow has to communicate to you so satisfactory, that I cannot help flattering myself it is likely to prove a very good auxiliary to Bath waters; and he seemed so much bent upon telling you his own story that I could not at any rate have discouraged his visit.[2]

"It appears to me that the principles in which it is now the great object of Russia to ascertain our concurrence are so completely our own, that there cannot be the smallest hesitation in contracting any provisional engagement with them that can but convince them of our determination to act with them fairly and decidedly. To reduce the French Power within its *ancient* limits (if possible) at least within *some*; is precisely the basis we wish to establish for any general concert. The restoration of the monarchy may become in the course of events, an object to be distinctly aimed at, but it certainly cannot be made itself

---

[1] Captain Wright's ship was captured by French gun-vessels during a calm.

[2] Vorontzoff [Woronzow] was Russian ambassador in England.

a substantive object in the first instance; and it is very satisfactory to see that in this important point there is no apparent difference in our sentiments.[1] The proposal for increasing our Hanoverian Corps, and forming one of Albanians, also tallies very much with the projects we have had in view, and may I think produce great facilities, by enabling them to increase the amount of their force destined to co-operate with Austria. I cannot help hoping too, from the manner in which one of the dispatches refers to the amount of force which Austria has demanded, that greater progress has been made towards some secret provisional engagement between the two Courts than we are apprized of. On the whole I think the communication promises better than anything we have yet seen, and gives a fair chance of our at last seeing some decided effort made adequate to the circumstances of the times. Your draft to Jackson[2] appears to be perfectly right, and I have only added a short postscript applying the principles it contains to the circumstances of his release. I am very sorry that the advantage which you appeared at first to derive from Bath, has been at all interrupted; but that ought not to discourage you from persevering. We shall none of us reckon that the experiment has been at all tried in less than a compleat three weeks; and not fairly unless, after coming up for a week when the Spanish answer arrives, you return for three weeks more before Parliament."

"Downing Street, Wednesday, Nov. 21st, 1804.

"You will receive from Hammond the account of our negotiation with Spain being broken off. As this will leave nothing to be done immediately of a diplomatic sort except preparing a Manifesto, I hope you will determine on remaining at Bath. But if you should think it necessary to come up (which I hope you will not) I trust at least that you will make your arrangements to return again without loss of time, and compleat your *six weeks*. You will have full time for this, as the state of money allows us again to postpone Parliament till the 15th; the appearance of war with Spain seems to me no reason for not doing so, as the inconvenience of meeting so soon after Christmas will be readily admitted as a sufficient reason for the delay."

"Downing Street, Wednesday, Feb. 6th, 1805.

"I received your letter this morning. The statement it contains is perfectly clear and satisfactory, and tallies entirely with

---

[1] This corrects Thiers' statement as to the differences between Russian and British policy.

[2] Francis J. Jackson (1770-1814), was British Minister at Berlin.

my recollection of the particulars as you communicated them to me by your letter to Walmer. The letter itself I am perfectly sure I destroyed; but that circumstance is not material, as I think without it we know exactly the state of the case, and I see no difficulty in any part of it. It is certainly not necessary to trouble you with any formal reference on the subject. Our whole case taken together is I think much strengthened by each additional volume of information which the Opposition have been so kind as to ask for, and I have no doubt that both our debate and division will be very triumphant. The day of battle however is again postponed till Monday, at the desire of Opposition, as several additional papers have only been presented to-day. I am grieved not to receive a better account of your own health, and shall be impatient to hear that it is thought prudent for you to make a fresh trial of Bath. There is nothing new at present and we are all going on very quietly and comfortably in spite of the ' Morning Chronicle.' "

"June 4th.

" What solution is there to the problem proposed in the private letter; or what is to be the conduct of Russia and G. Britain, if Austria declines the concert and a general war becomes impossible at present? I believe that we must remain at war, and Russia declare war, as the best chance of forcing the other Powers to a decision."

"Downing Street, Sept. 27th, 1805.

" I had another very full conversation before I left Weymouth, and again urged every topic that I thought could produce an impression, but with no better success than before; and I am convinced the resolution is fixed of running all chances, and never agreeing to take the step proposed but in case of actual necessity.[1] I see therefore nothing to be done but to prepare to fight the battle as well as we can. The prospect on the Continent is improving every day. I have desired Hammond to send you an account of the contents of yesterday's mail. The answer of Austria to Duroc's proposal, and the junction of the Bavarian force, are beyond our expectations. The next accounts will probably bring us the decision of Prussia, which I think will at least not be hostile.

" P.S. I do not see anything at present that should hasten your return to town, and I rather hope to make my excursion to Walmer in the beginning of next week."

[1] See Rose, " William Pitt and the Great War," p. 530.

"Downing Street, Oct. 15th, 1805.

" I came to town last night and hope to return again to Walmer in about a week. In the interval there are so many things to be discussed that as I know you are ready to move at a short warning I should be very glad if you can come to town, and we shall probably receive accounts interesting enough to make you not repent being on the spot. Our last letters from Berlin are of the 1st Oct. The march of the Russian troops thro Prussian territory was suspended till after an interview which was to take place between the Emperor and the K. of P. probably at Briesh, and about this time there is great reason to hope the result may ensure at least the fair neutrality of Prussia. If Russia would follow our advice, there would be some chance of co-operation. Denmark is assembling 26,000 men in Holstein, apparently with very favourable sentiments; and Sweden seems not unlikely to close with our last proposal and furnish 12,000 troops for active service. This force added to the Russians at Stralsund, and with some chance of Hessians (if Prussia is really neutral) affords no bad prospect of a considerable army in the North exclusive of Prussia. In the meantime France has nearly evacuated Hanover, and we are sending our Hanoverian force to the Elbe with about 5,000 British, to see whether they can be established with safety during the winter; and if not, with orders to return before the frost sets in, with whatever recruits in the interval they can draw from the country which will probably be numerous. The combined forces of Francis and Congreve will probably commence their operations on the opposite coast in a few days." [1]

"Downing Street, Oct. 17th, 1805.

" The accounts received last night from Berlin are so unexpectedly favourable and encouraging, that I cannot help sending you an abstract of them by a messenger for the chance of his meeting you on the road to town, or of following you in your tour through Needwood, if you should have set out before my letter of Tuesday reached you. You will not wonder that this intelligence increases my desire to see you, as I think the opening now given if properly improved may lead to everything we can wish. The whole fortune of the war, and the destiny of Europe may turn upon our having a person on the spot at Berlin in whom unlimited confidence can be placed, and who may turn the favourable disposition at Berlin to the best advantage, and communicate expeditiously from thence with both Emperors. I need not tell you who that person is. Pray revolve in your mind in your post-chaise whether it is possible

---

[1] An attempt on the Boulogne flotilla.

for him to undertake it. I would not propose it if I did not really feel it as important as I have stated. The business might probably all be compleated in six or seven weeks."

"Downing Street, Oct. 29th, 1805.

"The credentials I find are prepared and follow you by the messenger. I also send you the paper which Nicolai brought me containing the proposal of the Russian Finance Minister respecting the subsidies; and a memo. which has been sent to Leveson [1] in consequence, explaining why we cannot adopt that plan, and what are the measures we have taken. There is also a similar memo. as to the measures taken for Austrian subsidy, as well as a short abstract of the funds provided at Hamburg and the demands authorized to be made upon them up to the 15th of January, and a comparison of the proposed actual payments with the total amount of what is computed to fall due to each of the Imperial Courts within the same period. The latter computation must of course be uncertain until we know the precise period when the different Russian armies quitted their frontiers, and the actual amount of the Russian and Austrian force. The last of these I have probably estimated beyond the mark; but even allowing for the whole, you will see that provision is made for paying within the year or at furthest by the 15th Jany. the whole of the monthly subsidies, and nearly one half of the Russian and two thirds of the Austrian *mise en campagne*—of course this latter sum could not be expected to be paid at once. The payment I propose on account ought I think to be deemed to be very liberal; and the remainder may be completed early in next year. In addition to these payments, there may possibly be toward £100,000 for the different engagements to Sweden, making in the whole about £2,900,000. This will leave about £600,000 of our vote of credit disposable, but it may be desireable to reserve some small proportion of this for any demands from Naples which may go beyond what may be defrayed by secret service. On the whole I think (if absolutely necessary) you might safely stipulate for the actual payment of £500,000, and without any possible difficulty at least for £250,000 on account of Prussia and her Allies between the *middle* of *November* and the *middle* of *January*. And whatever be the times and proportions of actual payment, there seems no objection to agreeing that the monthly payments should be computed as due from the signature of any treaty you may conclude, or even (if Hardenberg should revert to that proposal

[1] Granville Leveson-Gower (1773-1846) was British ambassador at St. Petersburg. Compare this despatch with those of Mulgrave to Harrowby, Rose, "Third Coalition," pp. 207-220.

and insist upon it) from the 1st Oct. I hope you give as little implicit credit as I do to Commodore Robin's impertinent bulletin, and form as favourable conclusions from the intelligence in the private letter from Amsterdam, the substance of which was sent you by the post yesterday. We have nothing fresh to-day. I am not a little impatient for authentic news, but still more so for a west wind.

"P.S. I find the three first papers mentioned are sent already. I have enclosed the remainder."

"Downing Street, Oct. 30th, 1805.

"I enclose you a very gloomy account from one of our Dutch correspondents,[1] from which however I am inclined to deduct as he proposes at least one half. And though the remainder would be bad enough in itself, I see nothing in the consequences at all alarming, if Austria has the courage to pursue the only policy which is safe under such circumstances. Allowing for the great loss the French must evidently have sustained they must probably require some interval before they can move to the Inn, and that march must be from 100 to 150 miles. If the Austrians and Russians on the Inn, were to be 100,000 men by the 20th of this month, the further reinforcements they must probably receive from the Tirol and Salzburg, from such part of the Ulm army as may find its way to them, and from the Austrian reserves, must enable them to make a stout and probably an effectual resistance in that position. And they have still to expect a second army of fifty thousand Russians in no long time, and, I should hope, 40,000 more of the reserve originally intended by Russia to have been kept on the frontier of Lithuania, but which might surely now be converted into an active force. Add to this that if Bonaparte advances to the Inn, he will be at least 300 miles from his frontier, just about the time the Prussian force will be collected at Bayreuth, and his Allies probably advancing from Saxony and Hesse, the first of which places seems not more than 80 miles, the second 150 and the third 200 miles from points that would cut off all communication with Mentz, Manheim and Strasburg. I am only unreasonable enough to desire that the Prussian army may move for this object within five days from your arrival, and everything may yet take a decisive turn in our favour before Christmas. We are flattering ourselves that as the wind is nearly due north, you may be able to sail, but I take the chance of this finding you still at Yarmouth.

"P.S. It may be material to add that all we know of the writer

---

[1] Respecting the battle at Ulm.

of this intelligence is that he is the correspondent of a house in the City which will not disclose his name, and which house is known to Brooke in D. Hawkesbury's office, but the name of which he is not at liberty to communicate. The letter is not dated, but from the reference must be of the 26th. There is as you see no certain reliance on its being even an accurate statement of whatever may be the exaggerated official accounts published at the Hague. I cannot help even thinking that there is a very good chance of the Austrians and Russians having passed the Inn, and attacked the advanced corps under Bernadotte before the French army can move from Ulm."

"Downing Street, Nov. 6th, 1805.

" I cannot let Jackson[1] depart without one word to congratulate you on the glorious news of which he is the bearer. One hardly knows how in the first moment to enjoy the triumph, considering the sacrifice it has cost—but I trust the battle of *Trafalgar* will operate in no small degree even on the Continent to counterbalance the impression of that of *Ulm*, and will teach Bonaparte what his chance is of acquiring ' the ships and commerce and colonies' which he wants. It will not escape you to state how much the more we value this victory as it will enable us to co-operate with additional vigor in every effort on the Continent. We are still without any further intelligence from Berlin."

[On 9th November 1805 Harrowby announces to Pitt his arrival at Hamburg after long delays caused by fog.]

"Downing Street, Nov. 12th, 1805.

" I was sorry to learn by your letter from Hamburg which arrived this morning the accidents which retarded you, but happily what has been passing at Berlin has made the delay somewhat less material. We received late last night Jackson's despatches up to the 3rd, containing an account of the Treaty concluded between Russia and Prussia to which Austria was about to accede. Mulgrave sends you a despatch which contains all that occurs to us upon it; all of which and more you will have anticipated. I scarce think there is any prospect of Bonaparte's listening for a moment to a treaty proposed on such conditions and in such a manner. If however a negotiation should be opened, our right to be included is a point of great impor-

[1] Mr. Francis Jackson, British ambassador at Berlin, had been on furlough, but now returned to his embassy, the affairs of which had been entrusted to his younger brother, George, in the interval. (Rose, "Third Coalition," 220, and note.)

tance. I congratulate you most heartily on the progress already made as well as on the account of the firmness shewn by Austria since its disasters. The encouragement you are enabled to hold out, and the knowledge of our naval victories will I trust add all that is wanting to bring forth the full exertions of the Continent. In that case the past misfortunes, and even any that may happen in the interval of the next three weeks, will be soon repaired; and we shall still see Bonaparte's army either cut off or driven back to France, and Holland recovered *before Christmas*. Our object in wishing to disembark at Embden is to shorten our means of communication, and land whatever troops or stores we may send so much nearer the scenes of action, supposing any of the Allies to move immediately forward toward Holland.

" P.S. Local circumstances seem to make an attempt on Flushing at this season too precarious, but it is not quite clear that we may not find it possible if the weather proves favourable to try some diversion on the side of Voorn, and act from thence towards the Hague and afterwards Amsterdam, if the Allies should be advancing in force. We cannot, however, at all answer for being able to do this."

[For the rest of the Pitt-Harrowby correspondence see Rose, "William Pitt and the Great War," pp. 541-7; "Stanhope Miscellanies" (1863), pp. 29-39.]

(G.) LORD HARROWBY TO PITT

" It grieves me to the soul to think that your sanguine expectations of the immediate junction of Prussia are so likely to be disappointed. Whatever happens, our naval victories give us ample means of standing alone; and this must be our consolation. I cannot comprehend how our right to be joined in any treaty can now be brought forward. In the present trembling state of things it is impossible that our accession to the Congress should be insisted upon ; and it would not become our dignity to be merely proposed and rejected. Nor could this proposal come forward in the present stage of the negotiation. A succession of severe headaches have (*sic*) embarrassed my brain to such a degree that my anxiety upon all that is passing really makes me literally unfit either to do anything or to give an account of what I have done. If this lasts, I shall not (*sic*).

" P.S. This horrible secret article has finished me. It stood with its mouth open, and from mere cowardice I have run into it, and it will devour me. I am persuaded, however, that it would equally have caught me if I had run away. There is something however in every view of it which agonizes me. I am anxious beyond imagination to know what passes in England upon it, and conclude I shall by the next newspaper.

" Would it be impossible to prevail upon the King to listen to the idea of a sort of barrier treaty for Hanover, which would give Prussia a military frontier but not the territorial possession? In this unaccountable state of things I have hitherto found it impossible to communicate confidentially with Jackson, which adds not a little to all other miseries. I expect that I shall consider my orders as peremptory (?) to come away for the meeting. Therefore, pray have a frigate in waiting off the Elbe."

" I fear you will find that I have taken your instructions at any rate too much *à la lettre*; but, from the delay of your promised instructions from Mulgrave I have dreaded some rub about Hanover, and have felt such an anxiety to get some temporary arrangement forward before that insuperable bar intervenes, that I stopt at nothing.

"P.S. What can have stopt your decision on the treaty? Would to heaven it had come before I was driven to the wall by the fear of orders being given to Haugwitz to allow Austria to let its a[rmy?] down to nothing. The hope that I live upon is that you will have seen from my earliest letters home how miserable I was and how miserably I was doing and that you have before this time found out some way of sending for me."

"Berlin, Dec. 8, 1806 (*sic*).

"You will think my dispatches to-night wretchedly meagre, and so they are; but I have been so wretchedly ill for some days past with nervous headaches and sickness that I have been quite unequal to anything. I cannot yet execute that part of my instructions which relates to the admission of England to the treaty. They appear to me grounded upon two suppositions: one, that the negotiation takes a serious turn—of this as yet I know nothing. The other, that the terms will not be worse than those of the Treaty of Potsdam. After the present disorders they must be worse if there is any treaty at all.

"The Instructions also states (*sic*) that representations are to be made to the Allies. Now, the Allies have put affairs into the hands of a Prussian mediator and cannot act independently of him. How can I apply to Prussia, on whom we have no claims of present alliance, to insist upon the admission of an English negotiator to the Congress upon such terms, previously stated? All these embarrassments have led me hitherto (ill as I have been) to abstain from the subject. That and every other part has suffered even more than can be expressed from all I have suffered.

"Aulick is arrived, but does not stay many days, or perhaps hours, which I much regret. Your communication of my Instructions to W[oronzow] has also much embarrassed me. In spite of some prosperous circumstances you must not expect any treaty. I am persuaded that under the present gloom they will not sign any that I can sign.

"P.S. Don't forget the ship to be ready for us at the mouth of the Elbe, *i.e.*, for my coffin. Oh, I am serious, quite serious, a few more weeks must end me."

[For the letter of 12th December see Rose, "William Pitt and the Great War," p. 545.]

"Berlin, 23 Dec., 1705 (*sic*).

"The state of my dispatches will sufficiently show you the state of my mind. I have had some comfort in seeing Leveson

[Gower] for two days; but Anstruther is now going to the army and Hammond is grown not much less nervous than myself. Do not mention this to anybody. In this condition I only live in hopes of a recall, or of finding some ground on which I can with propriety be off. I feel that, if I could make up my mind as to the propriety of subsidising all this part of the world upon my own responsibility and without instructions, I ought to stay to do this great good or evil; but then I feel, on the other hand, that in my present state of mind and body it must be so done as to have no chance of being good and to be sure of being evil. If I am satisfied that I cannot take this upon myself without instructions, my stay would be utterly useless, unless I staid (*sic*) long enough to receive them; and this would both be awkward in appearance here, and put an end to the little chance there is of my renewing the operation. Before Leveson [Gower] goes I shall probably have decided this question, and am glad to hear that I shall find a frigate in the Elbe. If I am less dead on Wednesday, another newspaper will be to go and I will write again. Pray suggest to Mulgrave that Jackson should have full power to treat with Prussia (or Russia) as well as other States.

"You will judge of your situation altogether by the strange confusion of our dispatches and inclosures, and numbers; but pray make no observation upon it for heaven's sake at the office or elsewhere. Do not fancy, for you would fancy it most unjustly, that, if I can be of any use here, I will sacrifice that chance to any present wish of being at home. If I come away, it will be only upon a most complete conviction that I am fit only to do harm by staying."

(H.) CANNING TO PITT

[The first letter of Canning, then Under Secretary for Foreign Affairs, refers to the negotiations for peace with France conducted at Lille by Lord Malmesbury. The *coup d'état* of 18 Fructidor (4th September 1797) brought to power at Paris violent Jacobins who were opposed to peace, and soon broke off the negotiations. Aranjo, Portuguese envoy at Paris, had made a separate peace with France. Later on it was disavowed at Lisbon; but the event led Canning to suggest that we ought not to insist upon maintaining absolutely the integrity of the Portuguese possessions. Compare Canning's letters and Malmesbury's despatches in "Malmesbury Diaries," iii, pp. 461, *et seq.*]

"Spring Gardens, Sunday, Sept. 10, 1797.

[He states that he has stayed in town to hear the latest news of the negotiations at Lisle (*sic*). He is impatient at the delay there, and still more so at the delay here. As the situation there becomes more delicate, we ought to send to our envoy the fullest details.]

"If it was thought right a week ago to enable Lord M[almesbury] to soften and qualify in some degree the tone that has been taken about Portugal, or at least to put him in possession of the disposition there to do so if the case should require it, and to give him to understand that his last instructions upon the subject were not unalterable at a moment when there was known to be in part of the French government a desire not to push everything to extremities, nor to seek specious causes for a rupture, nor to avail themselves with eagerness of justifiable ones—and when it was likely or possible that a *contre projet* not wholly unfavourable to our views and wishes might be obtained—and when, to say the least, the *time* did not press so much, and it was not so likely as it is at this moment, that the accounts from Lisbon should anticipate any declaration from Ld. Malmesbury—I cannot conceive on what principle it is thought less right or necessary now to furnish Ld. M. with the means of explaining and conciliating (if there be room for it), or at least of giving distinctly to be understood what are the real sentiments and intentions of the Govt. here on the subject of Portugal, so as to prevent a rupture on grounds that we do not care about maintaining now, when, if the change (which we have

318

reason to believe) has taken place in France, there has succeeded to that apparent fairness with which Ld. M. had to treat before, a captious, and haughty and uncompromising spirit, which will be but too happy to seize the first opportunity of converting an amicable into an angry and hostile discussion, when all hopes of a moderate and acceptable *contre projet* (such as would enable us to go on in the negotiation, putting Portugal by as comparatively of no consequence) are for the present wholly at an end, and when, in point of *time*, if in no other, the case must necessarily have become urgent, so much so, perhaps, as hardly to leave the remedy any longer in our power. I cannot conceive on what principle this is to be defended unless upon a persuasion that if the violent party in France have got the better, there is no chance of the negotiation succeeding or being suffered to continue."

[He then suggests that, even if the new Directors, Rewbell and Barras, have gained all power at Paris, it is not well to facilitate the rupture on their part on the claims about Portugal "urged in the violent, unqualified, and indistinct manner in which Ld. M—— will be obliged to urge them." He would be in the painful and ridiculous position of not knowing his own Government's mind on that matter. Always to have to refer matters back to London would be humiliating to him. Canning concludes by saying that at least Malmesbury should be informed that the final decision about Portugal cannot yet be formed, and that the negotiation need not break off on that subject.]

[In a letter of 1st October 1797 Canning argues at length against publishing the despatches describing the rupture of the negotiations with France. For this purpose he puts himself in the place of a member of the Opposition.]

"Ashbourne, Thursday, Nov. 28, 1799.

[Canning refers to the possibility of another effort being made on the Continent against France, despite the failure of the Allies in Switzerland.]

"Supposing Austria to make peace and Russia to withdraw from the war, supposing us reduced to the limited system of exertion and the limited scale of expense, nothing, as it appears to me, could now be more easy than to keep up people's minds to the continuance of the war on the simple ground that it is neither safe nor now necessary or expedient to make peace with Revolutionary France, be the character of the Revolution under which she labours what it may. Do you apprehend that there is any man in this country, do you believe even that there is any man in France, to whom the first idea suggested by this last Revolution [the *coup d'état* of Brumaire] was any other than the restoration of the monarchy? Is it not plain that events are in full march towards that point? To me it seems indisputable that there is but one event (except a peace improvidently made by us), namely, the overthrow of Bonaparte by the violent party, and the consequent renewal of the Jacobin system, that can prevent, or much retard this conclusion. In that case of course there could be no peace made, and none could last that might have been made with the Consulate. But, supposing Bonaparte and Sieyès to consolidate their power (which is the only case in which you seem to apprehend a cry for peace might become troublesome), is it possible, think you, for any man, or any body of men, to persuade themselves that such a power can be lasting? That two persons linked together only by their common treachery to others, should have no fear of treachery from each other, and should not speedily find an opportunity of practising it? Whichever succeeds—no matter—is it to be conceived that the remaining despot can ever hope to maintain himself in a station so acquired without an hold upon the feelings or the prejudices of the people, in the midst of a multitude of factions all equally irritated against him, and all equally interested in overthrowing him? or that he can mean to make any other use of his power, while he holds it, than to bargain for impunity and perhaps reward, by the restoration of the Crown to its right owner? This is not subtlety or refinement of reasoning, God knows. It is the obvious irresistible inference in every plain man's mind from what he has now seen in France, compared with what he has read in his history of England; and this alone would be enough to bear up the spirits of the country long enough to give the experiment fair trial, *provided* (which I take for granted) there was no necessity for heavy additional burdens. . . ."

[He then states that France will try to stir up sedition again here; and, with Bonaparte whitewashed after gaining peace for France, the whole struggle will soon have to be done over again.]

"Where could be the objection to saying at once 'We will treat when monarchy is restored in the person of your lawful sovereign,' or, 'To your lawful monarchy we will give back everything—a cheap purchase for the peace and safety of the world.'"

"Ashbourne, Sat². Dec. 7, 1799.

"I think we differ even less than at the conclusion of your letter you seem to suppose as to the conduct to be pursued: the only point in which you do not completely satisfy me . . . is as to the language to be holden. Of the only two cases upon which you state your opinion as differing materially from what you understand mine to be—one, upon which you lay most stress in the beginning of your letter is proved before the end of it, by the inclosure which you pick up on your way, to be very little

likely to take place—I mean the establishment [in France] of a
moderate American kind of government, capable of maintaining
itself in any degree of respectability for any length of time, for
any time long enough to admit of the sending a courier and
receiving him back again at Paris, tho' with all the expedition
that kicking him back could communicate to his return.

"The plan of the new [French] constitution puts all ideas of
popular representation too much out of the question to leave
any room to suppose that a mixed Govt. is seriously intended,
and reduces therefore the chances of any Govt. that Bonaparte
and Sieyès can establish for themselves to the single one of a
military despotism, of the actual and manifest instability of which
you seem to entertain no doubt, nor of the facility with which
all notion of treaty with such a Govt. may be scouted.

"But further, the *Grand Elector for Life* is so like a constitutional King that it is difficult to conceive any otherwise of this
monstrous jumble of nonsense than as of an attempt to feel the
pulse of the nation as to the restoration of MONARCHY—limited
probably for the purposes of the personal ambition of those who
are to restore it, and, with the same view, probably, to be restored
not in the person of the right heir, but of the son of the Duke of
Orleans. . . . The other point on which you state your opinion
as if combating mine, is one upon which I think exactly as you
do; and I must have expressed myself very confusedly if I led
you to imagine that I thought otherwise:—'that we ought not
to commit ourselves by any declaration that the restoration of
royalty is the *sine quâ non* condition of Peace.'—Undoubtedly
we ought not; but surely it would be a very different thing from
this to say (as I would have you in case an offer from Paris
should make it necessary for you to say something), to accompany your refusal to treat now with a declaration, ' that you *would
treat* with a monarchy; that to the monarchy restored to its
rightful owner you would give not only peace, but peace on the
most liberal terms. . . .'

"You will send away at once without a hearing the scoundrell,
whom the present scoundrells, in their present or in any probable
state of their power, may send here to propose a treaty. That
assurance is enough to keep me quiet and comfortable for a long
time to come."

"Brooksby [near Leicester], Monday, Dec. 16, 1799.

"The letter which I enclose has just reached me, and I send
it to you as being the sequel of that which I sent you yesterday.
I do not feel myself to understand the subject enough to have
any opinion as to the reasonableness or policy of the suggestions
which it contains. The latter paragraph, about Nevis, reminds
me to remind you of the warrant. Nevis, if I am not much mis-

taken, is that which was *actually vacant*. Dominica, that which was expected to be so, and represented to be the more valuable of the two. But Nevis, by this description, is quite valuable enough, and in every respect the most desirable that could be found.

"The West Indies naturally lead me to the Slave Trade.[1] And here, in thinking over the arguments which I had to state to you in favour of the making the proposed Order in Council immediately, I find none to which you have not already perfectly assented, or which you have felt any reason for setting aside except (while it lasted) the chance of success from the expedition to Holland; and that impediment exists no longer.

"Pray tell me if there is any reason (except laziness) why the measure should not be announced at the first Cabinet, and executed at the first Council that meets? You have, as I understand you, nothing to apprehend in this instance from the traditionary wisdom and ancestral examples of Lord Liverpool, or from the sentimental and friendly opposition of Lord Westmorland. There are reasons in abundance for the measure, even if the Slave Trade were out of the question. Is it politic (does Lord Liverpool think) to take the colonies of our enemies for a a year or two, nurse them into prosperity, and restore them, formidable rivals to our own? Is it natural to invite the investment of British capital to an immense amount in foreign possessions in order (and for no other purpose that I can see) to make the restoration of them at a peace matter of clamour, and to make future wars with the Power to whom they are so restored (however just and necessary), matter of still more clamour, from the risque of British capital becoming exposed at once to British arms and to foreign confiscation? If we have already West Indian produce enough to glut the markets of Europe, is it wise in a national point of view to erect new sugar colonies for other countries to sell against those which shall remain to this country? Nay if (to admit Lord Westmorland's argument) the Slave Trade itself is a beneficial trade, is it expedient to send that British capital, which would otherwise be employed to extend the trade of Liverpool, the cultivation, and the slave population of our own islands, to lay the foundation of a rival Slave Trade from the ports of France, or Spain, or Holland? Would it not, in short (even if we looked to no other considerations except those of dry policy) be better to lay waste with fire and sword every colony that we have taken (I am sure it would be more humane), than to feed and fatten them at our own present cost

---

[1] Canning was for total and instant abolition (Bagot, "Canning and his Friends," i, p. 149). The Order in Council was to prohibit the import of slaves into the enemy's colonies conquered by us.

and to our own lasting detriment, and to restore them 1,000 per cent. more valuable than when they fell into our hands?

"When to these considerations are added that of the state in which the question of the Slave Trade now stands, the tacit agreement which the well disposed part of the West Indians conceive themselves to have made, to consent to the limitation of the trade in future to a certain percentage on the existing stock, and the pledge given by you to take care of the already vested interests of British proprietors—does not the allowing new investments of British interest to so enormous an amount to be made and a new stock to be created, pending the discussion and the interval between the announcing this principle and the application of it, look like carelessness, if not connivance at the increase of the evil which is to be remedied? And will not the old proprietors, who in their admission of the principle intended conscientiously to confine their demands to the keeping up their old estates, have some reason to complain that estates *begun* to be settled *since* the limitation was proposed, are considered (as I presume they must be) entitled to the same indulgence with those in which their interests have been vested for half a century? And when you propose to them to give the legislative sanction to this principle, which is necessary for carrying it into effect in our own old islands, will they not have a right to ask why, if you thought it so salutary, you have not already acted upon it wherever of your own mere authority you could so act? Why, while you are calling upon them to assist you in stopping the old Slave Trade, you have not, where you could do so without their assistance, prevented the growth of a new one?

" I have another reason, and I am not sure that it does not weigh with me as much as any of those which I have stated, for wishing that when next the question comes in any shape into discussion (in short, that as soon as possible), some step should be taken towards effecting that very moderate species of abolition to which all our projects are now restricted. I cannot bear to hear it gravely and pertinaciously doubted whether you really wish the accomplishment of the object or no. It is a doubt, in answer to which I can hardly speak with temper, and yet I have found, especially since Lord Westmorland's victory of last·year, and the intemperate and ostentatious use that has been made of it, many people, who I am sure mean well, professing to entertain such a doubt, and some (which is much the most provoking) candidly giving you credit for not intending so rashly as you have spoken. Nay, among the moderate West Indians (where such an opinion is most dangerous) I have found that, with the same professions as before of a readiness to *do their part* in any practicable scheme, they have evidently much less expectation of being speedily called upon to do it. I have eradicated this notion from the mind of the Ellises[1] (if it was harboured there) by telling them, with and under promise of strict secrecy, what, but for such a purpose I would not have told to them or to any body, the fact and the object of Smith's mission. They both approve most cordially of it, and both sincerely wish that the step had been taken many years ago. Charles [Ellis] has just told me that one great difficulty they find in talking to the generality of the West Indians upon the subject of any measure to be agreed on with Govt. for the restriction of the Trade, is to persuade them that Govt. has any serious intentions of that sort. Govt., they say, is at this moment planting new colonies, which will for years require a much larger Slave Trade than has been carried on for a long time back for the supply of the old islands. The greater part of the trade now carried on is for these new settlements, and yet we are made to bear the odium of the whole. Very unfairly indeed, but for an obvious reason, because, while the complaint is levelled against the old Slave Trade, it appears as if the evil were one which it is not in the power of Govt. to stop without the consent of the islands. If it were seriously meant to stop the evil, the greater part is such as Govt. might, without asking any one's consent, stop with a finger?

"How is this to be answered? I hope by the Order in Council. I am persuaded this measure (or something like it) must be the preliminary to any successful attempt in Parliament upon the question.

"And so, having disburthened my mind upon the subject, I do not desire you to take the trouble of writing to me about it, but I do earnestly entreat you to think it over seriously, and I cannot find ground to doubt of your decision."

[On 1st December 1803 Canning writes voluminously at his home, South Hill, Bracknell, Berks, charging Pitt, without proof, of having inspired statements in the " Accurate Observer " derogatory to him.]

"Whitehall, Tuesday evg., May 9, 1804.

"Upon consideration I think it much better to go out of town, in order to be out of the way of all the questions and conjectures that are going about and of the constructions and misrepresentations of my answers or my silence, which I am afraid would be not less multiplied now than they were three years ago. I shall set out therefore, to-morrow, for South Hill. But I shall be ready to come up at an hour's notice, if you should want to see me again. Before I go, I think it right to

---

[1] Canning was their guest at Brooksby. See, too, Bagot, *op. cit.*, i, 150.

assure you, which I do upon my honour, that I have mentioned what passed between us this morning to three persons only—Leveson, Morpeth and Borrington, and to these with the express prohibition not to communicate it further—not to Lord Stafford—not to Sturges;[1] which two names I specify because the opinions of the former (such as Leveson reports them to me[2]) *might* appear to be formed in concert with what he *might be supposed* to know to be mine. Whereas this is so far from being the case that when he put the question to me on Sunday of *what my conduct would be*, under the circumstances that were apprehended and have since occurred, I answered distinctly 'that I felt myself bound and pledged to obey any call that you might think proper to make upon me.' And with Sturges I have for obvious reasons cautiously abstained from dropping the slightest hint upon the subject. I indeed have rather repressed than encouraged in him and others the excessive desponding and lamentation over the failure of the broad system, almost, I believe, to the extent of incurring some suspicion that I did not in truth lament it as deeply as they do.

"I tell you all this thus minutely because I am earnestly desirous of anticipating all the attempts which (I do not say *will*, but) *may* be made, to impress you with a notion that I am either giving vent to ill humour (against *myself*—for myself only have I to blame) or seeking comfort in ostentation, or making myself party to any murmurs, loud or deep, of sorrow or indignation, against the limited scale, and especially against the rump part of your new Arrangement. I have done no such thing. And before you receive this to-morrow, I shall be out of the reach of any opportunities of doing this or any other mischief.

"Allow me before I close my letter to say one word, merely to remind you of poor Hammond. If either Ld. Grenville or Fox had come to the Foreign Office, his situation was secure. Whoever may come there will, I am pretty certain, find it very inconvenient, I believe nearly impossible, to go on without him. But they might not be aware of this. At least he thinks they might not, and has fears about himself, which, tho' I do not share them, I could not help promising to mention to you and to recommend him to your protection. His colleague, Arbuthnot, would not suffer himself to be preferred to Hammond, tho', if turned out, he would (I have no doubt) be glad enough to be turned into something else: but *he* is Hawkesbury's charge."

[Canning then recommends to Pitt's consideration Sir J. Sinclair, Sir R. Barclay, Burroughs and Ainslie.]

---

[1] Sturges Bourne was Secretary to the Treasury.
[2] Leveson-Gower was third son of Lord Stafford.

"Spring Gardens, Saty. morning, Aug. 28, 1801 [1804].[1]

"A night's reflection upon our conversation of yesterday has not produced the effect which you conceived to be most natural, of reconciling me more and more to your last proposal; my consent to which, the footing on which you placed it with respect to yourself, did extort from me at the instant, as it would to any much more distressing sacrifice to my personal feelings. That footing, as it is the only one, upon which I would accept, or hear of any the most tempting offers, such as should include the full and immediate gratification of my utmost ambition, so it is one upon which I should have found it difficult not to acquiesce in anything that you seemed to have so much at heart, however dear it might cost me to do it.

"But of one thing I confidently presume I may assure myself, that you do not value my acquiescence only in proportion to the struggle and mortification which it costs me, but that you would make any exertion on your part, which you yourself thought reasonable, and such as ought on a fair view of all circumstances, to be successful—to attain the same end at less expense of credit or feeling to me. In this confidence I cannot forbear stating to you as they now strike me—upon what I believe in my conscience to be as impartial and sober a consideration of them as if the case were another's—the circumstances of extreme and unnecessary unfairness to me in the last plan of Arrangement, which I think might be done away not only without any injustice to anybody but with the fullest admission of every claim that is placed in competition with mine—with *yours*, I should say, on my account.

"If the question were purely about what office I should take, I will own that your reasoning in favour of my old office immediately,[2] and by a vacancy to be made for the express purpose of giving it to me again—rather than the prospect of a higher one necessarily to be waited for to an uncertain period, and with the difficulty belonging to the interval which might elapse before it would be created—is satisfactory. But when this Arrangement is considered, not by itself, but with a reference to what is intended for Bragge,[3] I do think, and I am persuaded that any impartial man—that the Public at large—will think, that such a distribution of the two offices is grossly partial, and

---

[1] The date must be 1804. Canning went out of office with Pitt early in 1801 and became (unwillingly) Treasurer of the Navy in Pitt's Administration formed in May 1804.

[2] Probably that of Under Secretary for Foreign Affairs, which he resigned in March 1799.

[3] Charles Bragge had been Treasurer of the Navy in Addington's Administration.

that it will indicate such a disposition towards me, compared with others, as does not promise me very fair play in any subsequent competition. And this applies equally, whether the two offices are filled up precisely at the same time (as with a view to Sturges' succession I should certainly be glad that they were), or whether I take the Pay Office first, with the certainty that, as soon as the occasion offers, Bragge is to go *per saltum* (which you know is so very bad and wrong a thing) over my head.

"But do I therefore want the Treasuryship of the Navy with £4,000 a year? And is this the history of all my qualms and hesitations? I need not answer this to *you*; but I shall best answer it by showing what I think would be the best to all parties concerned, the most equitable arrangement. Why should not Yorke have the Treasuryship of the Navy?[1] Windham, you remember, was offered it, and would have taken it but for Dundas's reluctance to part with the House. Bragge, the Mint— £3,000 a year, and of rank so equal that Sir G. Yonge, you know, went from the War Office to it. And I, the Secretaryship at War? The scale of salary would then be—Yorke (already in possession) £4,000 a year, being a rise of £1,500, Bragge £3,000, and I £2,500, being not more in value than the Pay Office which is proposed to me. (And if further provision is wanted for Bragge, is there not Barré's office to fall within a period that cannot now be much protracted?)

"I feel perfectly assured that you cannot object to this as unfair or unreasonable. And I cannot but be persuaded that, if you suggest this arrangement.... I think it right to assure you that this is written previous to my communication with any of those whose opinions I know you would suspect, even more than my own, of partiality in my favour.... And now I have only to add that, whatever be the result of our meeting, in respect of this subject, I would not but have met, as we have done, for any consideration upon earth. Every other object of hazard or acquisition is light in comparison of that of which I have sometimes apprehended the loss, but which I do now trust that no decision, even no mistaken decision in what purely regards my own interest or happiness, can possibly take from me. I will say no more upon a subject on which my heart is full, but I shall be always in whatever situation, however separated, or however brought together, unalterably and most affectionately,

"Yours,
"G. C.

"P.S. I need not say that I shall be impatient to hear from you, and till I have heard from you upon the subject of this

---

[1] Charles Yorke had been Home Secretary under Addington.

letter, I trust you will not think me unreasonable in requesting that you will not *act* upon the decision of yesterday, even failing that which I have suggested here."

"South Hill, Nov. 7, 1805.

"I should like very much, before you take any step in the business of which we talked last week, to have one other quarter of an hour's conversation with you. I have great doubts, very great doubts, upon reflection, whether I *ought* to take advantage of your proposal, *ought* for your sake I mean, and I should not easily forgive myself, if, for any object personal to myself, I had suffered you, in the delicate and critical state in which your Government stands, and must stand, for the next six months, to do anything which might add to your difficulties or furnish ground for blame or cavil. What has passed between us on this occasion has left me no doubt of the fairness and kindness of your intentions towards me, but I must not avail myself of them at the hazard of your ease or advantage. As I shall endeavour to see you to-morrow, I need not enter into the detail of my reasonings and reflections here, but I write just to put you in possession of the nature and object of what I have to say to you. The decision shall be completely in your hands."

" *Private.*

"South Hill, Nov. 27, 1805.

"You will always find me here. I hope you will not suffer your Bath journey to be deferred till it is too late to do you much good. But I cannot wonder at your lingering in town under circumstances of so much expectation and anxiety. One must not venture to rely upon the length of the interval, after the intelligence with which the last suspension of arrivals from the Continent was followed; but the long continuance of that suspension now, and the absence of any unfavourable rumours do lead one to hope that the silence may this time be broken in a more satisfactory manner. Sunday was the termination (was it not?) of the month during which Austria was recommended to avoid an action, and at the end of which the Prussian armies were to be in a state to act? Or was the month given to Bonaparte to date only from the arrival at his headquarters of Haugwitz with the propositions for peace? That would carry on the date of the determination of Prussia so far that you could hardly look to know it by the meeting of Parliament, as it now stands fixed—hardly by the 21st, to which day I rather suppose you to meditate the prorogation. ' Ten days ' would bring it to Friday the 17th.

"Could you not arrange, before you leave town, to prepare the way for the actual accomplishment of the business which was settled when last I saw you? I ask, from no idle wish to have the thing hastened, or notorious. But, as when you now go, you will probably go to stay as long as you can; and as the time to elapse before the meeting of Parlt., even at the most distant supposable (*sic*) is not more than enough, I shall be anxious to have as much of it as is possible to look with my own eyes at all that has been doing—at least from the time of the beginning of Leveson's mission—which (especially in Hammond's absence) I cannot do comfortably, and to my full satisfaction, by sufferance, and while you are away still less.

"What do you do for Sir Richd. Strachan? I have been asked that question so often that I feel ashamed not to give any answer to it. O! that the Rendlesham Peerage could go to him, with promise of a dukedom, if you will, to The Worthy who is to have it—when you make English peers hereafter. Consider only what would be the difference of feeling to the whole Irish peerage—the whole Irish nation—at having such a man as T., such a name as Strachan's enrolled amongst them at their first vacancy—at having the *fashion set* (which once set will be followed) of making that order a reward of eminent merit, or a cheaper purchase—of jobbing support! I never felt more strongly convinced of the truth and of the importance of any proposition in my life. Pray, pray, pray think of it.

"*Private.*

"South Hill, Nov. 29, 1805.

"The silence has not been broken exactly in the way that would have been most agreeable. But it is not so much the fact of the French being at Vienna (especially as they appear to have got there without any very material action on their road), as their being there with a *month certain* of unmolested quiet and proffered negotiation before them, that fills me with despondency. It is very difficult now to persuade one's self that there is much chance of Prussia adhering to her promise of considering an indecisive answer as a signal for war. Indeed, one can hardly say that there could be any reasonable ground for her doing so. She had plenty of grounds for going to war at once without any negotiation at all. But to make the evacuation of Mantua by Bonaparte a *sine quâ non* of peace, at the moment when he is in possession of Vienna, has something in it so almost ridiculous, that (tho' I confess the notion did not strike me till events brought the two things directly into contrast, yet) reflecting that the *possible* occupation of Vienna *must* have been in their contemplation when Haugwitz's mission was determined upon, I cannot help entertaining more suspicion than I like, that the project of negotiation has all along prevailed over that of war in a much greater degree than they have been willing to confess to us. Nor can we hope (as it appears to me) that the Emperor of Russia will be much in the way of that decision. The leading fear which seems to occupy the mind of the Russians at all times is that of having their dignity compromised by an unsuccessful or ineffectual interposition. Now if he thinks it easier (as it probably may appear to him to be, though we may be persuaded it is not) to make a decent peace for the Continent, than to carry through a triumphant war, I very much fear that the Emperor of Russia will be glad enough to avoid the dangers of an actual trial of his arms, by taking advantage of the excuse which Bonaparte will cheerfully join in allowing him, that the very terror of them has answered his benevolent purpose, of imposing peace on Europe.

" As to Austria, though one must give full credit to her gallant resolution to brave all extremities of war, if supported by her allies, yet it would be idle to suppose that she could have a voice against the opening of a negotiation on whatever basis, if those allies concurred in recommending it.

"What then is the result? Why, I am afraid, this, that we ought to consider the interval (be it more or less) during which it is to continue in appearance doubtful whether a Congress shall assemble, or the war be renewed, with Prussia in the field—as the only opportunity remaining to us to make our own immediate home situation better in a military view, than it was before the diversion on the Continent raised the siege (*sic*) of invasion. I would have something attempted without delay. Boulogne, I suppose, is now out of the question—but I cannot think that Walcheren is, and I would make General M[oore?] (who has something of a Russian feeling about the compromise of his military reputation) reconsider his opinions—*not* as choosing between *that* expedition and *some other* more splendid and more easy one in which *he* would *equally* have a distinguished share, but as deciding between *himself* and some *other person*, which should take the command of *that* and that *alone*. In no other way would he come to the consideration of the subject, without prejudice.

" Surely the sending troops to Hanover cannot now be either necessary or desirable. *If* the war is continued, it is nothing to gain a month or two, or a whole winter for an object which (so long as Prussia is friendly) is in the keeping of a friend. But in the other alternative, can it be doubted that Prussia will have the offer of Hanover from France? Is there the smallest doubt of her accepting it? And then for what purpose would our troops be there, but to be civilly desired to walk out again, or to maintain themselves by force both against the enemy and against our allies? [1]

[1] The foresight evinced in this prophecy is very remarkable.

"On the other hand, if after the immense extent of the effort which you have made, you come back to Parlt. with no other fruits of the continental confederacy than the relief of a few months from the threat of invasion, and with that threat renewed at the moment when you are calling for the price of the confederacy, I cannot help fearing that the impression in the country and in Parliament will be very unfavourable indeed. And if, in addition to the fact, there appears reason to believe that a smaller expedition for objects so vital was kept back in order to accumulate force for an expedition on a greater scale to be commanded, *as such a force would be commanded*; or, that the force which was actually detached, was sent in preference to Hanover (which, according to these suppositions, you would be then either on the point of abandoning again, or compelled to maintain hostilely against Prussia), I do verily believe (what is dreadful to be uttered) that such a state of things, and of opinions in Parlt. and out of doors, would, in spite of your naval successes, be fatal to the Government. It is nothing, as I apprehend, to be able to prove, by all General M.'s arguments, that each particular object had its risque and chances of disaster. The plain naked fact will be. Here was an occasion, of three or four months' duration, when the enemy had no force, absolutely none, on any part of his coast. You had a disposable army of from 40 to 50,000 men. Nothing is done. The enemy returns at the end of his three months' war, and finds everything as he left it; and the invasion is renewed as closely as ever. What have we gained by our continental effort? If the answer is—'Nothing could be done'— only conceive what a tremendous and disheartening impression such a statement must make upon the country. By what unhoped-for concurrence of circumstances can a similar opportunity for *trying* what might be done, be afforded again? And is it a physical truth against which all our exertions must contend in vain, that the whole coast of the enemy from the Texel downwards, is absolutely unassailable, while there is scarce a point of it *from* which we may not be assailed? If this were true, would it be prudent to have it generally believed?

"The only other answer is, that our attention and our force has been otherwise occupied. How? In taking possession of Hanover, which (according to what has been supposed) we are not likely to hold—or in preparing for a grand expedition which (on the same supposition) can never take place. I am afraid these would not be palatable excuses. The recovery of Hanover by itself— not interfering with other what are considered more essential objects—would, I believe, be gratifying to the country. But the recovery of it by an army which might have been otherwise employed, and not with the consent of other Powers, but against their will, and liable to be wrested from us again, would be far otherwise.

" And, as to the other point I will not say that, supposing the war to go on briskly on the Continent, an army under the D. of Y[ork] might not be employed without creating dissatisfaction, so long (that is) as the pressure of the war is kept out of our sight and from off our own shores. But even then, if the D. should be unsuccessful, and in the case (of which we are speaking) of a Continental peace, I am bound in honesty to tell you (what I think you must hear from many other quarters) that the employment of the D. of Y., or the imputation of an intention to employ him on a great scale, and the keeping back or starving other services for that purpose, would, so far as one can judge from the language of *friends*, sooner than any other thing in the world hazard your popularity and perhaps your power.

" But this is beyond what I had in my mind when I began writing to you. If the war goes on, well. Then the occupation of Walcheren (or Boulogne) will not prevent your having a continental army with the D. of Y. at the head of it, if you think fit. If the war does not go on (which is the danger) there will be no such opportunity, and *then*, what I grudge, and do most earnestly hope may be avoided if possible—is the loss of this short interval, while Bonaparte is yet at a distance, and the failure of negotiation possible. A month—a fortnight—hence may be too late.

" P.S. Nothing from Harrowby?"

"South Hill, Jan. 4, 1806.

" If Sturges had not written to me yesterday, and I had only my newspapers of this morning to trust to, I should have made out a very good consolatory case from the materials which they furnish. But they are not altogether sufficient to counteract the impression of Sturges's first intelligence; and I must therefore refer to you for more substantial and certain consolation.

" 1. If the Emperor of Russia has not given up the game personally; and if he is still in a situation to communicate with the Emperor of Germany, I have hopes that his influence may yet induce the E. of G. to break the armistice, before it has led to peace. It is obviously (upon the map) the interest of Austria to do so.

" 2. My second hope is from the co-operation of Prussia, but that (which was my only hope yesterday) is a good deal weakened by the resolution which Sturges announced to me of the Russian army retreating through Hungary. Thro' Hungary! *Into* Hungary with a view to the first object, I can understand. But a retreat commenced thro' Hungary at the same moment with the offer to Berlin of the use of Russian armies is more perplexing than encouraging.

" 3. If the very worst happens that is now threatened—if Austria does make a separate peace, and is abolished as a Power, and if Prussia lies down and licks Bonaparte's feet, and is forgiven and gets Hanover assigned to her for her submission—still, with Russia unpledged to peace and committed in war, we are better off than we were before the Coalition took place. We must then, I think, set about making a new treaty with Russia with a view to joint negotiation *hereafter*. But still this is not the hopeless state of things in which (when we were looking at the possibility of it three months ago) we thought we should have nothing to do but to return an answer to Bonaparte's neglected letter of January last. Nothing like it.

" One of the greatest comforts that you could send me would be the intelligence that you are going on well and getting stout. I did not very much like the late accounts of you; but to-day I hear better accounts, and they, I believe, have contributed to make me see things in a less gloomy point of view than yesterday.

" Let me know also what your plans are. I take for granted you do not mean to attend the funeral.[1] You cannot afford a cold at this moment, either in point of health or of convenience. Do you stay on at Bath? If you move towards town, why should not you get *here* the first night.[2] (It is very easy, starting at ten, or eleven. I could have done it with my economical pair of horses) and stay here one day, during which Sturges or Huskisson, or whoever else you may want to see might meet you here. You must have a good deal to settle that would require a quiet day, and, once in town, you can hardly keep your door shut. . . ."

"South Hill, Tu. mng., Jan. 7, 1806.

" A thousand thanks for your letter, which comforts me a little as to the Continent, but disquiets me a good deal about yourself. . . . The account that you give me of yourself makes me still more desirous of doing so (*i.e.* going to meet him at Bath) if I thought you likely to feel it any comfort. But I should not be at all *affronted* at your not wishing it—as there are moments when one is best alone without disparagement to anybody. But again, you cannot indulge in absolute solitude very long, and there are so many things to be thought of and talked of that I cannot help renewing my offer. . . .

" P.S. Do not write if it is a trouble to you. Charles Stanhope[3] can let me know that you will, or will not, be glad to see me."

[1] Nelson's funeral, on 7th January, 1806, at St. Paul's.
[2] Canning's house, " South Hill," at Bracknell, was on the road from Reading to Putney.
[3] Lord Mahon. See Stanhope, iv, 368.

"South Hill, Thursday mng., Jan. 9, 1806.

"The wish which you express in your letter of yesterday (which I have this moment received) tallies so exactly with my proposal to Charles [Stanhope], that I hope nothing will prevent your putting them [*sic*] into execution. I write a line to Sir Walter [Farquhar] to enter into a solemn engagement with him not to talk with you, or (so far as I can help it) allow you to talk upon interesting subjects till you are fitter for it than you represent yourself to be. You shall have *south* rooms, entirely to yourself, and see as little, or as much of us, as you please. And we have room for Charles and for Lady Hester, and for Sir Walter as long as he chooses to stay, or whenever he chooses to come back to you, and moreover for Sturges, or Huskisson, or Castlereagh, or anybody else whom you may wish to see, whenever it is fit that you should see them.

"So pray come and stay till you are better able to bear the neighbourhood of town. I trust Parliament can be put off. God bless you. I need not tell you how anxiously Mrs. C. joins in my request."

SUGGESTIONS FOR THE ACT OF UNION

(I.) CAMDEN TO PITT

[N.B. I have not found Pitt's letter to Earl Camden (then about to retire from the Irish Viceroyalty), to which the following is an answer.— J. H. R.]

(*Endorsed*, " Rec⁴ 19 June 1798.")

"(1). It certainly will be proper that the great outlines of an Union should be digested and detailed as much as possible before it is attempted. This ought to be done by consultation with the principal persons in both countries, and it appears desirable if the English Government really look to the consideration of this question that the opinion of those who compose the King's Cabinet Council should forthwith be sounded, as it is not improbable there may be those who entertain considerable doubts upon it.

"(2). Those persons in whom confidence can be placed in Ireland should be privately consulted, and if the result of these deliberations should be to attempt the measure, no time should be lost in endeavouring to carry it into execution.

"(3). The manner in which the business should be first broached is subject to consideration by those who are better informed than I am in these forms. If the business is to be carried on with an intention of great liberality towards the Catholics, it might be proper that some of that persuasion should be included in the Commission, but it will be difficult to select the proper persons. The higher orders—such as Ld. Fingal and Ld. Kenmare have not information enough, and if any of the agitators are admitted (who really do understand the questions likely to arise) much mischief might ensue. The Chancellor [the Earl of Clare] should decidedly be consulted, and I can speak with confidence when I say that he is completely to be entrusted with the information of this delicate question being likely to be discussed. No man can so readily give a well founded opinion upon points in which legal knowledge is required, and he understands the feelings of the country, but in points of revenue and commerce he will not be enabled to give much information.

"(4). The Speaker [Foster] has very extensive and correct knowledge upon these subjects as far as Ireland is concerned, and his assistance in this measure is most important—he has a very great influence with commercial people, and is considered by the trading people in Ireland as much attached to their interests. He has also considerable weight in Parliament, and particularly with the Orange party, and would be more useful in matters of detail than any other person in that kingdom. Mr. Pelham [1] has been informed by a person, much in the Speaker's confidence, that an English peerage and a respectable provision would make a great impression upon his opinions. His services should forthwith be secured.

"If Lord Yelverton was disposed to take up this matter zealously he might be very useful. I know not the effect an Union would have on the Irish Bar, but it would lessen their importance, as the trade of Parliament is so much their object, and it is probable it would not therefore be relished. Mr. Saurin [2] has a very great influence with that body of men. Mr. Beresford could be extremely useful in matters of detail. I do not know his present sentiments; about a year ago they were much in favor of the measure—Lord Waterford is decidedly so. Lord Shannon and Lord Ely would object to the measure, as it lessens their importance, by which their decision, if they were not very much alarmed, would be chiefly directed, but negociation with them might probably succeed. There are men of less parliamentary weight, whose opinions in conversation are important, who ought to be secured. It is not necessary to name them here. No one understands Ireland better than Mr. Cooke. [3] The person alluded to [?] is amongst the most anxious for the measure but it is suppose[d] the idea of his alarm proceeds from the apprehension it is imagined he may entertain from the admission of Catholics, and most remarkable prejudice exists there, not too strong however if Ireland remains as she is—but it does not appear that the admission of Catholics into our Parliament can be mischievous, and nothing can so much weaken the Catholic cause in Ireland where alone it is to be dreaded. The R[oman] Catholics of Scotland ought to have the same privileges, whilst likewise provision should be made for the clergy of each sect. Our *Establishment* should receive every encouragement.

---

[1] Then secretary to the Lord-Lieutenant. Owing to illness he proceeded to England. Lord Castlereagh took his place as *locum tenens*, and a little later as Chief Secretary.

[2] Rt. Hon. W. Saurin was captain of a yeomanry corps, and strongly opposed the Union.

[3] Under Secretary of State.

"(5). The question of Reform will certainly be started; but, with liberal compensations to those who *may* be brought to give up their boroughs and a judicious mixture of boroughs to return members, that question does not appear very formidable at this —— [?] and revolutionists and Jacobins were never at so low an ebb either in England or in Ireland.

"(7). Great care should be taken that Scotland should be satisfied with the propositions which may be made to Ireland.

"(8). The French will not make peace until this country is so weakened as to be unable to disturb them, should the present Government continue in its present *form*. A new incentive to prolong the war is not therefore necessary.

"(9). Taking it for granted that the proposed Union shall be so arranged, as to give a decisive preponderance to the Protestant interest and the Establishments, it is presumed it ought to satisfy the Dissenters and Papists. They are given the same advantages as are bestowed upon the rest of the inhabitants of the 3 kingdoms. The hardship they complain of will be done away, of being governed by so comparatively small a number of a different persuasion in their own country. The majority will be Protestant and when it is felt that there is really a fair interchange of interests, the pretended grievances will cease with the real causes of discontent.

"(10). This remark is difficult to be answered. The principles of the Union ought therefore to be as much detailed as possible before the event actually takes place.

"(11). The expence will not be very much more considerable than in appeals from Scotland. The city of Dublin will feel most sensibly the removal of the Parliament and the Court from thence; and in case of the proposed Union the Lord Lieutenant, or by whatever name the Governor shall be called, ought to have such a salary as to be enabled to live in great splendour. Every inducement should be held out to persons of consequence to reside in Ireland when they are not called to England upon parliamentary duty. When they are so called, it is imagined the society and manners of the English will mix with their own, and they will return to Ireland with a desire to introduce English manners and customs there. When an Irishman now comes occasionally to England, he is considered as a foreigner and is not much taken notice of. By mixing more together and having a common interest, the jealousy of the lesser country will be eradicated and the contempt of the principal one taken off. Every possible arrangement should be undertaken to make the passage from one country to the other as easy and as expeditious as possible, and Government might provide passage boats of the greatest convenience free of expense to the passengers.

z

Many considerable offices should be left to induce the residence of principal persons.

"P.S. I have spoken to the Chancellor and to the Speaker upon the subject of your letter. They are so good as to lament that I am to leave the country and express their hopes with much anxiety that no alteration in the system to be pursued should take place, and I think it ought to be explicitly understood that Lord Cornwallis should adopt the same line of conduct I have done. Indeed all your opinions tend so much to that end, that I suppose he would not be entrusted with the Government unless it was perfectly understood he was to make no alteration in the system, and if he is immediately to pursue *mild measures,* my Government will be marked with much more harshness than it deserves, and it will not be advantageous to the country. I conclude Lord Cornwallis will very speedily take upon himself the government of Ireland and I imagine I shall hear forthwith upon that subject from the Duke of Portland."

POINTS TO BE CONSIDERED WITH A VIEW TO AN INCOR-
PORATING UNION OF GREAT BRITAIN AND IRELAND
(Anon. N.D. in Pretyman MSS.).

[Notes at the side are in the handwriting of Pitt. They are subjoined as footnotes with his initials.]

"(1). The King's authority, ecclesiastical, civil, and military, to be exercised as at present by a Lord Lieutenant resident in Ireland. (2). The two Parliaments to be incorporated on the plan of the Scotch Union. (3). The Courts of Justice to remain on their present footing in Ireland, and the Great Seal to remain there, with a Ld. Chancellor or Ld. Keeper as at present. (4). An appeal (in all cases where it now lies to the House of Lords) to lie to the Chancellor and three chief judges in Ireland, with power to them to permit a further appeal in doubtful cases to the House of Lords of the United Kingdom, and with power also to the House of Lords on special ground shewn, and for preserving uniformity in the law of the two Kingdoms, to remove the cause before them after the decision of that Court of Appeal. (5.) Power to the same Court to examine evidence and certify all parliamentary and other points for private Bills. This power might even be extended to the establishing certain provisions in particular cases according to some general principle [1] and on

---

[1] " Particularly in divorces and exchange of lands in settlement. I apprehend there are few or no Parliamentary Turnpike Bills. Query. How is it as to inclosures and paving and lighting Bills? These seem to be the prin-

grounds to be specified in the article. The object being as much as possible to diminish the objection of the expense and trouble of a resort to Parliament here for such private business as is now transacted by the Irish Parliament. (6). The greatest difficulty seems to arise from the impossibility of equalizing the systems of commerce, revenue and debt in the two countries. If the duties of import and export are made the same in Ireland as in England, it is conceived that the burthen would be intolerable to the former. If those of import only, without Excise, are extended to Ireland, still the consumer there would be burthened in many instances much beyond his present taxes. If the port and internal duties of both countries remain on their present footing, it will be impossible to abolish the duties on import from Ireland into England. The detail of the Irish Propositions [of 1785] will, if recurred to, furnish, it is apprehended, many other points of very difficult arrangement[1] (*sic*). Even if the whole of the present systems of revenue and debt could be left untouched and subjected only to the gradual amelioration or consolidation which an United Parliament might in the course of years provide for it, still there would be great difficulty[2] as to the funds for the interest of new loans here; since it may be doubted whether precisely the same taxes on internal consumption or on foreign trade, which may be necessary and easy here, would not overburden the Irish. This therefore must require the detailed discussion of commissioners; and the task will not only be arduous, but it may be to be apprehended that it will draw into length. Whereas the interest of both kingdoms and the success of the measure itself both require that after it is once on float it should proceed with the utmost possible expedition.

"(7). The details as to the frame of Parliament might be thus arranged. Putting the population of Scotland at 1,500,000 and that of Ireland at 4,000,000 of people, the scale of that proportion would give an addition of 40 peers and 120 commoners to the British Parliament.[3] But if the proportion be taken from that of the present population of the two islands it would be as 4 to 10, according to the best accounts of British population. Putting therefore the present House of Lords of Gt. Britain at

cipal classes of private bills. N.B. Query. Wharfs or Canal Bills, Parly. bounties, Election Committees?"—W. P.

[1] "Something approaching to this is indispensable to the scheme."—W. P.

[2] "Might not a certain proportion be fixed at once to be observed for a limited number of years, leaving it to commissioners to discuss in the meantime according to what rule the proportion should be regulated afterwards?"—W. P.

[3] "That is 15 : 40 : : 16 : 40 nearly. 15 : 40 : : 45 : 120."—W. P.

about 270 sitting members, and the House of Commons at 558, the addition on this ground must be 108 Peers and about 223 Commoners;[1] and the increase would be so great as to change in a very considerable degree the nature of both of those assemblies. It is presumed therefore that the former scale must be used. The Peers might either be chosen as the Scotch now are (and this seems the best[2] for many reasons), or the King might name those to whom, and to their heirs male, that right should belong, supplying vacancies as they arose from the remaining list, but leaving them in the interim on the footing of Commoners as to eligibility to sit in the House of Lords. The number of Irish peers who are now peers of Great Britain is not less than 40. Many of the others are now members of the House of Commons here. The Irish bishops might, according as one or the other of these two plans was adopted, choose from among themselves a certain number for each Parliament,[3] or a like number might be named by the King for the Parliament—or for their lives.

"For the House of Commons, if it was not thought that the addition of 150 was too large, that number, being the half of the present Irish Parliament, might be returned precisely in the present mode of election, only choosing one at each election, instead of two, and giving to Catholics as well as Protestants the right of eligibility under *effective* qualification laws of property in both kingdoms. The simplicity of this plan is a great recommendation of it. If the system of election in Ireland must be at all varied, this might still be done without altering the present rights of election, as follows, viz.:

PLAN I

32 counties, 2 members each	64
9 cities and towns, 2 members each	18
10 smaller towns, 1 each	10
99 boroughs, etc., to be united into sets of 3, with alternate casting votes, ⅓ each	33
Total	125

Or

---

[1] "That is 10 : 4 : : 270 : 108. 10 : 4 : : 558 : 223."—W. P.

[2] "Certainly. One of the great reasons for preferring this mode is its being actually in use, as one of the great objections to any new system would be the danger lest, if it were thought more advantageous to the Irish peerage than the present mode is to the Scotch, the latter might claim to be put on a similar footing."—W. P.

[3] "I suppose from 4 to 8."—W. P.

PLAN II

32 counties, 2 members each	...	...	...	...	...	64
12 cities, 2 members each	...	...	...	...	...	24
22 towns, 1 member each	...	...	...	...	...	22
84 boroughs, etc., to be united into sets of 3, with alternate casting votes, at ⅓ ...	...	...	...	...	...	28

Total 138

"But then would come the question of opening the elections in some of these places, particularly the populous towns, together with a host of pretentions and disputes in the arrangement of these classes. Any attempt to establish anything like a uniform system, on theories of population, contributions, etc., must, it is presumed, lead to confusion in both countries."

(J.) PITT'S LAST ILLNESS

"*Most Private.*

"Downing Street, Thursday, 16th Jan. 1806.[1]

"DEAR COURTENAY,

[On private matters]

. . . "As to myself, I am very heavy-hearted. Mr. Pitt has been worse ever since that abominable conversation which I told you he had on Monday with Lords Hawkesbury and Castlereagh. He complained to Lady Hester, after they were gone, that they had exhausted him too much—and Tuesday he saw Lord Wellesley, which would have been an agitating interview under any circumstances. He was pleased with Lord W's friendly and affectionate manner, and I rather expect, if things should go well, that he will take office. From what I can hear, he seems to lean to the Admiralty. Yesterday morning Mr. Pitt was still weaker. He could not keep even the light liquid nourishment, which he was able to swallow, upon his stomach, but grew better towards night. . . . He has been somewhat worried about the King's Speech. Hawkesbury and Castlereagh drew up one which he thought in many points objectionable, and, as he was not equal to any exertion himself, he desired Bourne and Huskisson, whom he saw on Tuesday, to correct it conformably to his ideas. But they found it so wrong throughout that they were obliged to frame an entire new one, with the assistance, I believe, of Canning; and I copied it out that it might be submitted to Mr. Pitt and sent to the Cabinet in my handwriting, as coming from himself. Bourne carried it down to Putney, but Mr. Pitt was too ill to see him. He could not leave his bed, and brings up everything, whether medicine or food, which he swallows, and is so excessively weak and exhausted that they have ordered him to see no person whatever, nor transact any business, however urgent or pressing it may be. We have one comfort left, which is, that the physicians think there is no immediate danger, and that he is not worse than he was when they saw him last Sunday. I trust in God this opinion is well founded, though it

---

[1] This letter is from William Dacre Adams, Pitt's private secretary, to his brother-in-law, J. P. Courtenay, private secretary to Mr. Long at Dublin.

contradicts one's own common sense. For my own part, I should rejoice beyond expression could we compound for his being out of office, if we could once more see him restored to health—and this is the distressing situation in which we are. Things cannot possibly remain so long. If Mr. Pitt does not get *much* better within a reasonable time, I have no idea but that his Administration must fall. I earnestly wish, as I have said, that *that* was the greatest evil which we have to apprehend. Perhaps I am too gloomy—I hope I am; but every publick and private feeling of my heart is so intimately blended with the preservation of that most excellent of men that I cannot look at his present state without the most trembling anxiety. You shall certainly hear again to-morrow.

"W. D. ADAMS."

"Downing Street, Tuesday, 21st January, 1806.

"DEAR COURTENAY,

"Last night the symptoms became less unfavourable than they were in the morning when I wrote to you. Sir Walter told Mr. Pitt that he ought to take some nourishment, and gave him his choice of a little jelly or an egg beat up with a spoonful of brandy. He preferred the latter, and liked it so well that he soon called for another, which he also eat (*sic*), and slept quietly afterwards till five o'clock. To-day, however, he is not *quite* so well—by no means out of danger, though certainly not in a state to give us such immediate alarm as we experienced yesterday.

"The Opposition, I find, mean to make a grand push to-day. Lord Henry Petty moves this amendment to the Address. They are exerting their utmost efforts to get a full attendance, and these circular pressing letters are signed *John McMahon*, the Prince of Wales's secretary. You who are fond of constitutional proceedings must admire the exertions of this kind of influence. You will naturally expect to hear, now that we are all in such confusion and distress, that my Lord Sidmouth could not witness such a scene without endeavouring to turn it to his own purposes. He is, I am told, by means of his emissaries, trying to persuade the King that nothing better can now be done than placing *him* again at the head of the Government. We are now in such a situation that *that* only could make us worse, and I trust we shall be delivered from it. I have no letter from you to-day, but I hope that Anne is going on well. Do send us some comfort from Ireland; we have none here.

"W. D. ADAMS."

[Adams' third letter, describing the death of Pitt, is in Earl Stanhope's "Miscellanies," (1863), p. 45.]

Printed in the United States
137333LV00002B/104/P

9 781408 691038